Mastering Resin

Richard Hightower
Joseph D. Gradecki

Wiley Publishing, Inc.

Vice President & Executive Group Publisher: Richard Swadley
Vice President & Executive Publisher: Robert Ipsen
Vice President & Publisher: Joseph B. Wikert
Executive Editor: Robert Elliot
Executive Editorial Director: Mary Bednarek
Editorial Manager: Kathryn A. Malm
Production Editor: Vincent Kunkemueller
Book Producer: Ryan Publishing Group, Inc.
Copyeditors: Elizabeth Welch and Tiffany Taylor
Compositor: Gina Rexrode

Published by Wiley Publishing, Inc., Indianapolis, Indiana

Published simultaneously in Canada.

Library of Congress Cataloging-in-Publication Data:

ISBN 0-471-43103-6

Printed in the United States of America

10 9 8 7 6 5 4 3 2 1

CONTENTS

Acknowledgments xi

About the Authors xiii

Introduction xv

Part I Introduction to Resin

Chapter 1 An Overview of Resin 1

What Is Resin? 4
Resin/Resin Enterprise Features 4
Resin Enterprise 8
What's Next 9

Chapter 2 Setting Up the Resin Server 11

Requirements for Installation 11
Support Software 11
Integrating Resin 12
Ports 13
Obtaining Java 14
IBM 14
Installing Resin on Windows 14
Windows Service Startup 16
Installing Resin on Unix/Linux 19
Executing Resin under Unix 19
Testing the Installation 21
Command-Line Options 22
Documentation 24
The Basic Configuration 24
The HTTP Port 26
Logging in Resin 3.x 26
The Java Compiler 27
The Error Page 29
The Server Restart Ping 30
What's Next 30

Part II Application Development with Resin

Chapter 3 Using JSP and Resin 31

Beginning JSP Usage 31
An Overview of JSP Technology 32
Resin Support for JSP 34
Page Placement 34

The JSP Hello World 34
Combining Java and HTML 37
JSP Variables 38
Using the Request Variable 38
Using the Response Variable 41
Response Redirection 41
Response Encoding 42
Using the Application Variable 42
Using the Session Variable 43
Directives 44
Imports 45
Sessions 45
Error Pages 46
Includes 46
Using Beans 46
Accessing Databases 49
JSTL and JSP-EL Support 50
What's Next 51

Chapter 4 Using Servlets and Resin 53

The Servlet Life Cycle 53
Configuring Resin 55
Web Defaults in Resin 3.x 55
Resin web.xml Elements 56
<servlet> 57
A Shortcut 59
Hello World Servlet 59
Using init Parameters 61
Servlet and Forms 62
Accessing the Database 64
Development 66
JSP Templates 67
Templates and Objects 68
What's Next 71

Chapter 5 Using XTP and StyleScript 73

The Hello World XTP 73
XML, XPath, XSL, and StyleScript 76
XML 76
XPath 77
XSL 82
Matching Tags with Attributes 89
Using XTP for Style Changes 92
Returning XTP from a Servlet 92
The Account History Example 93
StyleScript and XSL 94
What's Next 105

Chapter 6 Object-Relational Mapping with CMP 107

Resin-EE Features 108
Setting Up Your Database 108
Basic Database Access 109
  The login Table Entity Bean 109
  The EJB Descriptor 113
  Configuring the web.xml File 116
  Using the Entity Bean 116
  Deploying the Code 118
  Running the Code 118
Using EJB-QL and ejbSelect() 119
  Adding Finder Methods 119
  Using ejbSelect() 124
Changing Entity Values 126
Updating the Table 131
  Removing a Bean 134
Using Multiple Entity Beans 134
  Adding a Groups Bean 136
Relationships 137
  Relationship Types 138
  Building a Relationship between login and groups 139
Transactions 145
Using Stateless Session Beans 146
What's Next 149

Chapter 7 Using XDoclet with Resin 151

Installing XDoclet 151
Adding a New Entitlements Bean 152
The Ant Build File 155
The Files Ant Produces 157
Expanding a Bean 157
Resin XDoclet Tags 159
What's Next 161

Chapter 8 The Burlap Web Service Protocol 163

Downloading the Code 164
The Specification 164
  Serialization 164
  The <burlap:call> Tag 169
  The <burlap:reply> Tag 169
Using BasicAPI 170
Writing a Basic Client 171
  Executing the Code 172
Writing a Basic Service 173
  Creating the Interface 173
  The Build Interface JAR 174

Writing the Authentication Service 174
The Server Structure 175
Creating a Client for the New Service 176
What's Next 177

Chapter 9 Hessian Binary Web Service Protocol 179

Downloading the Code 180
Using BasicAPI 180
Writing a Basic Client 181
Downloading the Interface Class 182
Writing a Basic Service 183
Creating the Interface 183
Building the Interface JAR 184
Writing the Authentication Service 184
Server Structure 186
Changing Resin.conf 187
Changing web.xml 187
Starting the Server 188
Client for the New Service 188
Mobile Hessian 190
What's in the Code 193
Serialization Classes 194
Python Hessian 196
Hessian Mux 196
Hessian Specification 196
Serialization 197
Calls 198
Reply 198
What's Next 198

Chapter 10 Parsing 199

XML Parsing 199
DOM XML Parsing 200
SAX XML Parsing 203
Changing Parsers 204
HTML Parsing 205
What's Next 206

Chapter 11 Database Connectivity 207

Traditional JDBC Connectivity 207
Using Resin's JNDI Configuration 209
Basic Configuration Parameters 210
Library Placement 210
Using the Configuration 210
Connecting to MySQL 211

Connecting to Other Databases 213
Database Pooling 214
Database Reliability 216
Connecting through JSP 217
What's Next 219

Chapter 12 Debugging and Logging 221

Error Types 221
Compiler Parse Errors 221
Run-time Errors 222
Logic Errors 223
Just-In-Time Compilers 224
Tracing Your Code 224
Resin Logging 225
RootCause Exception 227
Thread Dumps 227
Resin and Debuggers 228
What's Next 229

Chapter 13 Security 231

Authentication 231
Providing Basic Authentication with XmlAuthenticator 231
Specifying a Password File 235
Session Timeouts 236
Storing Passwords in a Database with JdbcAuthenticator 236
Authentication API 239
Authorization 239
Logging Out 240
Using OpenSSL with Resin 240
Using JSSE with Resin 242
What's Next 243

Chapter 14 Page Caching 245

Overview of Page Caching 245
How Web Caches Work 246
HTML Metatags and HTTP Headers 246
Resin and Caching 248
Using Expires 249
Using If-Modified 250
Using Cache-Mapping 250
Setting Cache-Control 251
What's Next 251

Part III Resin Administration

Chapter 15 **Resin Server Configuration** 253

Details of resin.conf 253
XML Elements 254
Environments 254
High-Level Configuration Format 254
Using #include and app-default.xml 255
Default Path Values 255
Tag Definitions 256
Common Environment Tags 256
Web-App Tags 267
Application and Server Tags 276
<jsp> Configuration Elements 287
What's Next 288

Chapter 16 **Configuring Your Web Server** 289

URL-Dispatching 289
Apache 291
Installing and Configuring Apache on Unix 291
Installing and Configuring Apache on Windows 292
Configuring resin.conf 295
Testing Apache and Resin 295
Troubleshooting 296
Virtual Hosts 297
Error Pages 298
Using IIS with Resin 298
Testing IIS and Resin 300
Using Netscape iPlanet with Resin 300
Running Netscape iPlanet and Windows 301
Hosting a CGI without Apache 301
CGIServlet 301
FastCGIServlet 302
Resin and WebDav 303
Configuring for WebDav 303
Configuring Windows' My Network Places 304
What's Next 305

Chapter 17 **Exploring Virtual Hosting** 307

Basic Virtual Hosting 307
Virtual Hosting Using External Web Servers 309
IP Virtual Hosting 310
Providing JVMs per Host 310
What's Next 311

Chapter 18 Using Resin HardCore 313

Building the Module 313
Installing the Module 314
Running the Module 314
What's Next 314

Chapter 19 Load Balancing and Reliability 315

Sessions 315
 srun Indexing 316
 Distributed Sessions 316
 File-Distributed Sessions 319
Load-Balancing Options 319
 Hardware Load Balancing 319
 Using Resin as a Balancer 321
 Using srun-backup 323
Reliability Options 323
Conclusion 324

Part IV Appendixes

Appendix A Resin Sources 325

Appendix B Resin Status 329

Appendix C Resin and Eclipse 335

Installing the Eclipse Plugin 335
Using ResinProjectWizard 336
Using ResinLauncher 338
 Debugging 340

Appendix D Burlap and Hessian APIs 343

Package com.caucho.burlap 343
Package com.caucho.burlap.io 353
Package com.caucho.hessian 353
Package com.caucho.hessian.io 361

Index 363

Dedication

This book is dedicated to Christ, my wife and our sons.

Acknowledgments

I'd like to thank Scott Ferguson, Resin Architect, and Sam Heisz, Resin Software Engineer, for their excellent and thorough technical review of this book.

I'd like to thank Tim Ryan, Tiffany Taylor, and Liz Welch for their guidance and editing; also, thanks to everyone at Caucho for creating excellent products.

ABOUT THE AUTHORS

Richard Hightower is CTO of Trivera Technologies, a leading Java education company that offers online and classroom training, as well as consulting on enterprise Java application development. Rick is a software engineer by training who specializes in software development tools and processes, and developing enterprise applications using J2EE, XML, UML, JDBC, SQL, and open source technologies. Formerly he was the Senior Software Engineer for Java Architecture at Intel's Enterprise Architecture Lab. Rick is the co-author of the popular *Java Tools for Extreme Programming*. Rick has extensive experience in both developing with Resin and teaching classes about it.

Joseph D. Gradecki is a software engineer at Comprehensive Software Solutions, where he works on their SABIL product, a enterprise-level securities processing system. He has built numerous dynamic, enterprise applications using Java, AspectJ, servlets, JSPs, Resin, MySQL, BroadVision, XML, and more. He is the author of *Mastering JXTA* and the coauthor of *MySQL and Java Developer's Guide* (with Mark Matthews and Jim Cole). Mr. Gradecki holds Bachelor's and Master's degrees in Computer Science and is currently pursuing a Ph.D. in Computer Science.

Introduction

When the page layout function of HTML was combined with the power of Java, JavaServer Pages were born. To enhance the power and performance of JSPs, servlets were introduced, which removed Java code from the HTML page and placed it on the server itself. The Resin 3.x family of servers, including Resin Core and Resin-EE, all provide the ability to accurately and quickly process JSP and servlets, as well as deliver enterprise-level server functionality. Features of the Resin servers include:

- Full specification support for JSP and servlets
- Load balancing
- Built-in Web server with high-performance HTML processing
- Resin XTP templates for dynamic web page creation
- Virtual hosting
- Model-View-Controller support with JSP Templates
- Web services using Burlap and Hussein
- Resin Hardcore—incorporation of Resin into a Linux kernel
- J2EE and EJB support

All of these features and more await you with Resin servers.

Who Should Read This Book

This book is designed to be a comprehensive handbook for installing, administering, and developing Java Web applications with the Resin 3.x family of servers. All developers and administrators currently using Resin, or evaluating any application server (including Resin, Tomcat, and JRun) should use this book as a guide to Resin and its features. Developers using this book should have an understanding of Java and basic Internet programming concepts.

Book Organization

This book is organized into three parts. The first part is an introduction to Resin, including installation, setup, and explanations of how Resin works with various Java-based technologies. The second part covers application development with JSP, EJBs, templates, and other Java technologies. The third part covers advanced configuration of the Resin family of products, including enterprise-level features such as load-balancing.

Part I: Introduction to Resin

Chapter 1: Resin Setup

In this chapter we cover the requirements for installing the Resin server. The chapter provides detailed instructions for installing Resin Core on Linux Mandrake 8.2, as well as in a Windows environment using both Windows 2000 Server and Windows XP Professional. Each of the installations will be followed by a full test to insure the installation was completely successful. After the installation steps, the directory structure for Resin Core will be discussed, along with common errors encountered during installation.

Chapter 2: Resin and Java Technologies

This chapter examines the underlying architecture of the Resin server in order to provide an overall picture of its functionality. Following the architecture is a discussion of each of the primary Java technologies relevant to the Resin family of products: servlets, JavaServer Pages, JavaBeans, and EJBs.

Part II: Application Development with Resin

Chapter 3: JSP and Resin

The part of the book devoted to developing Web application development begins with a discussion of using JSP with Resin. We create a sample application to obtain information from a client, access a database, and display output using Resin. A discussion and example of using JavaBeans with JSP is also included.

Chapter 4: Servlets and Resin

JavaServer Pages is a great improvement over the static HTML page. Servlets pull the processing to the server with all the power of Java. This chapter will step through how to write servlets to be executed on the Resin server. This chapter also demonstrates how to access the database through a servlet and JSP support.

Chapter 5: Using XTP with XSL and StyleScript

Resin doesn't just rely on HTML, JSP, and servlets for content transformation and delivery; it includes a Native format called XTP or XML Template Pages. This chapter includes detailed coverage of XPath expressions, format of XTP, and using XTP for output translation. We will cover how to write stylesheets using both XSL and StyleScript syntax.

Chapter 6: Object-Relational Mapping with CMP

This chapter takes an in-depth look at the Resin-EE product which is designed to support CMP. Detailed steps for installing Resin-EE on both Windows and Unix/Linux machines are included. The focus of the chapter is building a comprehensive distributed application that demonstrates the power and functionality of Resin-EE.

Chapter 7: Using XDoclet with Resin

Now that we've just spent an entire chapter discussing how to write and deploy EJBs using Resin, we introduce Resin's support for XDoclet. Using Javadoc notation, EJBs can be written in a small percentage of the time normally required. This chapter includes installation instructions and describes the process of writing EJBs with XDoclet.

Chapter 8: Burlap Web Service Protocol

The Resin servers support two different kinds of Web services: Burlap and Hussein. In this chapter on Burlap, the discussion begins with a comparison between Burlap and SOAP. Next, an overview of the Burlap specification will take place and provide a complete understanding of how Burlap applies to Web services. The theoretical discussion will be followed by writing a Burlap service and a client to use the new service in Java. Next, the issue of how to serialize data through Burlap will be covered. The chapter will continue with the steps necessary to write Burlap clients in Python, Perl, and C#. Finally, a discussion of how Burlap and EJB interact.

Chapter 9: Hessian Binary Web Service Protocol

The second Web services protocol supported by the Resin servers is Hessian. This chapter begins with a detailed discussion of the Hessian Binary Web Service Protocol. The discussion will be followed with the steps necessary to write both a service and client using the Java language. This chapter includes details for writing clients in Python and C#. Finally, a discussion on the interaction between Hessian and EJB.

Chapter 10: Parsing

In this chapter, the Resin server includes a complete HTML parser. This parser can be used to pull HTML tags from HTML documents from an HTML editor or even from web pages pulled from the Internet. The parsing can be to a document or even a DOM object for further processing.

Chapter 11: Database Connectivity

The real power of a Web site was realized when it was married to a database. This chapter demonstrates how Resin allows access to several different databases including MySQL, Microsoft SQL Server, and Oracle. This chapter covers a wide range of database-related information, including using connection pools for efficient connections and a comprehensive look at database configuration.

Chapter 12: Debugging and Logging

This chapter explains the configuration settings for all logging; it also includes code that demonstrates how to log application activity.

Chapter 13: Security

This chapter explains how to use Resin with OpenSSL. Topics and code will include login configuration, authenticator support, and authorization setup.

Chapter 14: Page Caching

Caching is fundamental to any good Internet server. Resin includes full caching, and this chapter provides an overview of the Resin Cache, cache configuration operations, and demonstrates the effectiveness of the cache.

Part III: Resin Administration

Chapter 15: Resin Server Configuration

This chapter provides a comprehensive review of all Resin configuration options (except those for the internal Web server which are covered in the next chapter). The discussion begins with a full explanation of the resin.conf file. The configuration options covered are: general, servlet, database, Web application, and http. Other topics include threading, Linux boot start, and keepalives.

Chapter 16: Web Server Configuration

Resin can be configured to use either its own internal Web server or external Web servers such as Apache, IIS, and Netscape. This chapter will include a complete review of all configuration options for the internal Web server for both Windows and Linux platforms; it also explains how to configure Resin to work with external Web servers. Other topics include hosting CGI's written in PHP, Perl, and Python without using Apache; CGIServlet; FastCGIServet; and full coverage of Resin's WebDav.

Chapter 17: Virtual Hosting

This chapter includes complete instructions for installing and configuring Resin's built-in virtual hosting capabilities. The chapter also explains how to use Resin with external Web servers in a virtual hosting configuration.

Chapter 18: Resin Hardcore

An experimental but powerful feature of the Resin Core product is its ability to be incorporated directly into the kernel of the Linux OS. This chapter explains why incorporating Resin into the latest Linux kernel is a good performance option, and it provides detailed steps for performing the incorporation. The potential problems associated with the Resin-Linux kernel mix will be discussed as well as example code for testing the incorporation.

Chapter 19: Reliability and Load Balancing

This chapter provides an overview of Resin's approach to reliability and load balancing, as well as configuration details. Additional topics include handling sessions and persistence, as well as building multiple Web servers. Finally, the topic of server failure is discussed.

Part IV: Appendixes

Appendix A: Working with Resin Source Code

This appendix provides information on the Resin Source Code.

Appendix B: Resin Status

This appendix explains how to use Resin's built-in status servlet to obtain a wide range of information about the server. Related security issues are also discussed.

Appendix C: Resin and Eclipse

This appendix provides details of using Resin as your Web development platform from within the Eclipse IDE.

Appendix D: Burlap and Hessian APIs

This appendix is a concise, quick reference to Resin's Burlap and Hessian APIs.

CHAPTER 1

An Overview of Resin

During the early years of the Web, developers used a fairly small set of HTML document tags to manipulate the style and layout of each Web page. These static Web pages were usually stored on the same computer that was executing a Web server. When a user launched a Web browser on his or her local machine and pointed that browser to a Web server, a protocol-based exchange of information began. The page sent to the user was really just a text file with information and HTML tags embedded in it to present the information in a clear manner.

As time went on, it became clear that providing up-to-date and personalized information was going to be a developer's nightmare if using static pages was the only option. Keeping the static pages up-to-date was feasible, but personalizing that information manually was next to impossible. This meant that the pages had to be created on the fly in response to an action or request by the user. One early solution to this problem was called *Common Gateway Interface* (CGI). Figure 1.1 shows an example of how requests are made using CGI and a Web server.

Unfortunately, there were some problems with using CGI for dynamic Web page generation. First, the CGI protocol was designed to allow a Web server to communicate with an external program and not specifically for the generation of dynamic Web pages. The creation of the Web pages is actually a side effect of the CGI protocol. As shown in Figure 1.1, the protocol is written so that the Web server will create new process spaces in which the CGI application will execute. All information passed from the user's Web browser to the Web server is passed as environment variables to the waiting CGI application. All of these operations are expensive in terms of processor time as well as memory utilization.

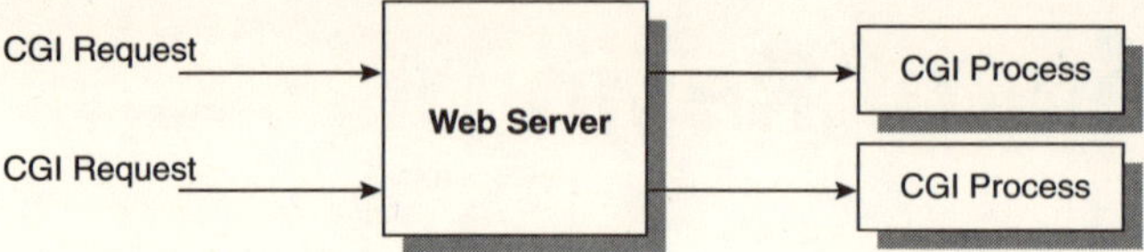

Figure 1.1 CGI request flow.

The second problem is the fact that most CGI applications were written in Perl, with C and C++ coming in second. Depending on your programming capability, Perl could be a stumbling block to Web development.

After the success of CGI became apparent, an alternative implementation of CGI was created called FastCGI. Figure 1.2 shows the request flow in FastCGI.

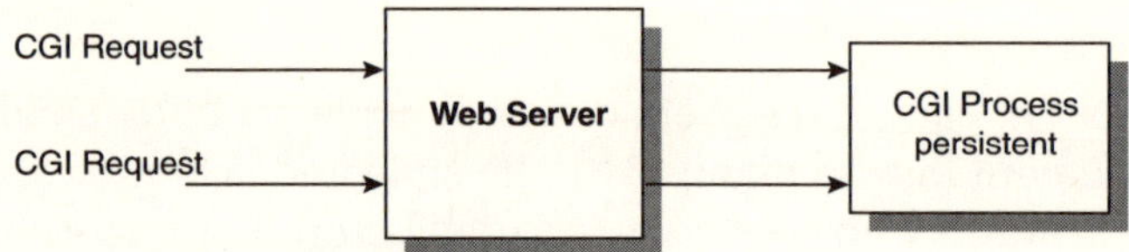

Figure 1.2 FastCGI request flow.

The primary difference between CGI and FastCGI is the creation of persistent processes in which the CGI application executes. By using persistent processes, the Web server doesn't have to expend processor time and memory constantly creating and destroying processes. The success of FastCGI led to the development of other products, like mod_perl and PerlEx, to address performance and interface issues.

The overall success of CGI was dependent on the fact that most Web servers on the market supported its use. This included open-source servers, such as Apache; Internet Information Services (IIS) from Microsoft; and iPlanet from Netscape. However, at the same time these Web servers started experimenting with newer technologies like Active Server Pages (ASP) and Server-Side JavaScript (SSJS).

Both ASP and SSJS solutions to the problem of dynamic Web pages employ the concept of embedding code into the HTML page where dynamic content is needed. ASP, for example, uses JScript or VBScript. Figure 1.3 shows the process flow for ASP and SSJS.

As Figure 1.3 shows, a user requests an ASP page from a Web server that supports ASP, usually IIS. The page is pulled into the Web server and processed.

The processing involves executing the ASP or SSJS code within the server and replacing the code with HTML tags and content. The resulting static page is sent to the browser.

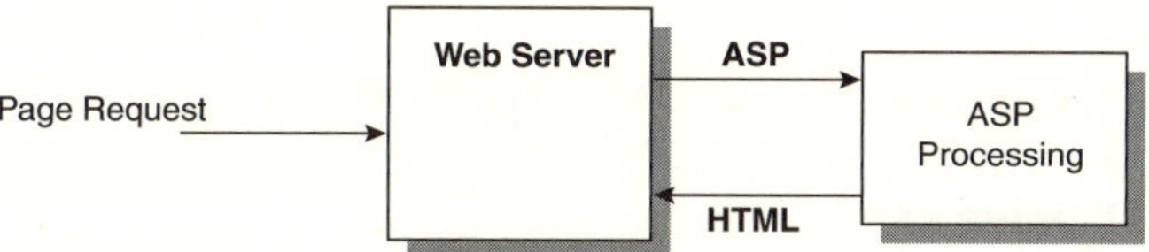

Figure 1.3 ASP/SSJS process flow.

One of my core beliefs is that all programming languages—both conventional and Internet based—should be compared with each other only when we're discussing a specific solution. Is Java better than Cobol? Well, for some applications clearly it is, but in some business situations, fancy GUIs and RMI just aren't needed. The same is true for things like ASP and servlets. Therefore, at this point, let's move to a discussion of JSP, servlets, and beans, which entered the scene after ASP and SSJS.

In the hierarchy of power, the JavaServer Pages (JSP) technology probably comes next. JSP pages are similar to both ASP and SSJS in that code is embedded in the HTML of a Web page. However, JSP isn't designed to be specific to one Web server. As long as a Web server can interpret the Java code embedded in the Web page, it will be able to handle JSP pages. Some of the real power in JSP comes from its ability to interact with JavaBeans. Beans are modular pieces of Java code designed to perform a specific job. Beans can be referenced from JSP pages and automatically instantiated on the server machine.

Finally, we have servlets. A servlet is an extension to a Web server written as a class that will be instantiated to provide additional functionality to the server. Figure 1.4 shows the process flow for a Web page that utilizes servlets.

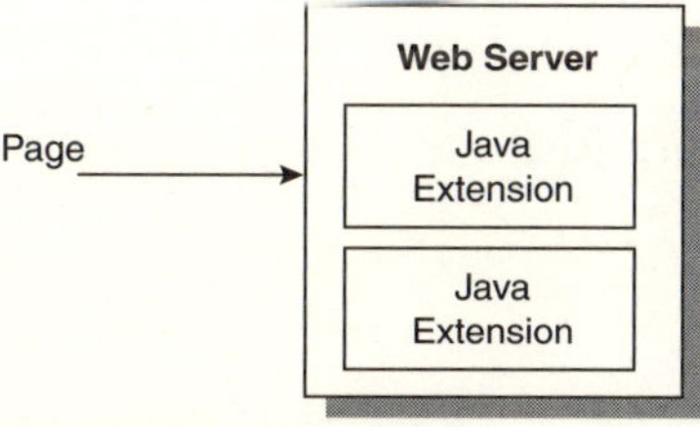

Figure 1.4 Servlet processing.

When a Web page that includes calls to a servlet is requested by a browser, the HTML is processed by the Web server and the servlet calls are farmed to a servlet engine. The servlet engine will instantiate the servlet code, process the request, and return any results to the Web server. Servlets are powerful because they:

- Remain in memory after the first instantiation.
- Are portable to any platform that can execute Java.
- Have access to the full power of the Java language and its supporting classes.

You can use servlets for database access, distributed access using Remote Management Interface (RMI) or Common Object Request Broker Architecture (CORBA), and a host of other operations.

In the remainder of this chapter, we cover the Resin server product family and take a more in-depth look at the features provided by the servers.

What Is Resin?

Resin is a high-performance XML application server for use with JSPs, servlets, JavaBeans, XML, and a host of other technologies. The 2.1.x line of servers is fully Servlet 2.3 and JSP 1.2 compliant and beats all of the competition in number of operations per second, as shown in the data obtained from www.caucho.com/articles/benchmark.xtp. Released in August 2003, Resin 3.x is JSP 2.0 and Servlet 2.4 draft compliant. As the drafts become standard, Resin 3.x will be updated to reflect any changes.

Over the past few years, the Resin family of servers has evolved with the needs of its users. As of this writing, two Resin application servers are available. Resin is the core product, and it supports all of the basic features defined in this chapter. Resin Enterprise enhances the core product with Enterprise JavaBeans (EJB) container-managed persistence (CMP) and database caching. Distributed objects are included using the Burlap protocol as well as full support for the EJB 2.0 specification. In the remainder of this chapter, we outline the major features of the Resin application server.

Resin/Resin Enterprise Features

The following features are available in both Resin and Resin Enterprise:

- JSP/servlet support
- Serif/XTP
- XML/XSL
- Internal and external Web servers
- Load balancing
- Distributed sessions
- Security
- Virtual hosting

- Web services
- JSP-EL
- JDK 1.4 Logging

Let's take a look at each of these features.

JSP

As mentioned earlier, the Resin application server fully supports the Java JSP 2.0 specification. JSP pages can use Java as well as JavaScript to embed code within the HTML tags and text on the page. However, beginning with Resin 3.x, JavaScript is not supported; therefore you will only want to use Java in your JSP pages. The server can handle XML-based JSP notation like the following:

```
<jsp:directive.page import="hello.Name" />
<jsp:useBean id="mybean" scope="page" class="hello.Name" />
<jsp:setProperty name="mybean" property="*" />

<html>
<head><title>Hello</title></head>
<body>

<h1>What's your name?</h1>

<form method="get">
<input type="text" name="username" size="25">
<br>
<input type="submit" value="Submit">
<input type="reset" value="Reset">
</form>
</body>
</html>
```

The Resin server allows you to create custom tag libraries to add better internal documentation to Web pages. Full support is provided for Web applications pulling together JSP pages, scripts, and beans.

XSL

JSP, servlets, and XML Template Pages can take advantage of Resin's ability to process Extensible Stylesheet Language (XSL) or Extensible Markup Language (XML) style sheets. By using XSL, basic XML can be transformed to HTML or another output, such as Wireless Application Protocol (WAP). Depending on the needs of the user, different style sheets can be created and used against XML to produce the desired output. In the following example, a JSP page instructs the Resin server to use the new.xsl style sheet against the provided XML:

```
<%@ page session=false contentType='x-application/xslt' %>
<?xml-stylesheet href='new.xsl'?>
<datarow>
 <title>Output Just For You</title>
 <data>data</data>
</datarow>
```

Web Server Support

Out of the box, Resin is a fully self-contained application server as well as a Web server. There is no need for any additional server software. The internal Web server is very fast and, in most cases, outperforms the competition. Resin also supports these external Web servers: Apache, Netscape, IIS, and O'Reilly WebSite.

Load Balancing

There's no need to worry about losing customers or visitors to your site when it's powered with a Resin server. Resin supports the use of a hardware load balancer for higher cost situations and a low-cost solution using Resin itself. The LoadBalanceServlet servlet is executed on one front-end machine, and it distributes user requests to numerous back-end servers. The Resin server also includes an HTTP proxy cache to make the entire system more efficient.

Distributed Sessions

For sites that must use sessions, Resin supports sticky and distributed sessions. Through file-based and in-memory hashtables, customer won't have problems with shopping carts when requesting transfers to different servers in a server farm or when a server crashes. There is support for database persistent sessions as well as TCP-based distribution.

Security

The Resin server includes four security mechanisms for use in applications:

Authentication through XmlAuthenticator—This allows username/password combinations to be placed in configuration files.

Authorization for protecting areas of a Web site—The areas of the site can be protected using various constraints: pattern-based for specific pages, roles-based for specific users, IP-based for keeping pages specific to specific machines, and transport-based for limiting pages to SSL. Further authorization can be constrained using custom controls.

Encryption of data—Resin supports OpenSSL for encrypting data. Full support is provided for certificates.

Security Manager for separating virtual uses in an ISP situation— The manager will put each Web application in its own separate security environment.

Virtual Hosting

If you are in a situation where numerous users or departments will be using Resin, it's a good idea to configure virtual hosting. In this mode, each host has its own directory structure. Advanced configuration allows each host to have its own Java Virtual Machine (JVM) for complete separation.

Web Services

The developers of Resin have incorporated two different Web service protocols to support this new Internet technology. The protocols are called Burlap Web Service Protocol and Hessian Binary Web Service Protocol.

Burlap

Burlap Web Service Protocol is designed to be a lightweight protocol for allowing EJB services to communicate with non-Java servers and clients. The underlying protocol is all XML-based for maximum interoperability. The protocol is simple, and using a Burlap service results in behavior similar to instantiating an object and calling a method. A basic client would look like this:

```
public class Client {
  public static void main(String[] args)
    throws Exception {
    BurlapProxyFactory factory = new BurlapProxyFactory();
    TestService test = (TestService) factory.create(
      TestService.class, "http://www.gradecki.com/burlap/TestSer-
vice");
    System.out.println("Call doIt(): " + TestService.doIt());
  }
}
```

Building a Burlap service is just like creating a standard Java class, with the public methods exposed or made available to remote clients. Here's the code for the service called by our client:

```
public class TestService extends BurlapServlet implements Basic {
 public String doIt()
 {
 return "called doIt()";
 }
}
```

You can use the protocol in Java 2 Micro Edition (J2ME) devices, and it also supports object serialization.

Hessian

The Hessian Binary Web Service Protocol is designed to be a simple protocol just like Burlap but is optimized for sending binary data between servers and clients. The API for Hessian is just as simple as Burlap, and it supports serialization as well.

Resin Enterprise

The remaining features are specific to Resin Enterprise:

- CMP
- XDoclet
- EJB-QL

CMP

For those of you who have written servlets—or just about any type of Web application that uses a database—the acronyms ODBC and JDBC may make you tremble. When writing servlets that connect with a database, JDBC is the common interface used. The developer is responsible for creating the connection to the database, building the SQL, and executing the calls. With EJB container-managed persistence (see http://java.sun.com/j2ee/tutorial/1_3-fcs/doc/EJBConcepts4.html#62950), most of the work is done for you. Resin helps even further by intelligently caching the database data. Full relations can be created between CMP beans like 1-n, 1-1, and others using a series of XML-based configurations.

XDoclet

Resin Enterprise supports XDoclet, which is an extension to JavaDoc available at http://xdoclet.sourceforge.net/. The custom Javadoc @tags created by Resin are: resin-ejb:entit-bean, resin-ejb:cmp-field, resin-ejb:entity-method, and resin-ejb:relation.

EJB-QL

The Enterprise server supports Enterprise JavaBeans Query Language (EJB-QL) in its use of container-managed persistence. EJB-QL (which is defined by

Sun at http://java.sun.com/j2ee/tutorial/1_3-fcs/doc/EJBQL.html) allows for support of portable data stores and maintains SQL '92 compliance.

What's Next

As we've seen, the Resin family of products is quite comprehensive and full of features. This chapter has only touched on the high points. In the next chapter, we begin the process of installing and learn how to bring out the best in the application servers.

CHAPTER 2

Setting Up the Resin Server

This chapter contains the information you need to install the base Resin server, whether you're a novice or an expert. As shown in the previous chapter, the fundamental component of the Resin server is code for handling Java servlets, JSP, and XTP templates. It just so happens that the developers also included an HTTP server for handling HTML, images, and other plug-ins. With the addition of an HTTP server, the Resin product can be installed in a matter of minutes and allows for rapid development and evaluation. For those of you who are already running a Web server, complete instructions for installing Resin using an external HTTP server can be found in Chapter 16, "Configuring Your Web Server."

Requirements for Installation

As with most all applications, there are minimum requirements for successful operation, and Resin is no different. Two of the most important considerations are ancillary software and physical server configuration.

Support Software

Resin requires that a Java Development Kit (JDK) be installed on the server where it will execute. The JDK version must be 1.4 or later; for the basic Resin server, you can use the Standard Edition rather than the Enterprise Edition. Note this isn't just a Java Runtime Environment (JRE) but the actual software development kit, including the Java compiler. To use the latest features of Java and Resin, install the 1.4 version of JSDK.

Tested Configurations

As of this writing, available Java versions include 1.2, 1.2.2, 1.3.1, and 1.4.x. We tested each of the installations on the Microsoft Windows and Linux platforms along with Resin and found that they worked as advertised.

Recommended Server Configuration

The Resin server itself is a fairly lightweight application, so the recommended server configuration primarily reflects the additional software needs. The following configuration is a base recommendation for a development platform:

- CPU: 300MHz or higher (Pentium II for Windows and Intel Linux)
- Memory: 128MB or higher
- Hard drive: 6GB or higher

For a production system, all three criteria will need to be expanded as appropriate. For the examples in this book, we used the following machine configurations:

Windows

- Windows 2000
- 600MHz Pentium III
- 768MB of RAM
- 40GB hard drive

Linux

- Mandrake 8.2
- 300MHz Pentium II
- 192MB of RAM
- 40GB hard drive

Integrating Resin

The Resin server's architecture is shown in Figure 2.1. The Resin system itself is written in Java with some JNI library code for advanced socket handling and OpenSLL support. The server executes as a standard application in relation to the operating system. All of the source code for the server is available on the Resin Web site, so you can examine it to see how it was implemented. Because the system is written in Java, a JRE is needed for basic execution.

If you use Resin to deploy servlets, JSP pages, or EJBs, you will need a Java compiler (e.g., the Sun Java SDK or jikes, an IBM Java compiler). When a request is made of a JSP or servlet, the compiler compiles the source code and places it into the appropriate application directory. Once compiled, the CLASS file will execute within a Java Virtual Machine (JVM).

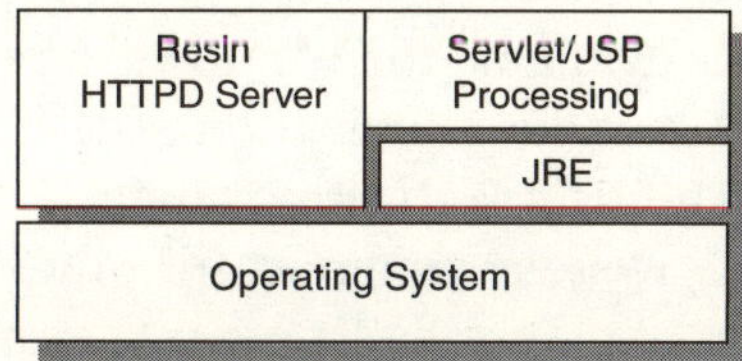

Figure 2.1 The Resin server architecture.

Ports

All requests to Resin will come from a Web browser using the HTTP protocol over the TCP/IP transport. The TCP/IP transport consists of an IP address and a port number. The IP address may temporarily be masked by a domain name, which is mapped to an IP address in due time. The traditional port for HTTP is 80. By default, the Resin HTTP server uses port 8080; this is done to maintain a cooperative environment in which other Web servers are executing on the same machine, as well as to accomodate development by providing a convenient port accessible without root access. In a production situation, the port should be changed to 80 to maintain consistency with Internet standards. Any Apache or IIS plug-ins are detected by Resin on port 6802.

This means that once Resin is installed, accessing the server will require the use of a port parameter in the URL. For example, if the server is installed on a machine with the IP address of 192.168.0.4, the URL would read

```
http://192.168.0.4:8080
```

As we will see in Chapter 15, "Resin Server Configuration," you can change the port number for the HTTP server when you use Resin in a production setting.

Obtaining Java

The most obvious place to obtain a JDK is from Sun at http://java.sun.com/j2se/. On this page links are available for 1.2.2, 1.3.1, and the latest 1.4.0 release of Java 2 Standard Edition (J2SE). At the top of the page are the download links for Windows, Linux, and Solaris versions of the SDK. Note the JRE link is also present on this page; ignore this link because you need the SDK. Further down the page is a link for an installation document, which you use to completely install Java.

IBM

It should be noted that IBM also has JDKs available for Windows, Linux, and other operating systems. Currently, the Linux kit is based on JDK 1.3.1 and the Windows kit is based on JDK 1.3.0. The IBM Web site includes 1.4.0 versions of the Java JDK for some operating systems; support for other OSs is coming soon. The Web site for the kits is:

http://www-106.ibm.com/developerworks/java/jdk/index.html?loc=j

The kits from Java and IBM differ in two ways. IBM features a reengineered JVM and a just-in-time compiler. If you're interested in high performance, check out the IBM kits; however, keep in mind that new features found in version 1.4 will not be present.

Installing Resin on Windows

Installing Resin on Windows begins with the installation of Java (which we just covered). Run all of the appropriate tests to verify that Java has been cleanly installed and is operational. The installation instructions that follow are based on Java 1.4.0_01 and Resin-EE 3.0.2. We set JAVA_HOME as a system-wide environment variable.

Start the Resin server installation by downloading the latest version compressed as a Zip file from www.caucho.com/download/. On this page, under the heading Latest Version, you'll see two versions: resin-3.0.2.zip and resin-ee-3.0.2.zip. Choose resin-ee-3.0.2.zip as it will provide you with all of the features needed for the examples in this book. Either launch the download or save it in an appropriate location on your hard drive.

When the file is uncompressed, it will save all of its contents in a root directory called \resin-ee-3.0.2. You have the option of placing this directory anywhere on your system. In most cases, you'll want to place the directory at the root or drive level, such as c:\resin-ee-3.0.2. Once the file is uncompressed, Resin creates a complete directory structure like the one shown in Figure 2.2.

Right now, the primary directory we are interested in is \bin—this is where the server executables are located. In a Windows environment, there are basically two ways to begin the execution of the server: manually and as a service.

For the manual approach, begin by double-clicking on the HTTPD.exe icon in the *<root directory>*/resin-3.0.2/bin directory. Or you can start a command prompt and execute the server by typing the command *httpd*. After you double-click or run the command from the command prompt, two dialog windows will appear. The first is a command prompt within which the Resin server begins execution, as shown in Figure 2.3. The second window, shown in Figure 2.4, is a small control panel that allows you to halt the server easily.

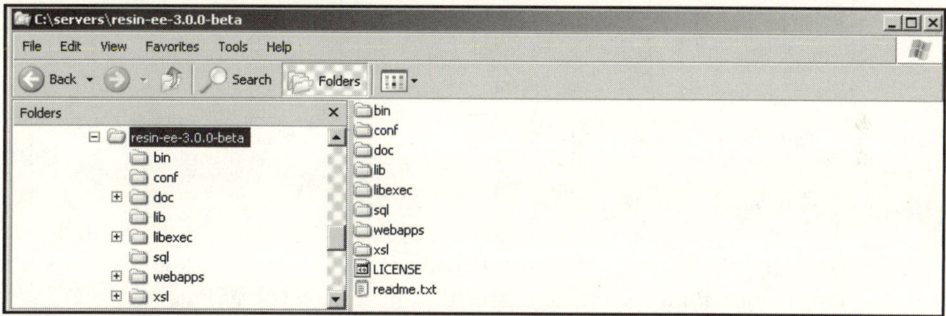

Figure 2.2 The Windows Resin installation directory hierarchy.

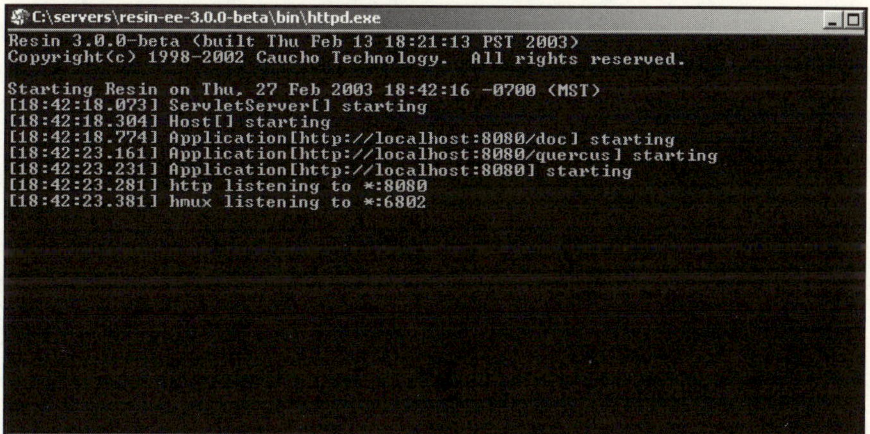

Figure 2.3 A command prompt within the Resin execution.

The server can be shut down by stopping the server process: simply click the Stop radio button, shown in Figure 2.4, and then click the Quit button. Figure 2.3 shows the initialization steps executed during the startup of the Resin Core server. Note the following:

- The server will automatically compile and initialize applications found in the directory hierarchy where Resin was initially installed.

- The server will begin listening on port 8080 of the host machine for HTTP requests.
- The server will automatically start listening on port 6802 for srun requests.

As we see later in this chapter, you can change the ports used for request listening.

Figure 2.4 The Resin launch control panel.

Windows Service Startup

The process we just described works well for server development needs and simple installations, but in a production setting (or whenever you don't want to deal with constantly starting the server manually), you can start Resin automatically by installing it as a Windows service under Windows NT, 2000, or XP.

To install Resin as a service, open a Windows command prompt and change to the /bin directory of the Resin installation. In this directory are two executables: httpd.exe (which we used earlier in our discussion) and a file called setup.exe, which includes several simple configuration options. In most cases, use the following command to start the service installation:

```
httpd –install
```

This command installs Resin into the service component of the operating system using the default configuration file (resin.conf) found in the /conf directory. The dialog box shown in Figure 2.5 confirms the installation was successful.

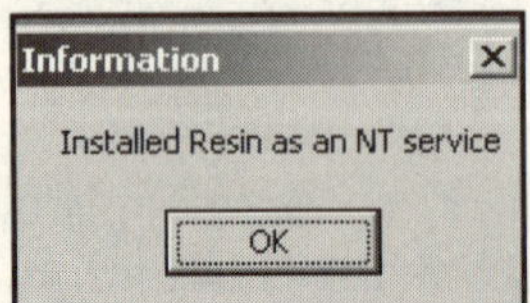

Figure 2.5 The service installation confirmation dialog box.

Once installed as a service, the server can be started and stopped using the Services dialog box in Administration Tools or by using command prompt commands. When executed, the Services application looks like Figure 2.6.

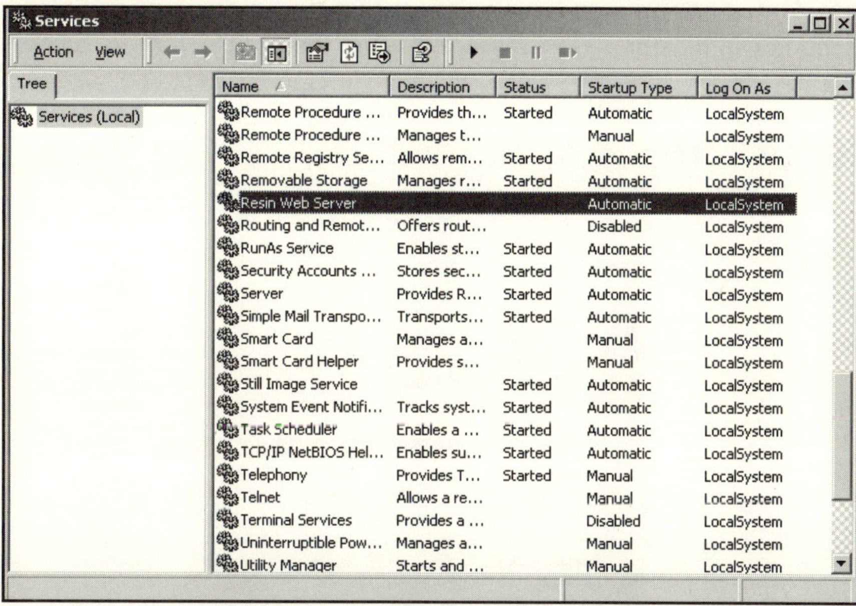

Figure 2.6 The Services application with the Resin server installed.

The service entry installed by the –install command-line flag used earlier is highlighted in Figure 2.6. When first installed, the service isn't actually started; it is just placed in the services system. Use this dialog box to start the service by right-clicking on the Resin Web Server entry and selecting the start option, as shown in Figure 2.7, or by pressing the black right arrow on the toolbar.

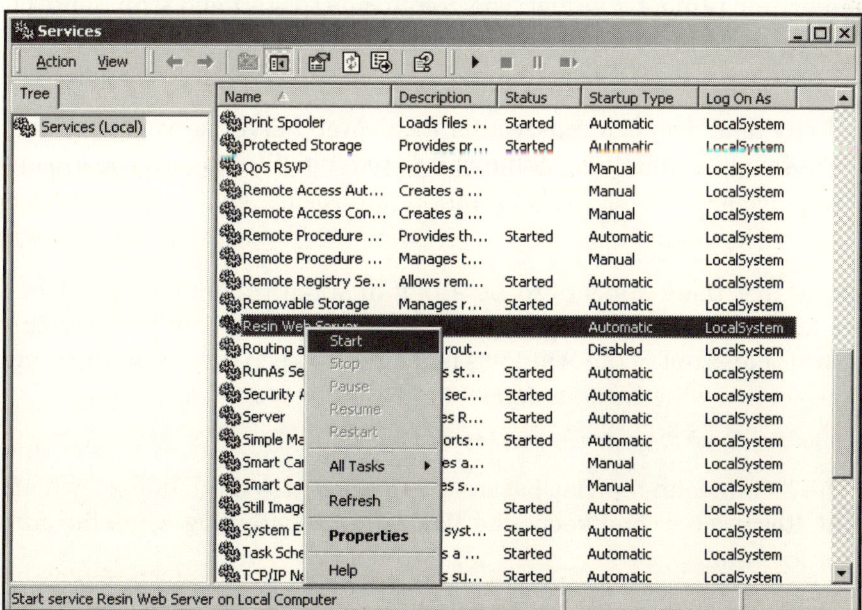

Figure 2.7 The right-click menu for the Resin Web server.

The Status column will have a value of Started, as shown in Figure 2.8. The service can be stopped or restarted using the toolbar button, also shown in Figure 2.8.

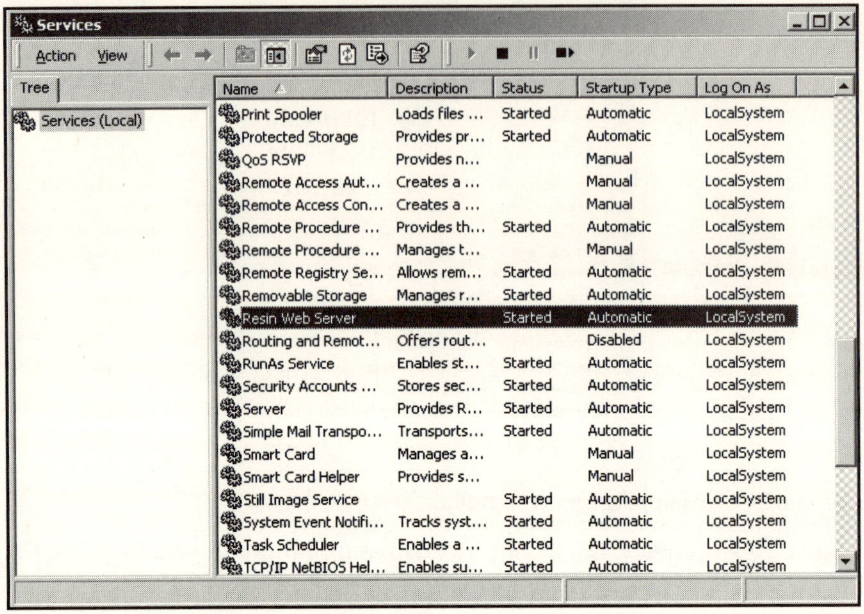

Figure 2.8 Running the Resin Web server.

The service can also be started and stopped using commands entered in a command prompt window. The commands to start and stop the service are:

```
net start resin
net stop resin
```

At any time, you can remove the Resin Web Server service from the system by issuing the following command in the /bin directory of the Resin installation:

```
httpd –remove
```

Note that there appears to be a bug in some versions of the JDK and the related JVM. In these versions, the JVM will stop executing when the administrator logs out of the Windows machine. To keep this from occurring, install the service with the command

```
httpd –install –Xrs –conf/myconf.conf
```

The X command-line flag passes the options rs to the JDK used when starting the Resin server and keeps the JDK VM from stopping when the administrator logs out.

Another bug has been reported in Windows 2000 that might occur when you install the service using the command-line option. For example, the following command starts the service and forces the server to use a specific configuration file:

```
httpd -install -conf conf/myconf.conf
```

In some cases, the system refuses to register the new service. In this instance, you can add command-line options to the Resin Web Server entry in the Service application by bringing up the right-click menu, selecting Properties, and adding the command-line option in the Path To Executable edit box.

Installing Resin on Unix/Linux

To demonstrate how to use the basic Resin server on Unix, we used a Mandrake 8.2 Linux installation. Resin requires you to install Java v1.2 or later on the machine where the server will execute. Our test environment used Sun Java Soft version 1.4.0 build92 SDK.

Start the process of installing Resin by downloading the most current Resin server from www.resin.com in the download area. If you are working on a headless Unix machine, you can also obtain the file from ftp.caucho.com in the /pub/resin directory. The downloaded file will have a name like

```
resin-3.0.x.tar.gz
```

where *x* is the latest revision of the code. Extract the files from the installation file using the command

```
tar -vzxf resin-3.0.2.tar.gz
```

This tar command uncompresses and untars the files located in the installation file. Alternately, you can use gunzip and tar in this sequence:

```
gunzip resin-3.0.2.tar.gz
tar -xf resin-3.0.2.tar
```

Once you extract the files, Resin places the directory structure shown in Figure 2.9 on the local drive. After installing the system, it is important to configure it:

```
/configure
make
```

The result is a system optimized for UNIX.

Executing Resin under Unix

Under Unix, the Resin server is executed using the shell script httpd.sh located in the /bin directory. You can launch the server using the shell script shown here:

```
resin@localhost.localdomain: /home/resin/resin-ee-3.0.0-beta
[resin@localhost resin-ee-3.0.0-beta]$ ls -l
total 404
drwxrwxr-x    2 resin    resin        4096 Feb 13 19:21 bin/
drwxrwxr-x    2 resin    resin        4096 Feb 13 19:21 conf/
-rw-rw-r--    1 resin    resin       39311 Feb 13 19:21 config.guess
-rw-rw-r--    1 resin    resin       27594 Feb 13 19:21 config.sub
-rwxrwxr-x    1 resin    resin      140520 Feb 13 19:21 configure*
-rw-rw-r--    1 resin    resin       20166 Feb 13 19:21 configure.in
drwxrwxr-x    2 resin    resin        4096 Feb 13 19:21 contrib/
drwxrwxr-x    4 resin    resin        4096 Feb 13 19:21 doc/
-rw-rw-r--    1 resin    resin        5598 Feb 13 19:21 install-sh
drwxrwxr-x    2 resin    resin        4096 Feb 13 19:21 lib/
drwxrwxr-x    4 resin    resin        4096 Feb 13 19:21 libexec/
-rw-rw-r--    1 resin    resin        3016 Feb 13 19:21 LICENSE
-rw-rw-r--    1 resin    resin       86948 Feb 13 19:21 ltconfig
-rw-rw-r--    1 resin    resin         125 Feb 13 19:21 Makefile.in
-rw-rw-r--    1 resin    resin        8857 Feb 13 19:21 missing
-rw-rw-r--    1 resin    resin         722 Feb 13 19:21 mkinstalldirs
-rw-rw-r--    1 resin    resin        4394 Feb 13 19:21 readme.txt
drwxrwxr-x    2 resin    resin        4096 Feb 13 19:21 sql/
drwxrwxr-x    3 resin    resin        4096 Feb 13 19:21 src/
drwxrwxr-x    2 resin    resin        4096 Feb 13 19:21 webapps/
drwxrwxr-x    4 resin    resin        4096 Feb 13 19:21 xsl/
[resin@localhost resin-ee-3.0.0-beta]$
```

Figure 2.9 The Linux Resin installation directory hierarchy.

The second way to execute the server—and more than likely the one you want to use in a development setting—is the shell script. You can launch the server using the shell script shown here:

```
$ ./resin-3.0.2/bin/httpd.sh
```

The first time the server is launched, you see the output shown in Figure 2.10 in the terminal window.

Note that the server isn't automatically launched into a background process. To make it execute in the background, use this command:

```
$ ./resin-3.0.2/bin/httpd.sh start
```

In the output shown in Figure 2.10, the server begins by checking all of the code in the example and tutorial directories to determine if compiled classes exist. If the classes aren't found for the corresponding source files or the source files have been changed since the last time the server executed, the system compiles the source. Once the files have been initialized, the server begins listening on port 8080 for requests. The system also listens on port 6802 for srun requests.

You can stop the server using the shell script as well. For example:

```
$./resin-3.0.2/bin/httpd.sh stop
```

The server can be restarted with this command:

```
$./resin-3.0.2/bin/httpd.sh restart
```

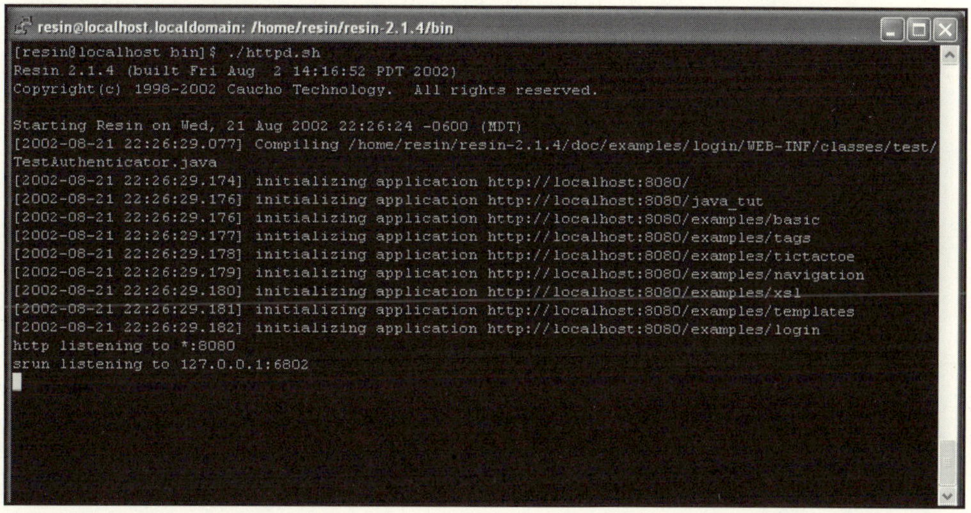

```
resin@localhost.localdomain: /home/resin/resin-2.1.4/bin
[resin@localhost bin]$ ./httpd.sh
Resin 2.1.4 (built Fri Aug  2 14:16:52 PDT 2002)
Copyright(c) 1998-2002 Caucho Technology.  All rights reserved.

Starting Resin on Wed, 21 Aug 2002 22:26:24 -0600 (MDT)
[2002-08-21 22:26:29.077] Compiling /home/resin/resin-2.1.4/doc/examples/login/WEB-INF/classes/test/
TestAuthenticator.java
[2002-08-21 22:26:29.174] initializing application http://localhost:8080/
[2002-08-21 22:26:29.176] initializing application http://localhost:8080/java_tut
[2002-08-21 22:26:29.176] initializing application http://localhost:8080/examples/basic
[2002-08-21 22:26:29.177] initializing application http://localhost:8080/examples/tags
[2002-08-21 22:26:29.178] initializing application http://localhost:8080/examples/tictactoe
[2002-08-21 22:26:29.179] initializing application http://localhost:8080/examples/navigation
[2002-08-21 22:26:29.180] initializing application http://localhost:8080/examples/xsl
[2002-08-21 22:26:29.181] initializing application http://localhost:8080/examples/templates
[2002-08-21 22:26:29.182] initializing application http://localhost:8080/examples/login
http listening to *:8080
srun listening to 127.0.0.1:6802
```

Figure 2.10 Launching the Unix Resin server.

Testing the Installation

After you've installed the server, you need to verify that things are working correctly. Launch a browser and browse to the page http://localhost:8080 (or http://<*server ip address*>:8080). For the remainder of the book, we assume that the Resin server is located on the local machine and we use the http://localhost:8080 URL. Once the browser makes a connection with the Resin server, the default home page of Resin will be displayed, as shown in Figure 2.11.

The first time you access the default home page, it will take a moment or two for the page to be displayed. During this pause, the Resin server is activating the Java compiler to convert the XTP-based dynamic pages to a static HTML page. When the page is accessed again, the server will not have to compile the dynamic code again, and subsequently the page will be displayed almost instantaneously. Once the compiling takes place, Resin leaves the resulting code for use when the server is shut down and restarted another time.

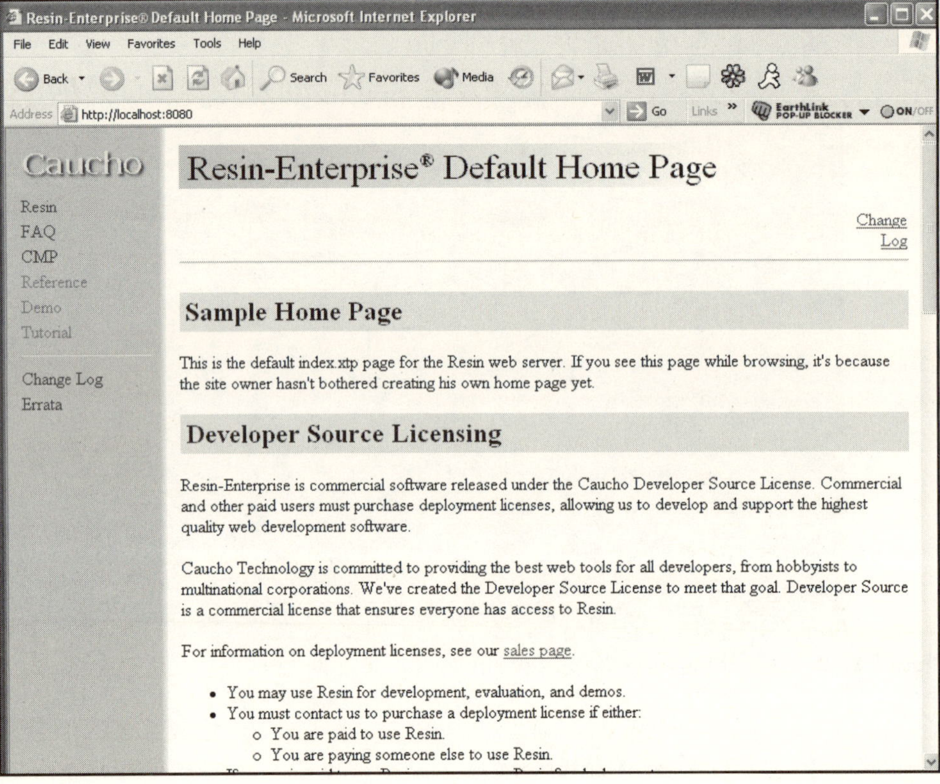

Figure 2.11 The Resin default home page.

Command-Line Options

As shown in Table 2.1, the Resin server includes several command-line options that let you customize the server when it is first executed. You can supply these options no matter how you start the server.

Table 2.1 The Resin Server Options (continues)

OPTION	DESCRIPTION	ARGUMENT	DEFAULT
–classpath	Adds new listings to the current classpath.	Paths to be added to the classpath	$CLASSPATH
–conf	Allows an alternative configuration file to be used when the server starts up.	Path to configuration file–i.e., conf/new.conf	conf/resin.conf

Table 2.1 The Resin Server Options (continued)

OPTION	DESCRIPTION	ARGUMENT	DEFAULT
–install	NT only; installs the Resin server as a service in NT, 2000, or XP. Does not automatically start the service.	None	None
–install-as	NT only; installs the Resin server as a service in NT, 2000, or XP as a named service. Does not automatically start the service.	name	None
–D	Sets the named Java system property to the supplied value.	name=value	None
–J	Passes the specific value to the JDK as an argument.	Command-line argument	None
–java_home	Sets the path to the Java environment the system should use when executing the server.	Path to Java installation directory –i.e., c:\j2sdk1.3.0	Checks for the JAVA_ HOME environment variable; if not found, it performs a search.
–nojit	Turns off the just-in-time compiler.	None	Enabled
–pid	Unix only; allows you to enter a path and filename where the system should store the application PID.	Path and filename for pid storage	Resin.pid
–remove	NT only; removes the Resin server from services.	None	None
–remove-as	NT only; removes the named Resin server from services.	name	None
–resin_home	Sets the path to the Resin installation directory.	Path to Resin installation	Parent of wrapper. pl or resin.dll file
–verbose	Using this argument causes the server to display information about the currently installed Java SDK as well as defined environment variables such as –classpath or JAVA_HOME.	None	Off
–X	Passes the specified option to the JDK	Java option	None

Documentation

The default installation includes documentation on the server as well as numerous example programs using servlets, JSP, XTP, and beans. From the home page of the installation site, the documentation consists of:

FAQ—This links brings up a page with high-level categories of questions and answers. The categories are:

- Installation
- SSL
- Class Loader
- Configuration
- JSP/Servlet
- Debugging
- Misc

Reference Guide—This link maps to a fairly comprehensive set of pages discussing reference topics like configuration, JSP, and XTP.

JavaDoc—This link looks at the various classes within the Resin server from the JavaDoc perspective.

Demo—This link displays the various example programs as mentioned in the discussion about the directory structure in the section "Testing the Installation." Examples are available using servlets, JSP, XTP, and JSP/XTP templates.

Tutorial—This link provides additional information about using Resin and programming in JSP and Java.

The Basic Configuration

The Resin server requires a configuration file to handle most of its basic settings. The configuration file, called resin.conf, is located in the /conf directory one level below where Resin has been installed. Listing 2.1 contains a basic configuration file with all of the options necessary to support an initial launching of the server.

```
<resin xmlns="http://caucho.com/ns/resin">
  <server>
```

Listing 2.1 A base configuration file. (continues)

```
      <http id='' host='*' port='8080'/>
      <resin:include href="app-default.xml"/>
      <host id=''>
        <document-directory>/home/gradecki/public_html</document-directory>
        <web-app id=""/>
        <web-app-deploy path="webapps" />
      </host>
    </server>
  </resin>
```

Listing 2.1 A base configuration file. (continued)

The Resin configuration file is based on XML and has a series of elements defined to handle all possible configuration issues. Each of the high-level elements, such as caucho.com and http-server, have additional elements defined. All of the elements available in the configuration file are shown in Appendix C. In this chapter, we discuss only the basic elements. In Chapter 15, "Resin Server Configuration," we define many more of the elements when we address advanced uses of the Resin server.

The Resin configuration file is designed for configuring the server itself. For the most part, all servlet configuration should be kept in a web.xml file located in WEB-INF. Many times, a servlet will need database information as well. The Resin system includes a file called resin-web.xml, also located in the WEB-INF directory, for setting server information for each servlet independently. We discuss both of these files as servlet examples later in Chapter 4, "Using Servlets and Resin."

The configuration shown in Listing 2.1 tells the Resin server many things about its operating environment. First, the <http> element specifies an attribute called port with a value of 8080. Obviously this tells the server that it should monitor port 8080 for all incoming HTTP requests. Notice the element itself doesn't have values associated with it but only an attribute—thus, the < /> closing tags are used. The <resin:include href="app-default.xml"/> tag pulls in a large number of server defaults which can be used as-is or overridden.

Next, the configuration file begins a section called <host>. This section deals primarily with the definition of a virtual host and specifies where the server can expect to find information on the local drives. In our example, the <host> element has a single attribute, called id. The id attribute lists hosts that could be used in the calling of a servlet. For example, multiple virtual hosts might be configured to handle the URLs http://www.yesone.com and http://www.unittest.com. For each of these URLs, you would need to set up separate directories. In our example, all URLs will use the same <host> definition. (See Chapter 17 for a discussion of virtual hosting.)

Within the <host> element are several subelements. The <document-directory> element is used to specify the document directory where source (HTML, servlet, etc.) files can be found. If this element is not present, the system will use the root directory where the server was installed. We recommend that you specify this element so the administrator of the machine has full control over file placement on the local drive.

The <web-app-deploy> element is used to specify the location of Web application resource files. By default no location is defined. The value defined in the element is appended to the document directory to form a complete directory structure. In our example, WAR files are placed in the directory /home/Gradecki/public_html/webapps. The file test.war is placed in the directory and auto-expanded to the directory webapps/test. Browsing to the application is accomplished with the URL http://localhost/test.

The HTTP Port

Within the <server> element is a subelement called <http> that lets you define the HTTP port to be used as the primary incoming channel. There are numerous attributes for this subelement, as shown in Chapter 15, but the most important is probably port. The port attribute is used to specify the port number to listen for incoming HTTP requests. The format of the subelement and attribute is as follows:

```
<http port=' '/>
```

If you want the port to be 80, just set it in the configuration file:

```
<resin>
  <server>
    <http port='80'/>
  </http>
</resin>
```

Logging in Resin 3.x

As discussed earlier, all configuration in Resin 3.x is based on a concept called the environment which allows for natural and logic separation of tasks within the configuration file. The logging definitions can be placed in several different Resin environments, including <resin>, <server>, <host-default>, <host>, <web-app-default>, and <web-app>. All logging in Resin 3.x is supported through the Logging API defined in Java 1.4. The primary element to define the logging is <log>:

```
<log
  name=''
  path=''
  level=''
```

```
    rollover-period=''
    timestamp=
/>
```

Let's break down the format of the <log> element:

name—defines a Java-like hierarchical name

path—where the logging should be sent. Valid values include stderr:, stdout:, and typical path names like '/usr/logs/resin/'

level—the log level designed to match the levels defined for Java 1.4 logging. The values available are shown in Table 2.2.

Table 2.2 Java 1.4 Logging Values

NAME	JAVA 1.4 LOGGING API	MEANING
off		no logging
severe	severe	severe issue with the application
warning	warning	possible problem has occurred and needs attention
info	Info	information only
config	Config	configuration issue
fine	Fine	course tracing information
finer	Finer	more detailed tracing message
finest	Finest	detailed tracing message
all		log everything

rollover-period—Specifies the frequency in days, weeks, or months before a new rollover file is created.

timestamp—Specifies the format for stamping each of the logging output lines. The format values are shown in Table 2.3. For example:

```
<resin xmlns=http://caucho.com/ns/resin>
  <log name='' path='stdout:' rollover-period='1W'/>
</resin>
```

The Java Compiler

The Resin server needs access to a Java compiler in order to compile JSP pages and build corresponding servlets. The <javac> element allows you to specify Java compiler information to be passed to the server. The format of the element is as follows:

```
<resin>
  <javac compiler=''
    compiler-args=''
    encoding=''/>
</resin>
```

In this format:

compiler—Specifies a path to a Java compiler like that supplied in the Java JDK or a just-in-time compiler. The default value is internal, which instructs the server to find a Java compiler based on where one would normally be found.

-args—Contains a string of additional arguments to pass through to the Java compiler when it is invoked.

encoding—Specifies the character encoding you want to use.

Table 2.3 Logging Timestamp Formatting Specification

VALUE	DESCRIPTION
%a	short weekday (mon)
%A	long weekday (Monday)
%b	short month (Jan)
%B	long month (January)
%c	date specific to executing locale
%d	day of month
%H	24-hour
%I	12-hour
%j	day of year
%m	month
%M	minute
%p	am/pm
%S	seconds
%s	milliseconds
%W	week of year
%w	day of week
%y	2-digit year
%Y	4-digit year

The Error Page

It is probably fair to say that everyone has experienced a Web site error in which a browser message appears with an error code (such as 404). Associated with the error code is a fair amount of descriptive text explaining what might have occurred. With some sites a missing page doesn't display a 404 error but instead displays a "nice" page with the site's graphics and logos. The Resin server allows a specific error page to be displayed in the event that a request fails. The <error-page> element handles the configuration:

```
<web-app id='/'>
  <error-page location=''
                  exception-type=''
                  error-code=''
  />
</web-app>
```

In this format:

location—Specifies the path to the file you want to display for a given exception or error code.

exception-type—Contains a string representing a valid Java exception.

error-code—Specifies a valid HTTP status code.

The <error-page> element is placed within a <web-app> element. The <web-app> element is used to define configuration parameters for applications being served by Resin (see Chapter 15). The tag <web-app id="/"> tells the Resin server to apply configuration information enclosed within the tag to all Web applications. For example, when the error code 404 is received it indicates that the page being requested cannot be found. The Web server generally returns a basic error page. You can place the following elements in the configuration file to display a more informative page when the error code is received:

```
<web-app id='/'>
  <error-page location='errors/404errorpage.jsp'
                  error-code='404'
  />
</web-app>
```

With this configuration, the page 404errorpage.jsp is displayed when a page cannot be found.

There are also times when a Java class will return an exception. Probably the most notable is the error java.lang.NullPointerException. Using the <error-page> element, you can display an error page for exceptions as well. For example:

```
<web-app id='/'>
  <error-page location='errors/404errorpage.jsp'
                        exception-type='java.lang.NullPointerException'
  />
</web-app>
```

It is possible to have a host-wide errorpage by including a <error-page> element under the <host> element.

The Server Restart Ping

During development work or in a production situation, the worst thing that can happen is to have your server crash or just become unavailable. To solve this problem, you can set up a monitor that can constantly ping the server to verify that not only is it alive but that a specific Web site is running on the server. The Resin server features this monitor capability, and you can set it up through the configuration file.

The monitoring of the server and hosted Web sites is accomplished using a separate thread, which acts like a simple Web browser to access a number of URLs. As long as the listed URLs return a result or HTTP status 200, it can be assumed the server and Web site are operational. If a failure does occur, the thread kills Resin and forces a restart of the server. Note that the separate thread executing to determine if the server is still alive executes in the JVM where the server is executing. If by chance the virtual machine hangs, the server will have essentially crashed without detection.

The ping functionality is handled through a resource. For example:

```
<resource jndi-name="ping" type="com.caucho.server.admin.PingThread">
  <init>
    <url>http://localhost:8080/index.jsp</url>
    <sleep-time>15s</sleep-time>
  </init>
</resource>
```

Using a <resource> allows the system to handle the execution of the ping thread and offload any special configuration. If you want to write your own ping class, place the newly created class name in the 'type' attribute.

What's Next

In this chapter, we've taken a comprehensive look at the installation of the Resin server on both the Unix and Windows platforms. In the next chapter, we begin the process of developing applications for Resin.

CHAPTER 3

Using JSP and Resin

When a Web site needs to move from the delivery of static information to the delivery of dynamic content, the developer must decide which scripting language to use to write the page. So many choices are available—JavaServer Pages (JSPs), PHP Hypertext Preprocessor (PHP), and Active Server Pages (ASPs), among others. Many of the choices are comparable to each other, and it's just a matter of selecting the language that fits the platform available and the philosophy of the shop where the language will be used. JSP is one of the more powerful options available.

In this chapter, we explore JSP and how to use it with the Resin application server to provide a comprehensive, dynamic computing environment.

Beginning JSP Usage

When the decision is made to move from a static page to dynamic, one of the consequences that comes into play is the mixing of presentation and business functionality. In many of the server-side scripting languages available, a dynamic page to retrieve information about the user might be structured in the following way:

```
<?
     'connect to database'
     'verify connection'
?>
<HTML>
```

```
<BODY>
   <!—display header information >!
   <h1>User: <? Get username ?> </h1>
   <?
      'Get more information'
      while (more accounts)
        'display account information'
      loop
   ?>
</BODY>
</HTML>
```

In this very simple example, we find the <HTML> presentation tags have had the scripting language tags directly inserted into them. While all of the server-side scripting languages require that the business tags be inserted into the HTML code, many languages put the large amounts of actual code in the tags instead of calls to the code necessary for a given piece of functionality. In other words, instead of having a method that connects to a database and verifies the connection, the scripting language shown here puts all of the connection code directly into the HTML code.

While this type of coding works, it means that both the Web designer and the Web developer have to change the same piece of code. When the designer has to alter the layout of the page, he or she will probably have to sit side by side with the developer in order to get the scripting language tags in the right place. When the development team needs to modify the functionality, they will have to read through all of the HTML code to find the scripting code. While this doesn't seem like a huge issue, it causes problems in a production setting. It would be much better to have a scripting language that takes advantage of an existing powerful language like Java and that allows minimal insertion into the HTML code. JSP is the right technology to provide this type of separation.

An Overview of JSP Technology

Before getting into the details of JSP and Resin, let's spend some time going over the technology behind JSP. As we mentioned earlier, using JSP allows you to add dynamic content to a Web page, which keeps the page from becoming old and stale. But you have to pay a price: You must add scripting code to pull the dynamic content from various files or a database.

Users will access the new JSP page using their browser just as they did when trying to access a static HTML page. Most of the differences between these two scenarios is the process occurring at the server. Figure 3.1 shows how the server handles the JSP page request.

The process starts with the user making an HTTP GET request for a JSP file located on our Web site, as shown by step 1. The request is processed by a server running Web server software. The Web server application processes the HTTP GET request and pulls the file indicated in the command, as shown in steps 2 and 3. In our case, the JSP file will have to be passed to another piece of software that can handle that file—traditional Web server software is designed to handle only HTTP requests.

The other piece of software in this process is the application server—in our case, Resin. We use Resin for both the Web and JSP part of the processing performed by the server machine. The Resin server examines the requested JSP file and performs one of two different processes. If the requested JSP file hasn't been requested since the application server began executing, the requested JSP file is transformed into a Java servlet file, compiled by the Java compiler on the server, and stored as a CLASS file. This is illustrated by steps 4 and 5, and represents the first process the application server can execute. The second process is the actual execution of the requested JSP file's servlet class, as shown by step 6. This step is executed regardless of whether the JSP file had to be converted and compiled. Finally, the Web server returns the appropriate HTML to the client as a code request found within the JSP's compiled servlet.

As you might expect, the first time a JSP file is requested by a user, the response time is slightly long as opposed to subsequent fetches. On the subsequent fetches, the application server doesn't have to compile the JSP page and simply executes the corresponding servlet class.

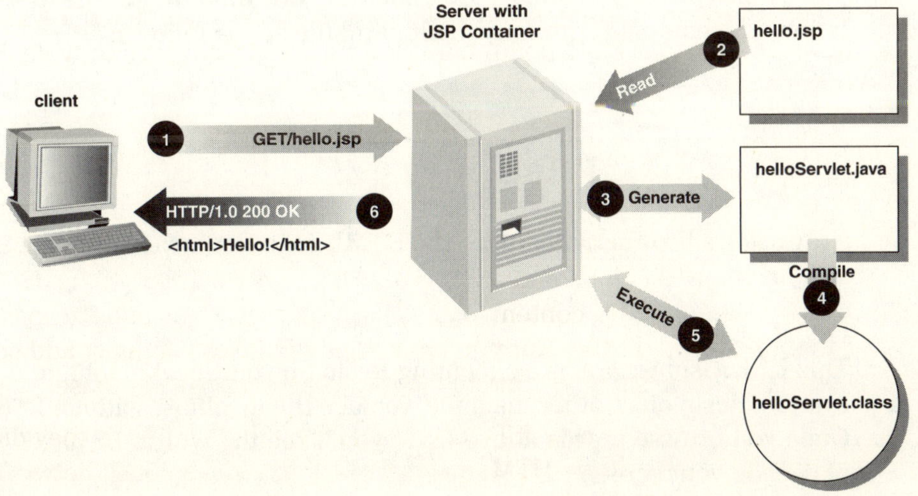

Figure 3.1 Handling a JSP page request.

Resin Support for JSP

The Resin server provides complete support for JSP 1.2 as defined in the Sun specification. All JSP pages must have template text, the HTML, and JSP actions represented by various tags and Java code. In the best cases, the JSP page consists of the <HTML> tags necessary to create the look and feel of the page, and JSP actions are used to execute code defined in both Java classes and JavaBeans. By putting the business logic in Java classes or JavaBeans, you achieve a better separation of functionality. Beginning with Resin 3.0, there is no longer any support for writing JSP pages using JavaScript.

Page Placement

Once Resin has been installed on your machine, it creates a directory called /doc to hold sample Web pages for smaller Web sites. For Web applications, the installation creates a directory called /webapps directory. This directory is designed to hold all of the Web applications and pages hosted by the server. In most cases, Resin creates separate directories for each individual site or application.

The JSP Hello World

To get a clear understanding of building a JSP page and hosting in Resin, let's build the classic Hello World as both an HTML page and a JSP page. First, let's build the HTML page. Using a text editor, create a file called hello.html and place it in a directory called hello under the /doc directory of the Resin installation. The contents within the hello.html file are as follows:

```
<HTML>
<BODY>
Hello, World!
</BODY>
<HTML>
```

Now using a browser, browse to the HTML page just created using a URL like this:

```
http://localhost:8080/hello/hello.html
```

This URL assumes you are executing Resin on your local machine. If you are running Resin on another machine, replace the localhost with an IP address. Once you browse to this above URL, you'll see the words *Hello, World!* displayed on your screen.

Now let's change the file to a JSP page by changing the .html extension to .jsp. Browse to the page again but replace *hello.html* with *hello.jsp*. Did you see any differences in the output? How about the response time? Instead of the *Hello, World!* text being instantaneously returned to the browser, there was a slight delay. This delay was the application server converting the JSP file to a servlet and compiling it. If you browse to the JSP page again, it should display the text without delay.

Now, building a JSP page without any Java in it isn't very useful, so let's add some. Change your hello.jsp file to read like this:

```
<HTML>
<BODY>
Hello World! <BR>
The time is now <%= new java.util.Date() %>
</BODY>
<HTML>
```

Save the file and browse to hello.jsp again. As you'd expect, there is a slight delay as the new JSP page is converted and compiled. Notice how the Resin server doesn't need to be shut down and restarted or otherwise told to reload the hello.jsp file. Resin senses the file has changed and automatically reconverts and compiles it. The result of this code is shown in Figure 3.2.

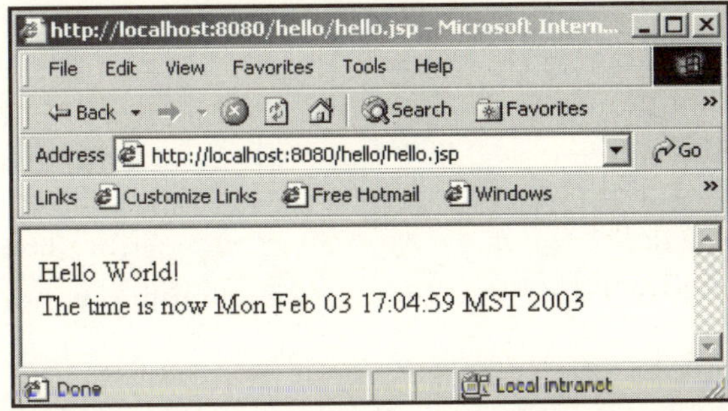

Figure 3.2 The output from the Hello World (with date) JSP.

Let's take a moment and discuss the code we just created and executed. The JSP page consists of both HTML template text and JSP code. The HTML template text consists of HTML tags and normal text. This information is passed from the server to the client browser without any changes to it. In order to differentiate the HTML from the JSP, special tags are used: <% and %>. The information contained within these tags is converted to Java code and placed within the servlet produced by the server. There are quite a few formats for the <% %> tags that cause the server to process the tagged information differently. Table 3.1 shows the four primary JSP tag combinations.

Table 3.1 JSP Tag Combinations

TAG	DESCRIPTION
<%@ ... %>	Directive
<%= ... %>	Java expression
<% ... %>	Java function
<%! ... %>	Java declaration

Of course, it's fairly hard to build a meaningful application just by pulling data information from the system. JSP allows you to use the special tags to enclose more than just expressions. Consider the following example:

```
<HTML>
<BODY>
<%
    java.util.Date localTime = java.util.Date();
    System.out.println("Pulled the correct date");
%>
Hello World! <BR>
The time is <%= date %>
</BODY>
<HTML>
```

In this new JSP page, we have added a scriptlet using the <% %> tags. A scriptlet is just a snippet of Java code that performs a specific function. In our case, we define a local script variable and assign it the current date/time. We also take advantage of the fact that we can use the System.out variable to output debug information to the console window where the Resin server was initially launched. Figure 3.2 shows the output to the Resin launch window created by the JSP page.

You might be curious about the difference between the System.out statement—which prints to the console window—and the HTML text and JSP expression tags <%= %>—which return output to the browser. Remember that all HTML tags and text are converted by the Resin application server into appropriate code within a servlet. The resulting code takes advantage of a system variable called out, which is a writer to the browser. So the HTML expression Hello World!
 will be converted to code like this:

```
out.println("Hello World!<BR>");
```

Our code can also take advantage of this variable to output specific text to the browser. For example:

```
<HTML>
<BODY>
<%
    java.util.Date localTime = java.util.Date();
    System.out.println("Pulled the correct date");
%>
Hello World! <BR>
The time is <% out.println(date.toString()); %>
</BODY>
<HTML>
```

In this example, we replaced the expression tags with function tags and included Java code to output the date string to the browser. The out variable is an object instantiated from the class javax.servlet.jsp.JspWriter.

Combining Java and HTML

In all of the examples to this point, the Java code and HTML have been separated for the most part. There will be times when you need to mix the Java and HTML xed to provide accurate output. For example:

```
<HTML>
<BODY>
<%
    java.util.Date localTime[10];
    for (int i=o;i<10;i++)
      localTime[i] = new java.util.Date();
%>
Time Array<BR>
<table>
<% for (int i=0;i<10;i++) { %>
  <TR><TD><%= localTime[i] %></TD></TR>
<% } %>
</table>
</BODY>
<HTML>
```

In this example, our scriptlet creates an array of Date objects and displays those objects in an HTML table. While the code could have been written with 10 JSP expression tags, the code would look terrible and thus need a second loop.

The display loop encloses the necessary table HTML tags along with a single JSP expression tag to pull the individual date values. The output is a table containing all of the date values. Mixing the JSP and HTML tags can get confusing at times, but by using proper formatting of the code, you reduce the confusion.

JSP Variables

The out variable isn't the only variable available to the developer. Table 3.2 shows all of the variables the Resin server provides to the JSP page.

Table 3.2 JSP Variables

NAME	DESCRIPTION	JAVA CLASS
application	Specifies the current application	javax.servlet.ServletContext
exception	For error pages, indicates the exception thrown from the broken page	java.lang.Throwable
out	Contains the buffered stream to the HTTP response	javax.servlet.jsp.JspWriter
pageContext	Indicates the state of the current page	javax.servlet.jsp.PageContext
request	Contains the request object	javax.servlet.http.HttpServletRequest
response	Contains the response object	javax.servlet.HttpServletResponse
session	Specifies the current session	javax.servlet.HttpSession

Using the Request Variable

One of the more powerful and useful variables provided by Resin is the request variable. Every time a browser makes a file request of the server, a request variable is created. This variable includes information such as the file being requested and the header for the request, as well as any user-entered values for an HTML form. Before we look at getting values from a form, consider the following example:

```
<HTML>
<BODY>
Request Information<BR>
Your IP is <%= request.getRemoteHost() %><BR>
The HTTP request was <%= request.getMethod() %><BR>
The URL requested was <%= request.getRequestURI() %><BR>
</BODY>
<HTML>
```

In this simple example, we use the Request object to obtain some generic information about the user making the request against the server. Of particular importance is the getRemoteHost() method. Unless you have made some extraordinary efforts, the administrator of the server you have accessed will have a record of the IP address from which you are browsing. This basic information is helpful, but the Request object also helps when using forms.

All of the requests to a URL contain numerous headers to hold information about the browser, user, and machine making the request. You can use the Request object to obtain the header both as a whole or individually. Consider the following code:

```
<HTML>
<BODY>
<table border='1'>
<tr><td>Header</td><td>Value</td></tr>
<%
Enumeration e;
e = request.getHeaderNames();

while (e.hasMoreElements())
{
    String key = (String)e.nextElement();
    String value = request.getHeader(key);
    out.println("<tr><td>");
    out.println(key);
    out.println("</td><td>");
    out.println(value);
    out.println("</td></tr>");
}
%>
<table>
</BODY>
</HTML>
```

This code puts all of the header names from the Request object using the method getHeaderNames() and places them in an Enumeration object. The names are cycled through using a loop and their values extracted using the get-Header(String key) method. Both the header name and values are displayed in a table, as shown in Figure 3.3.

If you need to look at a specific header, use code like the following:

```
<%
Enumeration e;
e = request.getHeaderNames();
String userAgent = null;

while (e.hasMoreElements())
{
    String key = (String)e.nextElement();
    if (key.equals("user-agent"))
    {
        userAgent = request.getHeader(key);
        break;
    }
}
%>
<html>
<body>
USER-AGENT is <%= userAgent %>
</body>
</html>
```

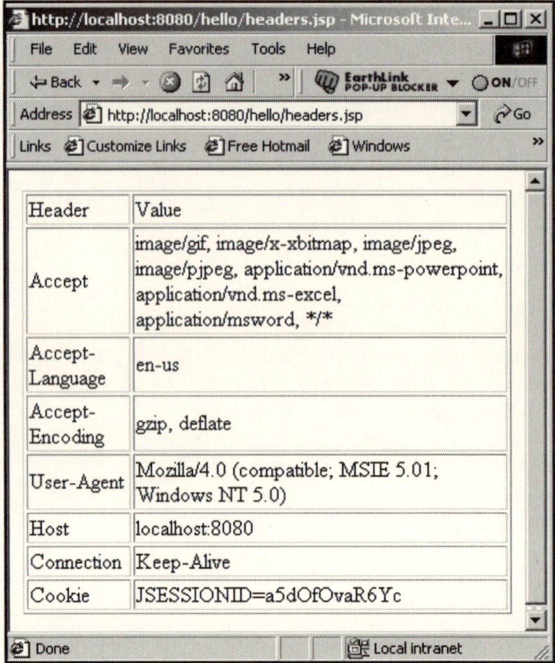

Header	Value
Accept	image/gif, image/x-xbitmap, image/jpeg, image/pjpeg, application/vnd.ms-powerpoint, application/vnd.ms-excel, application/msword, */*
Accept-Language	en-us
Accept-Encoding	gzip, deflate
User-Agent	Mozilla/4.0 (compatible; MSIE 5.01; Windows NT 5.0)
Host	localhost:8080
Connection	Keep-Alive
Cookie	JSESSIONID=a5dOfOvaR6Yc

Figure 3.3 Header names and values from the Request object.

JSP and Forms

An HTML form is used to obtain information about users and their possible intentions at a Web site. A typical form looks like this one, found in a page called name.html:

```
<HTML>
<BODY>
Please enter your Name:
<form method='post' action='name.jsp'>
<input type='text' name='username' size='35'><BR>
<input type='submit'>
</form>
</BODY>
<HTML>
```

Note two important things about our form. First, notice the page set in the action directive. We are letting the system know that when the user clicks Submit, the server should make a request of the name.jsp page. This is significant because, as we just learned, a Request object is created and the object includes all the information entered in the form. The second important part of our form is the name directive in the input for the username. The name is passed along with the information entered by the user.

Now let's see what name.jsp looks like:

```
<%
    String name = request.getParameter( "username" );
    String ip = request.getRemoteHost();
%>
<HTML>
<BODY>
Hey, <%= name %>, thanks for providing your IP address : <%= ip %><BR>
To continue to the next page, click <A HREF="address.jsp">here</A>
</BODY>
</HTML>
```

The Request object has a built-in container for the key/value pairs from the form. You can access the container in several ways, but the easiest is to use the getParameter(String key) method. This method requires that you provide the name of the field from the form and the method will return the value entered by the user. In our example, the value is assigned to a local variable and subsequently used to address the user directly.

Using the Response Variable

When an HTML response page is created by Resin, a Response object is attached with information about the page. The information includes numerous headers, date and timestamps, and possibly cookies. From the application's perspective, there are other uses for the Response object. Let's look at two of them: redirection and encoding.

Response Redirection

In most situations, a JSP page will handle some function needed by the user and return an appropriate page to the browser. The user works with the new page and is subsequently sent to another JSP page. At times, though, a JSP page will be processing information from the user and instead of that page being able to process the user's information, the system has to direct processing to another page. This redirection is accomplished using the Response object and the sendRedirect() method. For example, consider the following code based on the name.jsp page shown earlier:

```
<%
    String name = request.getParameter( "username" );
    String ip = request.getRemoteHost();
    if (ip.equals("192.168.1.1"))
      response.sendRedirect("noip.jsp")
%>
<HTML>
<BODY>
Hey, <%= name %>, thanks for providing your IP address : <%= ip %><BR>
```

```
To continue to the next page, click <A HREF="address.jsp">here</A>
</BODY>
</HTML>
```

In this code, the IP address of the requesting host is compared against the IP 192.168.1.1. If the IP matches, the user is directed to a page called noip.jsp where the user will be handled appropriately.

Response Encoding

When sites have to keep track of information about users, they will commonly use cookies. These small objects are stored on the hard drive of the remote machine. However, cookies can be turned off by the user; in this case, you must use a session ID. The session ID is attached to all of the URLs in the system. The session ID is attached to a URL using the Response object and the session ID is obtained using the Request object. In most cases, the system starts to attach the session ID to pages once a user logs. Consider this page, called authenticate.jsp:

```
<%
   String username = request.getParameter( "username" );
   String password = request.getParameter( "password" );

   if (check(username, password)) {
     String newURL = response.encodeURL("store.jsp");
     response.sendRedirect(newURL);
   } else {
     response.sendRedirect("login.jsp");
   }
%>
```

A user reaches this page after entering his or her username and password from a login page. If the username and password are valid, the code encodes the link store.jsp with the session ID of the Session object, which has been automatically created for the current user of the site. Once the URL has been encoded with the session ID, the sendRedirect() method is used to present the store.jsp page to the user. If the username/password combination isn't valid, the user is directed to the login.jsp page to try again.

Once the session ID has been attached to the URL, all links must use the session ID in order to maintain the Session object associated with the user. If the user goes to another page without the session ID, the session is lost.

Using the Application Variable

Another object associated with all JSP pages is the Application object. This object is global in scope and shared among all users of the JSP application.

The object has a container associated with it where objects can be stored for a time and utilized through the application. Objects are assigned to the Application object using the setAttribute(String, Object) method. For example:

```
<%
  java.util.Date date = new java.util.Date();
  application.setAttribute("today", date);
%>
```

This code could be executed by any page in the site. Likewise, any page could access the information in the object with code like the following:

```
<%
  java.util.Date date =
(java.util.Date)application.getAttribute("today");
%>
```

Using the Session Variable

In our code, we touched on the idea of sessions for the users who access our site. When a new user hits our site, the system automatically creates a new Session object for the user. The Session object is like the Application object in that it includes a container to hold information as well as other methods for session information. When the URL is encoded or cookies used, the system makes sure that the same session variable is associated with the same user at every page.

Since the Session object is kept unique per user, we can use it to store information like shopping carts or personal information. For example, we might expand our code from earlier to keep track of the user's name:

```
<%
   String username = request.getParameter( "username" );
   String password = request.getParameter( "password" );

   if (check(username, password)) {
     session.setAttribute("username", username);
     String newURL = response.encodeURL("store.jsp");
     response.sendRedirect(newURL);
   } else {
     response.sendRedirect("login.jsp");
   }
%>
```

When the user is redirected to the store.jsp page, we can extract the username and provide a more personalized visit for our customer:

```
<HTML>
<BODY>
Hello, <%= session.getAttribute( "username" ) %>
</BODY>
```

```
</HTML>
```

Directives

The Resin server and the JSP specification define a large number of JSP directives that you can use to change the preferences for a given JSP page. Table 3.3 lists those supported by Resin. Most of the options are self-explanatory, but we cover some of the more important ones here.

Table 3.3 JSP Directives Supported by Resin (continues)

DIRECTIVE	DESCRIPTION
<%@ include file="path" %>	The include directive combines the specified file with the current page before the JSP translation/conversion takes place.
<%@ page autoFlush="true" %>	The autoFlush directive tells Resin to automatically flush the output buffer when it gets full.
<%@ page buffer=sizekb %>	The buffer directive tells Resin the size of the output buffer used to generate the response from the JSP or servlet page.
<%@ page contentType="description" %>	The contentType directive sets the MIME type of the page.
<%@ page errorPage="path" %>	The errorPage directive defines a page to display if an error occurs in the JSP page.
<%@ page extends="Java class" %>	The extends directive specifies the parent class of the servlet produced from the translation of the JSP page.
<%@ page import="package" %>	The import directive specifies the packages used in the page.
<%@ page info="description" %>	The description directive specifies a description for the page.
<%@ page isErrorPage="true" %>	The isErrorPage directive specifies that the page is an exception page.
<%@ page isThreadSafe="true" %>	The isThreadSafe directive tells Resin whether or not the page can be accessed concurrently. The default is true, which means Resin assumes you have synchronized any sensitive data accesses. A value of false causes the page to be accessed sequentially and degrades performance.
<%@ page language="lang" %>	The language directive lets Resin know what

Table 3.3 JSP Directives Supported by Resin (continued)

DIRECTIVE	DESCRIPTION
	language is being used in the script code.
<%@ page session="true" %>	The session directive instructs Resin to associate a Session object with the page. The default is true. If the page doesn't need to be part of a session set, the value is false and resources will be saved.
<%@ taglib prefix="x" uri="foo" %>	The taglib directive specifies taglibs for the current page.

Imports

In most of the examples to this port, we've included the entire package path for the Java classes that we wanted to use. It would certainly be more helpful to have a mechanism that allows us to list the imports just like we do when writing a traditional Java application. You can use the import directive for this purpose. For example:

```
<%@ page import = "java.util.*" %>
<HTML>
<BODY>
<%
    Date localTime = new Date();
    System.out.println("Pulled the correct date");
%>
Hello World! <BR>
The time is <%= localTime %>
</BODY>
<HTML>
```

Using the import directive means you don't need to use the java.util.Date declaration—you simply use Date. If you have multiple packages, separate them using a comma. For example, you can use the following statement to import both the java.util and javax.sql packages:

```
<%@ page import = "java.util.*, javax.sql.*" %>
```

Sessions

By default, all requests for a JSP page result in the creation of a Session object. Using cookies or URL encoding, you can track the session. However, if you don't need sessions or have pages that should generate a Session object, you can use the session directive instead. For example:

```
<%@ page session="false" %>
```

This directive prevents a Session object from being created.

Error Pages

All JSP pages contain a certain level of Java code to help in the dynamic nature of the page. The Java code has the potential to produce errors when executed. When an error occurs in the page, we don't want the server to issue its own error; instead, we want to display an error page (that uses the look and feel of the site) to provide the user with helpful information. You can assign an error page to individual pages by using the errorPage directive. For example:

```
<%@ page errorPage="dberror.jsp" %>
```

This directive defines the dberror.jsp page, which will be used in the event an error occurs on the current page.

Includes

During development of JSP pages, you will likely come across pages where information has to be repeated. Instead of just using the cut-and-paste method, use the include directive. For example, if you have a header for each page, you can use a directive like this:

```
<%@ include file="header.jsp" %>
```

Using Beans

Once you become proficient at developing JSP pages, you'll realize that it would be helpful to encapsulate some of the data. Resin and the JSP specification provide this ability through the use of JavaBeans. Beans can be used to perform some specific functionality or handle the data from an HTML form. The Resin server is friendly to JavaBeans and will automatically compile them if they're placed in the WEB-INF/classes directory of the application directory. Throughout this chapter, we have been using the application directory called /hello. This means we need to create a WEB-INF/classes directory under the /hello directory and place all of our bean code in it. All of the JSP tags for beans are shown in Table 3.4.

Table 3.4 JSP Tags for Our Beans (continues)

TAG NAME	PURPOSE
<jsp:setProperty ... param="param"/>	Sets a bean property to a parameter value; requires a set method.
<jsp:setProperty ... value="value"/>	Sets a bean property to *value*; requires a set method.

Table 3.4 JSP Tags for Our Beans (continued)

TAG NAME	PURPOSE
<jsp:useBean id="name" ...>...	Creates a new bean and variable for the page.
<jsp:getProperty name="name" ... />	Prints a property defined in the bean; requires a get method.

Let's look at building a JavaBean that will keep track of the total visits to our Web site and display the count as needed. First, we write the JavaBean code:

```
public class Counter {
  private int hits;

  public int getHit()
  {
    return hits;
  }

  public void setHit(int i) {
    ++hits;
    //save in database or file
  }
}
```

The JavaBean code just looks like any other class you might write in Java; however, you must follow a specific format in order to use some of the JSP bean tags. Any property or attribute in the bean needs to have a set and get method if the JSP code will be setting and getting the properties value. The Resin server will automatically call the appropriate set and get methods depending on the property specified. We see this action in the next code snippet.

At this point, place the previous code in the /hello/WEB-INF/classes/Counter.java file. The Resin server automatically compiles it after it detects the new file. Now let's write code to access the JavaBean:

```
<jsp:useBean id='counter' scope='application' class='Counter'/>
<HTML>
<BODY>
Please enter your Name:
<form method='post' action='name.jsp'>
<input type='text' name='username' size='35'><BR>
<input type='submit'>
</form>
<BR>
<jsp:setProperty name="counter" property="hit" value='1'/>
Total Visits: <jsp:getProperty name="counter" property="hit"/>
</BODY>
<HTML>
```

Place this code in a file called login.jsp. Notice this code contains several new tags. The first is the <jsp:useBean> tag. This tag tells the Resin server that our JSP page will use a bean and that if the bean hasn't been previously created for the specified scope, it needs to be instantiated. The bean is specified by the class attribute of the tag. In this code, you tell the server the bean is called Counter and that it should be found in a file called Counter.java. The scope of the bean is specified by the scope attribute, which has a value of application. This means the bean should be created and placed in the Application object to be used by all the code in the application. Other possible values for the scope attribute are session and page. These two values further narrow the scope of a bean. Once the bean is instantiated, you are able to identify it through the code using the value assigned to the id attribute.

The HTML displays a username/password form and then performs two operations on our Counter bean. The first is found in the <jsp:setProperty> tag. In this tag, you tell the server that it should call the set method of the hit property of our Counter bean. The bean is identified by the name attribute and the property by the property attribute. The setProperty tag requires a value attribute, which is passed to the properties set method.

After calling the setHit() method, our code executes the <jsp:getProperty> tag. This tag obtains the value of a bean's property using the property's get method. To test the bean, browse to the URL http://localhost:8080/hello/login.jsp. In most cases, you will get an error on the browser saying the Counter bean isn't available. Check the /WEB-INF/classes directory and you find there is no CLASS file in the directory. This means the Resin server didn't compile the bean source file. This is because the Resin server has to know about the code you need compiled.

In order to get Resin to process the bean code, you must add an entry to the Resin configuration file letting the server know there is a new application being hosted by the server. An application is simply a directory with JSP, HTML, and bean files in it. The entry you need to add to the Resin.conf file is:

```
<web-app id='hello'/>
```

If the server is running, the change to the configuration file is automatically processed and the bean code is compiled. Try to browse to the application URL given earlier. You should see a form that displays *Total Visits: 0* at the bottom of the page. Hit the reload button a few times and you will see the count increment.

If you look at the bean code, you find that the set method for the hits attribute doesn't take advantage of the parameter value passed to it. Unfortunately this is how the JavaBean code works for the <jsp:setProperty> tag; a value is required. However, this doesn't mean you can't add your own methods to the bean. Consider the following code with an incHit() method added:

```
public class Counter {
  private int hits;

  public int getHit() {
    return hits;
  }

  public synchronized void incHit() {
    hits++;
  }
}
```

The new method accurately increments the hits property regardless of the number of simultaneous browses to the Web page. Now let's change the <jsp:setProperty> tag to a call on the new method. Consider the following:

```
<% counter.incHit(); %>
Total Visits: <jsp:getProperty name="counter" property="hit"/>
```

Here you add the appropriate JSP tags that allow you to execute Java code. You use the identity name of your bean and call the incHit() method directory. Change the login.jsp page and bean code to use the new method and then browse to the login.jsp page again. You will see the counter start at 0 again and increment as you reload the page. Obviously, you need to save the counter variable to either a file or a database row in order to keep the counter value persistent.

Accessing Databases

The ultimate tool in creating a dynamic Web site is utilizing a database to store the information to be presented to the user. Just like Amazon and a whole host of other sites, you can present dynamic information to your users based on their login. While there are many issues involved with building a dynamic site of the Amazon caliber, the first step is obtaining a connection to a database and retrieving information. Consider the following code:

```
<%@ page language="java" import="java.sql.* " %>
<html>
<body>
<%
  Class.forName("org.gjt.mm.mysql.Driver");
  Connection myConnection
DriverManager.getConnection("jdbc:mysql://localhost/mysql");

  myStatement = myConnection.createStatement();

  ResultSet myRS = myStatement.executeQuery("SELECT * FROM user");
  if (myRS != null) {
    while (myRS.next()) {
```

```
        out.println(myRS.getString("username"));
      }
    }

    myStatement.close();
    myConnection.close();
  %>
  </body>
  </html>
```

If you are familiar with using JDBC and Java, most of the code in this JSP page will look very familiar. The JDBC methods needed to communicate with a database are found in the java.sql package, which we have imported using the page directive at the start of the code. The Java code within the page pulls in a JDBC driver for the MySQL database and connects to the database. Next, a SQL statement is executed against the database and the information returned displayed to the user. Finally, the connection to the database is closed.

This example is about as simple as it gets. In a production system, you want to pull all of the database code and place it in a JavaBean to reduce the complexity of the JSP page. In fact, all of the database code should be transparent to the JSP code and utilized only through business objects.

JSTL and JSP-EL Support

JSTL is a specification for a library of tags that provide a collection of common functionality to Web designers using JSP. The JSTL specification can be found at http://java.sun.com/products/jsp/jstl/. The library was developed Some of the functionality provided in the tag library is:

- Core functions (e.g., session tracking, runtime conditions, looping, and importing content)
- XML processing
- Internationalization
- Database Access

The URIs for each type of functionality in the library are shown in Table 3.5.

Table 3.5 URIs for JSTL Functionality (continues)

FUNTIONAL AREA	URI	PREFIX
Core	http://java.sun.com/jstl/core	c
XML processing	http://java.sun.com/jstl/xml	x

Table 3.5 URIs for JSTL Functionality (continued)

FUNTIONAL AREA	URI	PREFIX
I18N capable formatting	http://java.sun.com/jstl/fmt	fmt
Database access (SQL)	http://java.sun.com/jstl/sql	sql

The Resin 3.x server line supports the JSTL specification. With JSTL, we can do things like:

```
<c:if test="${!empty cookie.userName}">
    Welcome back <c:out value="${cookie.userName.value}" />
</c:if>
```

Another important advance in the Resin 3.x server line is support for JSP-EL. JSP-EL is a simple language for accessing data in a JSP page. With JSP-EL, information can be stored in places like a pageContext or a request. For example:

```
<%
boolean newUser = true;
pageContext.setAttribute("userStatus", new Boolean(newUser));
%>
```

The stored variable can then be used later in the page:

```
<c:if test="${userStatus}">
User is new
</c:if>
```

In the spirit of JSTL, Resin includes support for tag files as defined in JSP 2.0. For example, we might have a tag file defined as:

```
<%@ attribute name="a" type="java.lang.String" required="true" %>
A sample tag: ${a}
```

The tag file should be used in a JSP file:

```
<%@ taglib prefix="x" tagdir="WEB-INF/tags" %>
<X:test a="Test 1"/>
```

What's Next

In this chapter, we looked at the process of writing and hosting JSP pages on the Resin application server. Using Java code and beans, you can present dynamic information to your users and build a fresh site each time the user visits. In the next chapter, we look at expanding the complexity of our site by learning how to use servlets with Resin.

CHAPTER 4

Using Servlets and Resin

In the previous chapter, we introduced the process of building dynamic Web pages using JSP pages. JSP pages allow you to mix Java code with HTML in a single file. While the JSP paradigm is powerful, you want to *completely* remove the Java code used for the business rules and database access from the presentation. The JSP page does a good job, but an even better way is through the use of servlets.

A servlet is a class designed to extend the server on which it executes. The servlet typically responds to HTTP requests, specifically GET and POST. Java's servlet support is found in two packages: javax.servlet and javax.servlet.http. Over the past few years, servlets have evolved into a Web service since they can be designed to handle requests from both a Web browser and another application.

In this chapter, we look at how servlets work and examine Resin's support of servlets. We also provide several examples to get you on your way to writing them yourself.

The Servlet Life Cycle

In the past, all Web pages had an extension like .htm or .html, but now you might have a JSP file on the server with an extension of .jsp. As we explained in the introduction, servlets are Java classes that extend the functionality of a Web server. These classes are kept on the server and normally don't have an extension—only the classname. This means that to use a servlet, you might have a URL like this:

```
http://localhost:8080/hello/loginServlet
```

Obviously, a normal Web server cannot handle this type of request; therefore, you must host the servlet with an application server—in our case, Resin. You have to configure the Resin server to both recognize the path to the servlet as well as invoke the servlet. We cover this configuration in the next section.

When the application server receives a request to execute a servlet, it first verifies the path to the servlet based on the server configuration. It then attempts to find the CLASS file for the servlet name. Remember that all servlets are Java classes and therefore must be CLASS files. Resin attempts to find the servlet starting at the WEB-INF/classes directory (unless a different directory is specified). As you saw in Chapter 3, Resin automatically compiles the Java source found in the WEB-INF/classes directory, so if you've previously placed the servlet source in that directory, more than likely Resin has already compiled the code.

Once the servlet CLASS file has been located or immediately compiled, Resin creates an instance of the class for execution. The first method called against the server is init(). The init() method is designed to contain constructor-like code. The method is executed only once during the lifetime of the Servlet object.

The signature for the init() method is:

```
public void init() throws ServletException()
```

The default init() method doesn't perform any work and should be overridden if the servlet requires resources or database access. If the initialization is unable to complete successfully and the functionality of the servlet cannot be used, the init() method throws UnavailableException.

After the call to init(), the servlet attempts to service the HTTP POST or GET request. The servicing takes place in either the doPost() or doGet() method, both of which are overridden methods. The method is passed a Request object (with information from the user) and a Response object (with a container to hold a response).

In most cases, the Servlet object is kept in the application server's memory for use by another request. Note that the init() method is not executed again. If the application server determines that it needs to remove the servlet from memory, it makes a call to the servlet's destroy() method before completely removing it.

Configuring Resin

As we mentioned earlier, servlets are typically found in the WEB-INF/classes directory of an application directory under the /doc directory of the Resin installation. The resin.conf file contains a <web-app> element, which has an id attribute with a path value to the application. For example, here's an entry for an application under the /hello directory of /doc:

```
<web-app id='/hello'/>
```

With this entry, Resin attempts to find application source files in the directory /doc/hello/WEB-INF/classes. The <web-app> element has many subelements for complete control over the application (see Chapter 15). You can either put the information from the application in the resin.conf file under the <web-app> element or create a web.xml file in the WEB-INF directory.

The web.xml file encapsulates all of the application's information. The following is a basic web.xml file for a servlet in the /hello application directory:

```
<web-app xmlns="http://caucho.com/ns.resin">
<servlet servlet-name='HelloWorld'
servlet-class='example.Hello'>

<servlet-mapping url-pattern='/hello'
servlet-name='HelloWorld'/>
</web-app>
```

In this sample web.xml file, the <servlet-mapping> element is used to perform a match against the URL passed to the server. If the URL includes the pattern "/hello", the "HelloWorld" servlet reference name should be used (note this isn't the name of the Java class that should be used). The "HelloWorld" servlet reference name is related to a classname using the <servlet> element. Within this element is an attribute called servlet-name, which relates to the name attribute in the <servlet-mapping> element. This reference name is mapped to the class test.HelloWorld. The Resin server attempts to load the class HelloWorld in the /WEB-INF/classes/test directory.

Web Defaults in Resin 3.x

With Resin 3.x, defaults can be applied to Web application using a new element called <web-app-default>. This element can be applied to the <server>, <host>, and <host-default> environments. Before a specific web.xml file is applied to a Web application, all of the tags defined within <web-app-default> will be applied first. The web.xml file will override any defaults defined for a specific server or host.

The <web-app-default> element can appear in the elements listed above or can placed in the file /conf/app-default.xml. When placed in the app-default.xml file, they are executed before any web.xml file. The elements available in <web-app-default> are shown in Chapter 15, "Resin Server Configuration." Following is an example:

```
<web-app-defaults>
  <class-loader>
     <compiling-loader path='WEB-INF/classes'/>
    <library-loader path='WEB-INF/lib'/>
  </class-loader>

  <servlet servlet-name="jsp"
              serlet-class="com.caucho.jsp.JspServlet"/>

  <servlet-mapping url-pattern="*.jsp" servlet-name="jsp"/>
</web-app-defaults>
```

Resin web.xml Elements

The Resin server recognizes many different elements within the <web-app> element in the web.xml file. Let's take a close look at those elements.

<servlet-mapping>

One of the most important things the web.xml file does is provide information about the mapping from a URL to a servlet. When a user or another Web page uses a URL containing a servlet, the Resin server must have a way to determine what servlet class to execute. The URL provided by the browser might specifically state the intended servlet classname, or it might be an arbitrary string. You use the <servlet-mapping> element to map possible servlet names to an actual classname.

Consider the following snippet:

```
<servlet-mapping>
  <url-pattern>/CA/*</url-pattern>
  <servlet-name>CAServlet</servlet-name>
</servlet-mapping>
```

In this mapping, you tell Resin to check the URL for a pattern like /CA/ that ends with any string value. If the URL looks like this sample pattern, Resin should execute the CAServlet servlet. The CAServlet is just a reference name; a <servlet> element is needed to find the actual servlet class. A <web-app> element can have any number of these <servlet-mapping> elements. For example:

```
<servlet-mapping>
  <url-pattern>/CA/CAServlet</url-pattern>
  <servlet-name>CAServlet</servlet-name>
</servlet-mapping>

<servlet-mapping>
  <url-pattern>/CA/Login</url-pattern>
  <servlet-name>CALoginServlet</servlet-name>
</servlet-mapping>
```

Here we have two specific servlets and the patterns a URL must have in order for Resin to execute them.

<url-pattern>

The <url-pattern> is very important; it is the only mechanism available to the server to match URLs. Matching will occur:

- On an exact match like /CA/Login
- Using wildcards, such as /CA/*
- With extension wildcards, such as /CA/*.srv
- By default with /

The / pattern can be important if you want to provide a page for users who don't supply a correct URL pattern. The /* pattern will override the *.srv pattern. If you need more control over the matching, you can use the <url-regexp> element (see Chapter 15).

<servlet>

Once a URL has been mined and matches against a servlet name, Resin matches the name against a <servlet> element. The <servlet> element acts as the link between the URL and the actual servlet class that Resin will execute. A typical <servlet> element looks like those in the following example:

```
<web-app xmlns="http://caucho.com/ns/resin" id="CA">
  <servlet servlet-name='CALogin'
           servlet-class='ca.Login'>
  </servlet>
  <servlet-mapping url-pattern='/login.html'
                   servlet-name='CALogin'/>
  <servlet servlet-name='cleanup'
           servlet-class='ca.Cleanup'>
  </servlet>
</web-app>
```

In this example, we see two different <servlet> elements. The first matches the directory with the <servlet-mapping> for the login.html URL. When a match is made, the <servlet-name> elements match each other and the ca.Login class is executed.

The <servlet> element can contain several subelements:

- <servlet-name>
- <servlet-class>
- <init-param>
- <load-on-startup>

<servlet-name>

You use the <servlet-name> subelement to define an alias name and to link the servlet to a URL through the <servlet-mapping> element. The name must be unique within the <web-app> element. It is entirely possible to have multiple servlets of the same classname but that have different aliases. In these cases, the <init-param> values are likely to be different.

<servlet-class>

The <servlet-class> subelement defines the actual Java class that Resin should execute when the alias is matched. Resin checks the WEB-INF/classes directory for the class by default (as well as the /WEB-INF/lib directory if a JAR file is involved).

<init-param>

Later in this chapter, we show you how to write a servlet that can obtain initialization parameters defined by the <init-param> subelement. The format of the element is

```
<init-param key='value'>
```

The servlet has the ability to request the value of the key parameter and use that value as needed in the servlet.

<load-on-startup>

The <load-on-startup> element tells the Resin server to automatically load and start the servlet when the server starts. The server finds the servlet, loads it, instantiates an object, and executes the init() method. Without this element, the server loads the servlet only when a request is made from a browser or application. The following is an example web.xml configuration:

```
<web-app id='/'>
  <servlet servlet-name='hello'
           servlet-class='example.Hello'>
    <load-on-startup/>
  </servlet>
  <servlet-mapping url-pattern='/hello'
                   servlet-name='HelloWorld'/>
</web-app>
```

Place the <load-on-startup> element within the <servlet> element to control the loading of individual servlets.

A Shortcut

In many cases, writing both the <servlet-mapping> and <servlet> elements separately is redundant. Resin lets you combine these two elements into the <servlet-mapping> element. For example, the following elements can be combined:

```
<web-app id='/'>
  <servlet servlet-name='hello'
           servlet-class='example.Hello'>
  </servlet>
  <servlet-mapping url-pattern='/hello'
                   servlet-name='HelloWorld'/>
</web-app>
```

The new <servlet-mapping> element is:

```
<web-app id='/'>
  <servlet-mapping url-pattern='/hello'
                   servlet-class='example.Hello' />
</web-app>
```

This shortcut is currently disabled in Resin 3.1, but it is expected to return in a future version of the server.

Hello World Servlet

With the configuration information out of the way, let's examine how to write a simple servlet (Hello World) and host it under Resin. Consider the following code:

```
package example;

import java.io.*;
import javax.servlet.*;
import javax.servlet.http.*;
```

```
public class Hello extends HttpServlet {
  public void doGet(HttpServletRequest request,
                    HttpServletResponse response)
    throws ServletException, IOException {

    response.setContentType("text/html");
    PrintWriter out = response.getWriter();

    out.println("<title>Hello, World!</title>");
    out.println("<h1>Hello, World!</h1>");
  }
}
```

When writing a servlet, keep in mind that the class must extend HttpServlet. The HttpServlet class includes four important methods, which can be overridden:

init()—Called when the servlet is first instantiated.

destroy()—Called when the servlet is removed by the server.

doGet()—Called when an HTTP GET request needs to be handled.

doPost()—Called when an HTTP POST request needs to be handled.

For our Hello World example, only the doGet() method needs to be overridden; there is nothing to instantiate or destroy, and the POST request won't be used. When the doGet() method is executed, the system passes in the Request and Response objects. The Request object isn't used in this example.

The first statement in the doGet() method sets the response type of the Response object to text/html; it's always a good idea to explicitly set the return type. Next, we obtain a PrintWriter object from the response in order to write HTML to be presented to the client browser. The println() method of the Out object is used to write appropriate HTML to the browser.

By itself, the servlet cannot do much without being configured into the server. First, the source code for the servlet is placed in the /hello/WEB-INF/classes directory. We expect to browse to the URL http://localhost:8080/hello, which in turn will launch our servlet.

In the resin.conf file, you need to add a default <web-app> with an id attribute set to the /hello directory:

```
<web-app xmlns=http://caucho.com/ns/resin" id="\hello">
```

You could add all of the servlet-specific elements to this <web-app> element, but it's cleaner to create a web.xml file with the following content:

```
<web-app xmlns="http://caucho.com/ns/resin">

  <servlet servlet-name='helloworld'
           servlet-class='example.Hello'>
```

```
    </servlet>
    <servlet-mapping url-pattern='/hello'
                     servlet-name='helloworld'/>
  <web-app>
```

Place the web.xml file in the WEB-INF directory. Once the servlet is located in the directory and you've configured it, a browser can be used to activate the servlet using the URL listed in the code. The browser makes an HTTP GET request, which calls the doGet() method. (If the browser were to use an HTTP POST request instead of GET, the response from the servlet would be nothing since we didn't override the default doPost() method.)

It just so happens that the code to handle a GET request and a POST request is the same for most servlets. Because of this similarity, servlets should include both the doGet() and doPost() methods. The traditional format is to write the servlet code within the doGet() method and have the doPost() method simply call doGet(). For example:

```
public void doPost(HttpServletRequest request,
  HttpServletResponse response)
  throws ServletException, IOException {
  doGet(request, response);
}
```

Using init Parameters

In our Hello World example, the *Hello, World!* text is compiled into the code and can be changed only by recompiling the servlet. We can use the <init-param> element to pass values into the servlet. Consider the following web.xml file:

```
<web-app>
  <servlet servlet-name='helloworld'
           servlet-class='example.Hello'>
    <init-param text="Hi All" />
  </servlet>
  <servlet-mapping url-pattern='/hello'
                   servlet-name='helloworld'/>
</web-app>
```

This web.xml includes an <init-param> element with a key of *text* and a value of "Hi All". To utilize the init parameter, use the servlet's init() method:

```
package example;

import java.io.*;
import javax.servlet.*;
```

```
import javax.servlet.http.*;

public class Hello extends HttpServlet {
  private String outputText;

  public void init() {
     outputText = getInitParameter("text");
  }

  public void doGet(HttpServletRequest request,
                    HttpServletResponse response)
    throws ServletException, IOException {

    response.setContentType("text/html");
    PrintWriter out = response.getWriter();

    out.println("<title>" + outputText + "</title>");
    out.println("<h1>" + outputText + "</h1>");
  }

  public void doPost(HttpServletRequest request,
    HttpServletResponse response)
    throws ServletException, IOException {
    doGet(request, response);
  }
}
```

This code includes the init() function for obtaining the parameter defined in the web.xml file. The code in the init() function uses the getInitParameter(String) method and the appropriate key string to pull the value stored in the file. In our case, the text key is passed to the method, which returns the *Hi All* text to the code. The string is saved in an object variable for later use. At this point, no requests have been made of the servlet but it has been fully initialized.

When either an HTTP GET or POST request comes through to the servlet, the text from the configuration file is output to the browser. Using the same technique as shown in this code, you can add any number of init parameters to the web.xml file.

Servlet and Forms

As you might expect, you can use the servlet to obtain information entered by a user on a form. This is desirable because it allows a clean separation between the presentation JSP and the business logic typically found in a servlet. Consider our login example HTML from the previous chapter:

```
<HTML>
<BODY>
  Please enter your Name:
  <form method='post' action='/hello/LoginServlet'>
    <input type='text' name='username' size='35'><BR>
    <input type='text' name='password' size='35'><BR>
    <input type='submit'>
  </form>
</BODY>
<HTML>
```

Here we have two inputs for a username and password. Instead of the form action being a call to a JSP or HTML page, we have the name of a servlet called LoginServlet using a path of /hello. Now let's look at the code for the servlet:

```
package example;

import java.io.*;
import javax.servlet.*;
import javax.servlet.http.*;

public class Hello extends HttpServlet {
  public void doGet(HttpServletRequest request,
                    HttpServletResponse response)
    throws ServletException, IOException {

    response.setContentType("text/html");
    PrintWriter out = response.getWriter();

    out.println("Username: " +
      request.getParameter("username"));
    out.println("Password: " +
      request.getParameter("password"));
  }

  public void doPost(HttpServletRequest request,
    HttpServletResponse response)
    throws ServletException, IOException {
    doGet(request, response);
  }
}
```

Note that in the <FORM> tag the method type is POST. This means that when the form's submit button is clicked, the Web browser sends the information provided by the user to the server using a POST request. In our servlet code, the doPost() method that handles the POST request simply makes a call to the doGet() method.

Within the doGet() method, the Response object is set up for an HTML MIME type and the PrintWriter is obtained. Next, the method returns the username and password to the user. In order to get the values entered on the form, the getParameter(String) method associated with the HttpServletRequest object must be used.

The getParameter(String) method takes as a single parameter the name of the <input> tag used in the form that initially called the servlet. If you look back at the <form>, you see that both <input> tags include an attribute called name, which is used as a key value to getParameter(). The response is a String object with the value the user entered into the form. (If that value is numeric, you need to cast the value to the appropriate type.)

Before you can browse to the HTML code, you need to make a change in the web.xml file so it looks like the following:

```
<web-app>
  <servlet-mapping url-pattern='/hello/LoginServlet'
                   servlet-class='example.LoginServlet'/>
</web-app>
```

With all of the configuration and source files in place, browse to the HTML page and you are presented with a form. After you enter a username and password into the form and click Submit, the LoginServlet servlet launches and returns an HTML response page with the username/password combination displayed for verification.

Accessing the Database

When you're building a dynamic site, the code will typically require access to the database to pull information for the current user. You can expand our earlier example to obtain information about users from the database after they have entered their username and password. Listing 4.1 contains the code for the database servlet.

```
package example;

import java.io.*;
import java.sql.*;
import javax.servlet.*;
import javax.servlet.http.*;
import javax.naming.*;
import javax.sql.*;

public class ViewAccount extends HttpServlet {
  DataSource pool;
```

Listing 4.1 The database servlet. (continues)

```
public void init()
 throws ServletException {
  try {
    Context ic = new InitialContext();
      Pool = (DataSource) ic.lookup("java:comp/env/jdbc/test");
    if (pool == null)
      throw new ServletException(
        "jdbc/test is an unknown DataSource");
  } catch (NamingException e) {
      throw new ServletException(e);
  }
}

public void doGet(HttpServletRequest request,
                  HttpServletResponse response)
  throws IOException, ServletException {

  response.setContentType("text/html");
  PrintWriter out = response.getWriter();

  Connection conn = null;
  try {
    conn = pool.getConnection();
    Statement statement = conn.createStatement();

    ResultSet rs = statement.executeQuery(
      "SELECT * FROM acc_acc WHERE username = " +
      request.getParameter("username") +
      " AND password = " +
      request.getParameter("password"));

    out.println("Full name: " + rs.getString("name"));
    out.println("Address: " + rs.getString("address"));
    out.println("City: " + rs.getString("city"));
    out.println("State: " + rs.getString("state"));

    conn.close();
      } catch(SQLException e) {
        out.println("There has been a database error");
      } finally {
        if (conn != null)
          conn.close();
      }

}
```

Listing 4.1 The database servlet. (continues)

```
   public void doPost(HttpServletRequest request,
     HttpServletResponse response)
     throws ServletException, IOException {
     doGet(request, response);
   }
}
```

Listing 4.1 The database servlet. (continued)

For a comprehensive discussion on using databases with Resin, see Chapter 11, "Database Connectivity"; we use some of the information from that chapter in this example. Probably the most important part of the database servlet code in Listing 4.1 takes place in the init() method. The code within init() is responsible for creating the connection to the database. For this example, we assume a Java Naming and Directory Interface (JNDI) definition is included within the web.xml or resin.conf file with a key of jdbc/test.

The servlet doesn't really care about the underlying database as long as it successfully obtains a connection. Once the connection has been established, the code will use the username and password passed through the HttpServletRequest object from the HTML form.

The servlet pulls information about the user from a database table called acc_acc, returned in a ResultSet object and displayed to the user through the Response object. Clearly the output generated for users can be uniquely tailored to their needs and personal profile. If the server does not find the username and password in the database, it redirects the user to a registration page.

Development

During the development cycle, it is often convenient to use a global invoker for all of the servlets in an application, as shown in the following <servlet-mapping>:

```
<servlet-mapping>
  <url-pattern>/servlet/*</url-pattern>
  <servlet-name>invoker</servlet-name>
</servlet-mapping>
```

In this mapping, all URLs that have the text *servlet* followed by another text string will be captured as servlets. The <servlet-name> uses a default value of invoker. By using invoker, you tell Resin to take the last string and use it as the servlet classname. For example:

```
/servlet/login
```

This URL attempts to find a servlet with a classname of login. We don't recommend using the invoker for the <servlet-name> value in a production environment because any string used in the URL is used as a possible servlet name. If you have a servlet named LoginServlet, the following URL works fine:

```
/servlet/LoginServlet
```

However, this one does not:

```
/servlet/aLoginServlet
```

The server returns an error stating that it can't find the URL.

JSP Templates

At this point, we've seen how to handle requests from a user using a servlet and how the servlet can use the PrintWriter object associated with the Response object to return information to the user. However, one of our goals is to separate as much as possible the jobs of the Web designer and the application developer. If we had to rely just on the PrintWriter object, the Web designer would constantly be getting into the source code of the developer. There must be a better way to send a response back to the user.

The solution is to take advantage of JSP templates. A JSP template provides the look and feel of a page on the site as well as some JSP to pull data out of the Application object. A servlet loads the template and dispatches it to the user. Fortunately, just before the JSP goes to the user, it is processed by Resin and all JSP is executed to produce a final HTML response page.

Consider the following servlet code:

```
package templates;

import java.io.*;
import java.util.*;
import javax.servlet.*;
import javax.servlet.http.*;

public class TemplateJSP extends HttpServlet {
  public void doGet(HttpServletRequest request,
                    HttpServletResponse response)
    throws ServletException, IOException
  {
    ServletContext app = getServletContext();
request.setAttribute("information", "All Good Things");
RequestDispatcher dispatch;
dispatch = app.getRequestDispatcher("/loginResponse.
jsp");
    dispatch.forward(request, response);
  }
}
```

In this servlet, several things are occurring. The line

```
ServletContext app = getServletContext();
```

obtains the Application object currently used for the running application. You can store information in the Application object that you want to transfer to a JSP template. To accomplish this, you use the app.setAttribute() method and assign a string value to the key "information".

Two lines of code follow that perform all of the JSP template work. The basic idea is that the servlet obtains a new Dispatch object and forwards its own Request and Response objects to the new JSP file. In this way, the servlet transfers control to the JSP file and the servlet is no longer responsible for the initial request from the user.

The code begins by obtaining a Dispatch object based on a call to the loginResponse.jsp page. This is followed by a call to the forward() method. The forward() method passes the current Request and Response objects to the new JSP page. The server then evaluates the code within loginResponse.jsp before passing the final HTML to the user.

The loginResponse.jsp page looks like this:

```
<% ServletContext app = getServletContext(); %>

<head>
<title>%{requestScope.information}</title>
</head>

<body bgcolor='white'>
<h1>%{requestScope.information}</h1>
</body>
```

For the JSP template page called loginResponse.jsp, the language of choice is JavaScript, primarily because there isn't any real need to use Java. Since all of the information for the page is found in the Application object, our code makes a call to the getServletContext() method and stores the resulting object in the app variable. Further down in the code, the information key set in the servlet is accessed in app.attribute.

Templates and Objects

In our example, the JSP template uses a text string added to the Application object by a servlet. It's also possible to attach Java objects to the Application object and have the JSP template use the object to display information. Probably the best example of this is using a servlet to obtain information from the database and passing the ResultSet object to a template. Let's look at an example where a servlet called ViewAccount is used to obtain all the orders from a database for a particular user in the system. The ResultSet from the query is attached to the Application object and passed to a JSP template called DisplayHistory.jsp. Let's look at the servlet first, shown in Listing 4.2.

```
package example;

import java.io.*;
import java.sql.*;
import javax.servlet.*;
import javax.servlet.http.*;
import javax.naming.*;
import javax.sql.*;

public class ViewAccount extends HttpServlet {
  DataSource pool;

  public void init()
   throws ServletException {
    try {
        Context ic = new InitialContext();
        Pool = (DataSource) ic.lookup("java:comp/env/jdbc/test");
      if (pool == null)
         throw new ServletException(
           "jdbc/test is an unknown DataSource");
    } catch (NamingException e) {
         throw new ServletException(e);
    }
  }

  public void doGet(HttpServletRequest request,
                    HttpServletResponse response)
    throws IOException, ServletException {

    response.setContentType("text/html");
    PrintWriter out = response.getWriter();

    Connection conn = null;
    try {
      conn = pool.getConnection();
      Statement statement = conn.createStatement();

      ResultSet rs = statement.executeQuery(
        "SELECT * FROM acc_his WHERE username = '" +
        request.getParameter("username") +
        "' AND password = '" +
        request.getParameter("password") +
        "'");
```

Listing 4.2 The ViewAccount servlet. (continues)

```
        ServletContext app = getServletContext();
        request.setAttribute("orderHistor;

         RequestDispatcher disp;
         disp = app.getRequestDispatcher("DisplayHistory.jsp");

        conn.close();
  } catch(SQLException e) {
    out.println ("There has been a database error");
  } finally {
    if (conn != null)
      conn.close();
  }

    }

    public void doPost(HttpServletRequest request,
      HttpServletResponse response)
      throws ServletException, IOException {
      doGet(request, response);
    }
  }
```

Listing 4.2 The ViewAccount servlet. (continued)

The ViewAccount servlet is called from an HTML form passing in a username and password supplied by a user. The values are used in a query of the acc_his table, where all the customer orders reside. The ResultSet object from the query is attached to the Application object using a key value of orderHistory. Finally, the servlet dispatches control to a JSP template called DisplayHistory.jsp.

The DisplayHistory.jsp file, shown in Listing 4.3, is responsible for displaying the values in the ResultSet object.

```
<%@ page language="java" import="java.sql.*" %>
<head>
<title>Order History</title>
</head>
<body>

<h1>Order History</h1>
<table border="1">
  <tr>
   <td><b>Date</b><td><b>Description</b><b>Price</b></td>
  </tr>
```

Listing 4.3 DisplayHistory.jsp. (continues)

```
<%
       ResultSet orders = %{requestScope.orderHistory}

while (orders.next()) {
  out.println("<tr><td>" +
    orders.getString("date") + "</td><td>" +
    orders.getString("description") + "</td><td>" +
    orders.getString("price") + "</td></tr>");
}
%>
</table>
</body>
```

Listing 4.3 DisplayHistory.jsp. (continued)

In our JSP page, the ResultSet containing all of the orders for this customer is pulled from the Application object and all of the orders are listed in a table. An example of the output is shown in Figure 4.1.

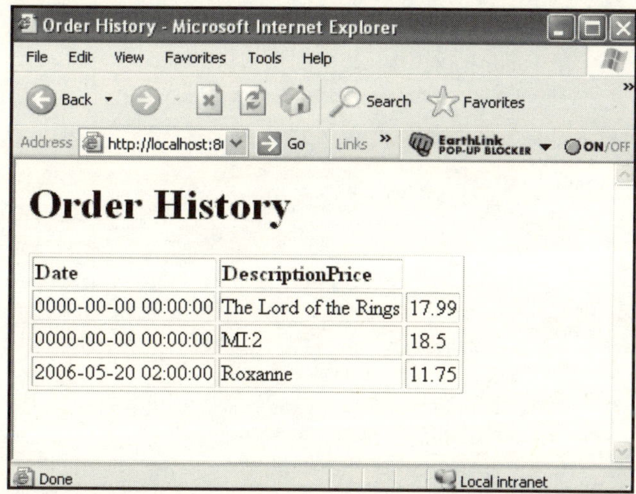

Figure 4.1 Output from the JSP template.

What's Next

In this chapter, we showed you how to develop and deploy servlets on the Resin server. Servlets are an important tool in the development of distributed Web applications. In the next chapter, we look at using XML Template Pages (XTP).

CHAPTER 5

Using XTP and StyleScript

Looking back at the last example in Chapter 4, you see that the JSP template used to display a user's account history has quite a bit of Java code embedded in it. If you want to accomplish the goal of providing good separation of tasks, you should remove as much of the Java code as possible and allow the Web designers to work with tags instead of code. Resin supplies a technology called XML Templates (XTP) to aid in this goal. In this chapter, we look at how XTP can be developed to give Web designers a host of tags for designing pages using data produced from business servlets in a full-featured system.

The Hello World XTP

Before we get into the details of cleaning up our account history example, let's look at our traditional Hello World application. The basic idea behind XTP is to create custom tags that you can use when creating presentation pages for a site and to hide all of the tag details. This allows the Web designer to use the tags in creating the presentation pages while giving the Web developer the ability to change the functionality of the tags or fix bugs without interference. The Resin server handles all of the details.

Figure 5.1 shows an example of an XTP page moving through the Resin server.

When users requests an XTP page using their Web browser, the Web server part of Resin or an external server acknowledges the existence of the XTP page by passing it to a Resin XTP processor. This processor is responsible for replacing all of the XTP tags with its underlying code. This processor uses an XSL style sheet, which it applies to the original XTP page. The result of the processing is a JSP page. The JSP is converted to a servlet and compiled. Finally, the resulting servlet is executed. The result is an HTML page sent to the user's Web browser. You create the tags for XTP using either StyleScript or XSL.

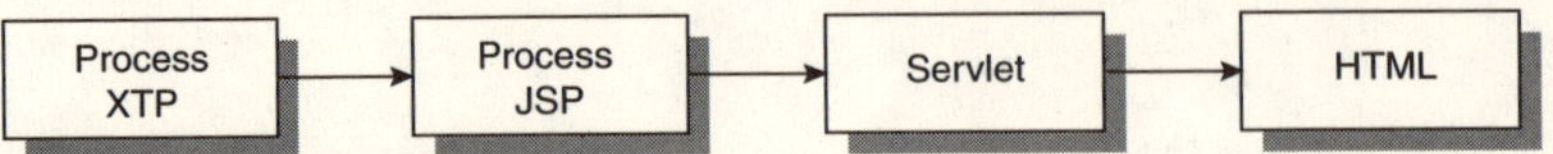

Figure 5.1 XTP processing through Resin.

To demonstrate how to use XTP, let's start with the basic design for a Web page written in HTML:

```
<HTML>
<BODY>
Current User Count:
</BODY>
</HTML>
```

In this Web page, we just want to display the current number of users on our site at any given time. The Web developer has placed the user count in an application variable called usercount. So, we could just change the HTML to JSP (using XML tags):

```
<HTML>
<BODY>
Current User Count:
<jsp:expression>
  application.attribute.usercount
<jsp:expression>
</BODY>
</HTML>
```

Of course, if the developer needs to change the variable name, decides to place the count in another value, or changes how the value is obtained, we have to modify the JSP page. In our example, this isn't much of a problem, but if there are HTML tags for the look and feel of the page throughout, problems could result. The solution is to convert the HTML to an XTP page. The new code might look like this:

```
<?xml-stylesheet href='usercount.xsl'?>

<HTML>
<BODY>
Current User Count: <usercount/>
</BODY>
</HTML>
```

In this example, we replaced the static JSP code with a new tag called <usercount/>. Obviously there are no tags in the HTML specification with this name, so we must have another way of defining it. The definition of <usercount/> is found in a file called count.xsl, shown here:

```
<xsl:stylesheet
xmlns:xsl="http://www.w3.org/1999/XSL/Transform" version="1.0">
<xsl:output disable-output-escaping='true'/>

<xsl:template match='*|@*'>
  <xsl:copy>
    <xsl:apply-templates select='node()|@*'/>
  </xsl:copy>
</xsl:template>

<xsl:template match='usercount'>
  <jsp:scriptlet>
    Integer usercount;
    usercount = (Integer) application.getAttribute("usercount");
    if (usercount == null)
      usercount = new Integer(1);
    out.println(usercount);
  </jsp:scriptlet>
</xsl:template>
```

The count.xsl file contains either Extensible Stylesheet Language (XSL) or StyleScript definitions. In our example, we are using XSL to match against the information found in the XTP page listed earlier. There are two groups of matching code: the first copies the input to the output with any changes, and the second matches on "usercount" and performs some operation. Let's look at each of the groups individually.

First we have the code that pulls in tags or text from the input file and transfers them to the output without any changes. Although this code group appears first in the file, the match occurs only if no other <xsl:template match=""> statements are executed. The *|@* tells the server to match any text and any attributes of existing tags.

The second group uses a match against the text string "usercount". If a tag is found in the input text and it has a value of usercount, the code within the <xsl:template> tag executes. When you're using the <xsl:template>, any text that you place within the tags will be copied to the output file. In this case, we output JSP XML tags, which themselves include Java code to execute.

Recall from our discussion on the XTP to JSP to HTML process that the XTP page will be converted to a JSP page. This means that all of the JSP code we put into the output will eventually be executed by the system.

The XSL file needs to be placed in a directory where the system can find it when the server pulls the XTP page. In our case, we added an xml-stylesheet tag to the XTP page to tell it which XSL file to use. You must place the XSL file in the WEB-INF/xsl directory or WEB-INF/classes. If no xml-stylesheet tag is found in the XTP page, the system attempts to look for a default.xsl file in these locations:

- The directory of the XTP file
- The application root
- WEB-INF/xsl
- The Java classpath

With our XTP and XSL files, we have a directory structure that looks like the following (assuming we placed them in an application directory called users):

```
/doc/users/users.xtp
/doc/users/WEB-INF/xsl/usercount.xsl
```

The code is executed by browsing to this URL:

```
http://localhost:8080/users/users.xtp
```

The result is text showing the total number of users on the system—in this case, just one. With JSP 2.0 and JSTL, we have to replace the Current User Count: <usercount/> tag with Current User Count: ${usercount}

XML, XPath, XSL, and StyleScript

All of our examples thus far are based on several technologies that you must understand before moving any further. These technologies include XML, XPath, XSL, and StyleScript. In this section, we discuss each of these technologies and explain how they work along with Resin to provide dynamic content to site users.

XML

You write XTP pages using HTML and other user-defined tags. For the most part, the XTP page can be fundamentally broken down into a format that resembles XML. By this we mean there are tags arranged in a pseudo-hierarchy, with attributes and enclosed values for some of the tags.

When the Resin server is presented with an XTP page, its first task is to parse the XML. Parsing the XML allows the system to "look" at each of the tags and determine if any action should take place. The parsing can be accomplished in two ways. The first is called the Document Object Model (DOM). In the DOM parsing methodology, a DOM tree is created that represents the entire XTP page. An alternative parsing method, called SAX, doesn't create an internal data structure but instead calls defined methods when various pieces of the XML are recognized. For instance, a method is called when a beginning tag is recognized.

Once the XTP page has been parsed using DOM, you can use a technology called XPath to match the nodes in the tree.

XPath

XPath is a specification-based language created for the express purpose of finding nodes in a DOM tree. As a defined language, XPath can be used independently of other technologies like XSL. The primary semantics defined in XPath revolve around matching patterns. The following is an explanation of the core patterns. Eventually, the patterns are used in either XSL or StyleScript to provide functionally to the system. As we examine the XPath pattern-matching syntax, consider the following example XML file:

```
<HTML>
<BODY>
  <table border='1'>
    <doTableHeader/>
    <handleRow/>
  </table>
  <table>
    <doTable2Header/>
    <handleRow value='0'/>
    <footer>2</footer>
  </table>
</BODY>
</HTML>
```

Although we haven't looked at XSL much yet, let's use the <xsl:template match='<pattern>' /> tag for our examples. This tag defines an action that needs to take place when the pattern found in the match attribute is successful. As mentioned, the following list provides an overview of the XPath pattern-matching syntax available to the developer when writing XSL.

/—Used as an absolute path to nodes within an XML document. For example:

```
/HTML
/HTML/BODY/table
```

/HTML represents the root element of our document. The string /HTML/BODY/table drills down into the document and selects the first <table> tag.

//—Used to select all nodes. For example:

```
//table
/table//handleRow
```

The first pattern example selects all <table> tags in the document. The second example pulls all of the handleRow tags but only when associated with a table tag. If there is a handleRow tag outside a table tag, it will not be returned.

<node>—Selects all elements within the document having a nodeName value of 'node'. For example:

```
<xsl:template match='handleRow'>
<xsl:template/>
```

When executed against our example document, the template matches on two <handleRow> tags. If we had another tag in the document called <handleRows>, it would not be matched because no wildcards are assumed.

*—Selects all elements within the document. For example:

```
<xsl:template match='//*'>
<xsl:template/>
```

This pattern returns all of the tags in the document. You can also use the * as a wildcard. For example:

```
<xsl:template match='/table/*'>
<xsl:template/>
```

This pattern selects all nodes under either of the <table> tags. You can place the wildcard between tags as well:

```
<xsl:template match='/HTML/*/table'>
<xsl:template/>
```

[<criteria>]—Selects a node based on criteria. For example:

```
/table[doTableHeader]
/table[1]
/table[footer=2]
/table[last()]
*[@border='1'][position()=last()-1]
```

In the first example, we are matching all <table> tags where one of the children is a doTableHeader tag. The second example matches <table> tags—but only the first one found in the document. The third example also matches <table> tags but a footer tag must be present and the value of the footer tag must be 2. In the fourth example, we are taking advantage of XPath functions available to the developer. (We list these functions later in this section.) For this match, only the very last <table> tag is used in the template. Finally, in the last example, we are matching all tags in the document but instead of just one criterion we have two. The first says that the matched tag must have an attribute called border set equal to 1, and the second criterion says the matched tag must be the second-to-last one found in the document.

.—Selects the current node. For example:

```
/table/.
```

When you want the value of a node to be returned, use the . character to signal the current node.

..—Selects a parent node. For example:

```
/table/handleRow/../footer
```

In this example, the .. pattern is used to move back up the tree hierarchy for the table node.

|—Used to match one node or another. For example:

```
/table/handleRow | /table/handleRow2
```

If you need to match two different nodes but perform the same action, use the | operator. In this example, we match on both handleRow and handleRow2 tags found as children to a <table> tag.

@<attribute>—Selects all of the attributes from a specified element. For example:

```
<xsl:template match='handleRow[@value]'>
<xsl:template match='//@border' >
<xsl:template match='handleRow[@value=2]' >
```

In this first example, we are looking for all handleRow tags where a value attribute is present. The pattern doesn't care what the value of the attribute is—just that it exists. In the second example, we attempt to match all tags in the document that have border attributes within them. In the third example, the matched tag must be called handleRow and have an attribute set equal to 2.

@*—Selects all attributes for the current node. For example:

```
<xsl:template match='handleRow[@*]' >
```

If you need to match on the handleRow regardless of the attributes, use the @* wildcard.

node()—Used to match a DOM node. For example:

```
<xsl:value-of select='node()' />
```

In this example, we use the <xsl:value-of> tag to obtain the value of the current node using the node() function.

text()—Used to match a text node. For example:

```
<xsl:value-of select='text()' />
```

In this example, we use the text() function to output the text() of the current node.

comment()—Used to match a comment node. For example:

```
<xsl:value-of select='comment()' />
```

The comment() function is used to pull any comment associated with the current node.

processing-instruction()—Used to match a processing instruction node. For example:

```
<xsl:value-of select='processing-instruction()' />
```

You can obtain processing instructions by using the processing-instruction() function.

Expressions

In most of the pattern-matching strings, you can use expressions to further clarify and narrow the selection of nodes in the document. Table 5.1 lists operators are available for formulating expressions.

Table 5.1 Available Operators

OPERATOR	DESCRIPTION
+	Addition
-	Subtraction
*	Multiplication
div	Division
mod	Modulus (division remainder)
=	Like (equal)
!=	Not like (not equal)
<	Less than
<=	Less or equal
>	Greater than
>=	Greater or equal
or	or
and	and

For example, we can match based on the value of an attribute:

```
//table[@border > '5']
```

This code matches when a <table> tag is found that has a border attribute greater than 5.

XPath Functions

In several of our examples, we use XPath functions such as last() and position() to give a level of dynamic selection to the processing. Table 5.2 lists the available functions.

Table 5.2 XPath Functions (continues)

FUNCTION NAME	PURPOSE
boolean(<object>)	Returns a Boolean value from converting <object>.
ceiling(<number>)	Returns the closest integer greater than <number>.
concat(<string1, string2, ...>)	Returns a new string by concatenating the supplied strings.
contains(<srcstring, substring>)	Returns True if the substring is found within the srcstring.
count(<node-set>)	Returns a total count of all nodes matching the supplied node-set pattern.
false()	Returns a value of False.
loor(<number>)	Returns the closest integer less than <number>.
id(<ref>)	Returns the node having id attribute equal to <ref>.
if(<condition>, <a>, <b>)	If <condition> is true, returns <a>, else returns <b>.
lang(<language>)	Returns True if xml:lang of context node is equal to <language>.
last()	Returns the total count of nodes matching the current pattern.
local-part(<node>)	Returns the local part of <node>'s name.
name(<node>)	Returns <node>'s name.
namespace(<node>)	Returns <node>'s namespace URL.
normalize-space(<string>)	Returns a new string with normalized whitespace in <string>.
number(<object>)	Returns a Java double based on converted <object>.
round(<number>)	Returns <number> rounded to the nearest integer.
starts-with(<srcstring>, <headstring>)	Returns True if <srcstring> starts with <headstring>.
string(<object>)	Returns a new string based on <object>.

Table 5.2 XPath Functions (continued)

FUNCTION NAME	PURPOSE
string-length(<string>)	Returns the length of <string>.
substring-after(<srcstring>, <substring>)	Returns a new string using the substring of <srcstring> after the matching <substring>.
substring-before(<srcstring>, <substring>)	Returns a new string using the substring of <srcstring> before the matching <substring>.
sum(<node-set>)	Returns a number based on the sum of all nodes designated by <node-set>.
translate(<srcstring>, <from>, <to>)	Returns a new string after converting characters using Unix 'tr' functionality.
true()	Returns True.

Many of the functions are used in XSL tags like <xsl:value-of> as well as in <xsl:template>. For example:

```
<xsl:template match="/table[if(@border>'5', bigTag, smallTag)]" >
 <xsl:value-of select="count(@border)" />
</xsl:template>
```

XSL

Now that you know all about matching tags in your XTP pages, let's look at the tags available in XSL that allow you to do something useful with the matches found. XSL consists of various tags starting with the prefix <xsl:. The following list of tags provides you with a steppingstone to fully utilizing the power found in XSL.

<xsl:apply-imports>—Allows an overridden XSL template to be used from an import when the template has been redefined in the current style sheet. For example:

```
<?xml version="1.0" encoding="ISO-8859-1"?>
<xsl:stylesheet version="1.0"
xmlns:xsl="http://www.w3.org/1999/XSL/Transform">

<xsl:import href="standard.xsl"/>

<xsl:template match="account">
 <font color='blue'>
   <xsl:apply-imports/>
  </font>
</xsl:template>
</xsl:stylesheet>
```

In this example, we import a style sheet called standard.xsl. In standard.xsl, there is a template with a match='account'. The style sheet defined here also has a template with a match on account. By using the <xsl:apply-imports/> tag, we can output the <font> HTML, then use the template defined in standard.xsl and finally close the </font> tag.

<xsl:apply-templates select="" mode="">—Called when the child nodes of the current node should be evaluated before proceeding with the actions defined for the current node. Here are its attributes:

- select—The pattern matching for the nodes to process.
- mode—Distinguishes between multiple templates of the same pattern. For example:

```
<?xml version="1.0" encoding="ISO-8859-1"?>
<xsl:stylesheet version="1.0"
xmlns:xsl="http://www.w3.org/1999/XSL/Transform">

<xsl:template match="account">
  <h1><xsl:apply-templates select="name"/></h1>
</xsl:template>

<xsl:template match="name">
 <xsl:value-of select="name"/>
</xsl:template>

</xsl:stylesheet>
```

In this example, we match on the account node and then attempt to match any child node with the name of 'name'.

<xsl:attribute name="" namespace="">—Adds a new attribute to the current element. Here are its attributes:

- name—The name of the attribute.
- namespace—Optional namespace for the attribute. For example:

```
<account>
  <xsl:attribute name="picture">
    <xsl:value-of select="images/pic" />
  </xsl:attribute>
</account>
```

This example shows how to add a new attribute to the account tag.

<xsl:attribute-set>—Creates a new attribute set for the current style sheet. It has one attribute:

- name—The name of the attribute-set. For example:

```
<xsl:attribute-set name="font">
 <xsl:attribute name="fname">Arial</xsl:attribute>
```

```
<xsl:attribute name="size">18px</xsl:attribute>
 <xsl:attribute name="color">blue</xsl:attribute>
</xsl:attribute-set>
```

In this example, we create an attribute set that includes the name of the set and individual <xsl:attribute> tags.

<xsl:call-template>—Performs a call to a specific template passing the current node. It has one attribute:

- name—The name of the template you want to call. For example:

```
<xsl:template match="address">
  <xsl:call-template name="city"/>
</xsl:template>
```

<xsl:choose>—Defines a switch-like structure with multiple if blocks. For example:

```
<?xml version="1.0" encoding="ISO-8859-1"?>
<xsl:stylesheet version="1.0"
xmlns:xsl="http://www.w3.org/1999/XSL/Transform">
<xsl:template match="/">
  <html>
  <body>
   <h2>Accounts</h2>
   <table border="1">
    <tr bgcolor="#9acd32">
      <th>Number</th>
     <th>Name</th>
   </tr>
    <xsl:for-each select="accounts">
    <tr>
          <td><xsl:value-of select="Number"/></td>
            <xsl:choose>
           <xsl:when test="number&gt;'99910'">
            <td bgcolor="red">
           <xsl:value-of select="name"/></td>
         </xsl:when>
         <xsl:otherwise>
           <td><xsl:value-of select="name"/></td>
         </xsl:otherwise>
        </xsl:choose>
      </tr>
      </xsl:for-each>
    </table>
  </body>
  </html>
</xsl:template>
</xsl:stylesheet>
```

This code uses the <xsl:choose> tag to display an account's number and name in a table. If the account number is greater than 99910, then the name is highlighted.

<xsl:comment>—Creates a new comment for the current element. For example:

```
<xsl:comment> This is a comment </xsl:comment>
```

<xsl:copy use-attribute-sets="">—Copies the current node only to the output. It has one attribute:

- use-attribute-sets—A comma-delimited list of sets to apply to the output. For example:

```
<xsl:template match="city">
 <xsl:copy>
   <xsl:apply-templates/>
 </xsl:copy>
</xsl:template>
```

This example uses the <xsl:copy> tag to copy all child nodes of the city node to the output without any processing.

<xsl:copy of>—Copies the specified subtree to the output. It has one attribute:

- select—The node pattern to send to the output. For example:

```
<xsl:variable name="header">
 <tr>
 <th>Name</th>
 <th>Number</th>
 </tr>
</xsl:variable>

<xsl:template match="/">
  <html>
  <body>
  <table>
  <xsl:copy-of select="$header" />
 </table>
 </body>
 </html>
</xsl:template>
```

In this example, we define an XSL variable and use <xsl:copy-of> to output the variable's contents as needed.

<xsl:element>—Creates a new element. It has one attribute:

- name—The name of the element. For example:

```
<xsl:template match="/">
  <xsl:for-each select="account">
```

```
 <xsl:element name="accountnumber">
 <xsl:value-of select="number" />
</xsl:element>
  <br/>
 </xsl:for-each>
</xsl:template>
```

This example looks through all of the nodes in the document with the name account. For each of those nodes, a new node is created in the DOM called accountnumber, with a value associated with the number node.

<xsl:for-each select="">—Loops through all nodes matching the specified child pattern. It has one attribute:

- select—The node you want to loop through. For example:

```
<xsl:template match="/">
 <xsl:for-each select="account">
    <xsl:value-of select="number" />
 </xsl:for-each>
</xsl:template>
```

The <xsl:for-each> tag is very useful in that it allows the style sheet to loop through all of the nodes based on a specific pattern match.

<xsl:if test="">—Produces selected output depending on the evaluation of a condition. It has one attribute:

- test—The condition that determines execution. For example:

```
 <xsl:if test="account&gt;'99910'">
  <tr>
          <td><xsl:value-of select="name"/></td>
          <td><xsl:value-of select="number"/></td>
        </tr>
</xsl:if>
```

Here the <xsl:if> tag is used to determine whether or not specific values are sent to the output.

<xsl:import href="">—Imports a new style sheet at the specified location in the current file. It has one attribute:

- href—The URI for the style sheet you want to import. For example:

```
<?xml version="1.0" encoding="ISO-8859-1"?>
<xsl:stylesheet version="1.0"
xmlns:xsl="http://www.w3.org/1999/XSL/Transform">

<xsl:import href="newXSL.xsl"/>

</xsl:stylesheet>
```

In this example, we import an XSL style sheet called newXSL.xsl into the current one.

<xsl:param name="" select="">—Creates a new XSL parameter. Its attributes are:

- name—The name of the variable.
- select—An optional default value for the variable

```
<xsl:variable name="header">
  <tr>
  <th>Name</th>
 <th>Number</th>
  </tr>
</xsl:variable>
```

In this example, we created a variable called header. We can use the variable throughout the XSL style sheet to display header information by using the <xsl:param> tag.

<xsl:processing-instruction name="">—Creates a new processing instruction. It has one attribute:

- name—The name of the processing instruction you want to add. For example:

```
<xsl:processing-instruction name="xml-stylesheet">
href="newstyle.css" type="text/css"
</xsl:processing-instruction>
```

In this example, the processing instruction xml-stylesheet is added to the DOM.

<xsl:sort>—Sorts nodes found in <xsl:apply-templates> or <xsl:for-each> based on the specified select. Its attributes include:

- select—Nodes you want to sort.
- lang—Language you want to use in the sort.
- data-type—The type of date (text or number).
- order—Ascending or descending.
- case-order—Upper-first or lower-first. For example:

```
<xsl:for-each select="accounts">
      <xsl:sort select="number"/>
     <tr>
    <td><xsl:value-of select="name"/></td>
  </tr>
</xsl:for-each>
```

Here we find all of the accounts, sort them by number node value, and display the name for each account.

<xsl:stylesheet>—Required top-level element of an XSL style sheet. Its attributes are:

- version—The version of the style sheet.
- extension-element-prefixes—A list of namespace prefixes sent to output.
- exclude-result-prefixes—A list of namespace prefixes not sent to output.
- id—A unique name for the style sheet. For example:

```
<xsl:stylesheet version="1.0"
xmlns:xsl="http://www.w3.org/1999/XSL/Transform">
```

<xsl:template>—An XSL construct for defining actions based on the matching pattern. Its attributes are:

- name—The name of the template.
- match—The node pattern you want to match for this template.
- mode—A unique mode name for possible duplicate templates.
- priority—The priority you want to apply to this template if multiple ones exist. For example:

```
<xsl:template match="/">
  <xsl:for-each select="account">
    <xsl:value-of select="number" />
 </xsl:for-each>
</xsl:template>
```

<xsl:text>—Copies text directly to output. For example:

```
<xsl:text>And I can't do that,</xsl:text>
```

<xsl:value-of select="" disable-output-escaping="">—Evaluates select and copies the result to the output. Its attributes are:

- select—The node for which you want to display the value.
- disable-output-escaping—Specifies yes or no; if no, then < would be < instead of <. For example:

```
<xsl:template match="accounts">
  <tr>
  <td><xsl:value-of select="name"/></td>
 <td><xsl:value-of select="state"/></td>
 </tr>
</xsl:template>
```

In this example, values are displayed for the name and state nodes defined as children under the accounts node.

<xsl:variable>—Assigns an XSL variable. It has one attribute:

- name—The name of the variable. For example:

```
<xsl:variable name="header">
 <tr>
 <th>Name</th>
 <th>Number</th>
  </tr>
</xsl:variable>
```

In this example, we created a variable called header. We can use the variable throughout the XSL style sheet to display header information by using the <xsl:param> tag.

Matching Tags with Attributes

Suppose you want to keep track of several different counts within the system and the Web designer wants to use those counts on the Web page. You could create new tags for each of the counts, or you could just create one tag and allow different attribute keys. Let's start the process by creating a JSP home page that will initialize two application variables called user and total. The user variable will increment each time the JSP page is executed, and the total variable will always be 1. The page will include a link to an XTP page called allcounts.xtp. The JSP code is:

```
<%
    Integer count;
    count = (Integer) application.getAttribute("user");
    if (count == null)
      count = new Integer(1);
    else
      count = new Integer(count.intValue() + 1);
    application.setAttribute("user", count);

    count = (Integer) application.getAttribute("total");
    if (count == null)
      count = new Integer(1);

    application.setAttribute("total", count);
%>
<a href="allcounts.xtp">Count Em</a>
```

When a user clicks the Count Em link, the system browses to the allcounts.xtp page:

```
<?xml-stylesheet href='count.xsl'?>

<HTML>
<BODY>
Current User Count: <count id="user"/><BR>
Total Count: <count id="total"/>
<BR>
```

```
<a href="index.jsp">Home</a>

</BODY>
</HTML>
```

The page includes a reference to the count.xsl stylesheet. The XTP page includes two new tags called <count>. The tags allow a single attribute called id. The id attribute is used to determine which count variable from the Application object should be displayed. The XSL file matches against the <count> element as well as the attribute. The XSL file is as follows:

```
<xsl:output disable-output-escaping='true'/>

<xsl:template match='*|@*'>
  <xsl:copy>
    <xsl:apply-templates select='node()|@*'/>
  </xsl:copy>
</xsl:template>

<xsl:template match='count[@id]'>
  <jsp:expression>
     <xsl:text>application.getAttribute("</xsl:text>
     <xsl:value-of select='@id'/>
     <xsl:text>")</xsl:text>
  </jsp:expression>
</xsl:template>
```

As you can see, we have the code which will pass selected text directly to the output in the XSL as well as an <xsl:template> tag matching against count[@id]. The [@id] represents the id attribute within the <count> tag. When this code is executed, the system outputs a JSP expression that looks like this:

```
application.getAttribute("user")
```

The value in the getAttribute() method call is based on the value of the id attribute in the <count> tag. The <xsl:value-of> tag is used to obtain the value of the id attribute using the @id key. The directory structure for all three files looks like this:

```
/users/allcounts.xtp
/users/index.jsp
/users/WEB-INF/xsl/count.xsl
```

Note that we placed a <web-app> element in the resin.conf file for the new application directory. The full element looks like:

```
<web-app id='/users' />
```

Browse to the index.jsp file using the URL

```
http://localhost:8080/users/index.jsp
```

You'll see the output shown in Figure 5.2.

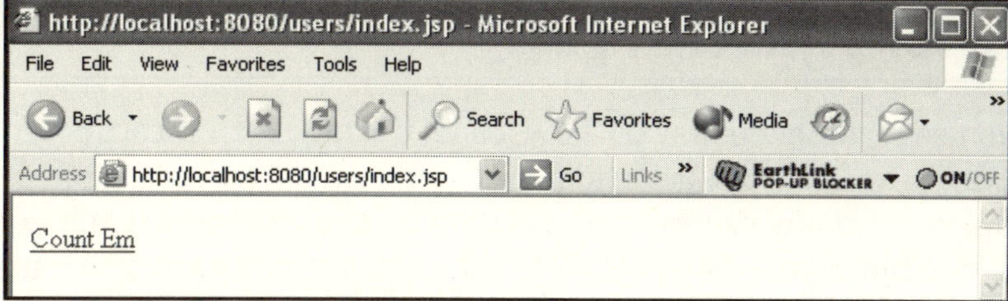

Figure 5.2 The index.jsp file's output.

The index.jsp file initializes or updates the application variables and displays a link to the allcount.xtp file. When the user clicks the Count Em link, the output shown in Figure 5.3 is displayed.

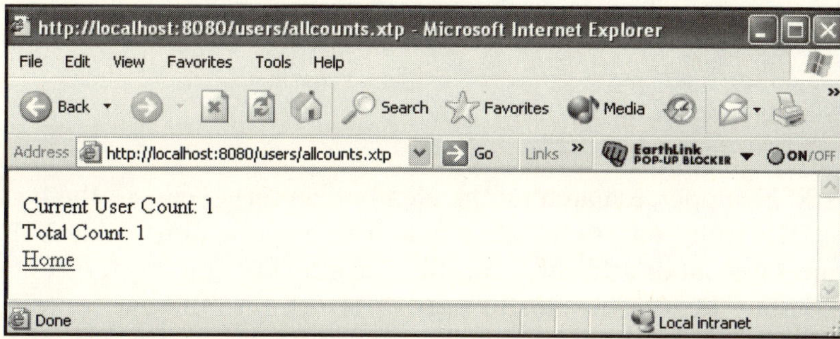

Figure 5.3 The allcounts.xtp file's output.

Once at the allcounts.xtp page, the user only has to click Home to return to the index.jsp file. This action causes the various application variables to be updated, as shown in Figure 5.4.

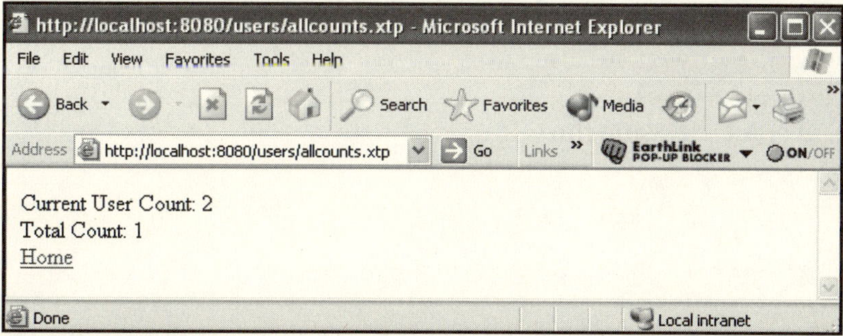

Figure 5.4 The updated allcounts.xtp output.

Using XTP for Style Changes

You can use style sheets to vary how a specific tag on an HTML page displays underlying text. XTP can be used in much the same way; you define tags that can implement many different types of style. For example, if you commonly use the combination <CENTER><B> for headings in a page, you can create a new tag called <centerbig>. The XSL file code might look like this:

```
<xsl:template match='*|@*'>
  <xsl:copy>
    <xsl:apply-templates select='node()|@*'/>
  </xsl:copy>
</xsl:template>

<xsl:template match="centerbig">
  <CENTER><H1>
    <xsl:apply-templates select="node()|@*"/>
  </H1></CENTER>
</xsl:template>
```

In this XSL snippet, a match on the element centerbig causes the tags <CENTER><H1> to be output. Next, a match is made against node()|@*, which pulls any element or attribute. This has the effect of copying the next element to the output. Finally, the closing tags, </H1></CENTER>, are output.

Returning XTP from a Servlet

In the previous chapter, you learned how to use a JSP template to customize output from a servlet by dispatching to the new page. You can use the same type of technique with XTP pages as well. Consider the servlet shown in Listing 5.1.

```
import java.io.*;
import java.sql.*;
import javax.servlet.*;
import javax.servlet.http.*;
import javax.naming.*;
import javax.sql.*;

public class ViewAccount extends HttpServlet {
  public void doGet(HttpServletRequest request,
                    HttpServletResponse response)
    throws IOException, ServletException {

    ServletContext app = getServletContext();
```

Listing 5.1 The ViewAccount servlet. (continues)

```
        RequestDispatcher disp =
          app.getRequestDispatcher("viewAll.xtp");
        disp.forward(request, response);
    }

    public void doPost(HttpServletRequest request,
        HttpServletResponse response)
        throws ServletException, IOException {
        doGet(request, response);
    }
}
```

Listing 5.1 The ViewAccount servlet. (continued)

When a request is made of the ViewAccount servlet, the code automatically forwards the request to the viewAll.xtp page, just like forwarding to a JSP page. In most cases, the servlet obtains information from a database or through variables stored for use by the XTP template.

The Account History Example

With all of this new information under our belts, let's look back at the account history example from the previous chapter. In that example, the JSP template file had quite a bit of JSP code in it. It would be nice to use an XTP page instead to remove much of the code and give the Web designers full control over it.

Here's a possible XTP page:

```
<?xml-stylesheet href='history.xsl'?>
<head>
<title>Order History</title>
</head>
<body>
<table border="1">
<order-history>
  <tr>
    <td>${orders.getString("date")}</td>
    <td>${orders.getString("description")}</td>
    <td>${orders.getString("price")}</td>
  </tr>
</history>
</table>
</body>
```

Here's the corresponding XSL file for the page:

```
<xsl:template match="loop-history">
        <jsp:scriptlet>
          ResultSet orders = (ResultSet)
            request.getAttribute("orderHistory");

          while (orders.next()) {
        </jsp:scriptlet>
            <xsl:apply-templates select="node()"/>
        <jsp:scriptlet>
          }
        </jsp:scriptlet>
      </xsl:template>
```

Or, actually, a better example might be:

```
<order-history>
  <tr>
      <td><order property="date"/></td>
      <td><order property="description"/></td>
      <td><order property="price"/></td>
  </tr>
</order-history>
```

Looking first at the XTP page, we see that all of the specific Java code found in the original JSP file has been replaced with a single tag called <order-history>. When the XTP page is browsed by a user, the XTP is processed along with the history.xsl file. The <order-history> tag causes the appropriate XSL to be executed with the proper results placed in the page. The result of the process is a JSP page and ultimately a servlet that produces the history of the current user.

StyleScript and XSL

As you've noticed, all of the XSL files for XTP use the traditional XSL syntax in order to grab the new tags added to the XTP file. Traditional XSL is very strict and follows all of the XML guidelines. You can learn about XSL in several books, including *XSL Essentials* by Michael Fitzgerald.

Resin has taken the liberty to lighten up the XSL syntax specifically for use with XTP files. XSLT-Lite or StyleScript doesn't follow the traditional XSL rules but vastly simplifies the verbosity involved. In this section, we cover a few examples to show how StyleScript relates to XSL.

First, consider this XSL declaration to match on a tag like <centerbig>:

```
<xsl:template match="centerbig">
  <CENTER><H1>
    <xsl:apply-templates select="node()|@*"/>
  </H1></CENTER>
</xsl:template>
```

If we convert this to StyleScript, it would look like this:

```
centerbig <<
<CENTER><H1>
   <xsl:apply-templates/>
</H1><CENTER>
>>
```

The matching string value typically found in the match="" of the <xsl:template> is used as a major heading in StyleScript using the << and >> symbols as beginning and end designators. StyleScript is easy to read because the template pattern has its own line. You can rewrite the XSL used to copy input to output using StyleScript:

```
node()|@*
<<
<xsl:copy>
  <xsl:apply-templates select='node()|@*'/>
</xsl:copy>
>>
```

As you can see, some <xsl:> tags are used in StyleScript. The following list provides examples of the major StyleScript pieces available with Resin.

$(expression)—Displays the value of an expression. The XSL equivalent is <xsl:value-of select="expression"/>.

XSL example:

```
<xsl:template match='count[@id]'>
     <xsl:value-of select='@id'/>
</xsl:template>
```

StyleScript example:

```
count[@id] <<
$(@id)
>>
```

$apply-imports —Calls an overridden template. The XSL equivalent is <xsl:apply-imports/>. For example, when a style sheet imports another style sheet with a match of the same pattern, the code importee will override the imported match. $apply-imports can be used to "call" the imported match.

$apply-templates—Applies template rules to the current element or the element's child nodes. The XSL equivalent is <xsl:apply-templates/>.

XSL example:

```
<xsl:template match="/">
  <html>
 <body>
<h2>CD Collection</h2>
 <xsl:apply-templates/>
</body>
 </html>
</xsl:template>

<xsl:template match="cd">
<p>
  new CD
 <xsl:apply-templates select="title"/>
  <xsl:apply-templates select="artist"/>
</p>
</xsl:template>
```

StyleScript example:

```
/ <<
 <html>
<body>
<h2>CD Collection</h2>
 $apply-templates
 </body>
</html>
>>

cd <<
  new CD
>>
```

$apply-templates(select)—Applies template rules to the current element or the element's child nodes based on a specific match pattern. The XSL equivalent is <xsl:apply-templates select=""/>.

XSL example:

```
<xsl:template match="/">
 <html>
 <body>
 <h2>CD Collection</h2>
  <xsl:apply-templates/>
 </body>
 </html>
</xsl:template>

<xsl:template match="cd">
<p>
 new CD
 <xsl:apply-templates select="title"/>
```

```
<xsl:apply-templates select="artist"/>
</p>
</xsl:template>
```

StyleScript example:

```
/ <<
 <html>
 <body>
 <h2>CD Collection</h2>
 $apply-templates
 </body>
 </html>
>>

cd <<
 new CD
$apply-templates(title);
$apply-templates(artist);
>>
```

$attribute(name)—Adds an attribute to the current element with 'name'. The XSL equivalent is <xsl:attribute name=""/>.

XSL example:

```
<xsl:template match="cd[@id]">
<cd>
  <xsl:attribute name="artist">
  <xsl:value-of select="artist" />
 </xsl:attribute>
</cd>
</xsl:template>
```

StyleScript example:

```
$template(cd{@id}) <<
<cd>
 $attribute (artist) <<
  $value-of(artist);
 >>
 </cd>
>>
```

$attribute-set(name)—Defines an attribute set called 'name'. The XSL equivalent is <xsl:attribute-set name="">.

XSL example:

```
<xsl:attribute-set name="font">
 <xsl:attribute name="color">red</xsl:attribute>
 <xsl:attribute name="weight">bold</xsl:attribute>
</xsl:attribute-set>
```

StyleScript example:

```
$attribute-set(font) <<
 $attribute(font-color) <<red>>
$attribute(font-weight) <<bold>>
>>

$template(lp) <<
 <cd xsl:use-attribute-sets='font'/>
>>
```

$call-template(name)—Calls template, 'name', and the passing current node. The XSL equivalent is <xsl:call-template name=""/>.

XSL example:

```
<xsl:template match="car">
  <xsl:call-template name="size"/>
</xsl:template>
```

StyleScript example:

```
$template(car) <<
$call-template(size)
>>
```

$choose(test) —Implements a select block where test evaluates to true but is optional. The XSL equivalent is <xsl:choose>.

XSL example:

```
<xsl:choose>
 <xsl:when test="price&lt;'25'">
 <td bgcolor="#ff0000">
 <xsl:value-of select="title"/>
 </td>
</xsl:when>
 <xsl:otherwise>
  <td><xsl:value-of select="title"/></td>
  </xsl:otherwise>
</xsl:choose>
```

StyleScript example:

```
$template(a) <<
 $choose() <<
   $when(price<25) <<
       <td bgcolor="#ff0000">
      $value-of(title)
      <td>
     >>
     $otherwise() <<
       <td>$value-of(title)</td>
```

```
        >>
      >>
    >>
```

$comment() << ..... >>—Adds a new comment. The XSL equivalent is <xsl:comment></xsl:comment>.

XSL example:

```
<xsl:comment>This is a comment</xsl:comment>
```

StyleScript example:

```
$template(a) <<
 $comment() << This is a comment. >>
>>
```

$copy() << .... >>—Copies the current node only to output. The XSL equivalent is <xsl:copy>.

XSL example:

```
<xsl:copy>
<xsl:apply-templates/>
 </xsl:copy>
```

StyleScript example:

```
$template(@*|node()) <<
$copy() <<
  $apply-templates(@*|node());
>>
>>
```

$copy-of(select)—Copies the 'select' subtree to output. The XSL equivalent is <xsl:copy-of select=""/>.

XSL example:

```
<xsl:variable name="header">
 <tr>
 <th>CD</th>
 <th>Title</th>
  </tr>
</xsl:variable>
<xsl:copy-of select="$header" />
```

StyleScript example:

```
$variable(header) <<
<tr>
 <th>CD</th>
 <th>Title</th>
 </tr>
>>
$copy-of(header)
```

$declaration—Adds declaration code.

StyleScript example:

```
$declaration <<
double area(double r)
{
 return 3.14 * r * r;
}
>>
```

$directive.page(attributes)—Sets the current pages directives using 'attributes'. The attributes available are:

- language—Determines the script language; the default is Java.
- session—Determines whether to use session; the default is false.
- errorPage—Specifies the page you want to display if an error occurs.
- import— Specifies the Java imports you want to use on the page.
- contentType—Specifies the defined content-type.

StyleScript example:

```
$directive.page(language=Javascript, session=true)
```

$element(name)—Adds a new element 'name'. The XSL equivalent is <xsl:element name="">.

XSL example:

```
<xsl:element name="performer">
<xsl:value-of select="artist" />
</xsl:element>
```

StyleScript example:

```
$template(cd) <<
  $element(performer)
    $value-of(artist)
>>
```

$expr(expression)—Prints the value of Java 'expression'.

StyleScript example:

```
$template(cd) <<
  $text() <<CD -  >>
 $scriptlet() <<
  String cd = "CD";
>>
 $expr(cd);
>>
```

$for-each(select) << .... >>—Loops through child nodes based on the 'select' pattern. The XSL equivalent is <xsl:for-each select="">.

XSL example:

```
<xsl:for-each select="cd">
<tr>
  <td><xsl:value-of select="title"/></td>
  <td><xsl:value-of select="artist"/></td>
</tr>
</xsl:for-each>
```

StyleScript example:

```
$template(contents) <<
 <ol>
$for-each(cd) <<
 <li>$value-of(@title);</li>
 <li>$value-of(@artist);</li>
>>
 </ol>
>>
```

$if(test) << .... >>—Executes the template if condition ‘test’ is true. The XSL equivalent is <xsl:if test="">.

XSL example:

```
<xsl:for-each select="cd">
  <xsl:if test="price&lt;'20'">
        <tr>
       <td><xsl:value-of select="title"/></td>
        <td><xsl:value-of select="artist"/></td>
      </tr>
 </xsl:if>
</xsl:for-each>
```

StyleScript example:

```
$template(cds) <<
 $for-each(@cd) <<
 $if(@price < 20) <<
 <tr>
        <td>$value-of(@title)</td>
        <td>$value-of(@artist)</td>
 </tr>
 >>
$else if (@price > 20) <<
 <td>Too Much</td>
  <td></td>
 $else <<
 <td>N/A</td>
  <td></td>
 >>
  >>
>>
```

$import(href)—Imports the 'href' style sheet. The XSL equivalent is <xsl:import href=""/>.

XSL example:

```
<xsl:import href="cds.xsl"/>
```

StyleScript example:

```
$import(cds.xsl)
```

$output(attributes)—Outputs control. The available attributes are:

- method—Determines the output type of the page; options include xml, html, and text.
- version—Specifies the XML version you want to use.
- encoding—Specifies the character set for final output.
- omit-xml-declaration—Specifies whether you want to use XML or HTML declarations; set to true or false.
- indent—If set to true, then pretty-print the output.
- media-type—Specifies the mime-type for the output.
- disable-output-escaping—If set to true, then special characters like < are printed as < instead of <.

StyleScript example:

```
$output(Method=xml, disable-output-escaping=true)
```

$param(name) —Declares a new XSL parameter called 'name'. The XSL equivalent is <xsl:param name="">.

XSL example:

```
<xsl:template name="test">
 <xsl:param name="title" select="double"/>
 <xsl:value-of select="title"/>
</xsl:template>

<xsl:template match="a">
<xsl:call-template name="test">
 <xsl:with-param name="title" select="new"/>
 </xsl:call-template>
</xsl:template>
```

StyleScript example:

```
$template(name=>test) <<
$param(title, select=>double);
$value-of($title);
>>

$template(a) <<
$call-template(test) <<
$with-param(title, select=>new);
```

```
>>
>>
```

$processing-instructions(name)—Adds a processing instruction called 'name. The XSL equivalent is <xsl:processing-instruction name="">.

XSL example:

```
xsl:processing-instruction name="xml-stylesheet">
 href="style.css" type="text/css"
</xsl:processing-instruction>
```

StyleScript example:

```
$processing-instruction(xml-stylesheet) <<
 href="style.css" type="text/css"
>>
```

$scriptlet() << statements >>—Adds an attribute to the current element with 'name.

StyleScript example:

```
$template(cdsearch) <<
$scriptlet() <<
 int count = Integer.parseInt(node.getAttribute("cds"));
 for (int i = 0; i < count; i++)
 out.print(title[i]);
 >>
>>
```

$sort(attributes) << .... >> —Sorts node from $apply-templates or $for-each. The XSL equivalent is <xsl:sort select="" />. The attributes are:

- select—Specifies the value you want to sort.
- order—The default is ascending.
- data-type—The default is text; values are text or number.

XSL example:

```
<xsl:for-each select="cd">
<xsl:sort select="artist"/>
<tr>
<td><xsl:value-of select="title"/></td>
 <td><xsl:value-of select="artist"/></td>
 </tr>
</xsl:for-each>
```

StyleScript example:

```
$for-each(cd) <<
$sort(artist)
<tr>
 <td>$value-of(title)</td>
 <td>$value-of(artist)</td>
</tr>
>>
```

$template(match) << .... >>—Creates new patterns and replacements. The XSL equivalent is <xsl:apply-templates>. The available attributes are:

- match—Specifies the required match pattern.
- name—Specifies the name for possible calls by another template.
- priority—Specifies an integer determining priority over other templates:

XSL example:

```
<xsl:template match="/">
<html>
<body>
<h1>CD Collection</h1>
 <xsl:apply-templates/>
 </body>
 </html>
</xsl:template>
```

StyleScript example:

```
$template(/) <<
  <html>
<body>
<h1>CD Collection</h1>
 $apply-templates(/)
 </body>
 </html>
>>
```

$text() << .... >>—Writes contents of the block to the output. The XSL equivalent is <xsl:text> </xsl:text>.

XSL example:

```
<xsl:text>, and </xsl:text>
```

StyleScript example:

```
$text() <<
, and
>>
```

$value-of(select)—Writes 'select' to the output. The XSL equivalent is <xsl:value-of select="">. For example:

XSL example:

```
<td>
<xsl:value-of select="title"/>
</td>
```

StyleScript example:

```
<td>
$value-of(title);
</td>
```

$variable(name)—Assigns value to 'name' XSL variable. The XSL equivalent is <xsl:variable name="" select="" />.

XSL example:

```
<xsl:variable name="color" select='"red"' />
```

StyleScript:

```
$variable(color, select=>red);
```

What's Next

In this chapter, we explored how to use XTP or XML templates to build dynamic sites without all of the strictness of XSL syntax. In the next chapter, we examine using XSL along with Resin.

CHAPTER 6

Object-Relational Mapping with CMP

When you're building dynamic Web sites using JSP or servlet technologies, two issues quickly come to the forefront: scalability and database access. As the traffic to a Web site increases, there comes a time when all of the functionality overwhelms even the fastest processor. In these instances, you need to change the single-tier architecture—Web, business, and database functionality all on one machine—so that different functionality is hosted on different machines. One of the most popular architectures is called *three-tier*, where Web, business, and database tasks are handled on three different machines. While you can create JSP and servlet pages to work in a three-tier environment by themselves, a better solution is to use Enterprise JavaBeans (EJBs). There is quite a bit of debate on whether a three-tier environment using EJBs is a good architecture or not. One of the primary issues is the volume of network communication that must take place to transfer data from the first tier to the second, then to the third, and finally back again. One of the purposes of Resin-EE is to create an environment where the remote calls and data transfer aren't needed.

The second issue that Web sites encounter is the hardcoding of SQL statements for database access. As you modify the underlying database, add or expand tables, or add new features, you have to change the SQL as well. When the SQL is strung throughout the application, maintenance becomes a real problem. EJBs come to the rescue here by encapsulating most database access within Java objects. When using EJBs, you employ various frameworks to handle all of the SQL automatically through the entity bean. By simply instantiating an entity bean, you gain transparent access to the database. Whether the Web site is on a single server or a hundred, EJBs simplify database access.

In this chapter, we introduce a product from Caucho called Resin-EE. Resin-EE is a server designed to use some of the best features of EJBs when you're developing smaller, mainly single-tier Web sites, although you can use it for larger sites as well.

Resin-EE Features

When you use EJBs, you realize that the effort put into the development needs to be balanced with the size of the sites. EJBs aren't designed to be used on single-machine architecture; they gain their power through scalability. This fact leads the developer of small and medium-sized sites to rely on ASP, JSP, and servlets and continue to write SQL—which might lead to problems down the road.

Resin-EE gets its power from its implementation of container-managed persistence (CMP). In CMP, the server does all of the hard work producing database access code. The developer is left the task of writing good object-oriented code. Since Resin-EE handles the database access, it can use advanced caching to push performance as high as possible.

Our goals in this chapter are to illustrate the features of Resin-EE and provide you with a full understanding of how to use CMP in a production environment.

Setting Up Your Database

For all of the examples in this chapter, you communicate with a MySQL database that has a number of tables. To access the database, you use a Java Naming and Directory Interface (JNDI) entry defined as:

```
<database>
    <jndi-name>jdbc/mysql</jndi-name>
    <driver type="org.gjt.mm.mysql.Driver">
    <url>jdbc:mysql://localhost:3306/test</url>
    <user></user>
    <password></password>
    </driver>
    <max-connections>20</max-connections>
    <max-idle-time>30s</max-idle-time>
    <xa>true</xa>
  </database>
```

We used the <xa> element to indicate the driver supports the concept of transactions, which are part of our examples.

Basic Database Access

To illustrate how to use Resin-EE and CMP, you will work through an example. Our example, called the Entitlements application, allows you to gather information about a login, including the login name, description, and position. It also lets you assign groups that the login is allowed to view. You can further break down the groups into subgroups. As we run through the features of Resin-EE, we expand our example. You will define a new application called login and place a new directory with the same name in the /doc directory of the Resin server; you'll also place the appropriate <web-app> entry in the resin.conf file.

Your first step is to query the primary login database called login. This table is used to store all of the information about a particular login without group or subgroup information. Use this SQL to create the table:

```
create table login (
     login varchar(64) not null primary key,
     ts timestamp,
     role varchar(32),
     description varchar(128),
     opendate datetime,
     closedate datetime
);
```

Then populate a couple rows so that you have some information to view:

```
insert into login values ('johnd', now(), 'owner',
  'owner john doe', '2002-10-10', null);
insert into login values ('janed', now(), 'CFO',
  'Chief Financial Officer', '2002-12-10', null);
```

The login Table Entity Bean

Resin-EE creates the connection between a database table and an object using a bean called *entity*. The Resin-EE entity bean is based on the EJB entity bean and, as such, contains a number of interfaces and classes that provide its functionality. The interfaces and classes are sparse because most of the work is handled by Resin-EE itself.

Entity beans have three classes/interfaces:

Local home interface—Allows the bean to be found and instantiated; typically called <*tableName*>Home.java.

Local interface—Describes the set/get and business methods available in the bean. The set or get method relates to the columns defined in the table the entity is representing. The interface is typically called <*tableName*>.java.

Implementation—Contains the logic behind the available methods; typically called <*tableName*>Bean.java.

Let's look at each of these classes individually and show the code in them that provides basic access to the login table.

The Local Home Interface

The local home interface has two primary tasks: creating and finding objects. Written as an interface, the local home interface extends EJBLocalHome for a format like this:

```
import javax.ejb.*;

public interface <InterfaceName> extends EJBLocalHome {
}
```

The name of the interface is typically a string that ties the entity bean to the table it is representing. For our case, use the interface name LoginHome. In this first attempt at creating the entity bean, you aren't going to create any new rows in the database table. (To learn how to create rows, see the section "Updating the Table" later in this chapter.)

In your local home interface, you first add the ability for the bean to find rows of data using the table's defined primary key. If you look back at the definition for the login table, you find that the primary key has been set as the login column. The login column has a type of varchar(), which you must use when building the primary key finder method.

All entity beans should have a method in the interface called findByPrimary(<type>) that returns a local interface object. The purpose of the method is to take a value in the primary key column of the table, search for the row, and return the appropriate result. As you might expect, the primary key is unique; therefore, the method returns either null or an object populated with the values from the database row. If there is an error, the method throws a FinderException exception. The parameter to the method must be the same type as the database table column (or one that can be properly cast by Java). Here's what your local home interface looks like for the login table:

```
package entitlements;
import javax.ejb.*;

public interface LoginHome extends EJBLocalHome {
  Login findByPrimaryKey(String id)
   throws FinderException;
}
```

As you can see, the LoginHome interface extends EJBLocalHome and includes a single method called findByPrimaryKey(string). The method returns a Login object (which you define in the next section). The parameter is a string that is compatible with the varchar() type of the primary key column.

Most entity beans should implement the findByPrimaryKey() finder method. However, it isn't the only one allowed. You might want a finder method that returns all rows, or one that searches on the opendate column. You add more finder methods to your local home interface in the section "Using EJB-QL and ejbSelect."

The Local Interface

The local interface exposes the methods available to clients that need to interact with the entity bean. This interaction includes getting values, setting values, and other business tasks. Let's break this down a little. When an application needs information from the login table, it might use the findByPrimaryKey (String) method you defined earlier. Let's say the application passes the login string "johnd" to the method. Since you know the database contains a row with this login, the findByPrimaryKey() method returns to the application a new object created from the local interface. The new object is populated with all of the values from the database row where the primary key is equal to "johnd". The values are stored in private attributes defined from the login database table. All of this happens automatically without you having to write the code.

The local interface includes methods that allow the application to access the values from the database row. In order to get the values, you need to provide getter methods appropriate for the login table. Because your table contains seven fields, you need seven getter methods.

The same is true for the setter methods. If you want to allow the user to change an attribute in the new object that will be reflected in the table automatically, you have to write setter methods for each of the table fields that can be changed.

Finally, you can write additional business methods that relate to the particular table. You might have a method called setNewRole() that automatically spell-checks a passed string. Another possibility is a method called changeOpendate() that makes sure the passed date is valid. You can create any number of business methods.

Before you can add the get/set and business methods, you must build the local interface by creating a new interface. You use the name of the table you are representing and extend the interface with the EJBLocalObject class:

```
package entitlements;
import javax.ejb.*;

public interface Login extends EJBLocalObject {
}
```

Now you can add the appropriate set/get methods. Let's assume that all of the fields from the row can be obtained and all but the login primary key can be set. Here's what the interface looks like:

```
package entitlements;
import javax.ejb.*;

public interface Login extends EJBLocalObject {

  String    getLogin();
  String getTs();
  String    getRole();
  String    getDescription();
  String    getOpendate();
  String    getClosedate();

  void      setTs(String t);
  void      setRole(String s);
  void      setDescription(string s);
  void      setOpendate(String  d);

  void      changeClosedate(String d);
}
```

That's all the code you need to set and get the values of the database row represented by this entity bean. Notice that you didn't include a public setClosedate() method but instead added a business method called changeClosedate (Date d). This allows you to provide some logic behind setting the closedate. You define the setCloseDate() method in the implementation class so it can only be called from within changeClosedate() if the provided date passes mustard.

The Implementation Bean

If Resin-EE writes all of the database code for you, why do you need to have an implementation file? The answer is that you need a foundation available for the server to fill out its own generated code as well as a place to put the code for your business methods. You include all of the set/get methods in the implementation file using the abstract designator. You add your business method with the code containing your custom logic. Here's an example:

```
package entitlements;
```

```
public abstract class LoginBean
  extends com.caucho.ejb.AbstractEntityBean {

  public abstract String    getLogin();
  public abstract String getTs();
  public abstract String    getRole();
  public abstract String    getDescription();
  public abstract String    getOpendate();
  public abstract String    getClosedate();

  public abstract void      setTs(String t);
  public abstract void      setRole(String s);
  public abstract void      setDescription(string s);
  public abstract void      setOpendate(String d);
  public abstract void      setClosedate(String d);

  public void      changeClosedate(String d) {
    if (d > getOpendate()) {
      setClosedate(d);
    }
  }
}
```

Notice the code extends a class called com.caucho.ejb.AbstractEntityBean. This is a convenience class provided by Caucho for handling default definitions of methods all entity beans must implement but hardly ever override. As you can see, all of the get and set methods are declared abstract and provided with the appropriate access scope.

You define the changeClosedate() method with logic for setting the closedate. You want to allow the closedate to be changed in the database table only when it is greater than the date the login was opened.

The EJB Descriptor

If you aren't familiar with Enterprise JavaBeans, you might be asking yourself how the server can generate all of the SQL necessary for finding rows based on the primary key as well as the setter/getter methods simply based on the three files you created earlier. Actually, you need to create an additional configuration file (using the extension .ejb) called the *deployment descriptor*. The EJB file isn't connected to just one entity bean, so the name of the file is usually tied to the application. For our example, call the file entitlement.ejb.

The entitlement.ejb, which is XML based, is used to describe both the entity bean you are building here as well as session beans (described later in the chapter). The format for the entity portion of the file is:

```
<ejb-jar>
  <enterprise-beans>
    <entity>
      <ejb-name>
      <local-home>
      <local>
      <ejb-class>

      <prim-key-class>
      <primkey-field>
      <persistence-type>
      <reentrant>
      <abstract-schema-name>
      <sql-table>
      <cmp-field><field-name>
    </entity>
  </enterprise-beans>
</ejb-jar>
```

Table 6.1 describes the specific tags.

Table 6.1 EJB Configuration Tags (continues)

TAG	MEANING
ejb-jar	Contains the top-level root element.
enterprise-beans	Indicates the bean configuration.
entity	Indicates an entity bean is being configured.
ejb-name	Specifies the name of the EJB being configured. This will be used for relationships.
local-home	Specifies the name of the class that should be used to define the local home interface.
local	Specifies the name of the class that should be used to define the local interface.
ejb-class	Specifies the name of the class that should be used to define the implementation of the bean.
prim-key-class	Specifies the Java data type that most closely matches the SQL type used for the primary key.
persistence-type	Specifies the type of persistence used for the bean: container or bean.
reentrant	Determines whether or not the bean may call itself.
abstract-schema-name	Specifies an abstract name for the bean. If the <sql-table> element isn't found, the server uses this name as the database table.
sql-table	Specifies the database table name to be used for this entity.

Table 6.1 EJB Configuration Tags (continued)

TAG	MEANING
primkey-field	Specifies the field in the table defined as the primary key.
cmp-field	Specifies a parent container element for each of the fields in the database table that will be managed.
field-name	Specifies the name of the field to be managed; if sql-column isn't found, the server uses this as the field name.
sql-column	Specifies the actual SQL column name for the defined field.

Using the descriptions from Table 6.1, define the EJB file for your Login bean. Here's the file:

```
<ejb-jar xmlns="http://caucho.com/ns/resin" >
  <enterprise-beans>
    <entity>
      <ejb-name>Login</ejb-name>
      <local-home>entitlements.LoginHome</local-home>
      <local>entitlements.Login</local>

      <ejb-class>entitlements.LoginBean</ejb-class>
      <persistence-type>Container</persistence-type>
      <prim-key-class>String</prim-key-class>
      <reentrant>True</reentrant>
      <primkey-field>login</primkey-field>

      <abstract-schema-name>logins</abstract-schema-name>
      <sql-table>login</sql-table>

      <cmp-field><field-name>ts</field-name></cmp-field>
      <cmp-field><field-name>role</field-name></cmp-field>
      <cmp-field><field-name>description</field-name></cmp-field>
      <cmp-field><field-name>opendate</field-name></cmp-field>
      <cmp-field><field-name>closedate</field-name></cmp-field>
    </entity>
  </enterprise-beans>
</ejb-jar>
```

As you can see, all of the interfaces and classes defined for the bean are listed, as well as all of the fields from the database. When the getOpendate() method is called against an object for this table, the system automatically removes the get and converts the first character after the get to lowercase in order to find the opendate field. If you were to define a setter method called setMyField, the server would convert this to my_field. The second, third, and so forth capital letters after the first one are considered delimiters but if you don't want them automatically separated use an underscore between the words.

Configuring the web.xml File

Well, you are almost ready to start using your new bean. First, though, you need to put an entry in the web.xml configuration file for your application. In the web.xml file you created for your database entry earlier in the chapter, you need to add configuration information about the entity bean:

```
<ejb-server jndi-name="cmp">
  <data-source>jdbc/entitlements</data-source>
  <config-directory>WEB-INF</config-directory>
</ejb-server>
```

Here you are defining a new resource reference element that lets the system know you are creating a new JNDI entry with the name /env/cmp. The new resource will be implemented by the class com.caucho.ejb.EJBServer. This resource will be the framework or container for handling all of your entity (and eventually session) beans. You are also setting the data-source parameter equal to the resource-ref for the database you created earlier.

Using the Entity Bean

At this point, you've created a database table, inserted rows into the table, created an entity bean, and configured the system to be aware of the bean. But how do you use it? One solution is to use a servlet.

If you elect to use this solution, then you must write a servlet (shown in Listing 6.1) that will find it, create it, and use the findByPrimaryKey() method you defined.

```
package entitlements;

import java.io.*;
import javax.servlet.*;
import javax.servlet.http.*;
import javax.naming.*;
import javax.ejb.*;

public class LoginServlet extends HttpServlet {
  private LoginHome home = null;

  public void init()
    throws ServletException {
    try {
      Context cmp = (Context)
        new InitialContext().lookup("java:comp/env/cmp");
```

Listing 6.1 Our servlet code. (continues)

```
        home = (LoginHome) cmp.lookup("Login ");
      } catch (NamingException e) {
        throw new ServletException(e);
      }
    }

    public void doGet(HttpServletRequest req,
                      HttpServletResponse res)
      throws IOException, ServletException
    {
      PrintWriter out = res.getWriter();
      res.setContentType("text/html");

      out.println("<h3>All Current Logins</h3>");

      try {
       Login login1 = home.findByPrimaryKey(''johnd');
       Login login2 = home.findByPrimaryKey(''janed');
       Login login3 = home.findByPrimaryKey(''joes');

       out.println(''Login: '' + login1.getLogin() + ''<br>');
       out.println('Opendate: ' + login1.getOpendate()
         + '<br><hr>');

       out.println('Login: ' + login2.getLogin() + '<br>');
       out.println('Opendate: ' + login2.getOpendate()
         + '<br><hr>');

       out.println('Login: ' + login3.getLogin() + '<br>');
       out.println('Opendate: ' + login3.getOpendate()
         + '<br><hr>');
  }
      catch (FinderException e) {
        throw new ServletException(e);
      }
    }
  }
```

Listing 6.1 Our servlet code. (continued)

Let's walk through the servlet code. After Resin-EE loads the servlet, it executes the init() method first. This method attempts to find the context associated with the /env/cmp reference. Once it does, the server uses a lookup() method to find the home interface to the Login entity bean. The "Login" string relates to the <ejb-name>Login</ejb-name> entry in your entitlements.ejb configuration file.

These lines of code are executed once so that the servlet has a reference object to the home interface for the entity bean related to the login table. By putting this code in the init() method, you save the system the time necessary to locate the home interface each time the servlet is used. It should be clear that no data is associated with the login table—there is only a reference to the home interface that can be used to obtain data. If you look back at the home interface code, you see that the only method defined is findByPrimaryKey(), so that is how you get data from the table.

All of the work for the servlet occurs in the doGet() method. Here the output from the servlet is prepared before trying to get data. Next, a call is made to the findByPrimaryKey() method of the home interface object using login name parameters. You know you will find data in the database with the two login strings. If there is a problem with the find, a FinderException will be thrown and caught by your code.

For each of the findByPrimaryKey() method calls, a unique entity bean is returned. Each object has a getter method used to obtain information stored in the object. You have queried a database for a specific row and displayed the data from the row.

Deploying the Code

Of course, to get all of this code to work, you must place it in the classes directory of your application. The Entitlements application hierarchy is shown in Figure 6.1.

```
/doc
   /entitlements
          /WEB-INF
             web.xml
             entitlements.ejb
             /classes
                /entitlements
                   EntLogin.java
                   EntLoginBean.java
                   EntLoginHome.java
```

Figure 6.1 The Entitlements application hierarchy.

Running the Code

With all of the code loaded in the right directories and the resin.conf file supplied with the appropriate <web-app> element, it's time to browse to the servlet. Use the URL http://localhost:8080/entitlements/LoginServlet; the result is shown in Figure 6.2.

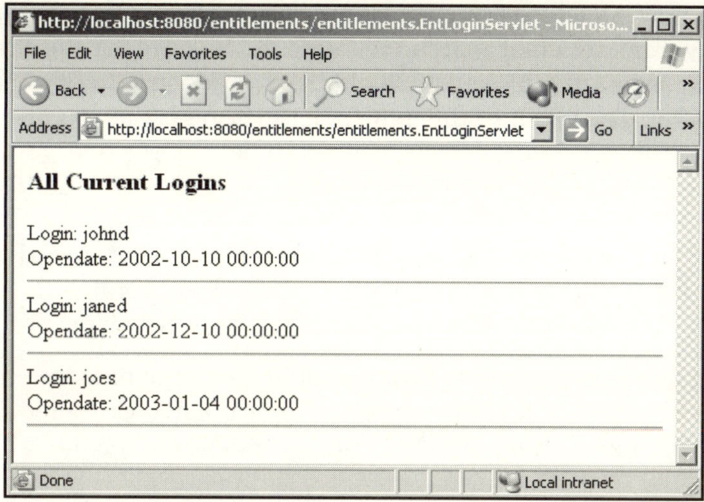

Figure 6.2 The servlet output.

Using EJB-QL and ejbSelect()

If you ran the example in the previous section or read through the code, you probably realize that having just a single finder method may not be enough. An application developer using the login entity bean probably wants more ways to query the table. In this section, we look at two ways to add query capabilities to your bean: adding a finder method and using ejbSelect().

Adding Finder Methods

As we saw earlier, you declare finder methods in the local home interface in order for them to be used in a manner that will return an actual Login entity bean. The findByPrimaryKey() finder is recognized by the server and takes advantage of the <primkey-field> element defined in the deployment descriptor to generate the necessary SQL.

Although easy to do, adding additional finder methods requires that you let the server know how to build the SQL using a language called Enterprise JavaBeans Query Language (EJB-QL). Two steps are involved when adding a new finder method:

1. Add the appropriate signature to the local home interface.
2. Add an EJB-QL entry to the deployment descriptor for the entity bean.

In step 1, the new signature typically starts with the string find. You include one or more parameters that match the fields in the table for the bean. The parameters are used to query specific fields of the database to find the result row you are after. The result of the new finder method is one of two types. If the result of the finder method is guaranteed to be a single row, you use the local interface Login as the return type (just as you did for the findByPrimaryKey() method). However, many queries return more than one result, therefore, you need to provide a result type that can handle a set of rows. For these results, you use the Java data-type Collection and an iterator that moves through the results. We show examples of this result a little later.

In step 2, you let the server know how it should query the database table for all of your new finder methods. The process uses a language called EJB-QL, which looks just like normal SQL but uses placeholders for the tables and parameters in the WHERE clause.

Finding All Logins

Now, let's add a query that returns a result with all of the rows in the login database. Call the finder method findAll(). No parameters are required; however, since the query returns more than one row, use the Collection type. Here's the code for the local home interface:

```
package entitlements;
import javax.ejb.*;
import java.util.*;

public interface LoginHome extends EJBLocalHome {
  Login findByPrimaryKey(String id)
   throws FinderException;

  Collection findAll()
   throws FinderException;
}
```

In your new local home interface, you've added a new method called findAll(), which returns all of the rows in your login table in a Collection object. The real work behind this query takes place in an entry called <query> (which you add to the <entity> element of your Login bean). Here's what the <query> entry looks like for your findAll() method:

```
<query>
  <query-method>
    <method-name>findAll</method-name>
  </query-method>
  <ejb-ql>SELECT o FROM logins o</ejb-ql>
</query>
```

Let's take a close look at two subelements of the <query> element. The first, <method-name>, tells the server which finder method defined in the local home interface this entry corresponds to. Use a value of findAll since this is the method name. The second element, called <ejb-ql>, has a value representing the SQL to be executed when the finder method is executed. The EJB-QL looks like standard SQL and has two placeholders to be handled by the server. We won't go into detail about EJB-QL; for a good explanation see http://java.sun. com/j2ee/tutorial/1_3-fcs/doc/EJBQL.html.

Of particular importance is the FROM clause. Use the <abstract-schema-name> value so that the server pulls the right value when determining which table the query should be used against.

Using findAll() in a Servlet

When changes are made to the deployment descriptor and local home interface, Resin-EE automatically compiles them and makes the entity bean ready for use. You need to change your servlet code to use the new finder method, as shown here:

```
package entitlements;

import java.io.*;
import javax.servlet.*;
import javax.servlet.http.*;
import javax.naming.*;
import javax.ejb.*;
import java.util.*;

public class LoginServlet extends HttpServlet {
  private LoginHome home = null;

  public void init()
    throws ServletException {
    try {
      Context cmp = (Context)
        new InitialContext().lookup("java:comp/env/cmp");

      home = (LoginHome) cmp.lookup("Login ");
    } catch (NamingException e) {
      throw new ServletException(e);
    }
  }

  public void doGet(HttpServletRequest req,
                    HttpServletResponse res)
    throws IOException, ServletException
  {
    PrintWriter out = res.getWriter();
    res.setContentType("text/html");
```

```
        out.println("<h3>All Current Logins</h3>");

        try {
          Collection c = home.findAll();
          Iterator iter = c.iterator();

          while (iter.hasNext()) {

            Login row = (Login)iter.next();

            out.println('Login: ' + row.getLogin() + '<br>');
            out.println('Opendate: ' + row.getOpendate()
              + '<br><hr>');
          }
        }
        catch (FinderException e) {
          throw new ServletException(e);
        }
      }
    }
```

In this new servlet, you have a call to the home.findAll() method; the results are set to the variable c. An iterator is obtained from the Collection and a loop runs through all of the rows displaying the login and opendate of the account. Figure 6.3 shows the resulting output.

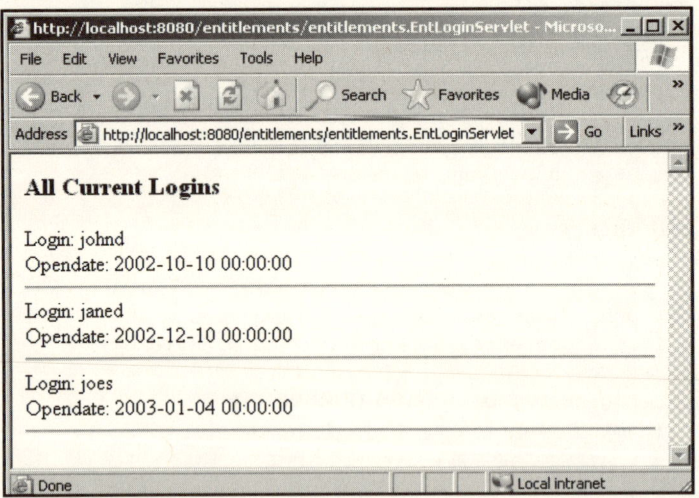

Figure 6.3 findAll()'s output.

Finding Logins by Open Date

Let's add another finder method that uses a parameter, the open date, for an account. The new finder method is called findByOpenDate() and its signature defined as

```
Collection findByOpenDate(String d)
   throws FinderException;
```

Place the signature in the local home interface and put a new <query> entry into the deployment descriptor, as shown here:

```
<query>
      <query-method>
        <method-name>findByOpenDate</method-name>
      </query-method>
      <ejb-ql>SELECT o FROM logins o WHERE o.opendate=?1
      </ejb-ql>
</query>
```

Note the addition of a WHERE clause. The WHERE clause allows you to narrow the results found in the database based on the fields and a specific value. In this case, you will be using the opendate field, as shown by the o.opendate text. The *o* will be replaced with an alias name for your database table. The opendate field is checked against a value denoted by *?1*. The value *?1* is a placeholder for the first parameter to the findByOpenDate() method.

At this point, modify the code in your servlet to use the new finder method:

```
try {
  Collection c = home.findByOpenDate('2002-02-12');
  Iterator iter = c.iterator();

  while (iter.hasNext()) {

    Login row = (Login)iter.next();

    out.println('Login: ' + row.getLogin() + '<br>');
    out.println('Opendate: ' + row.getOpendate()
      + '<br><hr>');
  }
}
catch (FinderException e) {
  throw new ServletException(e);
}
```

All of the rows in the table where the opendate field is *2002-02-12* will be returned by the findByOpenDate() method and displayed to the user.

Finding Logins by Open and Closed Date

Let's add one more finder method to illustrate how you can have more than one parameter in the method and EJB-QL query. The new method is called findByOpenCloseDate(String open, String closed). The full signature is:

```
Collection findByOpenCloseDate(String open, String closed)
   throws FinderException;
```

Again, the important work occurs in the deployment descriptor:

```
<query>
    <query-method>
      <method-name>findByOpenCloseDate</method-name>
    </query-method>
    <ejb-ql>SELECT o FROM logins o WHERE o.opendate=?1
       and o.closedate=?2</ejb-ql>
  </query>
```

The method call findByOpenClosedDate has two parameters that you must place in the query. Use standard SQL to build the WHERE clause (but number the parameters *?1* and *?2*, which relate to the open and close date parameters, respectively). The following snippet shows how to use the method:

```
try {
  Collection c = home.findByOpenCloseDate('2002-02-12',
    '2002-12-30');
  Iterator iter = c.iterator();

  while (iter.hasNext()) {

    Login row = (Login)iter.next();

    out.println('Login: ' + row.getLogin() + '<br>');
    out.println('Opendate: ' + row.getOpendate()
      + '<br><hr>');
  }
}
catch (FinderException e) {
  throw new ServletException(e);
}
```

Using ejbSelect()

Note that all of the finder methods return either a single instance of the Login class or a collection of Login classes. This is a requirement of the finder methods. It is possible to create methods that return a single field or a collection of fields from one or more tables based on a query of one or more tables.

The downside to the ejbSelect() method is that its scope is based within the bean itself. This is because you created its abstract signature in the bean implementation and not the local home interface. Business methods defined at the local interface scope typically use the ejbSelect() methods to provide intermediate results to the application.

To see how this works, let's create a select method that returns just the logins available in the table. The first step is to create a method in the bean implementation class:

```
public abstract Collection ejbSelectJustLogins()
  throws FinderException;
```

The ejbSelectJustLogins() method doesn't include any parameters, but it could if needed. You define the SQL to be executed by the select method in the deployment descriptor. Here's an example query for your new method:

```
<query>
      <query-method>
        <method-name>ejbSelectJustLogins</method-name>
      </query-method>
      <ejb-ql>SELECT o.login FROM logins o</ejb-ql>
    </query>
```

Now the only methods that can use ejbSelectJustLogins() are those business methods exposed by the local interface. So you need to create a new method signature and place it in the local interface class:

```
package entitlements;
import javax.ejb.*;
import java.util.*;

public interface Login extends EJBLocalObject {

  String      getLogin();
  String      getTs();
  String      getRole();
  String      getDescription();
  Date        getOpendate();
  Date        getClosedate();

  void         setTs(String t);
  void         setRole(String s);
  void         setDescription(string s);
  void         setOpendate(Date d);
  private void setClosedate(Date d);

  void         changeClosedate(Date d);
  Collection   pullLogins();
}
```

Here you've added a new business method called pullLogins() that returns a Collection containing all of the logins found in the system. Now you need to write the code behind the business method and place that code in the bean implementation:

```
public Collection pullLogins() {
  Collection c = null;
  try {
    c = ejbSelectJustLogins();
  } catch(FinderException e) {};
  return c;
}
```

After changing all of the bean code, you can make a call to the pullLogins() method from a servlet and get the output passed from the ejbSelectJustLogins() method. Here's the servlet snippet:

```
try {
  Login e = (Login)home.findByPrimaryKey("johnd");

  Collection c = e.pullLogins();
  Iterator iter = c.iterator();

  while (iter.hasNext()) {

    String row = (String)iter.next();

    out.println('Login: ' + row + '<br>');
  }
}
catch (FinderException e) {
  throw new ServletException(e);
}
```

Changing Entity Values

To show how the beans will work when both retrieving a row and changing it using just the code you've developed so far, let's create an HTML page that allows us to query the database for a specific row, display the values from the resulting bean, and change the values. The HTML is found in two files: getLogin.html and changeLogin.html. The code for getLogin.html is:

```
<HTML>
<BODY>
<TITLE>Login</TITLE>
<BR>
Enter Login name:
<form action="http://localhost:8080/entitlements/entitlements.Login-
MaintenanceServlet" method="post">
  Username: <input name="login"><BR>
  <input type="submit" name="submit" value="get">
</form>
</BODY>
</HTML>
```

The code for changeLogin.html is:

```
    <%@ page language='java' import='entitlements.Login' %>
<% ServletContext app = getServletContext();
   Login e = (Login)app.getAttribute("login");
 %>
<head>
```

```
<body>
<form action="http://localhost:8080/entitlements/entitlements.
  LoginMaintenanceServlet" method="post">
  Username: <input name="login" value = "
     <%= e.getLogin() %>"><BR>
  Timestamp: <input name="timestamp" value = "
      <%= e.getTs() %>"><BR>
  Role: <input name="role" value = "<%= e.getRole() %>"><BR>
  Description: <input name="description" value = "
     <%= e.getDescription() %>"><BR>
  Opendate: <input name="opendate" value = "
      <%= e.getOpendate() %>"><BR>
  Closedate: <input name="closedate" value = "
     <%= e.getClosedate() %>"><BR>
  <input type="submit" name="submit" value="update">
</form>
</body>
</head>
```

Both of the pages include a <form> that calls a single servlet called LoginMaintenanceServlet.java. The code for this servlet is:

```
package entitlements;

import java.io.*;
import javax.servlet.*;
import javax.servlet.http.*;
import javax.naming.*;
import javax.ejb.*;
import java.util.*;

public class LoginMaintenanceServlet extends HttpServlet {
  private LoginHome home = null;

  public void init()
    throws ServletException {
    try {
      Context cmp = (Context)
        new InitialContext().lookup("java:comp/env/cmp");

      home = (LoginHome) cmp.lookup("Login");
    } catch (NamingException e) {
      throw new ServletException(e);
    }
  }

  public void doGet(HttpServletRequest req, HttpServletResponse res)
    throws IOException, ServletException
  {
    PrintWriter out = res.getWriter();
    res.setContentType("text/html");

    String submit = req.getParameter("submit");
```

```
      if (submit.equals("get")) {
        try {
          Login e =
(Login)home.findByPrimaryKey(req.getParameter("login"));

          ServletContext app = getServletContext();
          request.setAttribute("login", e);

          RequestDispatcher dispatch =
            app.getRequestDispatcher("/changeLogin.jsp");
          dispatch.forward(req, res);
        } catch (FinderException e) {
          throw new ServletException(e);
        }
      } else if (submit.equals("update")) {
        try {
          Login e =
(Login)home.findByPrimaryKey(req.getParameter("login"));
          e.setTs(req.getParameter("timestamp"));
          e.setRole(req.getParameter("role"));
          e.setDescription(req.getParameter("description"));
          e.setOpendate(req.getParameter("opendate"));
          e.changeClosedate(req.getParameter("closedate"));
        } catch (FinderException e) {
          throw new ServletException(e);
        }
      }
    }
    public void doPost(HttpServletRequest req, HttpServletResponse res)
      throws IOException, ServletException {
      doGet(req, res);
    }
  }
```

As you can see, the servlet checks the value of the submit variable to determine what the user is trying to accomplish. If the action is an update, you create an entity bean from the system and set all of the appropriate fields of the row except the primary key. Obviously, you don't want to change the primary key because this could cause an error that your code doesn't handle at the moment.

Let's run through a query. In Figure 6.4, the user is asking to see the login for johnd using the getLogin.html page. Figure 6.5 shows the changeLogin.html page after the user has submitted the request to the LoginMaintenance-Servlet code. In Figure 6.6, we've changed the close date to 1-3-2003. Figure 6.7 shows the result of the change after we've used the getLogin.html page to lookup the johnd login a second time. The bean accepted the close date and either cached it or wrote the value to the database. In Figure 6.8, a query of the database shows that the date was stored in the database—without us having to write an INSERT SQL.

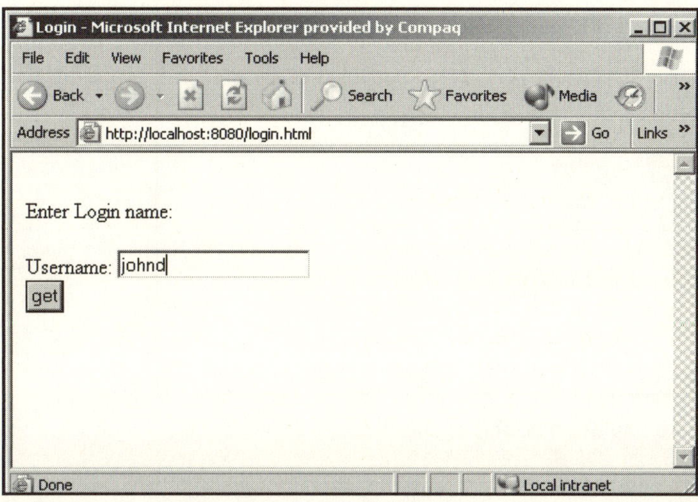

Figure 6.4 The getLogin.html page for login johnd.

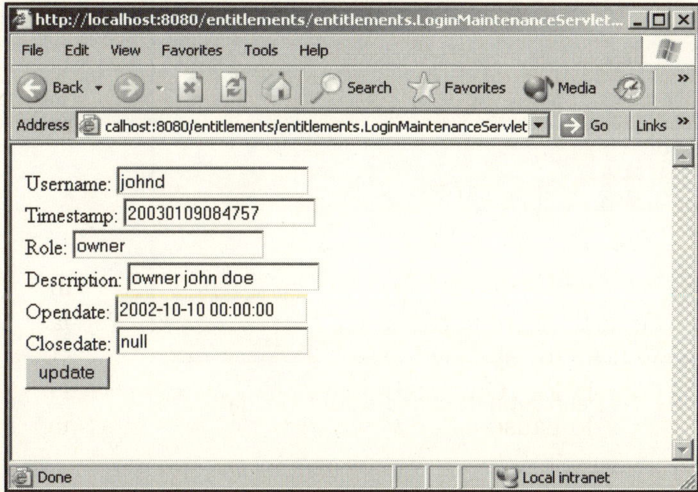

Figure 6.5 The result of getting the johnd login.

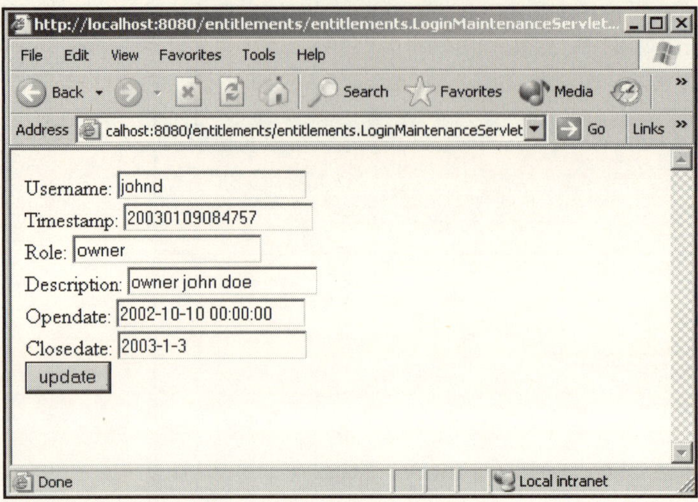

Figure 6.6 The close date has been added to the data.

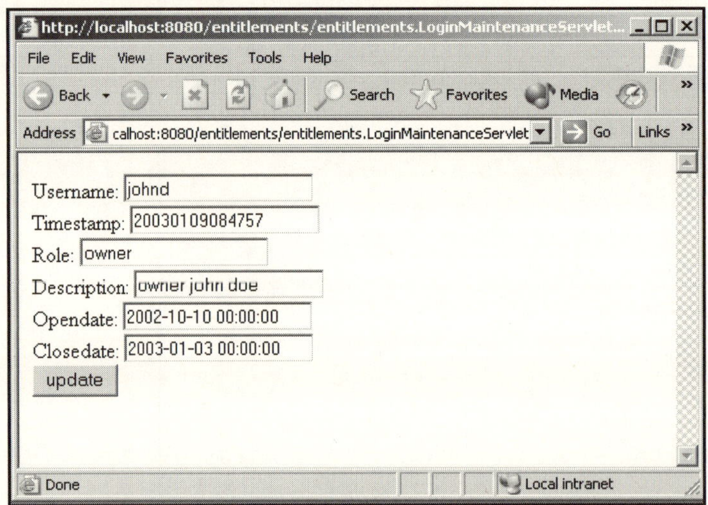

Figure 6.7 The close date has been submitted and stored in a database.

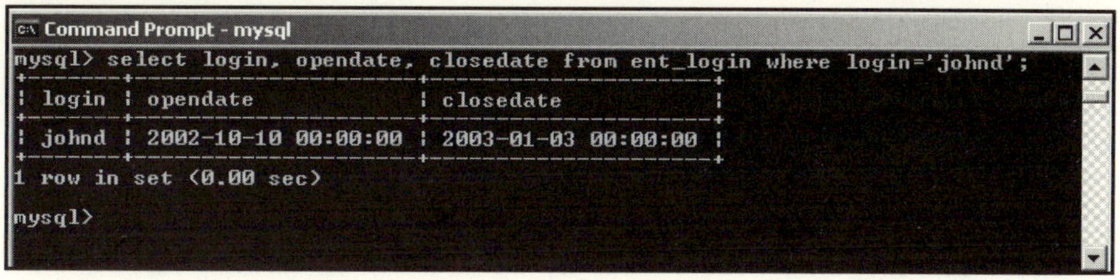

```
Command Prompt - mysql
mysql> select login, opendate, closedate from ent_login where login='johnd';
+-------+---------------------+---------------------+
| login | opendate            | closedate           |
+-------+---------------------+---------------------+
| johnd | 2002-10-10 00:00:00 | 2003-01-03 00:00:00 |
+-------+---------------------+---------------------+
1 row in set (0.00 sec)

mysql>
```

Figure 6.8 We queried the database to see the close date.

Updating the Table

Up to this point all you've been able to do is query for rows in the database and make changes to the data already stored. It would be nice to be able to add new rows to the table as well. Let's start from the user's point of view this time and expand your changeLogin.html page to allow a user to add a new login. This involves adding an Add User button to the <form> on the page. Here's the code:

```
<%@ page language='java' import='entitlements.Login' %>
<% ServletContext app = getServletContext();
   Login e = (Login)app.getAttribute("login");
 %>
<head>
<body>
<form action=
"/entitlements/entitlements.LoginMaintenanceServlet"
method="post">
  Username: <input name="login" value = "<%= e.getLogin()
%>"><BR>
  Timestamp: <input name="timestamp" value = "<%= e.getTs()
%>"><BR>
  Role: <input name="role" value = "<%= e.getRole() %>"><BR>
  Description: <input name="description"
    value = "<%= e.getDescription() %>"><BR>
  Opendate: <input name="opendate" value = "<%= e.getOpendate()
%>"><BR>
  Closedate: <input name="closedate" value = "<%= e.getClosedate()
%>"><BR>
```

```
    <input type="submit" name="submit" value="update">
    <input type="submit" name="submit" value="add">
  </form>
  </body>
  </head>
```

Now you need to change the entity bean so it can create a new row. You do this by adding a new method to the local home interface class. The method is simply called create(), and its signature is shown here:

```
Login create(String login,
             String ts,
             String role,
             String description,
             String opendate,
             String closedate
      )
   throws CreateException;
```

The create() method is a business method in its purest sense because you have to add some code in the implementation class to support its functionality. However, since it returns a local interface object, you must place it in the local home interface class.

You can pass into the create() method all of the fields of the table (as we've done here) or just some of the fields and handle the missing ones programmatically. Before we go any further, let's outline the code in the implementation class:

```
public String ejbCreate(String login,
             String ts,
             String role,
             String description,
             String opendate,
             String closedate
       )
  throws CreateException {
  setLogin(login);
  setTs(ts);
  setRole(role);
  setDescription(description);
  setOpendate(opendate);
  setClosedate(closedate);

  return login;
}

public void ejbPostCreate(String login,
```

```
                    String ts,
                    String role,
                    String description,
                    String opendate,
                    String closedate) {
        // since there are no relations, this is empty.
    }
```

Here, you add two methods to the implementation class. The first is called ejbCreate(), and it has the same parameters as the create() method you exposed in the local home interface class. When the create() method is called on the local home interface, a call is made to the ejbCreate() method, where individual setters are called to populate a new entity bean for the created row. You can place any business logic required during the creation of a new row in the ejbCreate() method. After the method is executed, a call is made to the ejbPostCreate() method, which handles any relationships set up between the current table and other tables in the database. We discuss relationships later in the chapter; for now, the ejbPostCreate() method doesn't have any code to execute.

If you have worked with databases for long, you know sometimes tables are created with an auto-incremented primary key. If the entity bean is related to such a table, you can eliminate the setter for the primary key in the ejbCreate() method. The server creates an appropriate SQL that passes a null to the database for the primary key, thus triggering the insertion of a new key value.

Now let's work on the servlet that will handle the Add Login button as well as the Update button on your changeLogin HTML page. Here's the code:

```
} else if (submit.equals("add")) {
  try {
    Login e = home.create(req.getParameter("login"),
                          req.getParameter("timestamp"),
                          req.getParameter("role"),
                          req.getParameter("description"),
                          req.getParameter("opendate"),
                           req.getParameter("closedate"));
  } catch(Exception e) {}
}
```

In this code, you now have three conditions to check: getting a login, updating a login, and adding a new login. Because you can use the code to handle the new login, it's just a matter of calling the create() method of the local home interface and passing the values for the new login. In return, the bean either returns a new Login bean or throws an exception. Figure 6.9 shows the database before a new row was added using our HTML and servlet code; Figure 6.10 shows the database after the new row was recorded.

```
mysql> select login, opendate, closedate from ent_login where login='johnd';
+-------+---------------------+---------------------+
| login | opendate            | closedate           |
+-------+---------------------+---------------------+
| johnd | 2002-10-10 00:00:00 | 2003-01-03 00:00:00 |
+-------+---------------------+---------------------+
1 row in set (0.00 sec)

mysql>
```

Figure 6.9 Before a new login.

```
mysql> select login, opendate, closedate from login where opendate > 0;
+-------+---------------------+-----------+
| login | opendate            | closedate |
+-------+---------------------+-----------+
| johnd | 2002-10-10 00:00:00 | NULL      |
| bobs  | 2003-01-10 09:51:27 | NULL      |
+-------+---------------------+-----------+
2 rows in set (0.02 sec)

mysql>
```

Figure 6.10 After the new login.

Removing a Bean

Probably the easiest task to code and perform with our entity bean is removing a row from the database. In fact, there is no code to write—removing the row occurs by simply calling the remote() method on the appropriate entity bean object. For example:

```
Login login = home.findByPrimaryKey('johnd');
login.remote();
```

In this code snippet, we use the findByPrimaryKey() method to obtain the table row with a login of johnd. Using the bean returned by the method, we call remove() to delete the row from the database.

Using Multiple Entity Beans

In order to show some advanced topics using beans, let's create another bean and database table. The new table is called groups. The groups table will be linked to the login table using a new field you'll add to login. First, though, the schema for ent_:

```
create table groups (
     group_Id Int not null primary key auto_Increment,
     groups varchar(3),
     ts timestamp
);
```

Now, populate a couple rows so you have some information to view:

```
insert into groups values(0, 'aab', now());
insert into groups values(0, 'bbc', now());
```

The result of these insertions is a table, as shown here:

```
mysql> select * from groups;
+----------+--------+----------------+
| group_id | groups | ts             |
+----------+--------+----------------+
|        1 | aab    | 20030109092527 |
|        2 | bbc    | 20030109092534 |
+----------+--------+----------------+
2 rows in set (0.00 sec)
```

You need to relate the rows in login to the rows in the groups table. This is accomplished in two steps:

1. Add a new column to login.
2. Update the rows in login.

First, add a new column to login with this SQL:

```
alter table login add column currGroup int;
```

This code adds a new column to each row in the login table. Now update the rows:

```
Update login set currGroup = 1 where login='johnd';
Update login set currGroup = 2 where login='janed';
```

With the new update statements, you have successfully linked the rows in the login table with the rows in the groups table, as shown in Figure 6.11.

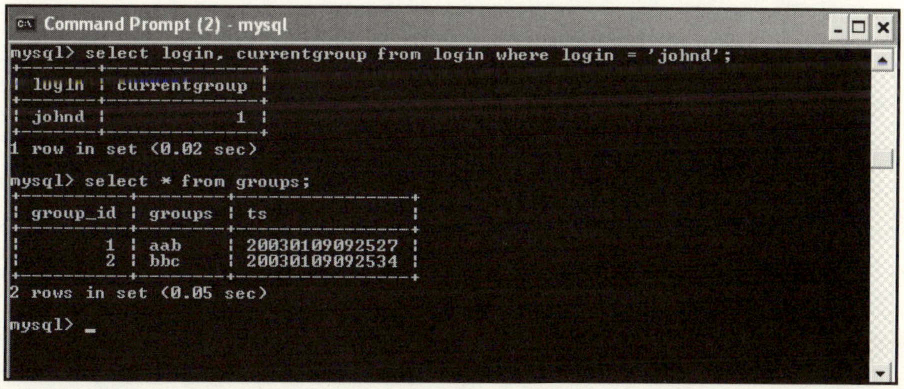

```
Command Prompt (2) - mysql
mysql> select login, currentgroup from login where login = 'johnd';
+-------+--------------+
| login | currentgroup |
+-------+--------------+
| johnd |            1 |
+-------+--------------+
1 row in set (0.02 sec)

mysql> select * from groups;
+----------+--------+----------------+
| group_id | groups | ts             |
+----------+--------+----------------+
|        1 | aab    | 20030109092527 |
|        2 | bbc    | 20030109092534 |
+----------+--------+----------------+
2 rows in set (0.05 sec)

mysql> _
```

Figure 6.11 The login and groups table relationship.

Adding a Groups Bean

To cut down on the code needed for the group bean, let's write a single finder method that will locate all rows in the groups table. Using everything you've learned so far, define the bean called Group for the groups table using the three files shown in Listings 6.2, 6.3, and 6.4.

```
package entitlements;
import javax.ejb.*;
import java.util.*;

public interface GroupHome extends EJBLocalHome {
  Group findByPrimaryKey(int id)
   throws FinderException;

  Collection findByLogin(String login)
   throws FinderException;
}
```

Listing 6.2 groupHome.java.

```
package entitlements;
import javax.ejb.*;
import java.sql.Timestamp;
import java.util.*;

public interface Group extends EJBLocalObject {

  int       getGroup_id();
  String    getGroups();
  String    getTS();

  void      setGroups(String g);
  void      setTS(String t);
}
```

Listing 6.3 groupHome.java.

```
package entitlements;

import javax.ejb.*;
import java.sql.Timestamp;
import java.util.*;
```

Listing 6.4 groupBean.java. (continues)

```
public abstract class GroupBean
  extends com.caucho.ejb.AbstractEntityBean {

  public abstract int        getGroup_id();
  public abstract String     getGroups();
  public abstract String     getTS();

  public abstract void       setGroups(String g);
  public abstract void       setTS(String t);
}
```

Listing 6.4 groupBean.java. (continued)

The entry in the deployment descriptor for the bean is:

```
<entity>
  <ejb-class>entitlements.GroupBean</ejb-class>
  <persistence-type>Container</persistence-type>
  <prim-key-class>int</prim-key-class>
  <reentrant>True</reentrant>
  <abstract-schema-name>groups</abstract-schema-name>
  <sql-table>groups</sql-table>
  <cmp-field><field-name>groups</field-name></cmp-field>
  <cmp-field><field-name>ts</field-name></cmp-field>
  <primkey-field>group_id</primkey-field>
  <query>
    <query-method>
      <method-name>findAll</method-name>
    </query-method>
    <ejb-ql>SELECT o FROM groups o</ejb-ql>
  </query>

  <local-home>entitlements.GroupHome</local-home>
  <local>entitlements.Group</local>
  <ejb-name>Group</ejb-name>
</entity>
```

Relationships

Relationships between tables are created when a column in one table is populated with values from another table. In our example, you created a relationship between the login and groups table by adding to login a column called currGroup that contains one of the primary key values from the groups table.

So, if you perform a query against login for the login johnd, you get a result like the following:

```
mysql> select login, role, currGroup, opendate
from login
where login='johnd';
+-------+-------+-------------+---------------------+
| login | role  | currGroup   | opendate            |
+-------+-------+-------------+---------------------+
| johnd | owner |           1 | 2002-10-10 00:00:00 |
+-------+-------+-------------+---------------------+
1 row in set (0.00 sec)
```

Now if you want to see the group associated with group 1, you run the query

```
mysql> select * from groups where group_id = 1;
+----------+--------+----------------+
| group_id | groups | ts             |
+----------+--------+----------------+
|        1 | aab    | 20030109092527 |
+----------+--------+----------------+
1 row in set (0.00 sec)
```

Using a SQL Join, you can return the values from both tables in a convenient single result:

```
mysql> select login, role, opendate, groups.groups
from login
left join groups
  on login.currGroup=groups.group_id
where login='johnd';
+-------+-------+---------------------+--------+
| login | role  | opendate            | groups |
+-------+-------+---------------------+--------+
| johnd | owner | 2002-10-10 00:00:00 | aab    |
+-------+-------+---------------------+--------+
1 row in set (0.00 sec)
```

Now you have all of your relationship information in a single result set. The question now is, How do you handle this in EJB and Resin? You handle the relationship primarily in the deployment descriptor, but before we get there let's consider some of the different situations that can occur in relationships.

Relationship Types

In our example, you created a one-to-one relationship between the login and groups table. The relationship is considered to be *unidirectional* because you are interested in the group with which a specific login is associated but you are not interested in which logins are associated with that group. You can create unidirectional relationships in the direction most appropriate for the application. If the business logic requires relationships in both directions between two tables, you create a bidirectional relationship.

In addition to one-to-one relationships, the following types are supported by Resin and EJB:

- One-to-one
- One-to-many
- Many-to-one
- Many-to-many

As you might expect, when a many relationship is involved, the code won't receive a single row from the database but several rows (or a Collection in the case of EJB).

Building a Relationship between login and groups

Now, let's see how you can change your beans to support the relationship between the login and groups tables. There are three basic steps to building an EJB relationship:

1. Add container-managed relation (CMR) fields to the appropriate bean definition.
2. Add <relationships> tag and subtags to the deployment descriptor.
3. Change the business code.

In the first step, you are changing the bean that is interested in the relationship to include a CMR field. In other words, the login table includes a field called currGroup that is a link to the groups table. You must define this field as a CMR field instead of just a CMP field. Consider the following local interface for the Login bean:

```
package entitlements;
import javax.ejb.*;
import java.sql.Timestamp;
import java.util.*;

public interface Login extends EJBLocalObject {

  String    getLogin();
  String    getTs();
  String    getRole();
  String    getDescription();
```

```
    String      getOpendate();
    String      getClosedate();
    int         getCurrGroup();

    void        setTs(String t);
    void        setRole(String s);
    void        setDescription(String s);
    void        setOpendate(String  d);
    void        setCurrGroup(int g);

    void        changeClosedate(String d);
    Collection  pullLogins();

    Group getCurrGroup();
    void     setCurrGroup(Group e);
  }
```

The CMR field for the currGroup column is shown in bold. When you add the field to the database table using the ALTER TABLE SQL command, you normally add the column to the local interface and bean implementation files immediately in the form of getter/setter methods. Looking back at the table definition, you see that the column type is int, so you use the following code:

```
int getCurrGroup();
void setCurrGroup(int group);
```

This code creates a CMP field for the bean. However, since the field is used in a relationship you need to add appropriate methods to handle getting and setting the field based on the relationship. When you execute the method getCurrGroup() against a Login object, you get a Group object in return. The Group object includes the row from the groups table in which the currGroup value is equal to the primary key. The same holds for setting the object. Now consider the LoginBean class, shown in Listing 6.5.

```
package entitlements;

import javax.ejb.*;
import java.sql.Timestamp;
import java.util.*;

public abstract class LoginBean
  extends com.caucho.ejb.AbstractEntityBean {

  public abstract String    getLogin();
  public abstract String    getTs();
  public abstract String    getRole();
```

Listing 6.5 The LoginBean class. (continues)

```
public abstract String    getDescription();
public abstract String    getOpendate();
public abstract String    getClosedate();
public abstract int       getCurrGroup();

public abstract void      setLogin(String l);
public abstract void      setTs(String t);
public abstract void      setRole(String s);
public abstract void      setDescription(String s);
public abstract void      setOpendate(String d);
public abstract void      setClosedate(String d);
public abstract void      setCurrGroup(int g);

public void      changeClosedate(String d) {
  setClosedate(d);
}

public abstract Group getCurrGroup();
public abstract void     setCurrGroup(Group e);

public abstract Collection ejbSelectJustLogins()
  throws FinderException;

public Collection pullLogins() {
  Collection c = null;
  try {
    c = ejbSelectJustLogins();
  } catch(FinderException e) {};
  return c;
}

public String ejbCreate(String login,
              String ts,
              String role,
              String description,
              String opendate,
              String closedate
      )
  throws CreateException {
  setLogin(login);
  setTs(ts);
  setRole(role);
  setDescription(description);
  setOpendate(opendate);
  setClosedate(closedate);

  return login;
```

Listing 6.5 The LoginBean class. (continues)

```
  }

  public void ejbPostCreate(String login,
              String ts,
              String role,
              String description,
              String opendate,
              String closedate) {
  }
}
```

Listing 6.5 The LoginBean class. (continued)

Again the added code is shown in bold. We listed the code in its entirety to show that no additional code is needed for the relationships. The container will be generating all of the code for you. However, you do need to give it some help—in the form of the deployment descriptor.

In the second step, you set up the relationship between the two beans by using a <relationship> tag. Here's the new descriptor:

```
<ejb-jar>
  <enterprise-beans>
       entity beans
  </enterprise-beans>

<relationships>
  <ejb-relation>
    <ejb-relation-name>LoginGroup</ejb-relation-name>

    <ejb-relationship-role>
      <ejb-relationship-role-name>LoginGroup</ejb-relationship-role-
name>
      <multiplicity>One</multiplicity>
      <relationship-role-source>
        <ejb-name>Login</ejb-name>
      </relationship-role-source>

      <cmr-field>
        <cmr-field-name>currGroup</cmr-field-name>
      </cmr-field>
    </ejb-relationship-role>

    <ejb-relationship-role>
      <ejb-relationship-role-name>LoginGroupPart
       </ejb-relationship-role-name>
      <multiplicity>One</multiplicity>
      <relationship-role-source>
        <ejb-name>Group</ejb-name>
      </relationship-role-source>
```

```
        </ejb-relationship-role>

      </ejb-relation>
    </relationships>
    </ejb-jar>
```

The <relationships> element includes quite a few new tags:

<ejb-relation>—A container element that encapsulates a single bean-to-bean relationship.

<ejb-relation-name>—The name of this specific bean-to-bean relationship.

<ejb-relationship-role>—The container element for one end of the relationship. The descriptor needs two of these for all relationships.

<ejb-relationship-role-name>—The name of this part of the relationship.

<multiplicity>—The type of relationship for this end of the relationship or bean.

<relationship-role-source>—The bean for this end of the relationship.

<ejb-name>—The name of the bean.

<cmr-field>—The relationship field for the bean.

<cmr-field-name>—The name of the relationship field.

When you create a relationship in the deployment descriptor, you must define two roles for each of the beans. Of particular importance is the <cmr-field-name> element. This element defines the CMR field relating to the setter/getter methods added to the local interface and bean implementation. You must define this field in the database table represented by the defined bean. If the relationship is unidirectional, there will be only one <cmr-field> for the entire <ejb-relation>. Obviously in a bidirectional relationship, a <cmr-field> appears in both <ejb-relationship-role> definitions.

In the third step, you'll make use of the CMR field entry added to the Login bean. For example, the LoginMaintenanceServlet allows you to GET the current values for a login. Let's make a quick change to the code that handles a GET as well as the JSP template that displays the information. (The update and insert will be left as an exercise.) The new code for the GET code is:

```
    if (submit.equals("get")) {
       try {
         Login e =
(Login)home.findByPrimaryKey(req.getParameter("login"));
         Group g = e.getCurrGroup();

         ServletContext app = getServletContext();
```

```
            app.setAttribute("login", e);
            app.setAttribute("group", g);

            RequestDispatcher dispatch =
    app.getRequestDispatcher("/changeLogin.jsp");
            dispatch.forward(req, res);
        } catch (FinderException e) {
            throw new ServletException(e);
        }
    }
```

At the beginning of the code, you obtain the Login object for the login provided by the user. Once it's found, the getCurrGroup() method is called on the object to obtain the Group object created from the relationship defined in the deployment descriptor. Essentially, the container executed the two SQL queries shown at the beginning of this section, but without you having to write the SQL. Both of the objects are added to the Application object.

The JSP for the output is dispatched. In the JSP, include support for the additional object:

```
<%@ page language='java' import='entitlements.*' %>
<% ServletContext app = getServletContext();
   Login e = (Login)app.getAttribute("login");
   Group g = (Group)app.getAttribute("group");
 %>
<head>
<body>
<form action="http://localhost:8080/entitlements/entitlements
.LoginMaintenanceServlet" method="post">
  Username: <input name="login" value = "
    <%= e.getLogin() %>"><BR>
  Timestamp: <input name="timestamp" value = "
    <%= e.getTs() %>"><BR>
  Role: <input name="role" value = "<%= e.getRole() %>"><BR>
  Description: <input name="description" value = "
    <%= e.getDescription() %>"><BR>
  Opendate: <input name="opendate" value = "
    <%= e.getOpendate() %>"><BR>
  Closedate: <input name="closedate" value = "
    <%= e.getClosedate() %>"><BR>
  Group: <input name="group" value= "<%= g.getGroups() %>"><BR>
  <input type="submit" name="submit" value="update">
  <input type="submit" name="submit" value="add">
</form>
</body>
</head>
```

Compare the previous code for the JSP template, and you can see that we changed the import directive to include all of the entitlements classes and added code to pull the Group object from the Application object. Finally, we used the Group object to pull the group description with the getGroups() methods previously defined for the Group bean.

With all of the code in place, you can test your relationship by browsing to http://localhost:8080/login.html. After entering the login johnd, you see the output shown in Figure 6.12. As you can see, the description aab is displayed for the group John Doe belongs to.

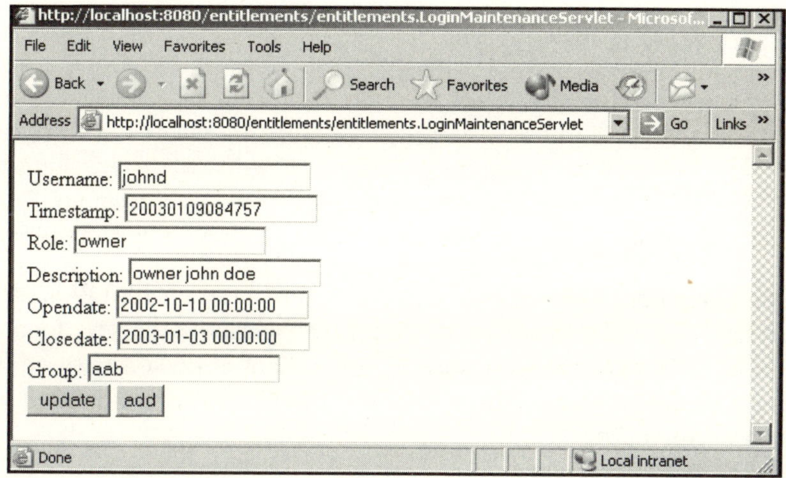

Figure 6.12 Group Output for Login.

Transactions

When working with beans, you may encounter a situation in which you need to perform multiple updates to several rows. In this case, you want to be sure all of the updates are successful; otherwise, you don't want any of them to succeed. This is called a *transaction* and is very common in the business world. Resin-EE supports transactions using the javax.transaction package.

Consider an example where you need to update all of the closedate fields in the database:

```
try {
  Collection c = home.findAll();
  Iterator iter = c.iterator();
  While (iter.hasNext()) {
    Login e = (Login)iter.next();
     e.setClosedate(–'2003-1-3ì');
  }
} catch(Exception e) {}
```

Now you want to make sure that all of the updates occur, so you add transaction support:

```
Context context = new InitialContext();
UserTransaction transaction =
(UserTransaction)context.lookup("java:comp/UserTransaction");
try {
  Collection c = home.findAll();
  Iterator iter = c.iterator();
  transaction.begin();
    while (iter.hasNext()) {
      Login e = (Login)iter.next();
       e.setClosedate('2003-1-3');
    }
  transaction.commit();
} catch(Throwable e) {
  transaction.rollback();
}
```

The code begins by obtaining an object pointer to the current context. Using the context, the JNDI entry to the UserTransaction object is located and assigned to a UserTransaction object. This object is tasked with controlling all updates to the database. Three important methods are associated with the UserTransaction class:

begin()—Begins the transaction.

rollback()—Causes all updates to be reversed because of an error or other situation.

commit()—Causes all of the updates to be committed to the database permanently.

Before you start doing any of the updates, you execute the begin() method to let the UserTransaction object know you are starting a group of updates that need to execute successfully as a unit. After all of the updates have finished, the commit() method is executed to make sure all of the updates are made permanent. If an error occurs during the updates, the rollback() method in the exception executes and all updates are removed.

Using Stateless Session Beans

Resin-EE provides support for instantiating stateless session beans in addition to entity beans. A stateless session EJB is basically an object that can be instantiated both locally or remotely to handle business-related issues within the application. The stateless session is like a servlet except it doesn't have the ability to handle state. The sessions are useful for the division of tasks within a servlet.

With the LoginMaintenanceServlet you created earlier, as you added each task to the servlet, more and more code was required. You can delegate each of the individual tasks to a stateless session EJB. Creating a stateless session bean is similar to creating an entity bean. Four steps are required:

- Create a remote interface.
- Create a local home interface.
- Create an implementation file.
- Create a deployment descriptor.

Since the stateless session can be instantiated remotely, you need a remote interface:

```
package entitlements;

import java.rmi.*;
import javax.ejb.*;

public interface LoginUpdate extends EJBObject {
  String getLogin(int e) throws RemoteException;
}
```

The only major difference here from your local interface is that the getLogin() method throws a RemoteException. Now the local interface:

```
package entitlements;

import java.rmi.*;
import javax.ejb.*;

public interface LoginUpdateHome extends EJBHome {
  LoginUpdate create() throws CreateException, RemoteException;
}
```

The local home interface has a single purpose: to create the remote object defined by the remote interface above. Now for the implementation code:

```
package entitlements;

import java.rmi.*;
import javax.ejb.*;
import com.caucho.ejb.*;

public class LoginUpdateBean extends AbstractSessionBean {
  private LoginHome home = null;

  public void ejbCreate() {
    throws ServletException {
    try {
      Context cmp = (Context) new
```

```
InitialContext().lookup("java:comp/env/cmp");

      home = (LoginHome) cmp.lookup("Login");
    } catch (NamingException e) {
      throw new ServletException(e);
    }
  }

  public String getLogin(int e){
    Login login = (Login)home.findByPrimaryKey(e);
    return login.getLogin();
  }
}
```

The code for the stateless session has two methods. The first is the ejbCreate() method, which is called when the session bean is first referenced. The method finds the local interface to the Login entity bean and stores it for later use. When a call is made to the getLogin(int) method, the bean accesses the home interface, calls the findByPrimaryKey() method to get a Login entity bean based on the passed key value, and returns the login string from the row.

You need to make sure the server knows about the bean by including an entry in the deployment descriptor:

```
<ejb-jar>
<enterprise-beans>
  <session>
    <ejb-name>LoginUpdate</ejb-name>
    <home>entitlements.LoginUpdateHome</home>
    <remote>entitlements.LoginUpdate</remote>
    <ejb-class>entitlements.LoginUpdateBean</ejb-class>
    <session-type>Stateless</session-type>
    <transaction-type>Bean</transaction-type>
  </session>
</enterprise-beans>
</ejb-jar>
```

Of course, you need to be able to remotely access the session bean. To do this, you will write a JSP page:

```
<%@ page import="com.caucho.burlap.*, entitlements.*, javax.ejb.*" %>
<%
HomeHandle homeHandle = new BurlapHomeHandle(
  "http://localhost:8080/entitlements/LoginUpdate");

// get the home stub
LoginUpdateHome home = (LoginUpdateHome) homeHandle.getEJBHome();

// create remote object
LoginUpdate login = (LoginUpdate) home.create();
%>
Login name for row 1: <%= login.getLogin(1) %>
```

As you can see, the code isn't very complex. First you attempt to make a connection to the remote server using Burlap. The URL is the same URL you might use in a browser. The outcome of the BurlapHomeHandle is a handle to the remote system. You use this handle to obtain the home interface of your session bean by calling homeHandle.getEJBHome(). A LoginUpdateHome object is returned. Using the home interface, you call the create() method to create the remote LoginUpdate bean and obtain a local object pointer or reference to the bean. Finally, you make a call to the getLogin(int) method to obtain the login name of the associated table row.

What's Next

In this chapter, we provided a comprehensive look at how Resin-EE makes writing object-oriented Web sites a breeze. If using beans isn't enough to reduce the amount of SQL written, you can take advantage of Resin's support of XDoclet to further reduce the code needed for the local home interface, home interface, and bean implementation, as you'll learn in the next chapter.

CHAPTER 7

Using XDoclet with Resin

In the previous chapter, we spent quite a bit of time discussing how to use EJBs with Resin. After we created the first bean using the local home interface, local interface, and implementation, building the Groups bean was fairly routine. When I wrote the code for the Groups files, I just copied the login files and changed what was needed. Wouldn't it be nice if there were an easier way to write the EJB files?

XDoclet is a technology that allows you to do attribute-oriented programming. Using JavaDoc-like tags, you can add meaningful metadata to Java source code and allow XDoclet to generate code or other output based on the specific meaning of the various tags. Caucho has produced its own set of metadata attribute tags for the generation of EJB code. In this chapter, we discuss how to install XDoclet and Resin extensions, and how to use the defined tags to generate bean code for us.

Installing XDoclet

A good deal of the work done by XDoclet is accomplished using Another Neat Tool (Ant), a build tool written in Java. So let's begin by installing Ant as well as XDoclet. Here are simple steps for installing all of the required tools:

1. Install Resin-EE.
2. Download Ant from http://jakarta.apache.org/ant and install it. The download is available as a .zip or .tgz file depending on your target system.

The download installs the application in a directory such as /jakarta-ant-1.5.1, but we will assume a default of /ant instead. (You can either rename your Ant installation directory or change the examples in the chapter.) For ease of use, the ANT_HOME environment variable is set to the installation directory, and an entry to the /bin directory is added to PATH.

3. Download and install XDoclet from http://xdoclet.sourceforge.net/install.html. Copy the XDoclet JAR files and dependencies (xdoclet.jar, log4j.jar) to the Ant lib directory (/ant/lib).
4. Download and install Resin XDoclet support from www.caucho.com/projects/xdoclet/resin-xdoclet.jar.

Adding a New Entitlements Bean

To show how to use XDoclet with Resin, let's accomplish two tasks. The first is to build a new bean based on a table called logs, and the second is to expand the login bean created in the previous chapter. First let's look at the new table:

```
create table logs (
  log_id int not null auto_increment primary key,
  application varchar(64),
  message varchar(128),
  ts timestamp);
```

If we were going to create an entity bean using what we learned from the previous chapter, we would need to create three files plus the deployment descriptor information. XDoclet and Resin's support allows us to write just the implementation file—the other files will be created automatically. Listing 7.1 contains the implementation file for our new entity bean.

```
package entitlements;
 /**
 * @ejb.bean                    type="CMP"
 *                              cmp-version="2.x"
 *                              name="LogsBean"
 *                              jndi.name="cmr.User"
 *                              view-type="local"
 *                              primkey-field="log_id"
 *
 * @ejb.pk                      class="int"
 *
 * @ejb.home                    generate="local"
 *                  local-class="entitlements.LogsHome"
```

Listing 7.1 Our new entity bean. (continues)

```
 *
 * @ejb.interface              generate="local"
 *                 local-class="entitlements.Logs"
 *
 * @resin-ejb:entity-bean      sql-table="logs"
 */
public abstract class LogsBean extends com.caucho.ejb.AbstractEntityBean {
  /** @ejb.pk-field
   *  @ejb.interface-method      view-type="local"
   *  @ejb.persistent-field
   *  @resin-ejb:cmp-field      sql-column="log_id"
   */
 public abstract String getLog_id();

  /** @ejb.persistent-field
   *  @ejb.interface-method      view-type="local"
   *  @resin-ejb:cmp-field      sql-column="description"
   */
 public abstract String getDescription();
  /** @ejb.interface-method      view-type="local"*/
 public abstract void setDescription(String description);

  /** @ejb.persistent-field
   *  @ejb.interface-method      view-type="local"
   *  @resin-ejb:cmp-field      sql-column="message"
   */
 public abstract String getMessage();
  /** @ejb.interface-method      view-type="local"*/
 public abstract void setMessage(String message);

  /** @ejb.persistent-field
   *  @ejb.interface-method      view-type="local"
   *  @resin-ejb:cmp-field      sql-column="ts"
   */
 public abstract String getTs();
  /** @ejb.interface-method      view-type="local"*/
 public abstract void setTs(String ts);

}
```

Listing 7.1 Our new entity bean. (continued)

As you can see, there is little code—and a whole bunch of tags. Starting at the top of the file, we find class-level tags. The first tag, called @ejb.bean, tells the system that we are building a new EJB. There are four important parameters to the @ejb.bean tag:

type="CMP"—Indicates that the bean should be container managed.

name="LogsBean"—Specifies the name of our bean.

view-type="local"—Indicates the view: local, remote, or both.

primkey-field="log_id"—Specifies the primary key for the table the bean represents.

After the class-level tags are tags that determine the additional classes created for the bean. The tags are:

@ejb.pk—Specifies the data type for the primary key of the table the bean represents.

@ejb.home—Indicates a home interface will be created and sets the name of the class.

@ejb.interface—Indicates the interface will be created with the provided classname.

@resin-ejb:entity_bean—Indicates the table associated with this bean. Note this is a Resin-specific tag and is supported only through the Resin XDoclet extension. All of the other tags to this point are supported by XDoclet itself.

Once the class-level tags have been taken care of, we need to define the methods in the implementation file, as well as provide tags so the appropriate methods are built in the interface files. The code starts with a method for accessing the primary key of the table. The tags are:

```
/** @ejb.pk-field
 *  @ejb.interface-method      view-type="local"
 *  @ejb.persistent-field
 *  @resin-ejb:cmp-field      sql-column="log_id"
 */
public abstract String getLog_id();
```

You will notice that we don't have a setLog_id() method. This is because the table auto-generates the key value. However, if it didn't, the tags would be:

```
  /** @ejb.persistent-field */
public abstract void setLog_id(int id);
```

The tags for the primary key accessors are:

@ejb.pk-field—Tells the system this is the primary key.

@ejb.interface-method—Tells the system to expose this method to the appropriate interface: local, remote, or both.

@ejb.persistent field—Tells the system this field is persistent.

@resin-ejb:cmp-field—Maps the field to the appropriate database column.

For all of the other accessor methods, we have a common pattern. The code for the get/set description field is:

```
  /** @ejb.persistent-field
   *  @ejb.interface-method      view-type="local"
   *  @resin-ejb:cmp-field      sql-column="description"
   */
public abstract String getDescription();
  /** @ejb.interface-method      view-type="local"*/
public abstract void setDescription(String description);
```

The tags are:

@ejb.persistent-field—Tells the system this field is persistent.

@ejb.interface-method—Tells the system to expose this method to the appropriate interface: local, remote, or both.

@resin-ejb:cmp-field—Maps the field to the appropriate database column.

That's all that you need to add to the bean implementation file. Now it's time to create an Ant build file that will use our implementation file to build all of the other required bean files.

The Ant Build File

At this point, let's create a build file, shown in Listing 7.2, that will take the implementation source file and produce all of the required files for our new bean. All of the work is accomplished with Ant tasks that use both XDoclet and Resin's XDoclet extensions.

```
<project name="resincmp" default="all">
  <property file="build.properties"/>

  <path id="resinclasspath">
       <pathelement path="${resinlib}/resin-ejb.jar" />
       <pathelement path="${resinlib}/ejb.jar" />
       <pathelement path="${xdocpath}" />
  </path>

  <target name="clean">
      <delete file="${webinf}/cmp-xdoclet.ejb"
failonerror="false" />
      <delete dir="${webinf}/classes"
failonerror="false"/>
  </target>

  <target name="ejbdoclet" >
```

Listing 7.2 Our Ant build file. (continues)

```
            <echo message="XDoc classpath = ${xdocpath}" />

           <taskdef name="resingendd"
                classname="com.caucho.xdoclet.ResinEjbDocletTask"
                classpath="${xdocpath}"
           />


           <resingendd
             ejbspec="2.0"
             sourcepath="${src}"
             ejbClassNameSuffix="Bean"
             mergedir="${src}"
                destdir="${src}"
                classpathref="resinclasspath"
           >

                <fileset dir="${src}">
                     <include name="${beans}" />
                </fileset>

                <localinterface/>
                <localhomeinterface/>
                <remoteinterface/>
                <homeinterface/>

                <entitypk/>

              <deploymentdescriptor
                destdir="${webinf}"
                destinationFile="cmp-xdoclet.ejb"
                validatexml="true" />
         </resingendd>
</target>

<target name="build" >
  <mkdir dir="${dest}" />
  <javac srcdir="${src}"
         classpathref="resinclasspath"
         destdir="${dest}"/>
  </target>
  <target name="all" depends="clean,build,ejbdoclet" />
</project>
```

Listing 7.2 Our Ant build file. (continued)

There are three primary targets for the build file: clean, build, and ejbdoclet. Most of the work is accomplished in ejbdoclet. Within this target, there is one primary task: resingendd. Within this task are several subtasks. The first, called localinterface, creates the local interface. The localhomeinterface subtask, as you'd expect, creates the local home interface. Finally, the deploymentdescriptor subtask creates the deployment descriptor for our new bean. In most cases, we have to cut and paste the information in the generated deployment descriptor file into our current descriptor file.

You might have to change two primary paths—Resinlib and xdocpath—on your own system. Check the build.properties file and verify all paths before issuing the command

```
ant buildfile.xml
```

The Files Ant Produces

After Ant has had a chance to process the build file, it produces four files:

cmp-xdoclet.ejb—The deployment descriptor.

logs.java—The local interface.

logsHome.java—The local home interface.

logsBean.java—The implementation file.

You can move all of the Java files to the /classes directory of your entitlement application and use them in servlets.

Expanding a Bean

One of the most popular options that you can add to a bean is a finder method. In this section, we add a finder method to the new LogsBean created earlier. Listing 7.3 contains our new implementation file with XDoclet tags added.

```
package entitlements;
 /**
 * @ejb.bean                        type="CMP"
 *                                 cmp-version="2.x"
 *                                 name="LogsBean"
 *                                 jndi.name="cmr.User"
 *                                 view-type="local"
 *                                 primkey-field="log_id"
 *
 * @ejb.pk                         class="int"
```

Listing 7.3 LogsBean with XDoclet tags added. (continues)

```
 *
 * @ejb.home                                generate="local"
 *                 local-class="entitlements.LogsHome"
 *
 * @ejb.interface                   generate="local"
 *                 local-class="entitlements.Logs"
 *
 * @resin-ejb:entity-bean               sql-table="logs"
 *
 * @ejb.finder
 *    signature="User findByApp(java.lang.String app)"
 *    query="SELECT DISTINCT OBJECT(log) FROM LogsBean log
 *     where log.app = ?1"
 *    result-type-mapping="Local"
 *
 * @ejb.finder
 *    signature="Collection findAll()"
 *    query="SELECT DISTINCT OBJECT(log) FROM LogsBean log"
 *    result-type-mapping="Local"
 */
 public abstract class LogsBean extends
com.caucho.ejb.AbstractEntityBean {
   /** @ejb.pk-field
    *  @ejb.interface-method      view-type="local"
    *  @ejb.persistent-field
    *  @resin-ejb:cmp-field      sql-column="log_id"
    */
  public abstract String getLog_id();

   /** @ejb.persistent-field
    *  @ejb.interface-method      view-type="local"
    *  @resin-ejb:cmp-field      sql-column="description"
    */
  public abstract String getDescription();
   /** @ejb.interface-method      view-type="local"*/
  public abstract void setDescription(String description);

   /** @ejb.persistent-field
    *  @ejb.interface-method      view-type="local"
    *  @resin-ejb:cmp-field      sql-column="message"
    */
  public abstract String getMessage();
   /** @ejb.interface-method      view-type="local"*/
  public abstract void setMessage(String message);

   /** @ejb.persistent-field
    *  @ejb.interface-method      view-type="local"
```

Listing 7.3 LogsBean with XDoclet tags added. (continues)

```
   *  @resin-ejb:cmp-field      sql-column="ts"
   */
  public abstract String getTs();
   /** @ejb.interface-method      view-type="local"*/
  public abstract void setTs(String ts);

}
```

Listing 7.3 LogsBean with XDoclet tags added. (continued)

Adding a finder to the bean is as simple as adding the @ejb.finder tag to the implementation file. The tag includes three important parameters:

signature—The signature for the finder method, including the return type and all parameters.

query—The actual EJB-QL query to use for the finger.

result-type-mapping—The scope of the finger: local, remote, or both.

That's it! Just build the implementation using Ant and XDoclet.

Resin XDoclet Tags

The following is a list of the EJB-relevant XDoclet tags defined within XDoclet and the Resin extension:

@ejb.bean—Defines the new EJB to be created. Its attributes are:

- name—Indicates the bean name as defined in the deployment descriptor file.
- view-type—Specifies the scope of the new bean. The values are local, remote, or both.
- reentrant—Indicates whether the entity bean is reentrant (True or False).
- type—Indicates CMP (for container-managed persistence) or BMP (for bean-managed persistence).
- schema—Specifies the value for the abstract schema name used in EJB-QL as defined in the deployment descriptor.
- primkey-field—Specifies the primary key field name as defined in the deployment descriptor.

@ejb.pk—Specifies the entity primary key definition as defined in the deployment descriptor. It has one attribute:

- class—The primary key classname.

@ejb.home—Starts the definition of the home interface. Its attributes are:

- generate—Determines which home interfaces to generate: remote, local, or both.
- local-class—Specifies the classname for the local home class.

@ejb.interface—Starts the definition of the interface. Its attributes are:

- generate—Determines which interface to generate: remote, local, or both.
- local-class—Specifies the classname for the local interface.

@ejb.finder—Creates a finger method. Its attributes are:

- result-type-mapping--specifies an optional result type mapping.
- query—Contains the query for the finder method using EJB-QL.

@ejb.select—Creates a select method. Its attributes are:

- signature—Indicates the select method signature with the return type and parameters.
- query—Contains the query for the select method using EJB-QL.

@resin-ejb:entity-bean—A Resin-specific tag for the use of the <sql-table> element. It has one attribute:

- sql-table—Specifies the physical SQL table name.

@ejb.interface-method—Include this attribute with the method in the interface.

@ejb.persistence—specified persistence information for a bean. It has one attribute:

- Table-name--the table to be mapped.

@ejb.pk-field—Include this attribute as a primary key.

@ejb.relation—Defines a relation. Its attributes are:

- name—Indicates the relation name; same if bidirectional.
- role-name—Specifies the name of the relationship.

@ejb.home-method—Include this with a home method. It has one attribute:

- view-type—Indicates local or remote.

@resin-ejb:cmp-field—Defines a Resin-specific persistent field. It has one attribute:

- sql-column—Specifies the name of the SQL column.

@resin-ejb:relation—A Resin-specific extension to @ejb.relation. It has these attributes:

- sql-table—Specifies the name of the table for n-m relations.
- sql-column—Contains the actual SQL column name.

What's Next

In this chapter, we showed you how to create and modify Resin EJBs using XDoclet without having to write the same basic code over and over. In the next chapter, we discuss Resin's support of taglibs.

CHAPTER 8

The Burlap Web Service Protocol

Enterprise JavaBeans (EJBs) require the ability to communicate between each other and the applications using them. The communication can involve sending something as simple as an integer or as complex as an entire Java object. To accomplish this communication, you must define a protocol—or more specifically, a wire protocol—that allows all types of information to be passed back and forth without developer intervention or complicated syntax.

The developers at Caucho looked at all of the options for a wire protocol when developing their EJB solution and determined that SOAP, CORBA-IIOP, and XML-RPC just didn't fit their goals for a protocol. However, those goals (summarized here) are outlined in the Burlap Web Service Protocol specification:

- It must serialize Java objects.
- It must support EJB.
- It must be fast, testable, and simple.

The Burlap Web Service Protocol is based on Simple Markup Language (SML), a subset of XML. In this chapter, we provide an overview of Burlap to give you an idea of how EJBs hosted in Resin are communicating with each other. In addition, we illustrate how you can use Burlap with independent applications.

Downloading the Code

Since Burlap is designed to be used with Resin as well as independently, Caucho has made it available as a separate download from the Resin servers. You can obtain the binary, source, and test JARs at www.caucho.com/burlap/index.xtp. As of this writing, the most current version is 2.1.6. The Caucho team is currently in the process of combining the Hessian and Burlap classes into a single download. You will see the download currently listed as a Hessian download, but this is expected to change in the near future.

Installing the protocol is simple. Download the JAR file named burlap-2.1.6.jar (or the latest version) and place it in your Java classpath.

The Specification

In this section, we examine some of the high-level details of the Burlap Web Service Protocol specification, including serialization and the <burlap:call> and <burlap:reply> tags. For a full discussion of the specification, visit www.caucho.com/burlap/burlap-draft-spec.xtp.

Serialization

As we mentioned earlier, the primary focus of the Burlap protocol is to transfer information between beans and/or applications. Since this is its most vital function, the task of serialization is very important. The current protocol defines nine serialization "primitives," two constructs to handle array-type data structures, one for null, and one for shared object references:

<boolean>

<int>

<long>

<double>

<base64>

<string>

<xml>

<data>

<remote>

<list>

<map>

<null>

<ref>

Let's examine each of these constructs and the resulting SML produced by the Burlap protocol when serialized.

<boolean>

The Java boolean is represented as the integer value 0 (for false) or 1 (for true). As a result, the Burlap tags are:

```
<boolean>0</boolean>
<boolean>1</boolean>
```

<int>

A 34-bit integer is represented in Burlap using the <int> tag. An integer can be positive, negative, or zero. For example:

```
<int>-34394</int>
<int>0</int>
<int>38943</int>
```

<long>

The <long> Burlap tag is used to represent all 64-bit integers. For example:

```
<long>2134445432</long>
<long>0</long>
<long>-2198748944</long>
```

<double>

The <double> tag represents 64-bit floating-point numbers. The floating-point number can be represented using formal IEEE notation. For example:

```
<double>2344.398e9</double>
<double>0.0</double>
<double>-3.1415924</double>
```

<date>

All dates passed using Burlap are converted to an ISO8609-encoded date. For example:

```
<date>20020709TO93848Z</date>
```

<string>

Strings passed in Burlap are encoded in UTF-8. Some escapes are allowed, including <, >, & and all &#*xx* values. All spaces in the string are also preserved.

```
<string>This is a string</string
<string>This string has escapes in it – 5 &lt; 9</string>
<string>How about another escape &#14;</string>
```

<xml>

The <xml> tag is used to encode an XML document using the same rules as <string>. All special characters are escaped, like the < and > of the XML document's tags. For example:

```
&lt;xml&gt;
     &lt;accounts&gt;
          &lt;account id='99910'&gt;
               &lt;name&gt;Steve&lt;/name&gt;
          &lt;/account&gt;
          &lt;account id='99920'&gt;
               &lt;name&gt;Pam&lt;/name&gt;
          &lt;/account&gt;
     &lt;/accounts&gt;
&lt;/xml&gt;
```

<base64>

Since binary date will also need to be passed between beans and applications, the Burlap protocol uses base 64 encoding to convert a binary stream to an alphanumeric string. For example:

```
<base64>
Aje8xc9Z9
</base64>
```

<remote>

The Burlap protocol is designed to allow both local and remote object reference. The remote references are particularly important for distributed beans and Web service implementation. Remote objects are distinguished using their type and the URL to the remote object. A remote reference is defined within Burlap as:

```
<remote>
     <type></type>
     <string></string>
</remote>
```

For example, suppose you have a Web service that exposes an Account object. The Burlap reference is:

```
<remote>
     <type>act.account</type>
     <string>http://www.mycompany.com/accounting</string>
</remote>
```

<list>

Other than the <remote> tag used for remote object references, all of the data structures have been primitive in nature. Burlap has the ability to represent two complex data structures: the list and the map.

A list is basically an array of a particular data type. It is represented by several characteristics:

Type—The type of list.

Length—The total number of elements in the list.

Objects—The actual elements contained in the list.

For example, we might have an array of doubles:

```
<list>
      <type>double</type>
     <length>4</length>
     <double>3.455</double>
     <double>1.3244e3</double>
     <double>34.344</double>
     <double>9393.44</double>
</list>
<ref>
```

<map>

The <map> tag is used to represent Hashtables and general serialized objects. An object or map is characterized by:

<type>—The map type or object.

objects—The elements that make up the map or object.

For example, you can create a HashMap() object and map account types to local application values:

```
HashMap acctMap – new HashMap();
acctMap.put(new Integer(455), "checking");
acctMap.put(new Integer(643), "savings");
```

You can pass the HashMap object to a client using the <map> tag:

```
<map>
     <type>java.util.HashMap</type>
     <int>455</int><string>checking</string>
     <int>643</int><string>savings</string>
</map>
```

You might also have a class for an account that needs to be passed to a client. You can define the class:

```
public class Account implements Serializable {
     String name;
int accountType;
}
Account newAccount = new Account("James", 643);
```

Notice that the class must implement the Serializable interface in order for Burlap to convert it to the following <map> tag:

```
<map>
     <type>Account</type>
     <string>name</string><string>James</string>

     <type>accountType</type><int>643</int>
</map>
```

<null>

The <null> tag is used to represent an object with no value or null pointer. Since SML doesn't allow the </null> tag, the null is represented as:

```
<null></null>
```

The <null> tag can be used to replace other burlap tags, including <string>, <xml>, <base64>, <list>, <map>, and <remote> as appropriate.

<ref>

When lists and maps are passed between the client and server, there might be references to the list or map in <tags> that come later. These references are typically circular, meaning that one of them will refer to the previously defined object itself. All references must be matched to the proper list or map sent between the systems. For example:

```
SpecialMap sm = new SpecialMap();
s.first = 5;
s.last = sm;
```

Here, the list attribute of the SpecialMap object sm is a reference back to itself. This object might be translated into the following map:

```
<map>
     <type>SpecialMap</type>
     <string>first</string><int>5</int>
     <string>last</string><ref>sm</ref>
</map>
```

The <burlap:call> Tag

Since the Burlap protocol is designed to handle remote invocations in bean or Web services arenas, it includes a way to invoke a method on a remote object: the <burlap:call> tag. As you saw with the <remote> tag, an object is defined by its URL, and all parameters to a method call on the object are serialized using the <burlap:call> tag. For example, suppose one of the methods of your Account object is called deposit(double). A call to this object is serialized by Burlap using the following:

```
<burlap:call>
     <method>deposit</method>
     <double>50.0</double>
</burlap:call>
```

Notice there is nothing in the <burlap:call> tag to specify the object on which the method should be invoked. This is handled by the code using Burlap, as you will see shortly.

The <burlap:reply> Tag

Of course, if you are able to make calls to a remote object, you need to be prepared for a response. There are basically two reponses Burlap is able to handle. The first is returning the object defined in the remote method's signature. The deposit(double) method returns a double indicating the new balance. The reply from the previous call is:

```
<burlap:reply>
          <double>4353.40</double>
</burlap:reply>
```

If the remote method fails, the system returns an error by way of the <fault> tag. The format of the <fault> tag is:

```
<burlap:reply>
  <fault>
    <string>code</string>
    <string>[code type]</string>

    <string>message</string>
    <string>[what failed]</string>

    <string>detail</string>
    <map>
      <type>[java exception]</type>
    </map>

  </value>
</burlap:reply>
```

Using BasicAPI

The Caucho Web server hosts a Burlap server designed around a simple interface called BasicAPI. This interface is designed to give new developers using Burlap a working test bed to become familiar with the code. The BasicAPI, which you can find at www.caucho.com/burlap/test/basic, fundamentally acts like a Web service by exposing various methods. Following is a list of the methods currently available. In this list we also indicate the interface exposed by the BasicAPI Web service hosted at Caucho.com; we describe each of the interface methods based on their purpose as well as the SML commands that are generated from the various interface methods; and we examine the SML commands in more detail later in this chapter.

Object echo(Object value)—Sends the method parameter to the server and waits for the server to return the parameter. This method illustrates the serialization of Java objects because the parameter to the method can be an object derived from java.lang.Object.

```
echo(1)

<burlap:call>
  <method>echo</method>
  <int>1</int>
</burlap:call>

<burlap:reply>
  <int>1</int>
</burlap:reply>
```

void fault()—Causes an application fault to occur by throwing an exception.

```
<burlap:call>
     <method>fault</method>
   </burlap:call>

   <burlap:reply>
     <fault>
       <string>code</string>
       <string>ServerException</string>
       <string>message</string>
       <string>test fault</string>

       <string>detail</string>
   <map>
           <type>java.io.IOException</type>
    <string>detailMessage</string>
    <string>test fault</string>
   </map>
     </fault>
    </burlap:reply>
```

String hello()—Returns a String object with the value of "Hello, World".

```
<burlap:call>
    <method>hello</method>
   </burlap:call>

   <burlap:reply>
     <value>
       <string>Hello,world</string>
     </value>
   </burlap:reply>
```

void nullCall()—No operation.

```
<burlap:call>
     <method>nullCall</method>
   </burlap:call>

   <burlap:reply>
     <value>
       <null></null>
     </value>
   </burlap:reply>
```

int subtract(int, int)—Returns the result of subtracting the second parameter from the first. Example: subtract(15,15)

```
<burlap:call>
  <method>subtract</method>
  <int>15</int>
  <int>15</int>
</burlap:call>

<burlap:reply>
  <value>
    <int>0</int>
  </value>
</burlap:reply>
```

Writing a Basic Client

Our first goal in this chapter is to write a client application in Java that allows you to use the BasicAPI service hosted on the Caucho.com Web site. Listing 8.1 contains the code for the client.

```
Line 1: import com.caucho.hessian.client.BurlapProxyFactory;
import com.caucho.burlap.test.BasicAPI;
import java.net.MalformedURLException;
```

Listing 8.1 A basic Burlap client for the BasicAPI Web service. (continues)

```
public class BasicClient {

  static String url =
    "http://www.caucho.com/burlap/test/basic";

  public static void main(String[] args) {
    BasicAPI basic = null;

    BurlapProxyFactory factory = new BurlapProxyFactory();
    try {
      basic = (BasicAPI) factory.create(BasicAPI.class, url);
    } catch (MalformedURLException e) {
       System.out.println("Bad URL");
    }

    if (basic != null)
      System.out.println("hello(): " + basic.hello());
  }
}
```

Listing 8.1 A basic Burlap client for the BasicAPI Web service. (continued)

Executing the Code

To test the code in Listing 8.1, you need to download the burlap-test.jar JAR file found on the Caucho Web site at www.caucho.com/burlap/index.xtp. This JAR contains the BasicAPI interface needed to build a local object reference to the Web service on the Caucho site. Once you have downloaded this JAR, place it in your classpath. (If you haven't already downloaded the burlap JAR, you can obtain it at the same URL.)

In the directory where you placed the code from Listing 8.1, compile the test code using the following command:

```
javac BasicClient.java
```

Now execute the code:

```
java BasicClient
```

You should see output shown in Figure 8.1.

So what did this small snippet of code do? In Listing 8.1, the code started by instantiating an object factory that allows you to create local references to remote services. At this point, you have only created a factory supplied by the Burlap implementation from Caucho.

Next, the code enters a try/catch block where an attempt is made to connect with the remote service and create an object. The object you are wanting to instantiate is called basic, defined as type BasicAPI. Web services provide the BasicAPI interface, defined in the burlap-test.jar file, to developers who want to use the service. All of the work for the remote instantiation takes place in this code:

```
basic = (BasicAPI) factory.create(BasicAPI.class, url);
```

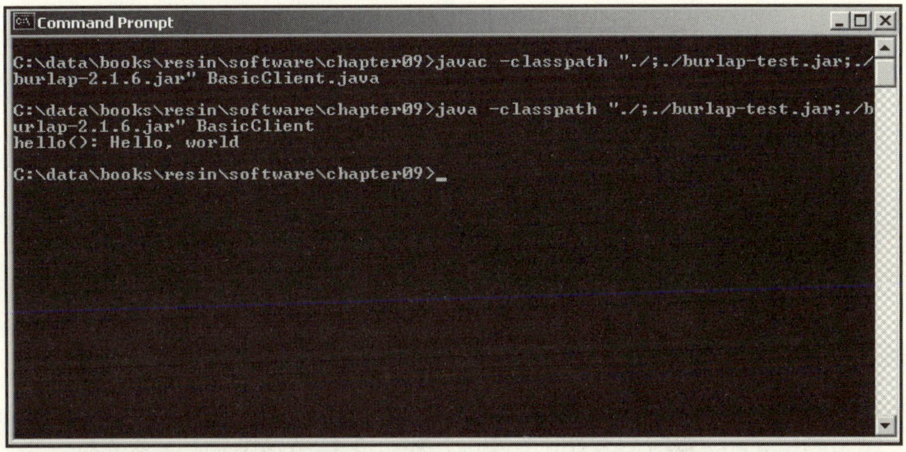

Figure 8.1 The Burlap BasicClient output.

Here you are asking the Burlap factory to connect to a service URL and attempt to instantiate an object of the BasicAPI.class type. If the protocol is successful, a reference to the remote object is returned and assigned to the basic variable. Finally, you use the newly instantiated object by calling the hello() method and displaying the output.

Writing a Basic Service

In the BasicAPI example, you saw only the client side of the protocol at work. Also hosted on the Caucho Web site is a Burlap Web service that handles all requests from potential clients. In this section, we look at the steps required to build your own service.

Let's build a Web service that allows you to get weather information about a city. The methods provided are:

```
double getRainTotals(city);
string getCurrentWeather(city);
```

Creating the Interface

The first step in writing your own service is to build the interface that can be shared with potential clients as well as used in building the service. Listing 8.2 shows an example of the API.

```
package weather;

import com.caucho.burlap.server.BurlapSkeleton;

public interface WeatherAPI {

  public double getRainTotals(String city);

  public String getCurrentWeather(String city);

}
```

Listing 8.2 The CAServiceAPI interface code.

The Build Interface JAR

Just as we saw in the BasicAPI example, you need to compile the interface and placed it in a JAR file for distribution. Here are the commands for accomplishing this task. First you have to save the code in Listing 8.2 in a file called WeatherAPI.java:

```
javac –d . WeatherAPI.java
jar –cf WeatherAPI.jar weather
```

Your Burlap service is going to be hosted by the Resin-EE server, so place the API JAR in the /resin-ee-<version>/lib directory so it can be found when needed.

Writing the Authentication Service

Now you need to write the actual code behind the server. Listing 8.3 contains the service code.

```
package weather;

import com.caucho.burlap.server.BurlapServlet;

public class WeatherService extends BurlapServlet implements  WeatherAPI {

  public WeatherService() {
  }

  public double getRainTotals(String city) {
  if (city.equals("Denver")) {
```

Listing 8.3 The CAService Web service. (continues)

```
      return 7.5;
    }
    else if (city.equals("Atlanta")) {
      return 15.35;
    }
  }

    public String getCurrentWeather(String city) {
    if (city.equals("Denver")) {
      return "Snow!";
    }
    else if (city.equals("Atlanta")) {
      return "Sunny and Warm";
      }
    }
}
```

Listing 8.3 The CAService Web service. (continued)

As you can see from the signature line for the WeatherService class, a class called BurlapServlet handles most of the work for the service—all you need to do is define your exposed methods. We show both the getRainTotals() and getCurrentWeather() methods with some example code in them.

Compile the new service using a command like this one:

```
java –d . WeatherService.java
```

Since the service uses servlets, you need to have Java 2 Enterprise Edition (J2EE) installed. In addition, include the WeatherAPI.jar and Burlap-<version>.jar files in your classpath.

The Server Structure

As you've seen, Resin requires that applications be placed in specific directories under the /doc directory. At this point, create a new directory structure like the following:

```
/doc/weather/WEB-INF/classes
```

Place the WeatherService.java file into the /classes directory. So that Resin can "see" the new application, add a new <web-app> entry to the resin.conf file:

```
<web-app id="weather"/>
```

When Resin is restarted or reads the change configuration file, the Web service will automatically be compiled and ready to be accessed.

Before you start using the new service, you also need to create a web.xml file in the new application directory. Create a file called web.xml in the /doc/weather/WEB-INF directory. Add the following to the file:

```
<web-app>
  <servlet-mapping>
    <url-pattern>/weather/WeatherService</url-pattern>
    <servlet-class>weather.WeatherService</servlet-class>
  </servlet-mapping>
</web-app>
```

This web.xml file tells your system to execute your weather.WeatherService servlet if a URL with the pattern /weather/WeatherService is found.

Creating a Client for the New Service

Using the code from the BasicAPI application as an outline, you can create a client for your weather service. The code in Listing 8.4 shows how to access the service.

```
import com.caucho.burlap.client.BurlapProxyFactory;
import java.net.MalformedURLException;
import weather.WeatherServiceAPI;

public class CAClient {

  static String url = "http://localhost:8080/weather/ /WeatherService";

  public static void main(String[] args) {
    WeatherServiceAPI weather = null;

    BurlapProxyFactory factory = new BurlapProxyFactory();
    try {
      weather = (WeatherServiceAPI)
       factory.create(WeatherServiceAPI.class, url);
    } catch (MalformedURLException e) {
        System.out.println("Bad URL");
    }

    if (weather != null) {
      try {
      System.out.println("Rain In Denver = "
        + weather.getRainTotals("Denver"));

      System.out.println("Current Weather In Atlanta = "
        + weather.getCurrentWeather("Atlanta"));
```

Listing 8.4 The CAService client. (continues)

```
        } catch (Exception e) {
          e.printStackTrace();
        }
      }
    }
  }
```

Listing 8.4 The CAService client. (continued)

As you can see, this code is similar to what you wrote in the BasicAPI client. Instead of using BasicAPI, though, you use the WeatherServiceAPI interface.

What's Next

In this chapter, we examined the Burlap protocol and showed you how to use it. In the next chapter, we present the Hessian protocol, which was designed in the same spirit as the Burlap protocol.

CHAPTER 9

Hessian Binary Web Service Protocol

The Hessian Binary Web Service Protocol is a simple protocol for the implementation of Web services that need to send binary data to and fro. A number of Web services can use this type of protocol, including publishers, image providers, and others. The primary catalyst for the development of the Hessian protocol was the amount of overhead in the more common protocols, such as SOAP. Using techniques like Huffman or Base-64 encoding, every byte of binary data results in 1.3 to 1.7 characters. This increase in the size of the binary data isn't an efficient use of the bandwidth connecting a client to a Web service.

Some of the goals during development of the Hessian protocol included:

- Small footprint
- Fast
- Support for object serialization
- Developers hidden from wire details

The entire protocol is implemented in a 30K JAR file that is used by both Web service clients and servers.

Downloading the Code

Before we get into the details of the protocol, let's write a couple of applications that will give you a feel for using it. Begin by downloading the JAR file needed for compilation of Web service clients and servers; the code is available at www.caucho.com/hessian/index.xtp. Near the bottom of the page is a table of binary, source, and test code. Select the option for the latest binary and download the JAR file into its own directory or into a directory on the classpath of the Java compiler and VM. For this chapter, we chose the location c:/data/resin/hessian for Windows and /home/resin/hessian for Linux.

Using BasicAPI

The developers at Caucho have provided a simple Hessian Web service written as an EJB at their primary Web site. This BasicAPI Hessian Web service is designed to let new developers access a service when writing a client. You will use the BasicAPI Web service when you build your first client in the next section. The location of the service is www.caucho.com/hessian/test/basic. The URL can be broken down in the following manner (you should use this format when writing your own services):

www.caucho.com/hessian. The first part identifies an EJB container on the specified site. If the Hessian Web service is hosted by Resin-EE, then *hessian* represents the servlet prefix.

test. The container specification is followed by the path of the request or the home interface. Because EJB containers can contain any number of beans, all requests must specify the right EJB home.

basic. The last part of the URL is the actual object to use.

Once the Hessian protocol has established a connection, you can use methods on the BasicAPI Web service. The current methods available are listed in Table 9.1.

Table 9.1 Hessian Protocol Methods (continues)

SIGNATURE	DESCRIPTION	HESSIAN COMMAND
Object echo(Object value)	Returns or echoes the method parameter back to the caller	
void fault()	Causes an application fault to occur	

Table 9.1 Hessian Protocol Methods (continued)

SIGNATURE	DESCRIPTION	HESSIAN COMMAND
String hello()	Returns a String object with the value "Hello, World"	c x01 x00 m x00 x05 hello z r x01 x00 S x00 x0c Hello, world z
void nullCall()	No operation	c x01 x00 m x00 x08 nullCall z r x01 x00 N z
int subtract(int, int)	Returns the result of subtracting the second parameter from the first	c x01 x00 m x00 x03 sub I x00 x00 x00 x07 I x00 x00 x00 x03 z r x01 x00 I x00 x00 x00 x04 z

The important parts of the table are the signature and description of each service method. Later in the chapter, we'll discuss the command Hessian uses to represent the method call.

Writing a Basic Client

Your first goal in this chapter is to write a client application in Java that will let you use the BasicAPI service hosted on the caucho.com Web site. The code for the client is shown in Listing 9.1.

```
import com.caucho.hessian.client.HessianProxyFactory;


import com.caucho.hessian.test.BasicAPI;
import java.net.MalformedURLException;

public class BasicClient {

  static String url =
    "http://www.caucho.com/hessian/test/basic";

  public static void main(String[] args) {
    BasicAPI basic = null;

    HessianProxyFactory factory = new HessianProxyFactory();
    try {
      basic = (BasicAPI) factory.create(BasicAPI.class, url);
    } catch (MalformedURLException e) {
       System.out.println("Bad URL");
    }
```

Listing 9.1 Basic Hessian client for the BasicAPI Web service. (continues)

```
Line 20:    if (basic != null)
      System.out.println("hello(): " + basic.hello());
  }
}
```

Listing 9.1 Basic Hessian client for the BasicAPI Web service. (continued)

Downloading the Interface Class

To write a client using the Hessian protocol and the BasicAPI service, you must download the interface class for BasicAPI from the Caucho Web site. The URL for the download is www.caucho.com/hessian/download/hessian-test.jar. Place the file hessian-test.jar in a directory where the client can be built.

Next, put the code from Listing 9.1 in the same directory and compile the code with this command:

```
javac -classpath ".\hessian-3.0.2.jar;.\hessian-test.jar" Basic-
Client.java
```

Execute the code with the following command:

```
java -classpath ".\hessian-3.0.2.jar;.\hessian-test.jar;" BasicClient
```

You should see the text *hello(): hello* on the console window.

Let's walk through the code:

Line 1 imports the class used for building a proxy to the Web service object you are using. Line 2 imports the interface built for the Web service with which you are connecting. This is a very important step, because your application needs to know the methods made available by the remote object.

Lines 7 and 8 represent the URL where the Web service has been made available. The URL follows the naming guidelines presented earlier, so you know the object you're accessing is called *basic*.

Line 11 creates an object of type BasicAPI, which is the name of the class made available at the Caucho Web site. The object is set to NULL for the time being.

Line 13 instantiates an object factory provided by the Hessian protocol. This factory is used to build a proxy object in the local machine to act as a representation of the remote object.

Line 15 does the actual work of attempting to create a new local object based on the remote object.

Lines 20 and 21 check to make sure the object creation was successful and make a call to the hello() method of the remote object. Notice that the call is no different for the remote object than for a local object.

Writing a Basic Service

A client is half the story; the plot lies in the Web service. In this section, we will look at the steps necessary to build a new Web service based on the idea of authentication. The service provides four methods:

- **createNewAccount(username, password)**—Sets the username and password with the service
- **baseAuthenticate(username, password)**—Returns true if the username and password match those in the service
- **secureAuthentication(username, password, certificate)**—Returns true if the username, password, and provided certificate match those in the service
- **provideCertificate(username, password)**—Returns a vector with a vector for the supplied username/password

Creating the Interface

Once you've defined the methods for the service, you place them in a simple interface structure. Listing 9.2 shows the interface used for the new CAService authentication service.

```
package authentication;

import com.caucho.hessian.server.HessianSkeleton;
import java.util.Vector;

public interface CAServiceAPI {

  public boolean createNewAccount(String username, String
password);

  public boolean baseAuthenticate(String username, String
password);

  public boolean secureAuthentication(String username,
```

Listing 9.2 CAServiceAPI interface code. (continues)

```
    String password, Vector certificate);

  public Vector provideCertificate(String username, String
password);

}
```

Listing 9.2 CAServiceAPI interface code. (continued)

Building the Interface JAR

Now that you've written the interface code, you need to build it. The command to compile the interface is as follows:

```
javac -d . CAServiceAPI.java
```

Once you've built the class file, place it in a JAR file for use by the service as well as client code. Because the code for the interface is contained in a package, you need to put the entire hierarchy for the class in the JAR file, as well. The command to built the JAR file is

```
jar -cf CAServiceAPI.jar authentication
```

As we will cover in Chapter 14, the Resin server can automatically compile source code within its directory structure. In a few paragraphs you will see where to place the service source code about to be built; but in the case of the CAServiceAPI.jar file, you need to put the file in a location where the Resin server can find it. All class library files should be placed in the directory *<installation drive>*/resin-ee-3.0.2/lib.

Writing the Authentication Service

With the interface built, you can write the code to handle requests made of the Web service. The code in Listing 9.3 sets up the service and builds out the methods.

```
Line 1: package authentication;

import com.caucho.hessian.server.HessianServlet;

import java.util.Vector;
import java.util.Random;

public class CAService extends HessianServlet implements
 CAServiceAPI {
```

Listing 9.3 CAService Web service code. (continues)

```
private String storedUsername = null;
  private String storedPassword = null;
  Vector vec = null;

  public CAService() {
    vec = new Vector();
    Random random = new Random();

    for (int i=0;i<15;++i) {
      vec.add(new Integer(random.nextInt(50)));
    }
  }

  public boolean createNewAccount(String username, String
   password) {
    storedUsername = new String(username);
    storedPassword = new String(password);

    return true;
  }

  public boolean baseAuthenticate(String username, String
   password) {
    if (storedUsername.equals(username) &&
        storedPassword.equals(password)) {
      return true;

    }
    return false;
  }

  public boolean secureAuthentication(String username, String
   password, Vector certificate) {
    if (storedUsername.equals(username) &&
        storedPassword.equals(password)) {
      if (certificate.equals(vec)) {
        return true;
      }
    }
    return false;
  }

  public Vector provideCertificate(String username, String
   password) {
    if (storedUsername.equals(username) &&
        storedPassword.equals(password)) {
      return vec;
```

Listing 9.3 CAService Web service code. (continues)

```
        }
        return null;
    }
}
```

Listing 9.3 CAService Web service code. (continued)

The code begins by importing the HessianServlet class in line 3. This class is the foundation for the Web service and makes the Web service act as a servlet when hosted on the Resin-EE server. Lines 7 and 8 create the CAService class that implements the CAServiceAPI interface and extends HessianServlet. All Hessian Web services are required to both implement an interface and extend HessianServlet.

The rest of the class looks like any other Java class. In this case, the methods from the interface are fully coded, and you add a constructor for class initialization. When the createNewAccount() method is called, the username/password parameters are saved in the service object. Each of the remaining methods works against the saved username and password, returning a boolean value based on the code in the method.

At this point, you can make sure the code compiles correctly. An example build command is shown here:

```
java -d . -classpath ".\;.\CAServiceAPI.jar;.\hessian-
3.0.2.jar" CAService.java
```

Server Structure

Within the Resin-EE directory structure, all Web applications are placed in the /doc directory as discussed booking Chapter 6, "Object-Relational Mapping with CMP." To launch the Web service, you need to place a new directory in /doc. This example uses the directory hessian. Within this new directory, the server expects a directory called WEB-INF. Within the WEB-INF directory, you need to create another directory called classes. Because the code was built with a Java package hierarchy, it must be duplicated within the classes directory; this means adding a new directory called authentication. Move the CAService.java code from above into the directory called authentication. When you're finished, you should have the directory structure shown in Figure 9.1.

Figure 9.1 Authentication Web service directory hierarchy.

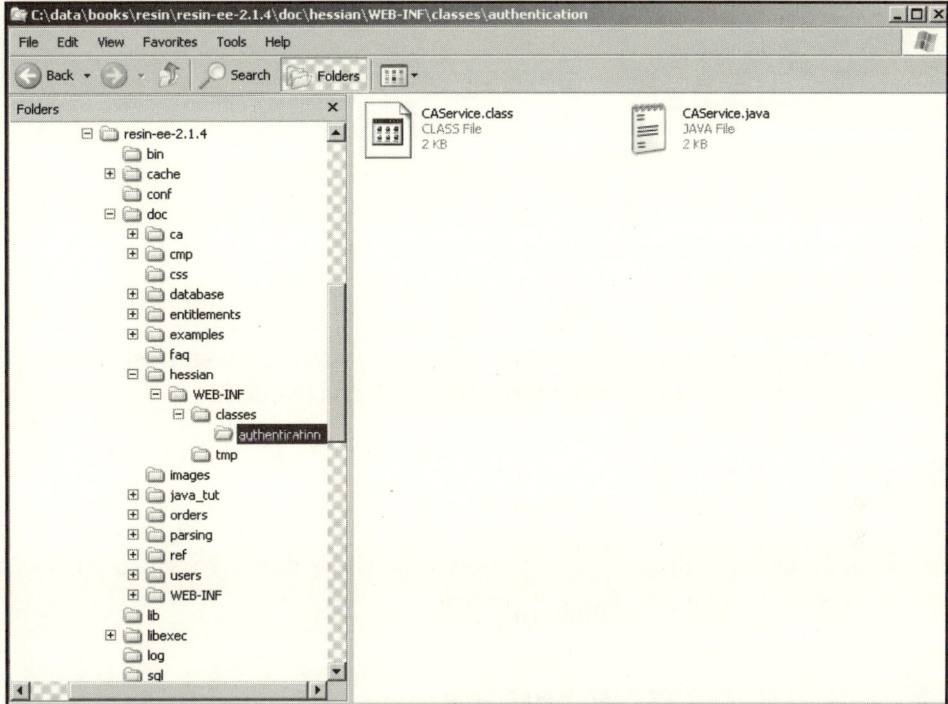

Changing Resin.conf

The next step in getting the Web service up and running is to let the Resin server know about the existence of the new service. You do so by modifying the resin.conf file located in the /conf directory of the Resin-EE installation.

Add the following line in the <host> element of the configuration file:

```
<web-app id='hessian'/>
```

Changing web.xml

The <web-app> element added to the configuration file doesn't have any subelements attached to it. As you've learned previously, this means the server expects to find an xml.conf file in the WEB-INF directory. The web.xml file defines the specifics of your new Web service.

Create a text file called xml.conf in the WEB-INF directory and put in the file the XML from Listing 9.4.

```
<web-app>
  <servlet servlet-name='certService'
           servlet-class='authentication.CAService'>
```

```
  </servlet>
  <servlet-mapping>
    <url-pattern>/authentication/CAService</url-pattern>

  <servlet-name>certService</servlet-name>
  </servlet-mapping>
</web-app>
```

Listing 9.4 Xml.conf file contents.

This XML tells the Resin server to check whether the URL ends with /hessian/authentication/CAService. If it does, then the system should execute the servlet found in the authentication.CAService class.

Starting the Server

The last step in getting the new service up and running is to start the Resin-EE server. The console window will show any errors produced when the server recognizes the new service.

Client for the New Service

Now that your new authentication service is up and running, it's time to write a client to use the provided methods. The code in Listing 9.5 shows how to access the methods using the same techniques found in the BasicAPI client.

```
import com.caucho.hessian.client.HessianProxyFactory;
import java.net.MalformedURLException;
import java.util.Vector;


import authentication.CAServiceAPI;

public class CAClient {

  static String url =
"http://localhost:8080/hessian/authentication/CAService";

  public static void main(String[] args) {
    CAServiceAPI basic = null;

    HessianProxyFactory factory = new HessianProxyFactory();
    try {
      basic = (CAServiceAPI) factory.create(CAServiceAPI.class,
url);
```

Listing 9.5 CAService client code. (continues)

```
    } catch (MalformedURLException e) {
      System.out.println("Bad URL");
    }

    if (basic != null) {
      try {
      System.out.println("newaccount creation status = "
        + basic.createNewAccount("username", "password"));

      System.out.println("check basic authentication with
        username/password = " +
        basic.baseAuthenticate("username", "password"));
      System.out.println("check basic authentication with
        username1/password1 = "
        + basic.baseAuthenticate("username1", "password1"));

      Vector vec = (Vector)basic.provideCertificate("username",
       "password");
      System.out.println("First 10 values in vector");
      for(int i=0;i<10;i++)
        System.out.print(vec.elementAt(i) + " ");
      System.out.println("");

      System.out.println("check basic authentication with
        username/password = "
        + basic.secureAuthentication("username", "password",
         vec));

      } catch (Exception e) {
        e.printStackTrace();
      }
    }
  }
}
```

Listing 9.5 CAService client code. (continued)

As you look through the code in Listing 9.5, you will find that it looks like the BasicAPI client, except instead of using BasicAPI as the interface class, it uses CAServiceAPI instead. The code in the client exercises all the methods of the authentication service. When you compile and execute the client, it is imperative that both the hessian-3.0.2.jar and the CAServiceAPI.jar files be found in the classpath. If the JAR files aren't in the classpath, the client will produce an error. Figure 9.2 shows the output from an execution of the client code.

Figure 9.2 CAClient execution output.

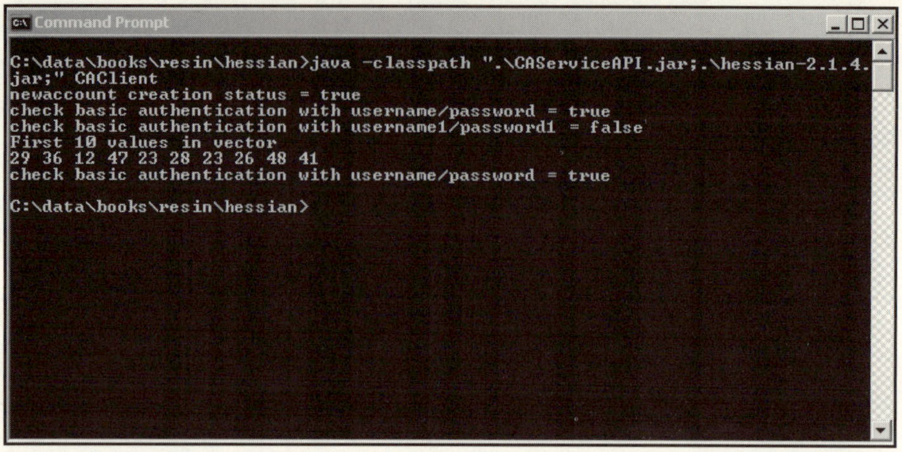

```
Command Prompt
C:\data\books\resin\hessian>java -classpath ".\CAServiceAPI.jar;.\hessian-2.1.4.
jar;" CAClient
newaccount creation status = true
check basic authentication with username/password = true
check basic authentication with username1/password1 = false
First 10 values in vector
29 36 12 47 23 28 23 26 48 41
check basic authentication with username/password = true

C:\data\books\resin\hessian>
```

Mobile Hessian

The Hessian protocol is so small and efficient that it can be used for communication between mobile devices and a service. The process for using Hessian in a mobile device isn't as straightforward as the online documentation would suggest. This section leads you step by step through the process of creating a J2ME client to access both the BasicService and the Authentication Service previously coded as a traditional application. The following steps include the full process:

1. The first and most important step is installing J2ME from Sun on your development machine. For these examples, we used J2ME Wireless Toolkit 2.0, available at http://java.sun.com/products/j2mewtoolkit/download.html. We used J2SE version 1.4. Download the toolkit, execute the installer, and follow all the steps to install J2ME.
2. The next step is hinted at on the Caucho site under Hessian. To use Hessian for mobile devices, you must remove many of the objects in the Hessian-3.0.2.jar to produce a JAR file that contains only those classes needed for J2ME. Here are the steps to create a micro version of the JAR:
   - Using a command prompt, move to the directory where Hessian-3.0.2.jar currently is located.
   - Unjar the file with the command jar –xf Hessian-3.0.2.jar to produce a directory structure of the classes in the JAR file. The only directory in the local directory from the JAR extraction will be /com.
   - Move into the /com directory and down the hierarchy until you get to a level that has the directories hessian and services.
   - Delete the services directory.

- Move into the hessian directory.
- Delete the directories client, server, and mux.
- Move into the io directory.
- Remove all class files except HessianProtocolException.class, HessianRemote.class, and HessianServiceException.class.
- Go back to the root directory where you did the previous JAR command.
- Create a new JAR file with the command jar –cf microhessian-3.0.2.jar com.

3. Various tools were installed with the J2ME toolkit. One is KToolbar, which is a simple application to build and execute an emulator which will run a J2ME application. In a Windows installation, you can launch KToolbar by clicking Start/Programs/J2ME Wireless Toolkit 2.0/KToolbar. The application is shown in Figure 9.3.

Figure 9.3 KToolbar dialog.

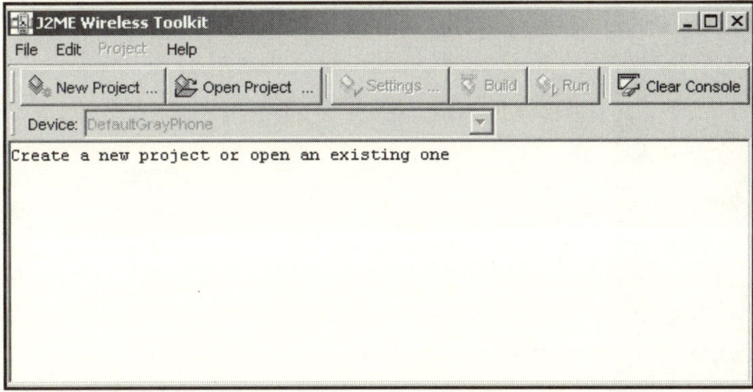

4. The J2ME product includes instructions for using KToolbar, so the following instructions are simple:

   - Create a new project by clicking New Project. Enter a name for the project (it becomes a directory under *<installation drive>*/WTK104/apps directory); use *hessian*. Enter a name for the class to be used to build the mobile application; use *Hello*. Click Create Project, and the application will build the appropriate directories for the project.
   - The project directories are in the directory *<installation drive>*/WTK104/apps/hessian. Two of the directories are immediately important to use. The system expects to find any non-Java-standard class libraries in /lib; this is where you need to put the microhessian-

3.0.2.jar file created in step 2.

- You need to place a Java source file in the second directory, /src. In this directory, create a file called Hello.java and enter the code from Listing 9.6.
- Click the Build button in KToolbar. After a successful build, click Run. A cell phone emulator will appear, as shown in Figure 9.4. Click the middle button among the arrow keys on the emulator to launch the hessian application.
- You should see the familiar Hello World, just as you saw in the BasicAPI example earlier in the chapter.

Figure 9.4 Cellphone emulation.

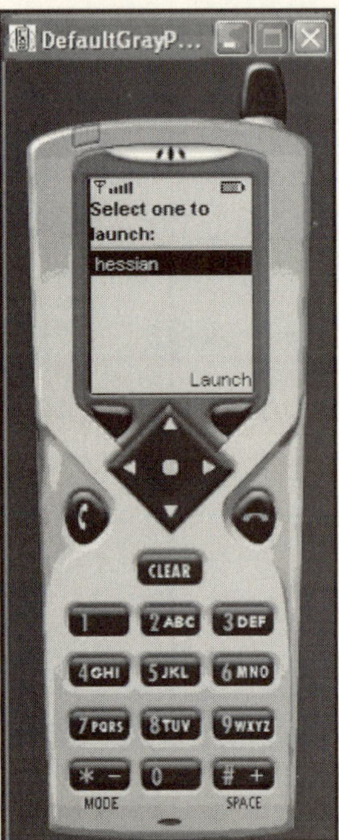


```
import javax.microedition.midlet.*;
import javax.microedition.lcdui.*;
import javax.microedition.io.*;
import com.caucho.hessian.io.*;
import com.caucho.hessian.micro.*;
import java.io.*;
```

Listing 9.6 MicroHessian BasicAPI code. (continues)

```
public class Hello extends MIDlet {
  private Display display;

  public void startApp() {
    display = Display.getDisplay(this);
    try {
      String url = "http://www.caucho.com/hessian/test/basic";

      HttpConnection c = (HttpConnection) Connector.open(url);
      c.setRequestMethod(HttpConnection.POST);

      OutputStream os = c.openOutputStream();
      MicroHessianOutput out = new MicroHessianOutput(os);
      out.startCall("hello");
      out.writeNull();
      out.completeCall();

      InputStream is = c.openInputStream();
      MicroHessianInput in = new MicroHessianInput(is);

      in.startReply();
      String value = in.readString();
      in.completeReply();

      TextBox t = new TextBox("Http Test", value, value.length(), 0);
      display.setCurrent(t);
    } catch (Exception e) {}
  }

  public void pauseApp() {
  }

  public void destroyApp(boolean unconditional) {
  }
}
```

Listing 9.6 MicroHessian BasicAPI code. (continued)

What's in the Code

Let's discuss the Mobile Hessian code in Listing 9.6, because it is little different from the previous Hessian client code. All the code for using the BasicAPI Web service is found in the startApp() method, as required by the J2ME specification.

The first statement in the startApp() method obtains an object pointer to the cell phone display and stores it in the *display* variable. Next, the code attempts to create an HTTP connection to the Web service using the HttpConnection class.

Once the connection is opened, an OutputStream object is attached to the connection as well as a MicroHessianOutput object. The object's startCall() method is used to pass the method you want to access—in this case, the hello() method.

After the call is made, the reply from the Web service is obtained using the following statements:

```
in.startReply();
String value = in.readString();
in.completeReply();
```

Finally, the reply is written to a textbox and displayed on the cell phone. Although this is a simple example, it shows how even small devices can be used to access Web services and transfer information back and forth.

Serialization Classes

As part of the process for sending objects between the Hessian client and service, serialization must occur. The Java Class Library includes functionality for serialization, but it is specific to the Java language. For this reason, the developers at Caucho wrote their own code to support Hessian as well as for general use in any implementation language. An object can be serialized in Java but deserialized in Python, as long as the Hessian specification is used in the serialization code.

In serialization of objects, two actions are required: serialization and deserialization. Both operations require the use of a stream object from the OutputStream and InputStream class hierarchies. Serialization is simple to do, as shown in Listing 9.7.

```
Line 1: import com.caucho.hessian.io.HessianOutput;
import com.caucho.hessian.io.HessianInput;
import java.util.Vector;
```

```
import java.util.Random;
import java.io.*;

public class Serialization {

  public static void main(String[] args) {
Line 10:     Vector vec = new Vector();
    Random rand = new Random();

    for(int i=0;i<10;i++) {
```

Listing 9.7 Hessian serialization example. (continues)

```
        vec.add(new Integer(rand.nextInt(50)));
        System.out.print(vec.elementAt(i) + " ");
      }
      System.out.println();

      try {
Line 20:      OutputStream os = new
          FileOutputStream("test.txt");
        HessianOutput out = new HessianOutput(os);
        out.writeObject((Object)vec);
        os.close();
      } catch(Exception e) {}

      vec.clear();
      try {
        InputStream is = new FileInputStream("test.txt");
Line 30:      HessianInput in = new HessianInput(is);
        vec = (Vector)in.readObject(null);
        is.close();
      } catch(Exception e) {}

      for(int i=0;i<10;i++) {
        System.out.print(vec.elementAt(i) + " ");
      }
      System.out.println();
    }
Line 40:}
```

Listing 9.7 Hessian serialization example. (continued)

The code in Listing 9.7 begins by creating a Vector object and populating it with 10 Integer objects, each containing a random integer value. At the same time the objects are added to the vector, the integer values are displayed on the console. Once the Vector has been populated, the serialization process begins. The Object is serialized and saved in a file called test.txt on the local drive.

Line 20 begins the process by creating a FileOutputStream object with the filename you want to use. On line 22, a HessianOutput object is created, using the FileOutputStream object as a parameter. The HessianOutput object performs the serialization of an object using its writeObject() method, as shown in line 23. The Vector object is cast to an Object and supplied as an argument to the writeObject() method. This method converts the provided Object into a format that can be easily saved in a file, transmitted on the Internet, or put into a database. Line 24 closes the previously open file.

Next, the Vector object is cleared of all stored values. The code begins the deserialization process by creating a FileInputStream object to the file just saved with the serialized Vector object. On line 30, a HessianInput object is instantiated to handle the deserialization process. The Vector object is pulled from the file and brought back to its original state using the readObject() method. The file you were using is closed, and the contents of the new object are displayed. As you can see in Figure 9.5, the original Vector and the object pulled from the file are identical. The figure also shows the original compile and execution statements used in the process.

Figure 9.5 Hessian serialization.

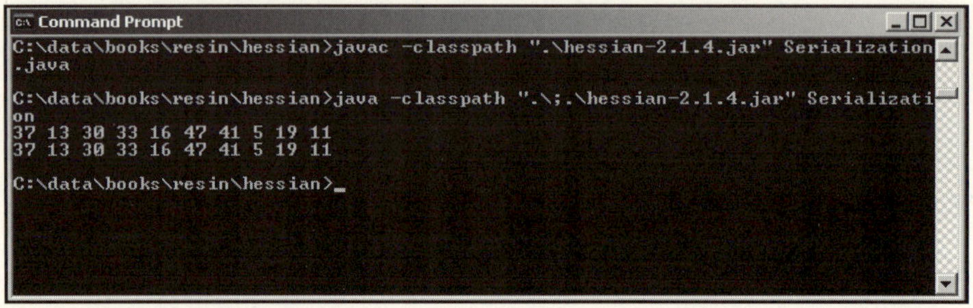

```
C:\data\books\resin\hessian>javac -classpath ".\hessian-2.1.4.jar" Serialization
.java

C:\data\books\resin\hessian>java -classpath ".\;.\hessian-2.1.4.jar" Serializati
on
37 13 30 33 16 47 41 5 19 11
37 13 30 33 16 47 41 5 19 11

C:\data\books\resin\hessian>_
```

Python Hessian

The Hessian protocol is not designed to be specific to one language. In order to show this, the developers at Caucho provide an implementation in Python. As of this writing, the Python code is lagging behind the Java implementation. The code is available at www.caucho.com/hessian/download/hessianlib.py.

Hessian Mux

At the time of this writing, the developers at Caucho are in the process of defining a protocol and implementation code called Hessian Mux. Mux will allow for peer-to-peer communication using the Hessian protocol. This specification has the benefit of the simple and efficient Hessian protocol. Further information for the developing specification can be found at www.caucho.com/hessian/hessian-mux.xtp.

Hessian Specification

All of the work you've done to this point is based on a specification developed by Caucho for the Hessian protocol. The protocol is based on tokens followed by data for serialization, calls, replies, and messages. In this section we detail what Hessian is doing behind the scenes.

Serialization

All data that needs to be sent from a client to a service or from the service to the client is *serialized* into a token and possibly additional data. The conversions for the supported structures are as follows:

NULL—Represented by a single byte 'N'.

boolean—Represented by the byte 'T' or 'F'.

int—Represented by the bytes 'I' 0x01 0x02 0x03 0x04, where the bytes of the 32-bit integer are represented by the 0x01, 0x02, 0x03, and 0x04.

long—Represented by the bytes 'L' 0x01 0x02 0x03 0x04 0x05 0x06 0x07 0x08.

double—Represented by the bytes 'D' 0x01 0x02 0x03 0x04 0x05 0x06 0x07 0x08.

string—Represented by chunks of data using 'S' and 's' bytes. The 'S' byte represents a final chunk of data, and 's' is the initial chunk. If there is only one chunk of data, the 'S' byte is used. The first two bytes after the 'S' or 's' is the length of the string in 16 bits. The string is 16-bit Unicode UTF-8 encoded.

xml—An XML document is sent in the same manner and format as a string, but the token bytes are 'X' and 'x'.

date—Represented by a 64-bit long consisting of the milliseconds since the epoch. The token byte is 'd'.

binary—Represented by chunks, using 'B' as final and 'b' as initial chunk tokens. Each token is followed by 16-bit length bytes.

list—Represented by the token 'V', then 't', followed by a length of the format l 0x00 0x00 0x00 0x03, and then the type value itself; for example, V t l 0x00 0x00 0x02 AB. The 't' is undefined in the spec and is available for use by the application. After this initial header information, the values in the list are represented using the values already defined. The last token is a 'z' to indicate the end of the list.

map—Used to represent serialized objects as well as Map objects. The format is 'M', 't' followed by a 16-bit length and the type value itself. In a serialized object, the type name is the object name. In a map, the 't', length, and value may be blank. After this initial header information, the values in the object or map are listed using the values already defined. The last token is a 'z' to indicate the end of the list.

ref—A reference to a previous map or list is represented by 'R' followed by an integer indicating the position where the map or list previously appeared.

remote—A reference to a remote object is represented by ‘r’ ‘t’ 16-bit length *<object type>* ‘S’ length *<utf-8 URL>*.

Calls

A call from a client to a service indicates the client's desire to invoke the remote object and an appropriate method. All parameters to the method are serialized using the rules outlined in the previous section. The call is represented by this sequence:

```
c 0x01 0x00 <header> m <16-bit length> <method name> <parameters> z
```

The *<header>* is a placeholder for adding name/value pairs to a method call. An example might be a transaction.

Reply

A call to a service method always results in a reply. There are two possible replies: valid and fault. The valid reply is designated by this sequence:

```
r 0x01 0x00 <header> <serialized return value> z
```

The fault reply is designated by this sequence:

```
r 0x01 0x00 <header> <fault> z
```

The fault is a serialized map containing code, message, and detail values for the fault.

What's Next

This chapter has provided a comprehensive overview of the Hessian protocol and its use in both applications and mobile devices. In Chapter 10, we discuss HTML and XML parsing.

CHAPTER 10

Parsing

In addition to supporting the hosting of dynamic pages for Web sites and providing an advanced Web services infrastructure, the Resin Server family has a large class library you can use during development of pages and services. One area of support in the class libraries is document parsing. The parsing classes are broken into three areas: DOM XML, SAX XML, and HTML. In this chapter, we will discuss each of the parsing methodologies and show through example code how to use the provided libraries. This information is important to understand, because XML is used increasingly often and you will use it in industry software development.

XML Parsing

The current standard interface for XML processing in Java is Java API for XML Processing (JAXP). By way of imports, a servlet can use XML functionality while being hosted within a Resin server. To maintain platform independence, all applications that need XML processing should stick to the API provided by JAXP. You can find more information about JAXP at http://java.sun.com/xml/ jaxp/index.html.

Before any processing of an XML document can take place, the document must be parsed. There are currently two methods for parsing XML: Document Object Model (DOM) and Simple API for XML (SAX). JAXP provides an API for both methods with a class defined by the package javax.xml.parsers. With the package are two factories—SAXParserFactory and DocumentBuilder-Factory—that produce SAXParser and DocumentBuilder objects for parsing XML documents.

This isn't rocket science. What makes JAXP such an interesting API is the fact that the included Factory classes for DOM and SAX don't limit you to using only Sun-provided parsing code; instead, they allow you to use third-party plug-in parsers. If third-party parsers aren't used, the default reference implementations are used. You will use both the reference implementation and Resin's fast parsers, which are designed for performance.

DOM XML Parsing

DOM parsing involves building a node hierarchy representing the elements in the XML document. The code in Listing 10.1 is the simplest for building a DOM object from an XML document on the local hard drive.

```
package servlet;

import java.io.*;
import javax.servlet.http.*;
import javax.servlet.*;
import javax.xml.parsers.*;
import org.w3c.dom.*;
import com.caucho.xml.*;

public class Parsing extends HttpServlet {
  public void doGet(HttpServletRequest request,
    HttpServletResponse response)
    throws IOException, ServletException {

    try {
      DocumentBuilderFactory factory =
        DocumentBuilderFactory.newInstance();
      DocumentBuilder parser = factory.newDocumentBuilder();

      Document doc = parser.parse("test.xml");

      PrintWriter pw = response.getWriter();
      FileOutputStream os = new FileOutputStream("out.xml");

      XmlPrinter printer = new XmlPrinter(pw);
      XmlPrinter oprinter = new XmlPrinter(os);

      printer.printHtml(doc);
      oprinter.print(doc);
```

Listing 10.1 DOM XML parsing servlet. (continues)

```
Line 30:
      pw.close();
      os.close();

    } catch(Exception e) {
       e.printStackTrace();
    }
  }
}
```

Listing 10.1 DOM XML parsing servlet. (continued)

Some setup steps are involved in executing the code in Listing 10.1. First, add the line

```
<web-app id='parsing'/>
```

to the resin.conf file. Second, under the /doc directory of the Resin server installation, create a directory structure that looks like Figure 10.1.

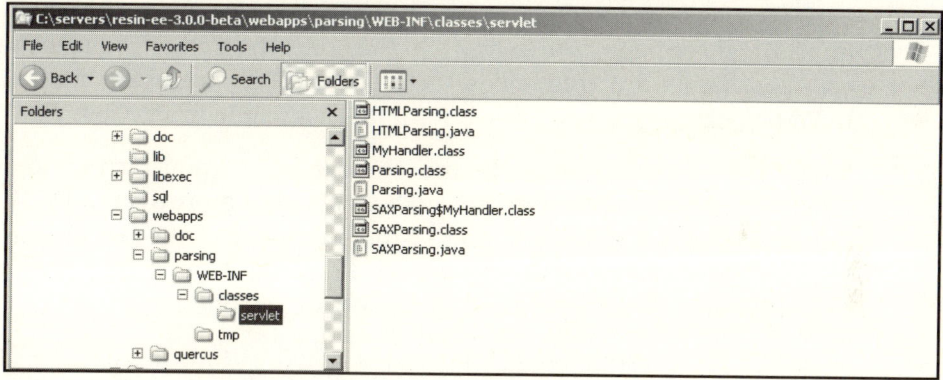

Figure 10.1 Directory structure for the DOM XML parsing servlet.

The web.xml file in the WEB-INF directory looks like this:

```
<web-app>
  <servlet-mapping>
    <url-pattern>/servlet/*</url-pattern>
    <servlet-name>servlet/Parsing</servlet-name>
  </servlet-mapping>
</web-app>
```

In the main Resin server directory, create a file called test.xml that contains a sampling of XML. Execute the servlet by browsing to the following location:

```
http://localhost:8080/parsing/servlet/Parsing
```

Once you compile and execute the servlet, two outputs are created: a file called out.xml in the main Resin server directory; and XML from the test.xml file, which is sent to the Web browser. Figure 10.2 shows the source sent to the browser.

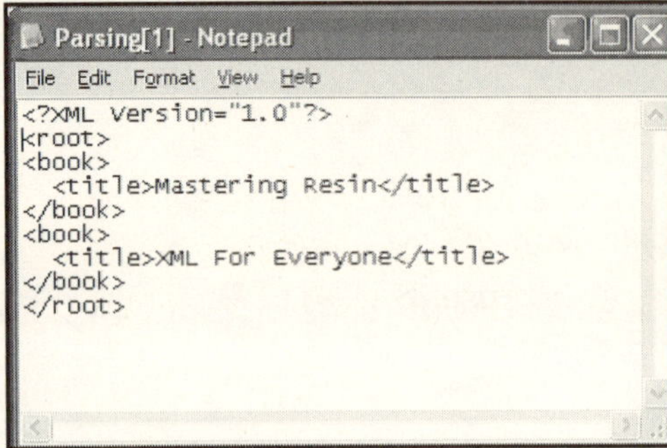

Figure 10.2 Parsing output.

Let's take a moment and look at the code. It begins starts with a number of imports necessary to support three primary functions: I/O, servlet, and XML. For XML, three imports are shown in the code: the first references the parser classes, the second references the DOM classes necessary for building a DOM object, and the last is used for a Resin-specific print class.

Lines 10 through 13 define the doGet() servlet method for the application. When the servlet is activated through a call from a browser, a DOM factory object is obtained in lines 16 and 17 through a call to the DocumentBuilder-Factory class's newInstance() method. From the factory instance, a parser object is instantiated with a call to newDocumentBuilder().

In line 20, the parser's parse() method is called with the path to an XML document supplied as the single parameter. The parse() method attempts to build a new Document object based on the XML found in the supplied file. If the method is successful, the new DOM object is assigned to the *doc* variable.

In a production-level application, the DOM object would be used to process the imported XML document as needed by the business logic of the problem being solved. In this case, you return the XML document to the browser that made the call to the servlet, and output a new file with the DOM object contents.

Line 22 retrieves a PrintWriter object from the response object used to send text back to the browser. Line 23 creates an object to a server-based file called out.xml. Lines 25 and 26 create separate XmlPrinter objects with parameters based on the response PrintWriter and the FileOutputStream, respectively.

The XmlPrinter class is provided by Caucho to enable easy printing of XML documents. As shown in lines 28 and 29, the class includes methods for a variety of printing. The full class structure is outlined in the Javadoc pages at www.caucho.com/resin/javadoc/com/caucho/xml/XmlPrinter.html.

Once the printing has been accomplished, the FileOutputStream and PrintWriter objects are closed and the application ends. Although this is a simple example of parsing, it shows the basic operation.

SAX XML Parsing

SAX parsing can also be performed with the JAXP API and either the reference implementation provided with JAXP or a parser provided with Resin. Listing 10.2 shows a simple servlet that uses SAX for XML document parsing.

```
package servlet;

import java.io.*;
import javax.servlet.http.*;
import javax.servlet.*;
import org.xml.sax.*;
import org.xml.sax.helpers.DefaultHandler;
import com.caucho.xml.*;

public class SAXParsing extends HttpServlet {

  private class MyHandler extends DefaultHandler {
    public void startElement(String namespaceURI,
     String localName,
     String qName, Attributes atts) {
      //Do something with element start
    }

  public void endElement(String namespaceURI, String localName,
                                  String qName) {
      //Do something at element end
    }
  }

  public void doGet(HttpServletRequest request,
    HttpServletResponse response)
    throws IOException, ServletException {

    try {
      Xml xml = new Xml();

      xml.setContentHandler(new MyHandler());
```

Listing 10.2 Simple SAX XML parsing. (continues)

```
        xml.parse("test.xml");

    } catch(Exception e) {
      e.printStackTrace();
    }
  }
}
```

Listing 10.2 Simple SAX XML parsing. (continued)

The code for SAX parsing is quite different from that of a DOM parser. In the DOM code, the entire XML document is kept in the application's memory. If the XML document is large, the corresponding DOM object will also be large. In addition, the amount of time necessary to build the object increases as the XML is parsed. On the other hand, when an XML document is parsed using SAX, content handler methods are called based on points hit during the parsing of the document, such as the start and end of an element.

Lines 10 through 23 define a private class that extends the DefaultHandler class. This new class is used to override the content handler methods for SAX processing. This example overrides startElement and endElement so the system can process specific elements. Next comes the code for the servlet doGet(). Line 30 instantiates a new SAX parser. Line 32 associates the private content handler class with the new SAX parser. Finally, line 34 performs the actual parsing of an XML document. As each element in the XML document is encountered, the appropriate content handler methods are executed. In this case, most of the methods are null, except startElement and endElement.

Changing Parsers

If you aren't happy with the functionality found in the reference DOM and SAX parsers, you can swap them with other third-party parsers. The Resin server provides an easy way to configure which parser is used for either SAX or DOM parsing. Once the parsers are swapped, you don't need to do anything except restart the application—as long as you use the API provided in the JAXP package, you don't have to change any code. To specify which parser the factory classes should use, set the following properties in the resin.conf file:

```
<web-app>
  <system-property javax.xml.parsers.DocumentBuilderFactory=
      "dom" />
  <system-property javax.xml.parsers.SAXParserFactory=
      "sax" />
  <system-property javax.xml.transform.TransformerFactory=
      "trans" />
</web-app>
```

As you can see, you place the parser and XSL system properties in the <web-app> portion of the configuration file.

Although we don't discuss the transformation aspect of JAXP in this chapter, note that Resin includes its own XSL processor, which can replace the reference implementation used in JAXP. The dom, sax, and trans values are replaced by the full hierarchy name of the class to use. To use the implementations provided by Resin, replace the values as follows:

```
dom = com.caucho.xml.parsers.XmlDocumentBuilderFactory
sax = com.caucho.xml.parsers.XmlSAXParserFactory
trans = com.caucho.xsl.Xsl
```

The Resin documentation cites two other possible replacements, which we list here for completeness. For Xalan/Xerces, use the following:

```
dom = org.apache.xerces.jaxp.DocumentBuilderFactoryImpl
sax = org.apache.xerces.jaxp.SAXParserFactoryImpl
trans = org.apache.xalan.processor.TransformerFactoryImpl
```

For the parsers and transformer provided with Java 1.4, use these values:

```
dom = org.apache.crimson.jaxp.DocumentBuilderFactoryImpl
sax = .apache.crimson.jaxp.SAXParserFactoryImpl
trans = org.apache.xalan.processor.TransformerFactoryImpl
```

HTML Parsing

The last parsing mechanism we will cover is HTML parsing, which allows an application to process the HTML tags found in an HTML document. You can use this functionality to write spider applications, simple editors, and other applications that need access to HTML. Listing 10.3 shows a small example of reading an HTML document from the hard drive and parsing it. All the parsing is performed with Resin-supplied classes.

```
package servlet;

import java.io.*;
import javax.servlet.http.*;
import javax.servlet.*;

import org.w3c.dom.*;
import com.caucho.xml.*;

public class HTMLParsing extends HttpServlet {
```

Listing 10.3 HTML parsing example. (continues)

```
    public void doGet(HttpServletRequest request,
      HttpServletResponse response)
      throws IOException, ServletException {

      try {
        Html parser = new Html();

        Document doc = parser.parseDocument(
          "c:/data/resin/resin-ee-3.0.2/sample.html");

        FileOutputStream os = new
          FileOutputStream("newsample.xml");
        XmlPrinter printer = new XmlPrinter(os);

        printer.printHtml(doc);
        os.close();

      } catch(Exception e) {
         e.printStackTrace();
      }
    }
  }
```

Listing 10.3 HTML parsing example. (continued)

The code in Listing 10.3 shows how to parse an HTML document using the Resin-supplied HTML parser. The primary class for the parser is Html; it doesn't require the use of a factory. Once the object is instantiated, the parseDocument() method is called and given the path to a sample HTML file. This method parses the document and places it in a DOM object. In the sample code, the XmlPrinter outputs the HTML to another file.

You can find the full API for the Html object at: www.caucho.com/resin/javadoc/com/caucho/xml/Html.html. The Html parser can be used to parse into a DOM object using both a file and a String object as well as using SAX.

What's Next

This chapter covered the use of JAXP as well as numerous Resin classes for parsing. This parsing includes both XML and HTML. In Chapter 11 we'll discuss how to interface Resin with a backend database server.

CHAPTER 11

Database Connectivity

Databases use a common language called Structured Query Language (SQL) to manipulate data stored in tables. During the early days of database use, SQL wasn't standardized; but in 1992, a body came together and standardized how SQL should be represented and used. Although this standardization is helpful for the manipulation of data, it doesn't do anything for the connection to the database from an application (which is usually the first step in using a database).

To help make connectivity as portable as possible, a new interface was created: Open Database Connectivity (ODBC). ODBC is a C-based API that exposes a common framework for connecting to a database. A database vendor that wants to provide access using ODBC writes a bridge driver hooking the API to the vendor's database. The bridge driver is different for each specific database vendor.

ODBC has served the C and C++ community well, but it doesn't help the Java community. Java Database Connectivity (JDBC) is an answer to ODBC, and by using it, Java applications can connect to databases in a portable fashion.

Traditional JDBC Connectivity

Before we dive into the details of what Resin brings to the table for advanced database connectivity, let's look at the traditional way a Java application connects to and manipulates a database. Listing 11.1 shows a simple application for communicating with a MySQL database.

```
package servlet;

import java.io.*;
import java.sql.*;
import javax.servlet.*;
import javax.servlet.http.*;

public class Traditional extends HttpServlet {
  public void doGet(HttpServletRequest inRequest,
   HttpServletResponse outResponse)
    throws ServletException, IOException {

    Connection myConnection = null;
    Statement myStatement = null;
    ResultSet myResultSet = null;

    outResponse.setContentType("test/html");
    PrintWriter out = outResponse.getWriter();

    try {
      Class.forName("com.mysql.jdbc.Driver");

      myConnection = DriverManager.getConnection(
        "jdbc:mysql-caucho://192.168.1.25/products?user=spider
         &password=spider");
      myStatement = myConnection.createStatement();
      myResultSet = myStatement.executeQuery("SELECT title,
        price FROM product");

      out.println("<HTML><HEAD><TITLE>MySQL Example</TITLE></HEAD>");
      out.println("<BODY>");
      out.println("<UL>");

      while (myResultSet.next()) {
        out.println("<LI>" + myResultSet.getString("title") + " "
          + myResultSet.getString("price"));
      }

      out.println("</UL>");
      out.println("</BODY></HTML>");
    } catch(ClassNotFoundException e) {
  out.println("Couldn't load driver");
} catch(SQLException e) {
  out.println("SQLException catught: " + e.getMessage());
} finally {
  myConnection.close();
}
  }
}
```

Listing 11.1 Traditional JDBC MySQL connectivity.

Before we move to Resin specifics, let's discuss this traditional JDBC code. On the local test network is a Linux machine at IP 192.168.1.75 running MySQL. MySQL has a database called products. This database contains a small table called product that has two fields: title and price.

The code in Listing 11.1 connects to the database, pulls the title and price information, and displays the information to the user. To make the connection to the database, you must have a JDBC driver specifically for MySQL. The primary MySQL JDBC driver is called MySQL Connector/J (formerly called MM.MYSQL) which is available directly from MySQL AB at www.mysql.com/products/connector-j.

When the servlet is executed, the first JDBC-oriented statement is a call to load the JDBC driver. If the class or respective JAR file isn't found, an exception is thrown, indicating the error. Once the driver is pulled into the address space of the application, a connection can be made to the MySQL database. The connection string is defined as follows:

```
interface:driver name:ip/database<options>
```

In the code, the fully defined string is

```
jdbc:mysql://192.168.1.25/products?user=spider&password=spider
```

The connection to the database occurs with the getConnection() method of the DriverManager static class. Once the connection is established, SQL can pull the necessary information.

What makes JDBC so powerful is the ability to change from MySQL to Oracle or any other JDBC-compliant driver. Of course, the code in this example would require you to change the driver class name and the connection string in the source code and recompile the code each time you use a new driver. This problem isn't too significant when you consider that Resin automatically recompiles source code that has changed on the server; however, constantly changing source code can lead to problems. Fortunately, Resin has a better solution.

Using Resin's JNDI Configuration

The Resin server supports the use of Java Naming and Directory Interface (JNDI). JNDI provides an application with a global naming tree designed for storing factory objects and configuration variables. The goal is the extreme separation of configuration information from an application. An application can use JNDI to pull a factory object and grab an object for use by the application. By using a configuration file, you can exchange databases with little fanfare and—more importantly—without any changes to the source code.

Basic Configuration Parameters

The basic database configuration uses the <database> element as a number of sub-elements. A complete list of the sub-elements can be found in Chapter 15. Following are the most used ones:

<name>—The JNDI path relative to java:comp/env.

<driver-class>—The JDBC driver class. (Required)

<driver-url>—The location of the database as either an IP, localhost, or domain name. (Required)

<user>—Default is an empty string. The username to use when connecting to the database.

<password>—Default is an empty string. The password to use when connecting to the database.

<max-connections>—Default is 20. The maximum number of allowed connections to the database.

Library Placement

When you're using the JNDI configuration, you must place the driver class or JAR in an appropriate location where the server can find it. As you saw earlier in the chapter, one of the first places the system attempts to find the driver is on the global classpath. If the driver isn't on the classpath, the system looks in the /lib directory of the server. In most cases, this is the best place to put the driver because it is specific to the server. You have the option of putting the driver in the application's WEB-INF/lib or WEB-INF/classes directory if you want it to be more aligned with the specific application.

Using the Configuration

The JNDI information is put into the Resin configuration file under the <database> element. The database connectivity information used in Listing 11.1 can be converted into a JNDI configuration as shown here:

```
<database>
    <jndi-name>jdbc/mysql</jndi-name>
    <driver type="org.gjt.mm.mysql.Driver">
    <url>
      jdbc:mysql://localhost:3306/products
    </url>
    <user>spider</user>
    <password>spider</password>
    </driver>
    <max-connections>20</max-connections>
    <max-idle-time>30s</max-idle-time>
  </database>
```

You place this configuration in the resin.conf configuration file for access by an application.

Connecting to MySQL

With the JNDI configuration set in the Resin configuration file, all an application has to do is access it. Listing 11.2 shows the code from Listing 11.1 changed to use the JNDI information.

```
package servlet;

import java.io.*;
import java.sql.*;
import javax.servlet.*;
import javax.servlet.http.*;
import javax.naming.*;
import javax.sql.*;

public class JNDI extends HttpServlet {
  DataSource _ds;

public void init()
  throws ServletException {
  try {
    Context ic =
      (Context) new InitialContext();

    _ds = (DataSource) ic.lookup("java:comp/env/jdbc/mysql");

    if (_ds == null)
      throw new ServletException("'jdbc/mysql' - unknown");
    }
  }

  public void doGet(HttpServletRequest inRequest,
    HttpServletResponse outResponse)
      throws ServletException, IOException {

    Connection myConnection = null;
    Statement myStatement = null;
    ResultSet myResultSet = null;

    outResponse.setContentType("test/html");
    PrintWriter out = outResponse.getWriter();

    try {
      myConnection = ds.getConnection();
      myStatement = myConnection.createStatement();
```

Listing 11.2 MySQL connection using a JNDI configuration. (continues)

```
        myResultSet = myStatement.executeQuery("SELECT title,
          price FROM product");

        out.println("<HTML><HEAD><TITLE>MySQL
           Example</TITLE></HEAD>");
        out.println("<BODY>");
        out.println("<UL>");

Line 50:       while (myResultSet.next()) {
          out.println("<LI>" + myResultSet.getString("title")
          + " " + myResultSet.getString("price"));
        }

        out.println("</UL>");
        out.println("</BODY></HTML>");
      }
      catch(SQLException e) {
    out.println("SQLException caught: "+ e.getMessage());
  } finally {
    myConnection.close();
  }
Line 60:  }
}
```

Listing 11.2 MySQL connection using a JNDI configuration. (continued)

The results of the application are shown in Figure 11.1.

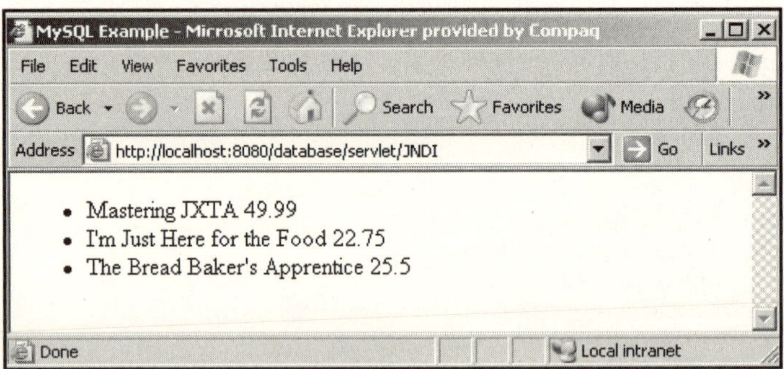

Figure 11.1 MySQL JDNI application output.

In the initial database access code, the application was responsible for loading the driver class as well as creating the connection to the database. In Listing 11.2, things are quite different. First, notice the addition of the init() method in lines 13-26 as well as the DataSource attribute in line 11.

These new pieces of code are used when the servlet is first called into action. The init() method handles finding the JNDI entries for the database and setting up the application to use the entry. The real work begins in line 17, where an InitialContext object is instantiated. This object pulls the configuration information added to the resin.conf file. In line 19, a call is made to the lookup() method to find the value represented by jdbc/mysql. Recall that this value was used in the res-ref-name element of the JNDI information put into the resin.conf file.

If the lookup() method can't find an appropriate entry in the configuration file, the DataSource variable *_ds* is set to null and an exception is thrown. If the lookup() method is successful, the DataSource variable *_ds* is assigned the values found as part of the matched jndi-name element. This is where all the JNDI magic takes places: A simple lookup populates an entire object with the information found. In this case, the DataSource class contains all the information necessary to create a connection to the database.

Once the init() method has finished, the doGet() method processes the call from the client's Web browser. Line 40 is the only other change made to the code from Listing 11.1. In this line, a Connection object is instantiated from the DataSource object. If the getConnection() method is successful in obtaining a connection with the associated database, a new Connection object is returned from the method. After this line, all the code is the same, and information is extracted from the database.

Connecting to Other Databases

Given all the configuration information we've presented in the last few sections, allowing an application to access databases besides MySQL using JNDI should be a snap. Here are the configurations for some other popular databases:

Oracle

```
<database>
  <jndi-name>jdbc/oracle</jndi-name>
  <driver type="oracle.jdbc.pool.
OracleConnectionPoolDataSource">
  <url>jdbc:oracle:myschema:@localhost:product</url>
  <user>username</user>
  <password>password</password>
  </driver>
</database>
```

Postgres

```
<database>
  <jndi-name>jdbc/mypostgre</jndi-name>
  <driver type="org.postgresql.Driver">
  <url>jdbc:postgres://localhost/product</url>
  <user>username</user>
  <password>password</password>
  </driver>
</database>
```

Database Pooling

One of the most interesting things about the DataSource object used in the JNDI example is the fact that the underlying driver can be written to perform three different levels of connection:

- A basic implementation returns a Connection object based on an attempt to communicate with the database when the getConnection() method is called.
- A connection pooling implementation returns a Connection object obtained from a pool with possible connections already made.
- A distributed transaction implementation returns a Connection object obtained from a pool that allows transactions.

Depending on the underlying database, support for distributed transactions may or may not be available. The modes available depend on the implementation of the database driver. In the case of the Resin MySQL driver, database pooling is available. The system includes a number of parameters for making full use of pooling:

- **max-connections**—Determines the total connections; defaults to 20.
- **max-idle-time**—Determines the idle time of a pooled connection before it's removed; defaults to 30 seconds.
- **max-active-time**—Determines the maximum connection time; defaults to 6 hours.
- **max-pool-time**—Determines the maximum time a connection is kept in the pool; defaults to 24 hours.
- **connection-wait-time**—Determines the time to wait for an idle connection; defaults to 10 minutes.
- **max-overflow-connections**—Determines the number of overflow connections when a connection times out; defaults to 0.

All the times used in the parameters can be represented in several different ways. Here are the values to use:

s = seconds

m = minutes

h = hours

D = days

If a value for a parameter isn't one we've listed, the default used is seconds.

Let's see how the JNDI configuration for a database driver can use pooling. Note that nothing from the server side tells you whether pooling is being used; you simply configure for its use, and, if it's available, the DataSource object and the database driver handle the details. Consider the following configuration:

```
<database>
    <jndi-name>jdbc/mysql</jndi-name>
    <driver type="org.gjt.mm.mysql.Driver">
    <url>
      jdbc:mysql://localhost:3306/products
    </url>
    <user>spider</user>
    <password>spider</password>
    </driver>
    <max-connections>20</max-connections>
    <max-idle-time>30s</max-idle-time>
    <connection-wait-time>15</connection-wait-time>
  </database>
```

This configuration uses the Resin MySQL driver and sets several pooling options, including the maximum number of connection, the maximum idle time for a connection object, and the time a new connection will wait for a connection object from the pool. Listing 11.3 shows a snippet of code based on Listing 11.2; it builds five threads, each with a new connection to the database.

```
private class Csql implements Runnable {
  Connection connection;
  int time;

  public Csql(Connection localConnection, int t) {
    connection = localConnection;
    time = t;
  }

  public void run() {
    try {
      Thread.sleep(time*1000);
      Statement statement = connection.createStatement();
      ResultSet rs = statement.executeQuery("SELECT title,
       price FROM product");
    } catch(Exception e){}
    System.out.println("Done = " + time);
  }
}
```

Listing 11.3 Code with multiple connection objects. (continues)

```
...

    try {
      for (int i=0;i<5;i++) {
        myConnection = ds.getConnection();
        Csql s = new Csql(myConnection, i);
        Thread t = new Thread(s);
        t.start();
      }
```

Listing 11.3 Code with multiple connection objects. (continued)

As each thread is launched, it removes a thread from the thread pool and executes some SQL. Notice, though, that the connection isn't closed; this is done to show that 20 pool connections are indeed available. After the code executes four times, the following message appears in the browser:

```
SQLException caught: Can't open connection with full database pool
(20)
```

This small program has used all the pool connection objects.

Most databases can view the processes currently executing on them. MySQL has two commands that show the current connections to the database: show status and show processlist;. At the end of the show status command is a *Threads_connected* variable. When you execute the previous code, the value is 21: 20 connections from the servlet and 1 from the administrator. The show processlist; command lists all the current connections, the current user, machine, database accessed, current status, and current idle time. After the servlet executes four times, the show processlist; command details 21 threads: 20 threads come from the Resin server and 1 comes from the administrator.

You can change all the pooling options to find the right combination for both the Resin server and the database server. Too many connections will bog down the database, and too few can potentially cause a connection attempt failure error.

Database Reliability

In a production setting or even in a development shop, it's important to know the database is alive. Resin can test whether a database is alive by using a very simple SQL query called a *ping query*. You can use the ping test with objects in a connection pool. It is represented by the following SQL:

```
select 1 FROM <defined table>
```

This SQL attempts a select on a specific table defined in resin.conf for the database driver. The JNDI configuration options available are as follows:

- **ping-table**—The database table used for pinging; note that the table is in the database specified in the configuration.
- **ping-on-reuse**—A pool object tests for a live connection before being used or allocated in an application; default is false.
- **ping-on-free**—A pool object tests for a live connection before being put back into the pool; default is false.
- **ping-on-idle**—A pool object tests for a live connection randomly; default is false.

In all cases, if the connection attempt fails, the object shuts down its current connection and reattempts to connect with the database. To see database reliability in use, consider the following JNDI configuration:

```
<database>
    <jndi-name>jdbc/mysql</jndi-name>
    <driver type="org.gjt.mm.mysql.Driver">
    <url>
      jdbc:mysql://localhost:3306/products
    </url>
    <user>spider</user>
    <password>spider</password>
    </driver>
    <max-connections>20</max-connections>
    <max-idle-time>30s</max-idle-time>
    <connection-wait-time>15</connection-wait-time>
    <ping-table>product</ping-table>
    <ping-on-reuse>true</ping-on-reuse>
  </database>
```

This configuration tells the Resin server to perform a ping query on the product table found in the products database. The pool connection objects ping just before they are allocated for use by the server. You can test the ping query by executing the servlets shown in any of the listings. Once the results are presented to the client browser, shut down the database where the code is making connections. This action will cause all the pool connection objects to have stale information. If the object attempted to execute SQL, they would fail if the ping query wasn't in place. Because ping query attempts are made just before the pool objects are allocated to an application, a new connection is made with the database, and the code executes without error.

Connecting through JSP

This chapter wouldn't be complete without a simple example of connecting to a database using a JSP page. The code in Listing 11.4 is a JSP page to pull the same data as in Listing 11.1.

```
<%@ page import='java.sql.*, javax.sql.*, javax.naming.*' %>
<HTML>
<HEAD>
<TITLE>MySQL JSP Example</TITLE>
</HEAD>
<BODY>
<%
  Context ic = new InitialContext();
  DataSource ds = (DataSource)
  ic.lookup("java:comp/env/jdbc/mysql");

  Connection conn = ds.getConnection();

  try {
    Statement stmt = conn.createStatement();
    ResultSet rs = stmt.executeQuery("SELECT title,
      price FROM product");
%>
<UL>
<%
  while (myResultSet.next()) {
%>
  <LI>
<%
    myResult.getString("title") + " "
      + myResultSet.getString("price));
  }
%>
  </UL>
</BODY>
</HTML>
<%
} catch(SQLException e) {
    out.println("SQLException caught: "
     + e.getMessage());
  }
} finally {
    conn.close();
  }
%>
```

Listing 11.4 JSP database access.

As you can see, a JSP page with embedded Java can use the JNDI configuration information provided in the resin.conf file. Once the database information has been obtained, the database is queried and the results are output to the browser, just as in the servlet code.

What's Next

In this chapter, we have taken a comprehensive look at various ways to access databases through Java servlets and JSP pages. The Resin server provides JNDI support for database configuration as well as comprehensive pooling and reliability checks. In Chapter 12, we will cover many of the options available for debugging applications executing with a Resin server.

CHAPTER 12

Debugging and Logging

As you begin to write larger and more complex applications, the possibility of errors will exist. Well, your code *will* contain errors, and debugging them may not always be easy. In this chapter, we will cover some of the errors you can expect to experience as well as the various options available for finding their cause. First let's look at some of the error types you are likely to see.

Error Types

Four types of errors are encountered in the development and execution of a software application: compiler parse errors, run-time errors, logic errors, and user errors. Of these errors, the first three are under your control as a developer. Let's examine how Resin works with you to identify these error types.

Compiler Parse Errors

Consider the following JSP code as an example of compiler parse errors:

```
<%
    String username = null;
    out.print("The user's name is " + username + "<BR>");

    out.print("Calculation of 5 / 0 = ", 5/0 | "<BR>");

    if (1 < 2)
```

```
        write("1 > 2");
      else
        out.print("1 < 2");
%>
```

When you browse to a page containing this JSP code, you get the output shown in Figure 12.1.

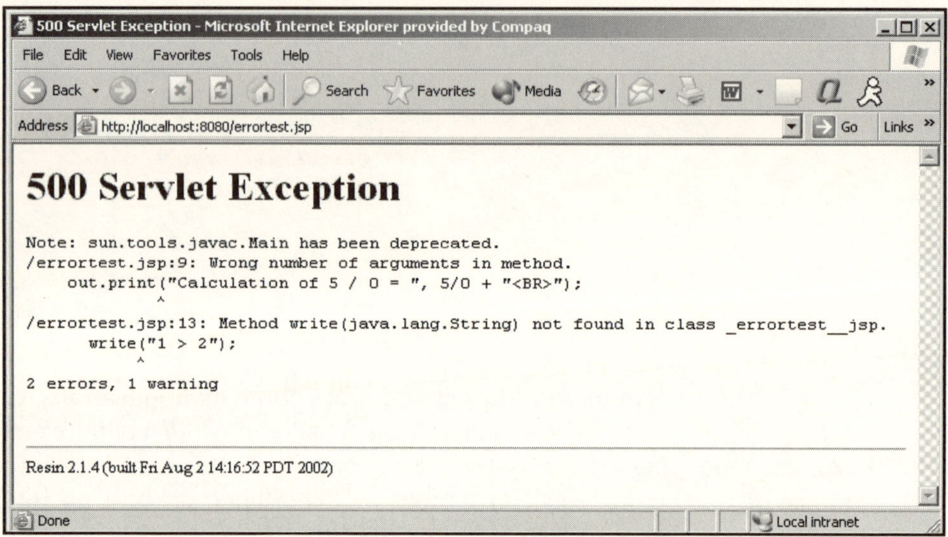

Figure 12.1 Compiler parse errors.

In Figure 12.1, the Resin server has attempted to compile the JSP code so it can be executed. Unfortunately, the code contains a couple of errors, so the Resin server returns a 500 Servlet Exception error and a listing of the code with possible error locations. The first error results because the code uses a comma (,) character instead of a plus (+) to concatenate values in a print statement. The second error is the use of the statement write instead of print (the system doesn't know about a write command). Once you fix these two errors, the code will execute.

Run-time Errors

Once your code executes, you may encounter another error type: a run-time error. A run-time error occurs when an error is found in the executing code. Figure 12.2 shows the run-time error information produced by the example JSP.

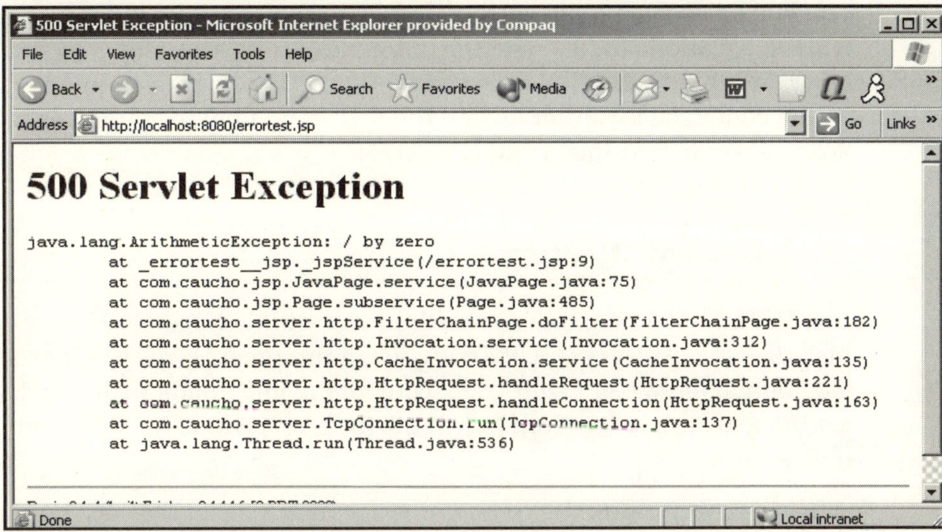

Figure 12.2 Example run-time error.

If you look at the example JSP code, you will see that one of the out.print lines includes code to divide 5 by 0; this code causes an error because you cannot divide by zero. The Resin server returns to the client a 500 Servlet Exception error along with a stack dump showing where the error occurred. The first line of the dump shows that the error occurred on line 7 of the errortest.jsp page.

Logic Errors

Once you fix the division-by-zero error, you can reload the page. As you can see in Figure 12.3, the pages executes successfully. Unfortunately, there is a problem with the output.

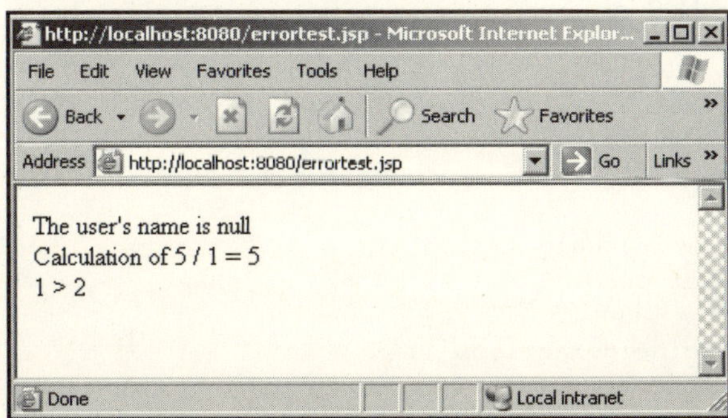

Figure 12.3 Logic error example.

The output appears to be correct, but the original JSP includes a comparison with an equation (1 < 2)—and the output is (1 > 2). This an example of a logic error, which is by far the hardest error type to recognize and find in the application code. The Resin server and the Java compiler are completely unable to determine whether this result is an error.

Just-In-Time Compilers

Just-In-Time (JIT) compilers wreck havoc with debugging. If your Java Virtual Machine (JVM) uses a JIT compiler, a run-time 2 error won't produce the nice output shown in Figure 12.2, with all the line numbers. Instead, you will get the text (Compiled Code) in all the locations where the line numbers currently exist.

JITs are great for production systems because they let the Java code get performance numbers almost as fast as code compiled to the native hardware. But the extra compiling isn't helpful for debugging, so it is a good idea to turn off JITs during development. You do so by appending the command-line flag -nojit to the execution of the Resin server. For example:

```
httpd.exe –nojit
```

The flag is passed through the Resin server to the underling JVM.

Tracing Your Code

One of the ways you can determine what is happening in a servlet is to produce milestone indicators to either the client browser or the console. Resin allows this type of tracing, but you should use it only with smaller projects because of its inefficiency. Consider the following piece of JSP code with milestones written to System.err:

```
<%
 System.err.println("Handling username");
    String username = null;
    out.print("The user's name is " + username + "<BR>");

System. err.println("Doing calculation");
    out.print("Calculation of 5 / 1 = " + 5/1 + "<BR>");

System.err.println("Doing comparison");
    if (1 < 2)
      out.print("1 > 2");
    else
      out.print("1 < 2");
%>
```

This code example contains milestones that use the System.err.println() statement. When the system encounters these statements, it prints the text to the current location for System.err. On Resin, the default path for System.err is the console window where the server was started. Depending on the output received on the console, you can match the last text with its location in the source code. Unfortunately, you should limit your use of System.err because the code might be executing on a shared server, and the output will go to the primary console window.

A better solution is to use a log file, which can be incorporated in the source code and turned on or off based on the deployment of the code. In production, the log is turned off. In the Resin server, logging is accomplished with a combination of a stream, entries in the config file, and code.

Resin Logging

Resin includes a logging mechanism built into the Server, which provides the ability to write to a stream. You set up the log in the Resin configuration file and write to it in a servlet or JSP page.

First, let's consider the configuration file. The logging element is called <log>, and it includes a number of attributes:

- **name**—The name of the debugging section.
- **path**—The destination file.
- **timestamp**—Format for the timestamp in the file.
- **rollover-count**—Number of different log files to keep; default is 2.
- **rollover-period**—How often to create new log files, typically using days (D), week(W), or months(M).

The name value can be a custom value such as /testdebug; this value indicates that debugging data from the testdebug class should be logged to the specified file. You could use mycompany.com/jsp to log all debugging data from the JSP files from the mycompany.com domain. Other values specific to the server are as follows:

- "**com.caucho.jsp**"—Debug JSP files.
- "**com.caucho.java**"—Debug Java compilations.
- "**com.caucho.xsl**"—Debug XSL processing.
- "**com.caucho.server.port**"—Debug TCP connections.
- "**com.caucho.server.clustering**"—Debug clustering.
- "**com.caucho.sql**"—Debug all database connection pooling.

- **"com.caucho.http"**—Debug all HTTP information.
- **"com.caucho.server.session"**—Debug HTTP sessions.

Let's debug the simple JSP application from the beginning of the chapter. This JSP file is called testdebug.jsp, so the configuration file information is as follows:

```
<caucho.com>
  <log name='/testdebug'
       path='logging.txt'
       timestamp='[%Y-%m-%d %H:%M:%S.%s]'/>
</caucho.com
```

This configuration information tells the system that a file called logging.txt should be placed in the root Resin server directory if an application opens the log ID with the name testdebug. Here's what the logging code looks like:

```
<HTML>
<BODY>

<resin xmlns="http://caucho.com/ns/resin">
  <log name="testdebug" path="logging" />
</resin>

<%@ page import="java.util.logging.*" %>
<%!
  static Logger debug = Logger.getLogger("testdebug");
%>
<%
if (debug.isLoggable(Level.FINE))
  log.fine("printing name");
if (debug.isLoggable(Level.FINE))
  log.fine("doing calculation");
out.print("Calculation of 5/1 = " + 5/1 + "<BR>");
if (debug.isLoggable(Level.FINE))
  log.fine("doing comparison");
if (1 < 2)
  out.print("1 > 2");
else
  out.print("1 < 2");
%>

</BODY>
</HTML>
```

You must include a couple of important pieces of code in either a JSP or servlet application. First, you must import the java.util.logging.* class hierarchy, which imports the JDK 1.4 logging API. First, you must import the java.util.logging.*, which imports the JDK 1.4 logging API. Next, you set up a JSP declaration and instantiate a variable of type Logger through the call to getLogger() of the Logger static variable. The single parameter to the getLogger() method is the log ID, found in the configuration file.

When the code is executing, it checks the isLoggable() method to see if the log is configured for writing. The output from the page should be:

```
[2002-09-16 21:06:35.961] printing name
[2002-09-16 21:06:35.961] doing calculation
[2002-09-16 21:06:35.961] doing comparison
```

RootCause Exception

During the development of JSPs and servlets, you may trigger exceptions in the code. At times the resulting output from the exception is what caused the error in the first place, because the server is overriding the original exception to provide some information. You really want to know the underlying cause of the error. The Resin server allows you to access this rootCause exception. Consider the following code:

```
catch (Exception e)
{
  debug.log(Level.WARNING, e.toString(), e);
  Throwable rootE = e.getCause();

  if (rootE != null)
    debug.log(Level.WARNING, e.toString(), e);

}
```

This code includes a normal try/catch block that catches all Exception types. The information about the exception will be logged to the Resin logging system.

Thread Dumps

If you need to know what your Resin server is doing within its threads, you can obtain a dump as follows:

Windows. Open a command prompt and start the server by changing to the installation's /bin directory and running the command httpd.exe. When the server has started and processed the pages you are interested in, press Ctrl-Break. The server will shut down and display where and what all the threads are currently doing.

UNIX. Open a command prompt and type *kill –QUIT <PID>*. The PID is one of the child processes for IBM's JDK and the parent process of all the threads in Sun's JDK.

Once you kill the server, output will be generated similar to that shown in Figure 12.4. Pay particular attention to the threads in the waiting-on-monitor stage, because several threads may be waiting on each other—thereby producing a deadlock.

```
Command Prompt
        at java.lang.Object.wait(Native Method)
        - waiting on <02F8B460> (a java.lang.ref.ReferenceQueue$Lock)
        at java.lang.ref.ReferenceQueue.remove(ReferenceQueue.java:111)
        - locked <02F8B460> (a java.lang.ref.ReferenceQueue$Lock)
        at java.lang.ref.ReferenceQueue.remove(ReferenceQueue.java:127)
        at java.lang.ref.Finalizer$FinalizerThread.run(Finalizer.java:159)

"Reference Handler" daemon prio=10 tid=0x0003E7F8 nid=0x9d4 in Object.wait() [aa
df000..aadfd8c]
        at java.lang.Object.wait(Native Method)
        - waiting on <02F8B4C8> (a java.lang.ref.Reference$Lock)
        at java.lang.Object.wait(Object.java:426)
        at java.lang.ref.Reference$ReferenceHandler.run(Reference.java:113)
        - locked <02F8B4C8> (a java.lang.ref.Reference$Lock)

"main" prio=5 tid=0x00036058 nid=0x918 runnable [7f000..7fc40]
        at java.net.SocketInputStream.socketRead0(Native Method)
        at java.net.SocketInputStream.read(SocketInputStream.java:129)
        at java.net.SocketInputStream.read(SocketInputStream.java:182)
        at com.caucho.server.http.ResinServer.waitForExit(ResinServer.java:907)
        at com.caucho.server.http.ResinServer.main(ResinServer.java:1133)
        at com.caucho.server.http.HttpServer.main(HttpServer.java:103)

"VM Thread" prio=5 tid=0x009E5568 nid=0x9c8 runnable

"VM Periodic Task Thread" prio=10 tid=0x009E8328 nid=0x9e4 waiting on condition

"Suspend Checker Thread" prio=10 tid=0x009E8D28 nid=0x9e8 runnable
closing server
```

Figure 12.4 Resin thread dump output.

Resin and Debuggers

Considerable attention has been given within the Resin mailing list groups to the subject of using stand-alone debuggers like jdb, JPad Pro (www.modelworks.com), Java Platform Debugger Architecture (JPDA; www.javasoft.com/ products/jpda), and others with Resin. If you are interested in this topic, we suggest that you visit the Resin site (www.caucho.com) and search on the topic of debugging. You will be directed to a results page with hundreds of articles from the mailing lists about using these tools with Resin. Some of the comments include complete instructions, which we won't duplicate here.

What's Next

In this chapter, we covered some types of errors you can expect to experience when working with JSP and servlets. We also discussed several different ways to produce debugging or logging information about your application. In Chapter 13, we will cover how to implement security in your server and pages.

CHAPTER 13

Security

Security is one of the most talked-about aspects of the Internet today. When you're developing a site or Internet-based application, you must concern yourself with providing access security, encryption of sensitive data, and other security topics. In this chapter, we will look at tools Resin provides in the following areas:

- **Authentication**—Who can access.
- **Authorization**—What can be accessed.
- **OpenSSL**—Keeping data secure.

Authentication

Authentication is defined as the process of determining the identify of a user. Typically, the user is trying to access a password-protected part of an application or site; for example, they may be logging in to a site that has personalized content. In this section we will look at three Resin techniques you can use instead of writing your own authentication code.

Providing Basic Authentication with XmlAuthenticator

If you are interested in password protecting part of your site or application, the XmlAuthenticator will do the work for you. The XmlAuthenticator code pulls username/password combinations from the user and matches them against combinations listed in the Resin configuration file. Let's look at the configuration code first:

```
<authenticator type="com.caucho.server.security.XmlAuthenticator">
  <init>
    <user>usergroup:group54:user</user>
    <password-digest>none</password-digest>
  </init>
</authenticator>

<login-config auth-method="basic"/>
<security-constraint>
  <url-pattern>/users-only/*</url-pattern>
  <role-name>user</role-name>
</security-constraint>
```

This configuration information is added to a <web-app> element to control access to the application files in the Web application. In the default Resin configuration file, you file a <web-app> for the tutorials defined as <web-app id="\java_tut" \>. By putting the previous configuration in the <web-app> element, the users-only directory is protected and a username/password is required for access. When you attempt to browse to one of the example template files in the java_tut/users-only directory, a username/password dialog appears on the screen, as shown in Figure 13.1.

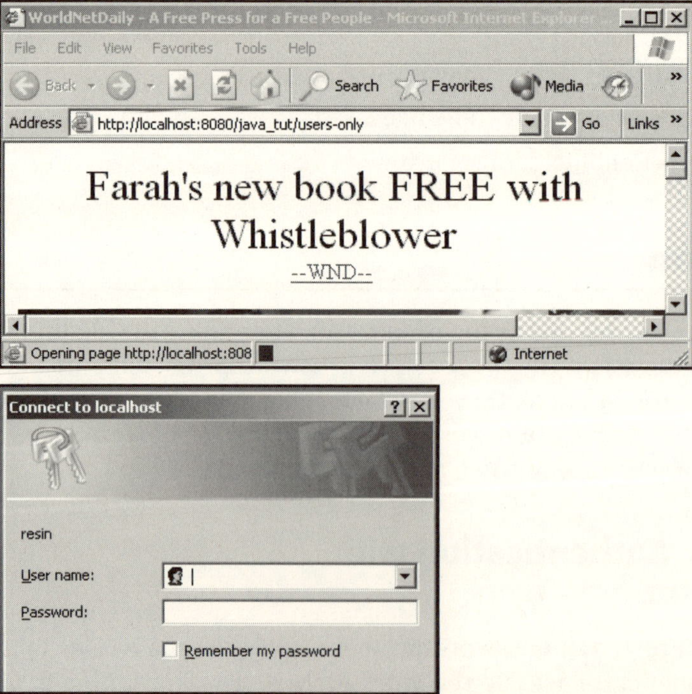

Figure 13.1 Basic authentication using XmlAuthenticator.

Let's look at the configuration to determine what it's doing. The <login-config> element is the primary root for the configuration information. This element has an attribute called auth-method; in this example, it is set to basic. The basic value tells the system to pop up a username/password dialog. (In a moment you will see two other values that can be used.) Next, the configuration uses an <authenticator> element to choose the type of Resin authenticator class to use. (You will see other choices later in the chapter and look at the API to write your own authenticator class.) The <init> element lists the username:password:role values for the authentication. Notice that all the information is plain text. After the authenticator is chosen, the <security-constraint> element picks the directory where protected code resides and the role necessary to gain access to the code.

When you browse to your Web application and use a path with the user-only text in it, the system prompts for a username/password. Keep in mind that the username and password are passed over the network as plain text and can be easily hacked.

Note that the username/password/role information can also appear in the web.xml files located in each of the Web application's directories.

Digest Authentication

We've mentioned that the password in the basic authentication scheme is kept in a clear-text format in the Resin configuration file or the web.xml file. Resin provides the ability to encrypt the passwords stored in the various files. Consider the following authentication configuration:

```
<authenticator type="com.caucho.server.security.XmlAuthenticator">
  <init>
    <user>segroup:8b7dchPDKI261QvH9Cw:user</user>
    <password-digest>MD5-base64</password-digest>
    <password-digest-realm>resin</password-digest-realm>
  </init>
</authenticator>

<login-config auth-method="digest">
  <realm-name>resin</realm-name>
</login-config>
```

In this configuration, the auth-method attribute has been changed from basic to digest. In the <authenticator> element, a new <init-param> element has been added, using the password-digest attribute and a value of MD5-base64. This element tells the system that the authenticator is using the MD5 algorithm for the encryption/decryption of stored passwords. In the <init-param> for a user, you will see that the password is no longer plain text but instead is encrypted. To determine what the password should be, you can use the following application:

```
import com.caucho.http.security.PasswordDigest;
import java.io;

public class CreatePassword {

  public static void main(String[] args) {
    PasswordDigest digest = new PasswordDigest();
    digest.setAlgorithm("MD5");
    digest.setFormat("base64");
    digest.setRealm("resin");

         System.out.println(digest.getPasswordDigest(args[0],
args[1]));
  }
}
```

The application takes two command-line arguments: the username and the password. The result is output to the console. Unfortunately, you must execute this program manually each time you want to add a username and password combination to the password file. This process isn't very productive for new users to your site or application. As you will see later in the chapter, you can also use the database to store passwords.

Form Authentication

Both basic and digest authentication use the popup dialog shown in Figure 13.1 to obtain the username and password from the user. Many times, you'll want to obtain the username and password using a form with associated graphics on the page. Resin lets you use an authenticator class, as in the basic and digest mechanisms, but also a form. First consider the configuration:

```
<authenticator type="com.caucho.server.security.XmlAuthenticator">
  <init>
    <user>usergroup:group54:user</user>
    <password-digest>none</password-digest>
  </init>
</authenticator>

<login-config auth-method="digest">
  <realm-name>resin</realm-name>
</login-config>
```

Here the configuration is changed to use an auth-method of form as well as a password-digest through the user= parameter. The real works takes place in a form placed on a Web page. The form must contain several specific values in order to work correctly.

You can add an additional element to the configuration to help define the form values to be used when a user wants access to a secured page. The <form-login-config> element contains a number of attributes for defining which page to display when a password is needed (form-login-page) and the page to display if the user is denied access to the page (form-error-page).

Here are the page and form to use as an example:

```
<HTML>
<BODY>

<FORM action='j_security_check' method='POST'>
<TABLE>
<TR><TD>User:<td><input name='j_username'></TD></TR>
<TR><TD>Password:<td><input name='j_password'></TD></TR>

<TR><TD><input type=submit>
</TABLE>
</FORM>

</BODY>
</HTML>
```

An HTML form needs to use a number of elements specific to Resin and the form authentication. The action value for the form must be the string j_security_check. When the form is submitted to the Resin server, the code defined as j_security_check executes. The code looks for a username defined by the name j_username and a password defined as j_password. These two values are compared against the defined username/password combinations stored in the configuration file.

If the username/password combination is found in the configuration file, the user is directed to the page they originally tried to access; otherwise, the user will see the error page. You have the option of embedding the name of the page where the user should be directed when they enter the correct username/password, by adding the following <input> tag and supplying the correct values:

```
<input name='j_uri' type='hidden' value='index.jsp'>
```

Specifying a Password File

When you're using the XmlAuthenticator class and configuration, you can specify a password file. For example:

```
<authenticator type="com.caucho.server.security.XmlAuthenticator">
  <init>
    <path>init/password.xml</path>
    <password-digest>MD5-base64</password-digest>
  </init>
</authenticator>
```

```
<login-config auth-method="digest">
  <realm-name>resin</realm-name>
</login-config>
```

In this configuration file, the path attribute is used in an <init-param> tag to indicate the exact location and filename where passwords can be found. The format of the file is as follows:

```
<authenticator>
  <user name='segroup' password='8b7dhcPDKI261QvH9Cw' role='user'/>
</authenticator>
```

Session Timeouts

At some point, you have probably experienced an interruption while shopping online. When you return to your shopping, one click on the site causes the system to ask you to log in again. This is called a *session timeout*. You don't want users to be continually logged in to the system, regardless of the idle time for the session. Resin lets you set configurations where the user is automatically logged out when the session times out.

Consider the following configuration:

```
<authenticator type="com.caucho.server.security.XmlAuthenticator">
  <init-param>
    <path>init/password.xml</path>
    <password-digest>MD5-base64</password-digest>
    <logout-on-session-timeout>true</logout-on-session-timeout>
    <user>segroup:8b7dhcPDKI261QvH9Cw:user</user>
  </init-param>
</authenticator>

<login-config auth-method="digest">
  <realm-name>resin</realm-name>
</login-config>
```

The new line in the configuration is the <init-param> element that has a logout-on-session-timeout attribute with a value of True. This attribute causes the system to log out the user for this specific Web application.

Storing Passwords in a Database with JdbcAuthenticator

As we've noted several times, the username/password combinations are stored in the various configuration files or another file on the server. Although this setup works, it doesn't handle adding new combinations easily. Resin provides another option: You can use a backend database to store the password information. Just about any database can be used, as long as it can be connected to by a JDBC driver.

Consider the following configuration:

```
<authenticator type="com.caucho.server.security.JdbcAuthenticator">
  <init>
    <data-source>jdbc/logins</data-source>

<password-query>
SELECT password FROM PASSWORD WHERE username=?
</password-query>

<cookie-auth-query>
SELECT username FROM PASSWORD WHERE cookie=?
</cookie-auth-query>

<cookie-auth-update>
UPDATE PASSWORD SET cookie=? WHERE username=?
</cookie-auth-update>

<role-query>
SELECT role FROM PASSWORD WHERE username=?
</role-query>

    <logout-on-session-timeout>true</logout-on-session-timeout>
  </init>
</authenticator>

<login-config auth-method="digest">
  <realm-name>resin</realm-name>
</login-config>
```

You can use the JdbcAuthenticator class to obtain a password from a JDBC-compliant database. As you can see in the previous configuration, access to a restricted page causes a form to be displayed to the user; this form is found in the login.html Web page. The form's HTML is as follows:

```
<HTML>
<BODY>

<FORM action='j_security_check' method='POST'>
<TABLE>
<TR><TD>User:<td><input name='username'></TD></TR>
<TR><TD>Password:<td><input name='password'></TD></TR>

<TR><TD><input type=submit>
</TABLE>
</FORM>

</BODY>
</HTML>
```

As required, the action on the form is j_security_check; but the names of the input values have been changed since you first saw the form authentication of username and password. When the user clicks the Submit button, the values are passed to the JdbcAuthenticator for use in various SQL statements. The statements are listed in the previous configuration.

The first element for defining access to a database where passwords are stored is <pool-name>. This element defines the datasource to be used for access to the password database. In this example, the datasource value is jdbc/logins. This value relates to a <resource-ref> element in the configuration file. Here's an example <resource-ref> element used as a test:

```
<database>
     <jndi-name>jdbc/logins</jndi-name>
      <driver type="org.gjt.mm.mysql.Driver">
      <url>jdbc:mysql://localhost:3306/users</url>
      <user></user>
      <password></password>
      </driver>
      <max-connections>20</max-connections>
      <max-idle-time>30s</max-idle-time>
</database>
```

Once the authenticator has access to a database, it expects to find a database and table with the password information. The schema defined in the JdbcAuthenticator code is as follows:

```
CREATE TABLE password (
 username VARCHAR(250) NOT NULL,
 password VARCHAR(250),
 cookie VARCHAR(250),
 role VARCHAR(250),
 PRIMARY_KEY(username)
 )
```

Once access has been established with the appropriate database, SQL is executed to obtain the correct information for the provided username and password. There are four SQL definitions:

- **<password-query>**—Requires a SQL statement that returns the password for a provided username.
- **<cookie-auth-query>**—Provides the username for a specific cookie value.
- **<cookie-auth-update>**—Allows the system to update the cookie for a specific username.
- **<role-query>**—A SQL statement that returns a role value for a specific username.

The specific SQL statements should use the <input> tag names from the HTML form used to obtain the username and password.

If the username and password aren't found in the database, the error.html page is executed. In a production system, the error page will probably add the user to the database as appropriate.

Authentication API

If you don't want to use XmlAuthenticator or JdbcAuthenticator, you can build your own authenticator. The fundamental goal of an Authenticator class is to accept a username and password and return a UserPrincipal object if the username/password matches stored combinations.

All new authenticators should extend the AbstractAuthenticator class. The specific methods that need to be implemented can be found at www.caucho.com/ resin/javadoc/index.html under the com.caucho.http.security.AbstractAuthenticator entry.

Authorization

All the authentication schemes we've documented here are activated only when some part of a site or application needs to be secured and designated as such. You cause this designation to occur by setting up a constraint. A Web application can define a set of secured pages or even a single page using the <security-constraint> element. This element contains a number of other elements that help determine who has access to the pages.

Consider the following example configuration:

```
<security-constraint>
  <web-resource-collection>
    <url-pattern>/confidential.jsp</url-pattern>
    <url-pattern>/safe/*.jsp</url-pattern>
  </web-resource-collection>
  <auth-constraint role-name='user'>
  <ip-constraint>152.168.1.0/24</ip-constraint>
  <user-data-constraint>
    <transport-guarantee>CONFIDENTIAL</transport-guarantee>
  </user-data-constraint>
</security-constraint>
```

The configuration begins with the high-level <security-constraint> element, which holds all other elements. Next, the <web-resource-collection> element defines which pages are restricted from anonymous access. A <url-pattern> element defines the pattern to use when matching page requests; this example restricts access to the confidential.jsp file as well as all JSP files in the safe directory. If a user attempts to access any of these pages, an authenticator will attempt to obtain a username/password from the user. The <web-resource-collection> element can also include a <method> element to restrict the HTTP request types, such as GET or POST.

Next, an element called <auth-constraint> further restricts access to the pages. In this element, the role-name attribute tells the system that even if the user enters the correct username/password, their role must still be of type user. The role value is an arbitrary string defined in the configuration file for the XmlAuthenticator or database for JdbcAuthenticator.

If the user gets past the username/password combination and the role, they are hit with a restriction on the IP address of the requesting machine. The <ip-constraint> element lets you restrict IPs based on an IP pattern or a specific IP address. Finally, a constraint based on the element <user-data-constraint> says the transport must be CONFIDENTIAL, which means SSL—the user must have accessed the pages using an HTTPS request instead of just HTTP. If you don't want to restrict the transport type, you can leave the element out or use a value of NONE.

Logging Out

The current implementation of the Authenticator classes doesn't provide a comprehensive way to log out of the site. However, you can accomplish a log-out a couple of ways. First, you can invalidate the user's session with a call to invalidate():

```
HttpSession session = request.getSession(false);
session.invalidate();
```

Another way to log out is to remove the login name:

```
HttpSession session = request.getSession(false);
session.removeValue("com.caucho.servlet.login.name");
```

Using OpenSSL with Resin

In order to use SSL with Resin, you must have OpenSSL installed on your server. OpenSSL is an open-source implementation of the Secure Socket Layer and is available at www.openssl.org. Once it is downloaded, you can compile the /bin/resin application on a Linux box, which is required to use Resin and SSL. You don't need to do any additional work on a Windows Resin installation.

After OpenSSL is installed, you need to create the various keys for your machine. Follow these steps:

1. Create a private key for the server where Resin and SSL will execute. The openssl executable is used to create the key. The following options tell the application to generate a DES3 RSA key with a size of 1024 bits, and the resulting key is placed in the file serverkey.key:

   ```
   openssl genrsa –des3 –out  serverkey.key 1024
   ```

2. Create a request to have the certificate signed, again using the openssl executable:

   ```
   openssl req –new –key serverkey.key –out serverkey.csr
   ```

3. Obtain a certificate from a Certificate Authority (CA). A few CAs will provide a certificate so you can use SSL on your box. There is a charge for the certificate. Several CAs will provide temporary certificates. Try the following companies:

   - **Thawte**—www.thawte.com/html/RETAIL/ssl/index.html
   - **Verisign**—www.verisign.com/products/site/index.html

4. Receive a test or real certificate file with the extension .crt. Place the original key file and the new .crt file from the CA in the certs directory of the OpenSSL installation.

5. Add the following information to the Resin configuration file. In the <certificate-file>, you place the UNIX or Windows path to the location where the .crt file is installed. In the <certificate-key-file>, you place the UNIX or Windows path to the location where the original .key file is installed:

   ```
   <http port='443'>
     <openssl>
     <certificate-file>
       /usr/local/ssl/certs/keyserver.crt
     </certificate-file>
     <certificate-key-file>
       /usr/local/ssl/certs/keyserver.key
     </certificate-key-file>
     <password>password</password>
   </http>
   ```

6. Launch Resin using the resin executable on Linux or httpd.exe on Windows. The system will indicate that it is listening to port 443 for HTTPS files.

7. Add a page on your server like the following to determine if everything works:

   ```
   <HTML>
   <BODY>
   Are we secure? <%= request.isSecure() %>
   </BODY>
   </HTML>
   ```

Using JSSE with Resin

If you or a client aren't comfortable using an open-source produce like OpenSSL, you may be satisfied with Sun's Java Secure Socket Extension (JSSE) product, which provides an implementation of SSL. The following discussion provides a step-by-step look at using JSSE. You can find complete information at http://java.sun.com/products/jsse/install.html. Note that JSSE is really a specification, which can and has been implemented by vendors other than Sun.

To use JSSE, follow these steps:

1. Download JSSE from http://java.sun.com/products/jsse/. If you are using JDK 1.4, skip to step 4; JSSE has been incorporated into the latest release.
2. Extract the files from the JSSE download. Put the files jsse.jar, jnet.jar, and jcert.jar in either the classpath or the $JAVA_HOME/jre/lib/ext directory.
3. Change to the directory $JAVA_HOME/kre/lib/security and open the file java.security. Make sure the .1 and .2 security provider entries look like the following:

   ```
   security.provider.1=sun.security.provider.Sun
   security.provider.2=com.sun.net.ssl.internal.ssl.Provider
   ```

4. Use the JSSE keytool to build a test server certificate. Figure 13.2 shows a progression through the keytool application.

```
resin@localhost.localdomain: /home/resin/resin-2.1.4/keys
[resin@localhost resin-2.1.4]$ cd keys
[resin@localhost keys]$ keytool -genkey -keyalg RSA -keystore server.keystore
Enter keystore password:  password
What is your first and last name?
  [Unknown]:  Frank Smith
What is the name of your organizational unit?
  [Unknown]:  Smith Inc.
What is the name of your organization?
  [Unknown]:  Smith and Jones Co
What is the name of your City or Locality?
  [Unknown]:  Dallas
What is the name of your State or Province?
  [Unknown]:  TX
What is the two-letter country code for this unit?
  [Unknown]:  US
Is CN=Frank Smith, OU=Smith Inc., O=Smith and Jones Co, L=Dallas, ST=TX, C=US co
rrect?
  [no]:  y

Enter key password for <mykey>
        (RETURN if same as keystore password):  password
[resin@localhost keys]$
```

Figure 13.2 Keytool progression.

5. Change the Resin configuration file as shown here:

```
<http port=443>
 <jsse-ssl>true</ssl>
 <key-store-file>keys/server.keystore</key-store-file>
 <password>password</password>
</http>
```

6. Launch Resin using the resin executable on Linux or httpd.exe on Windows. The system will indicate that it is listening to port 443 for HTTPS files.

7. Add a page on your server like the following to determine if everything works:

```
<HTML>
<BODY>
Are we secure? <%= request.isSecure() %>
</BODY>
</HTML>
```

What's Next

In this chapter we've taken a comprehensive look at providing security in the Resin server environment. You can add security in the form of username/password combinations pulled from a file or database. Data can be kept secret using OpenSSL or JSSE. In Chapter 14, we will look at how Resin handles page caching.

CHAPTER 14

Page Caching

When the usefulness of the Web became apparent after the flurry of activity in the late 1990s, site developers suddenly had to worry about staleness of a site, response times, bandwidth consumption, server usage, and other such topics. The fundamental theme today is to make the Web faster (with better performing servers) and less expensive to implement and maintain. All of these topics revolve around page caching.

Overview of Page Caching

Although it might seem like a simple topic, page caching is important because it brings advantages to the Web without much effort on the developer's part. Some of these advantages are as follows:

- **Reduced page latency**—Users quickly gets the information they are seeking.
- **Less backend hardware**—Cached pages don't need as many databases and Web servers.
- **Reduced bandwidth**—Pages cached on the browser don't need server access.

Caching can occur on both the client and server as well as in a semi-middle tier. On the client, the cache is found in the Web browser; it handles storing pages returned from a server. The cache can typically be sized according to the needs of the user; the size can range from a single megabyte to many hundreds. The performance of built-in Web caches isn't always the best, so third-party extensions are available to increase size and performance.

When you browse to a large and potentially busy Web site, you may see a URL redirection away from the primary site to a proxy location where a proxy cache is used to store pages. The proxy cache is situated between the client and the server, typically near a network gateway. If the proxy cache is located near a gateway, users on the local network don't need to traverse the entire Internet to retrieve pages.

The last cache is found in the Web server. These caches are usually called *proxy caches*; you can find them built into the Web server or as a separate product in front of the Web server. Clients hit the cache before hitting the server.

How Web Caches Work

The functionality of most caches is governed by rules established in the HTTP protocol. These rules work with the page passed from the Web server to the client browser to determine whether the page should be cached. Some of the rules are as follows:

- Secure pages are not cached.
- Authenticated pages are not cached.
- If a page says to not cache it, the page isn't cached.

A page is cached if:

- The expiration date on the page is valid.
- The page has been in the cache before, and the cache only checks once a session.
- The modification date is well in the past.

Let's examine how a page tells the Web browser all these things.

HTML Metatags and HTTP Headers

One of the least common tags used by page developers is the metatag. A metatag provides attributes about the page that are read by the Web browser. Unfortunately, metatags are generally read by browser caches and aren't used by most proxy caches. The proxy cache doesn't read the Web page the way a Web browser does, because the Web browser needs to display the information contained in the page.

One of the most likely candidates for inclusion in a Web page by Web designers is the pragma: no-cache metatag. Its format is as follows:

```
<META HTTP-EQUIV="Pragma" CONTENT="no-cache">
```

This metatag is designed to be read and followed in a manner such that the page isn't stored in the cache. Unfortunately, because many caches won't see the tag and some won't honor it, it is a waste of page space.

The alternative to metatags is to use HTTP headers that pass caching information. You don't place an HTTP header directly in Web page; instead, you add it to page content dynamically at the server. All Web pages begin their transfer from the server to the Web browser with an HTTP header, which is seen by any proxy caches and the Web browser.

Here's an example:

```
HTTP/1.1 200 OK
Date: Fri, 13 Sep 2002 13:50:24 GMT
Server: Apache/1.3.3 (Unix)
Cache-Control: max-age=3600, must-revalidate
Expires: Fri, 13 Sep 2002 14:50:04 GMT
Last-Modified: Mon, 29 May 2002 03:23:54 GMT
ETag: "5c23-763-2333accd"
Content-Length: 1045
Content-Type: text/html
```

After this information comes the HTML for the served Web page. As you can see from the header, there are two powerful cache headers: Cache-Control and Expires. The Expires header is recognized by most caches and Web browsers; it lets you specify for the cache a time period when the page is still fresh and can be served to clients without asking the server for a new copy. Setting a long expires value lets clients and proxy caches store your pages and allows for quick responses. The value provided in the Expires header is always a date/time stamp supplied in GMT time. A value in the past (by even a second) will cause the page to be marked uncacheable.

The Cache-Control header was introduced in the HTTP 1.1 protocol to help caches do their job of caching pages. The Cache-Control header can contain a number of attributes:

- **max-age=[seconds**—The maximum time a page is fresh and can be served from the cache. The seconds start from the time the page was requested.
- **s-maxag[seconds]**—Same as max-age, but used for proxy caches.
- **public**—Allows a normally uncached page to be cached.
- **no-cache**—Indicates that the page should not be cached by either the Web browser or the proxy cache.
- **must-revalidate**—Forces the cache to be strict with the Cache-Control attributes. (The HTTP protocol allows caches to fudge some on the serving of cached pages.)
- **proxy-revalidate**—Same as must-revalidate, but for proxy caches only.

You can find complete information in the HTTP 1.1 specification at www.ietf.org/rfc/rfc2616.txt. Now, let's see how to use this information with XTP, JSP, and servlets in the Resin server.

Resin and Caching

The Resin server provides a built-in advanced proxy cache. Per our previous discussion, the Resin proxy cache works with the HTTP headers to determine which pages should be cached. The default setup for the cache is to not cache any pages unless specific HTTP header information is present. The Resin server will not cache pages that use sessions and have cookies associated with them. If your site uses cookies for anonymous or users who don't log into a site, the pages will not be cached. This is an important consideration when you're designing site pages.

One of the Resin cache's powerful features (which most proxy caches don't allow) is the partial caching of JSP pages that contain includes. The includes allow you to write a page like that shown in Figure 14.1 as follows:

```
<%@ page session=true %>
<% if (! session.isNew()) { %>
  <h1>Here's Your Personalized New Page!</h1>
<% } %>
<jsp:include page="menu.jsp"/>
<jsp:include page="body.jsp"/>
<jsp:include page="footer.jsp"/>
```

This code snippet represents the personalized page called news.jsp. In Figure 14.1, the gray boxes represent pages that can be cached because they aren't personalized. A normal proxy cache can't break apart the pages, but the Resin cache can. The menu.jsp and footer.jsp pages set session=false, so they can be cached by the Resin server. In the remainder of the chapter, we will show you how to set various HTTP header values to facilitate caching in both JSP and servlet code.

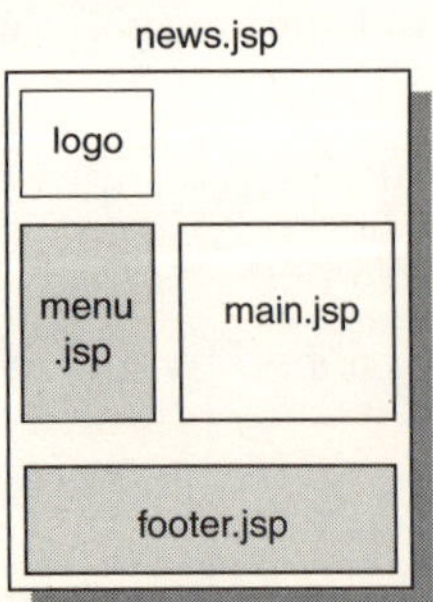

Figure 14.1 Included page caching.

Using Expires

If you have pages that don't change often, it is a good idea to let Resin cache the pages in order to boost performance. If changes to the pages are produced on a regular basis, they can still be cached for a period of time—even if the time is short. To achieve page caching for a time period, use the Expires HTTP header. The following listing shows how to set the Expires HTTP header in JSP:

```
<%@ page session=false %>
<%
    long currentTime = System.currentTimeMillis();
    response.setDateHeader("Expires", currentTime + 30000);
%>
<H1>Headline 1</H1>
More Text to output
```

This code snippet begins by making sure the *page session* variable is set to false; otherwise the rest of your efforts are useless. Next, you obtain the current time in milliseconds and store the value in the *currentTime* variable. Now the response object's setDateHeader() method is called, to add the Expires header. The first parameter indicates your desire to use the Expires HTTP header, and the second parameter is the value to be assigned to the Expires. The value is the current time plus 30 seconds, represented in total as milliseconds. The method handles converting the milliseconds into a time string outlined by the HTTP protocol. The remainder of the snippet is HTML and text to use with the page. When this page is served to a client's browser, Resin caches the page for a total of 30 seconds. At the next page request, the server checks the Expires time against the current time and obtains a new copy of the page if the current time is greater.

You can use the same type of code in a servlet. The following snippet shows how:

```
import javax.servlet.*;
import javax.servlet.http.*;
import java.io.*;

public class CacheServlet extends HttpServlet {

  public void doGet(HttpServletRequest request,
                    HttpServletResponse response)
    throws IOException, ServletException {

    long currentTime = System.currentTimeMillis();
    response.setDateHeader("Expires", currentTime + 30000);

    PrintWriter out = res.getWriter();

    out.println("<H1>Your News</H1>");
  }
}
```

Using If-Modified

Although its useful to set a specific expiration date on a file, another useful technique involves caching a page until it is modified on the server. You can use the If-Modified HTTP header to do this.

To use this technique, you override the getLastModified() method of a servlet or a JSP page. Here's what the code might look like for a servlet:

```
import javax.servlet.*;
import javax.servlet.http.*;
import java.io.*;

public class CacheServlet extends HttpServlet {

  public long getLastModified(HttpServletRequest request)  {
    return new
      File(request.getRealPath("news.jsp")).lastModified();
  }

  public void doGet(HttpServletRequest request,
                    HttpServletResponse response)
    throws IOException, ServletException {

    PrintWriter out = res.getWriter();

    out.println("<H1>Your News</H1>");
  }
}
```

The getLastModified() method is overridden. Within the method, the path to the server file news.jsp is obtained, a File object is created, and the lastModified() method is called. This method returns the last modified date, which is subsequently returned to the caller. Resin uses the method to determine whether the page on the server has been changed because the page in the cache was cached. A JSP page looks similar, as shown here:

```
<%@ page session=false %>
<%!
  public long getLastModified(HttpServletRequest request)  {
    return new File(request.getRealPath("news.jsp")).lastModified();
  }
%>
<H1>Headline 1</H1>
More Text to output
```

Using Cache-Mapping

If you want to store a page on the browser, you can include an Expires metatag using a server configuration option called cache-mapping. The

Expires metatag is applied to pages sent to the browser, but only if some rules are followed:

- The page must be cacheable.
- The If-Modified code must be applied as shown in the previous section.
- The browser Expires will have no effect on pages that automatically set the Expires HTTP header.

The configuration option looks like the following:

```
<web-app id='/'>
  <cache-mapping url-pattern='*.jpg'
                 expires='12h'/>
</web-app>
```

Here the configuration option is applied to all pages as noted by the id='/' attribute of the <web-app> element. The <cache-mapping> element says to apply the Expires metatag to all files with the extension JPG. The total cache time is 12 hours.

Setting Cache-Control

If you have a page that doesn't use sessions but you absolutely don't want it to be cached, you should use the Cache-Control HTTP header. Set the no-cache attribute with this code:

```
response.setHeader("Cache-Control","no-cache");
```

As of this writing, Resin only recognizes the no-cache attribute for the Cache-Control HTTP header. Resin ignores any other header combination for Cache-Control, and the internal cache is disabled. Recognizing and using the other attributes of the Cache-Control HTTP header have been submitted to Caucho as an enhancement request.

What's Next

In this chapter, we've explored how Web pages are cached and Resin's contribution to the caching. We showed you how to add caching capability to pages served by Resin. In Chapter 15, we will cover advanced configuration of Resin servers.

CHAPTER 15

Resin Server Configuration

If you've read all the pages in this book up to this chapter, you have gained quite a bit of experience with the Resin configuration file found in the installation's /conf directory. However, we have only scratched the surface of the available options. In this chapter, our goal is to present the entire Resin configuration file, the possible settings, and how they affect the execution of the server and supported applications. In areas such as databases and logging, we will point you to the appropriate chapters where the information is covered.

Details of resin.conf

The Resin configuration file is commonly found in the /conf directory of the installation path. By default, the filename is resin.conf. If you need to use a different configuration file (such as in a development situation), you can tell the server about the new file using the –conf *<filename>* command-line option. For example:

```
httpd.exe –conf c:\resinconfs\dev.conf
```

When you open the configuration file, all the information is provided as XML elements, attributes, and associated values.

XML Elements

You can add comments to the configuration file using the <!-- --> combination:

```
<!-- this is a comment -->
Comments can also span multiple rows
<!-- this is a comment
    - on multiple lines
-->
```

The XML in the configuration file can be used in both canonical and attribute formats. Consider the following XML element layout:

```
<root>
     <sub> value </sub>
</root>
```

The same information can be converted to use attributes and represent the same hierarchy and data:

```
<root sub='value' />
```

Environments

The Resin configuration incorporates the concept of an environment. Environments are allowed to incorporate element tags that relate to resources or properties which might change from host to host or Web application to Web application. Some of the high-level information that can be incorporated in an environment includes:

- Classloaders
- Resources
- Logs
- Properties
- JNDI
- Other miscellanous tags

In this chapter we discuss a variety of tags, pointing out which ones can appear in environments and which ones cannot. The environments are defined within the <resin>, <server>, <host-default>, <host> and <web-app-default>, and <web-app> elements. When there are multiple environments, an inner environment will inherit the parent elements.

High-Level Configuration Format

To give you a feel for the amount of configuration information that can be stored in the Resin configuration file, Listing 15.1 shows the high-level elements under the root element. Of particular note is the <web-app> element hierarchy. All the information in this element can be placed in the web.xml files found in each Web application's WEB-INF directory. Only the high-level <web-app> with the ID attributes needs to be in the Resin configuration file.

```
<resin xmlns="http://caucho.com/us/resin">
  <database>
  </database>
  <server>
    <host-default>
    </host-default>
    <resin:include path="app-default.xml"/>
    <host>
      <web-app>
      </web-app>
    </host>
  </server>
</resin>
```

Listing 15.1 Resin configuration high-level hierarchy.

Using #include and app-default.xml

If you look at any of the Resin configuration files, you will see that they can be large and cumbersome. The developer or system administrator has the option of breaking apart the configuration file into smaller chunks by using the resin:include statement. The <resin:include> tag will automatically pull in the contents of the provided file name and place them where the tag is located. Looking at Listing 15.1, you will see a <resin:include> tag has been used to pull in a file called app-default.xml.

The app-default.xml file is usually placed in the same directory as resin.conf. The file contains an environment for all Web applications hosted by Resin. The idea behind the file is to place default information that all Web applications will be able to use without defining their own tags. If a Web application needs to override a tag value, it just places a duplicate in its <web-app> element. Since Resin works in environments, the <web-app> environment will override the default environment.

Default Path Values

Throughout the configuration file are attributes for defining an id or href path. The value for the href/id can be an absolute path or a relative one. Resin also defines a number of global variables that you can use in the path definition. In addition to the following variables, the paths can contain JSP-EL expressions:

- **$resin_home**—The default installation directory of the Resin server.
- **$server-root**—The root of the server instance.
- **$host-root**—When used with the <host> element, contains the application directory.
- **$app-dir**—When used with the <web-app> element, contains the application directory.
- **$var**—The value for System.getProperty("var").

Tag Definitions

In the remainder of this chapter, each of the tags defined in the Resin configuration will be outlined. An attempt has been made to keep the tags separated by their placement in the Resin configuration file and environments but realize that many of the tags can cross environments. This fact will be noted where appropriate.

Common Environment Tags

The environment defined within Resin has the following format:

Classloaders

- class-loader
- compiling-loader
- library-loader
- make-loader
- simple-loader

Clustering

- cluster
- cluster-definition

Resources

- database
- ejb-server
- env-entry
- jndi-link
- reference
- resource
- resource-ref

Logging

- log
- stderr-log
- stdout-log

Authenticator

- authenticator

Miscellaneous

- system-property
- javac
- dependency-check-interval
- character-encoding
- case-insensitive
- temp-dir
- work-dir

As stated previously, environments can appear under the tags: <resin>, <server>, <host-default>, <host> and <web-app-default>, and <web-app>. The details of each tag are discussed in the following section.

<class-loader>

Element defines a dynamic classloader for the current environment. There are four possible sub-elements: compiling-loader, library-loader, make-loader, and simple-loader. For example, the following uses the <compiling-loader> subelement.

```
<class-loader>
    <compiling-loader path="WEB-INF/classes"/>
</class-loader>
```

<compiling-loader>

Element which automatically compiles Java code into CLASS files; it has five attributes associated with it:

- **path**—path for the loader.
- **source**—directory for java source.
- **args**—arguments to pass to the Java compiler.
- **encoding**—internationalization encoding for the Java compiler.
- **require-source**—if true all CLASS files without Java code will be removed (default is false).

<library-loader>

Element adds JAR files found to the CLASSPATH; it has a single attribute:

- **path**—path where loader should look for JAR files.

<make-loader>

Element which configures a make-style loader; it is currently undefined.

<simple-loader>

Element which loads CLASS files without compiling; it has two attributes:

- **path**—path for the loader.
- **prefix**—class package prefix to filter those classes found.

<cluster>

Element defines a cluster of Resin server for load balancing – defined in Chapter 19, "Load Balancing and Reliability." There are four attributes for <cluster>:

- **id**—identifier for naming the cluster.
- **srun**—configures the srun port and protocol for cluster server.
- **cluster-group**—configuration for sub-clusters.
- **cluster-ref**—identifier of a previous defined cluster.

<cluster-definition>

This element defines a cluster to be referenced from a <cluster> element; its attributes are:

- **id**—identifier for naming the cluster.
- **srun**—configures the srun port and protocol for cluster server.
- **cluster-group**—configuration for sub-clusters.

Resources

Resources are components such as a database used by a web-application, host, or the server. Since they exist in an environment, each web-application can defined their own resources, including resources that override previously defined defaults.

<database>

The <database> element is primarily designed to define database pooling configurations. The defined resource is a DataSource in a JNDI context as well as ServletContext. You should place the database JDBC driver associated with the resource in either the system classpath or the /lib directory associated with the Resin server installation. You can also place the driver in the WEB-INF/lib or WEB-INF/classes directory, but this is a secondary choice.

The <database> element has numerous sub-elements for defining the database resource.

- **<jndi-name>**—the JNDI path relative to java:comp/env.
- **<driver>**—the JDBC driver class (required).

    <url>—the location of the database as either an IP, localhost, or domain name. (Required)

    <type>—the type of database driver being used.

- **<user>**—the username to use when connecting to the database. Default is an empty string.
- **<password>**—the password to use when connecting to the database. Default is an empty string.
- **<max-connections>**—the maximum number of allowed connections to the database. Default is 20.
- **<max-idle-time>**—the maximum amount of time an idle connection is kept open. Default is 30 seconds.
- **<connection-wait-time>**—the total amount of time the system waits for an idle connection to be returned to the database pool. Default is 10 minutes.
- **<max-overflow-connections>**—the number of possible connections to keep in an overflow state while waiting for an idle connection. This assumes the connection wait time has timed out. Default is 0.
- **<ping-table>**—a table to be used for a simple ping test. A value of false disables the ping test.
- **<ping-on-reuse>**-defines whether the database should be pinged through a connection before the connection is provided to the application. Default is false.
- **<ping-on-free>**—defines whether a connection should be tested before replacing the connection in the pool. Default is false.
- **<ping-on-idle>**—defines whether a connection should be randomly tested for a live connection. Default is false.
- **<xa>**—defines whether pooling is performed on the database. Values are true and false.

<ejb-server>

This element is used to define a CMP server for using EJBs under Resin. For example,

```
<ejb-server jndi-name="java:comp/env/cmp">
    <data-source>java:comp/env/jdbc/AccountsDB</data-source>
</ejb-server>
```

The attributes for the CMP server are provided using the <init-param> element. The available parameters are shown in Table 15.1.

Table 15.1 <init-param> Parameters

PARAMETER	DEFAULT	MEANING
auto-compile	true	EJB code will be automatically generated
config-directory	Directory to search for *.ejb files	WEB-INF
create-database-schema	false	if tables for entity beans aren't in the database—create them
data-source	java:comp/env/jdbc/test	JNDI name
entity-cache-size	8192	total entity beans cached
entity-cache-timeout	inf.	Total time a bean is cached
resin-isolation	database	if database then use database's isolation, otherwise row-locking
jdbc-isolation	db default	the JDBC isolation for an update
transaction-timeout	60	timeout for a transaction
queue-connection-factory	none	JNDI name for QueueConnectionFactory
topic-connection-factory	none	JNDI name for TopicConnectionFactor

<env-entry>

When a non-servlet class needs access to a JNDI parameter, you can use <env-entry> to define the parameter. The parameters and associated values are accessible from within an application. You can define as many <env-entry> elements as needed for the environment. The element has three attributes:

- **env-entry-name**—an entry name defined as a JNDI path relative to java:comp/env.
- **env-entry-type**—the Java type of the value in the env-entry-value attribute.
- **env-entry-value**—the JDNI variable value.

Here's an example of a JNDI-defined variable:

```
<resin>
  <env-entry env-entry-name='server' env-entry-type='java.lang.String'
env-entry-value='internal.company.com' />
</resin>
```

This code can be used to access the variable:

```
Context c = (Context) new InitialContext().lookup("java:comp/env");
String server = (String) c.lookup("server");
```

<jndi-link>

The <jndi-link> element lets Resin instantiate external EJBs defined in foreign containers. For a large number of examples, including Hessian, Burlap, WebLogic, CORBA, Inprise, Orion, jBoss, and JOnAS, check www.caucho.com/resin/ref/ejb.xtp. The attributes of <jndi-link> are as follows:

- **jndi-name**—the pathname for the link.
- **property-file**—a property used to obtain the context.
- **factory**—the name of the factory class used to instantiate beans.
- **init-param**—values used to obtain the initial context.
- **foreign-name**—the path used for the foreign context.

<reference>

This element is used when a JDNI ObjectFactory is needed by the server, host or web-application. For example,

```
<reference>
  <jndi-name>accounts/link</jndi-name>
  <factory>accounts.LinkFactory</factory>
  <init url="http://localhost:8080/accounts/link"/>
        type="account.LinkHome"/>
</reference>
```

The attributes for the element are:

- **jndi-name**—JDBC name.
- **factory**—class name for Factory.
- **init**—initialization for the instantiation for the factory.

<resource>

This element will create a bean that can be instantiated and accessed within an application. The implementation class must be bean compliant. The beans created are stored in JDBC. For example:

```
<resource name="env/login">
  <type>app.RegisterForm</type>
  <init>
    <username>all</username>
    <password>none</password>
  </init>
</resource>
```

The attributes for the element are

- **name**—resource name.
- **type**—Bean class.
- **init**—Bean-style initialization.

Logging

Logging can be defined within the environment and redefined at lower levels as needed for a web-applicaton or a host.

<log>

This element defines logging using JDK 1.4 Logging. A description of the element can be found in Chapter 2 under the section "Logging in Resin."

<stderr-log>

When an application produces output using System.err, the corresponding text is directed to a system file. The < stderr_log> element has the following attributes:

- **path**—the path and filename for the output file.
- **rollover-period**—the time period that can elapse before the log file is rolled over. Values are in days (D), weeks (W), or months (M). Default is no rollover. (Optional)

- **rollover-size**—the maximum size of the log file before it is rolled over. Rollover occurs if the size reaches the maximum before the rollover period is reached. Default is 1 megabyte.
- **timestamp**—a timestamp defined in format from Table 2.3 add to each line.

The following example illustrates use of the stderr-log <host> element level. There is no <log> element. The file storecomstderr.log stores the output from stderr for all Web applications defined in the store.com host:

```
<host id='store.com'>
<stderr-log path='/opt/logs/storecomstderr.log'
rollover-period='1W' rollover-size='10M'/>
</host>
```

<stdout-log>

When an application produces output using System.out, the corresponding text cannot be displayed on a console (in a production setting, there is no console window). The <stdout-log> element has four attributes:

- **path**—the path and filename for the output file. (Required)
- **rollover-period**—the time period that can elapse before the log file is rolled over. Values are in days (D), weeks (W), or months (M). Default is no rollover. (Optional)
- **rollover-size**—the maximum size of the log file before it is rolled over. Rollover occurs if the size reaches the maximum before the rollover period is reached. Default is 1 megabyte.
- **timestamp**—a timestamp defined in format from Table 2.3 add to each line.

The following example illustrates the use of stdout-log. The file storecomstd-out. log stores the output from stdout for all Web applications defined in the store.com host:

```
<host id='store.com'>
<stdout-log path='/opt/logs/storecomstdout.log'
rollover-period='1W' rollover-size='10M'/>
</host>
```

You can also have individual files for Web applications:

```
<web-app id='/storefront'>
<stdout-log path='/opt/logs/storefrontstdout.log'
rollover-period='1W' rollover-size='10M'/>
</web-app>
```

<access-log>

All requests to the Resin server can be logged at various server levels. For each request, you can create configurable output to display the information important to you. The <access-log> element can be defined at several levels of the hierarchy:

- At the <web-app> level, all requests for the designated application are output to the specified log file.
- At the <host> level, all requests for the designated host are output to the specified log file if <access-log> isn't defined at the <web-app> level.
- At the <http-server> level, all requests for the designated host are output to the specified log file if <access-log> isn't defined at the <web-app> or <host> level.

The <access-log> element has six attributes:

- **path**—defines the path and filename for the log file. The log is relative to $RESIN_HOME. (Required)
- **format**—defines the format of the output to the log. The individual values are shown after this list and follow the Apache standard. Default string is "%h %l %u %t \"%r\" %>s %b \"%{Referer}i\" \"%{User-Agent}i\"". (Required)
- **rollover-period**—the time period that can elapse before the log file is rolled over. Values are in days (D), weeks (W), or months (M). Default is no rollover. (Optional)
- **rollover-size**—the maximum size of the log file before it is rolled over. Rollover occurs if the size reaches the maximum before the rollover period is reached. Default is 1 megabyte.
- **bean-class**—allows a custom developer-created class for logging. The class must implement AbstractAccessLog. No default.
- **init**—parameters are passed to the log as bean parameters and are accessible from a class that implements AbstractAccessLog.
- **archive-format**—name used for archive files.

The format attribute defines how each request appears in the log file. Before we show you all the options, consider the following example of an access-log definition for all pages in a storefront Web application:

```
<web-app id='\storefront'>
  <access-log id='e:/log/access.log' rollover-period='10D' format='%h
%r"/>
</web-app>
```

The output is stored in a file called access.log in a /log directory on the E: drive. Each request from a client browser records the remote IP address and the requested URL. The format values are as follows:

- %**b**—Result content length.
- %**h**—Remote IP address.
- **%{*X*}I**—Request header *X*.
- **%{*X*}o**—Response header *X*.
- **%{*X*}c**—Cookie value *X*.
- **%n**—Request attribute.
- **%r**--Request URL.
- **%s**—Status code.
- **%{*X*}t**—Request date with optional time format string.
- **%T**—Time of request in seconds.
- **%u**—Remote user.
- **%U**—RequestedURI.

Authenticator

Authentication be defined globally for the server or host and redefined as needed by a web-application.

<authenticator>

This element will define a authentication resource in the current environment. The authenticator uses a class that extends com.caucho.server.security. AbstractAuthenticator. For example:

```
<authenticator>
<jndi-name>accounts/login</jndi-name>
<class>AccountAuthenticator</class>
<init>
  <configtype>5</configtype>
</init>
```

The attribute for the element are

- **name**—JDBC name for the authenticator – default is /caucho/auth.
- **class**—class for the authenticator.
- **init**—Javabean style configuration.

Miscellaneous

For following elements aren't specific to any host or application but provide miscellaneous information to the server.

<system-property>

The Resin server lets you set system properties in the configuration file using the <system-property> element:

```
<resin>
  <system-property titleClr='red' />
  <system-property maxConn='60' />
</resin>
```

<javac>

The most important external application used by the Resin server is a Java compiler. Each time a servlet or JSP is accessed, the Java compiler may need to compile the code. Every code change definitely invokes the compiler. In a development environment, the compiler associated with the Java Development Kit (JDK) is perfectly suitable to the task. However, in a production situation, we recommend a faster compiler. One of the best Java compilers is IBM's Jikes (www-124.ibm.com/developerworks/oss/jikes/); if you install this compiler, you should use it instead of the JDK compiler.

By default, the Resin server uses the internal compiler found in the JDK, as noted by the <javac> element provided in the resin.conf file:

```
<javac compiler="internal" compiler-args=""/>
```

The <java> element is found in the <caucho.com> root element and has three attributes:

- **compiler**—defines the path to a specific Java compiler to be used with the system or *internal* for the JDK compiler. Default is *internal.*
- **args**—compiler arguments to be passed through to the compiler as needed. No default.
- **encoding**—the character encoding used. No default.
- **max-compile-time**—the total time the Resin server will allow for the compiling of an application. Default is 30 seconds.

Here's an example of a <java> configuration using Jikes:

```
<resin>
  <java compiler='e:/jikes/jikes' compiler-args='-g' max-compile-
time='60' />
</resin>
```

<dependency-check-interval>

This element defines how often the environment contexts will be checked for changes. The default is every 2 seconds. For deployment, use a larger value like 60s or 1h.

<case-insensitive>

If you have worked with both UNIX and Windows, you know that UNIX is case-sensitive and Windows is not. For both the <servlet-mapping> and <filter-mapping> elements, matches need to be made on URLs. The Resin server can treat the matching in a case-sensitive or case-insensitive manner. The default is true for Windows and false for Unix. These defaults can be changed as needed:

```
<web-app>
  <case-sensitive>true</case-sensitive>
</web-app>
```

<temp-dir>

A temporary directory is available to all Web applications and associated with the variable javax.servlet.context.tempdir. The default value for the temporary directory is WEB-INF/tmp. You can change the directory for each Web application using this format:

```
<web-app>
  <temp-dir>e:/$app-dir/app/temp</tmp-dir>
</web-app>
```

In a servlet, you can obtain the temporary directory using the following code:

```
File dir = (File) getServletContext().getAttribute("javax.servlet.con-
text.tempdir");
```

<work-dir>

All Web applications have an associated work directory for placement of server-compiled code. The default directory is WEB-INF/work. To change the directory, use the <work-dir> element:

```
<web-app>
  <work-dir>e:/$app-dir/app/work</tmp-dir>
</web-app>
```

Web-App Tags

Web applications are key to the use of Resin; therefore, there are quite a few tags available to configure their operation. The tags are divided into two areas: basic configuration and servlet definitions.

Basic Configuration

<web-app-default>

This element defines specific elements that are designed to be used for all Web applications. All of the elements defined earlier for the <web-app> can be used within this element. The <web-app-default> element can be used within <server>, <host-default>, and <host>.

<web-app-deploy>

This element is used to define the directory where a WAR file is expanded. The attributes available are:

- **path**—path to the webapp directory.
- **url-prefix**—prefix to add to all expanded webapps.
- **expand-path**—directory where WAR files are expanded.
- **lazy-init**—if true, then Web applications should be initialized only when first requested by a user. Default is false.

<web-app>

This element defines a new web-application to be used in the system. The sub-element can include those for an environment listed above, as well as the elements under the section "Servlet 2.4 Definitions" below.

<cache-mapping>

When you set up a cache on the Resin server, specific pages in a Web application can be assigned different cache intervals. Basically, the <cache-mapping> element enables the developer or system administrator to control an application's pages in the cache for better management. The elements attributes are:

- **url-pattern**—a pattern for matching a specific URL.
- **url-regexp**—a regular expression for matching a URL.
- **expires**—a time interval representing the number of seconds a page lives in the cache. The value in the attribute can use the following time values: seconds (S), minutes (M), hours (H), and days (D). There is currently no default time for the expires attribute. Defaults to seconds.

The following example shows how to use the <cache-mapping> element to keep pages in the cache for different periods of time:

```
<web-app id='\store'>
  <cache-mapping
    url-pattern='\storefront\*.jsp'
    expires='120S' />
```

```
  <cache-mapping
    url-pattern='\storefront\images\*'
    expires='15M' />
</web-app>
```

<path-mapping>

The <path-mapping> element maps URL patterns to a real path value. The attributes in the element are:

- **url-pattern**—the string used to match a URL.
- **url-regexp**—the regular expression to match a URL.
- **real-path**—the real path. Can use variables from a regular expression.

Here's an example:

```
<web-app id='/store'>
  <path-mapping
    url-pattern='/storefront'
    real-path='e:/webs/store' />
</web-app>
```

<strict-mapping >

By default, the Resin server lets a <servlet-mapping> violate the Servlet 2.4 specification by allowing .jsp extension paths like /store/my.jsp/storefront.jsp. To ensure strict Servlet 2.4 <servlet-mapping> elements, set the value to true. For example:

```
<web-app>
  <strict-mapping>true</stict-mapping>
</web-app>
```

Servlet 2.4 Definitions

<description>

This tag is currently not defined.

<display-name>

This tag is currently not defined.

<distributable>

This tag is currently not defined.

<context-param>

When you need to define variables for a Web application at the server level, you can put them in the resin.conf or web.xml file using <context-param>. Any number of variables may be added to the configuration files. This element has two attributes:

- **param-name**—the name of the variable.
- **param-value**—the value of the variable.

There are two ways to add the <context-param> element:

```
<web-app id='/storefront'>
  <context-param max='50' />
  <context-param>
    <param-name>title</param-name>
    <param-value>My New Store</param-value>
  </context-param>
</web-app>
```

<filter>

When you need to define a filter, you can use the <filter> element to create an alias commonly used in a <filter-mapping>. The <filter> element associates a filter class with a common alias name. The attributes available in the <filter> element are as follows:

- **filter-name**—the filter name or alias.
- **filter-class**—the actual filter class to associated with the alias name.
- **init-param**—initialization parameters for the filter class.

As example of using the <filter> element appears in the <filter-mapping> section that follows.

<filter-mapping>

The <filter-mapping> element is designed to match a URL-pattern and a filter. When a URL is found that matches the URL pattern, the listed alias is matched with a filter class and the filter is applied. The <filter-mapping> element contains six attributes:

- **url-pattern**—a pattern for matching a specific URL.
- **url-regexp**—a regular expression for matching a URL.
- **filter-name**—the servlet name to match, thus combining the functionality of the filter with the <servlet-mapping> element.
- **dispatcher**—Multiple <dispatcher> tags are allowed. REQUEST, INCLUDE, FORWARD, and ERROR are defined. If no <dispatcher> is defined, the filter-mapping uses REQUEST.

- **filter-name**—either an alias defined in a <filter> element or a specific servlet class.

Here's an example of using the <filter-mapping> element:

```
<web-app>
  <filter
    filter-name='product-filter'
    filter-class='store.product-filter' />
  <filter-mapping
    url-pattern='/products/*'
    filter-name='product-filter' />
</web-app>
```

<listener>

This tag is currently not defined.

<servlet>

The Resin server allows a servlet to be mapped from a URL pattern to a specific servlet. For example, the string /storefront.html should be mapped to a servlet called storefront, which in turn represents a servlet class store.storefront. The <servlet> element is used to associate a servlet name with a specific servlet class called an *alias*. The attributes for <servlet> are:

- **servlet-name**—the servlet name.
- **servlet-class**—the name of the servlet's class. Default is the servlet-name value.
- **init-param**—necessary initialization parameters for the servlet.
- **load-on-startup**—defines whether the servlet should be instantiated and initialized upon server start.
- **run-at**—determines when the server should be automatically executed. Examples include 3:00, 3:15, and so on.

Here's an example of an alias for a time servlet that runs at 1:00 a.m. each morning:

```
<web-app id='/utilities''>
  <servlet
    servlet-name='time'
    servlet-class='time.utilities.setup'
    run-at='1:00'
  />
</web-app>
```

<servlet-mapping>

As mentioned earlier, you can map a URL to a servlet using the <servlet-mapping> element. This means you can define a URL pattern like \store* to execute a servlet. The element has four attributes:

- **servlet-name**—name of servlet.
- **url-pattern**—the url pattern to match.
- **url-regexp**—the url pattern to match based on a regular expression.
- **servlet-name**—the servlet name can using replacement vars or the name.

For example:

```
<web-app>
  <servlet
    servlet-name='storefront'
    servlet-class='store.storefront'
    run-at='1:00'
  />

  <servlet-mapping>
    <url-pattern>\store*</url-pattern>
    <servlet-name>storefront</servlet-name>
  </servlet-mapping>
<web-app>
```

You can combine the <servlet> and <servlet-mapping> elements into one. Here's an example:

```
<web-app>
  <servlet-mapping
    url-pattern='\store*'
    servlet-class='store.storefront' />
<web-app>
```

<session-config>

When a Web application uses sessions, you can use the <session-config> element to configure how the sessions act and maintain themselves. The attributes available in the element are as follows:

- **session-timeout**—the length of time before a session times out. Default is 30 minutes.
- **session-max**—the maximum number of active sessions allowed. Default is 4096.
- **enable-cookies**—defines whether cookies are used with sessions. Default is true.

- **enable-url-rewriting**—defines whether URL rewriting may occur. Set enable-cookies to false to force URL rewriting. Default is true.
- **cookie-version**—the current cookie spec used for sessions. Default is 1.0.
- **cookie-domain**—the cookie domain. Default is none.
- **cookie-max-age**—the maximum age allowed for session cookies. Default is none.
- **cookie-length**—the maximum length of a cookie. Default is integer.MAX_VALUE.
- **file-store**—defines whether a file store should be used for sessions.
- **jdbc-store**—defines whether a JDBC store should be used for sessions.
- **tcp-store**—defines whether a distributed ring should be used for sessions.
- **always-load-session**—defines whether session data should be reloaded upon each request. Default is false.
- **always-save-session**—defines whether session data should be saved upon each request. Default is false.
- **save-on-shutdown**—defines whether session data should be saved only on shutdown. Default is false.
- **reuse-session-id**—defines whether a session id should be reused regardless of whether the session has timed out. Default is true.
- **ignore-serialization-errors**—defines whether objects that don't implement java.io.Serializable should be ignored when a session is saved. Default is false.
- **persistant-path**—TBD.
- **cluster-store**—if persistent sessions are used, the cluster will be used for storage.
- **invalidate-after-listener**—TBD.

<mime-mapping>

Most of the popular file extensions have automatic mime-types associated with them, as found in com.caucho.server.http.Application. If you have specific file extensions that need to be associated by the server, use the <mime-mapping> element. The element has two attributes:

- **extension**—a url to match.
- **mime-type**—the mime-type to associate with the specific extension.

As an example, the following element associates the extension .xxm to an html mime-type:

```
<web-app>
  <mime-mapping
    extension='.xxm'
    mime-type='text/html' />
</web-app>
```

<welcome-file-list>

The <welcome-file-list> element defines the pages that can be used when the user doesn't specify an actual filename. A user typically enters the URL www.mycompany.com and expects a page to be returned. By default, the Resin server attempts to find three different pages: index.xtp, index.jsp, or index.html. If none of these files are found, a 404 error is returned. This element enables you to define other pages as defaults using one or more <welcome-file> elements. Here's an example:

```
<web-app id='/storefront'>
 <welcome-file-list>
  <welcome-file>store.html</welcome-file>
  <welcome-file>store.jsp</welcome-file>
  <welcome-file>storefront.jsp</welcome-file>
 </welcome-file-list>
</web-app>
```

The files can also be listed as follows:

```
<web-app id='/storefront'>
  <welcome-file-list>store.html, store.jsp, storefront.jsp />
</web-app>
```

<error-page>

As you've seen several times in previous chapters, the default behavior for Resin as well as other application and Web servers when an error occurs in a page request is to display a generic 404- or 500-type error. The error information may include a stack dump in the case of servlets. Although errors do occur, you don't want to scare users with such a dull error presentation. Instead, you can provide a page that looks like the rest of the site and offers users help with the error. The <error-page> element allows this type of flexibility. The attributes in the element are as follows:

- **location**—defines the path and filename of the error page.
- **exception-type**—causes the location page to be executed when the specified exception is thrown.
- **error-code**—causes the location page to be executed when the specified HTTP status code is found.

The following example shows how to catch some of the more common errors:

```
<web-app id='/'>
    <error-page
     error-code='404'
           location='/errorpages/file_not_found.html'/>
    <error-page
            exception-type='java.lang.NullPointerException'
           location='/errorpages/nullpointer.html'/>
</web-app>
```

<jsp-config>

This tag is currently not defined.

<resource-env-ref>

This tag is currently not defined.

<message-destination-ref>

This tag is currently not defined.

<resource-ref>

This tag is currently not defined.

<security-constraint>

The developer of a site doesn't necessarily have to use authentication to secure areas of the Web site; you can use the <security-constraint> element. The element includes several subelements:

- **<web-resource-collection>**—Defines which areas of a site have a restriction. This element has two attributes:

  url-pattern—the directory and possible files to be restricted.

  method—HTTP methods to be restricted.

- **<user-data-constraint>**—defines the transports that must be used to access the restricted files. It has one attribute:

  transport-guarantee—the transport type: NONE, INTEGRAL, or CONFIDENTIAL. SSL requires the CONFIDENTIAL value.

- **<auth-constraint>**—used when authenticated users have a role. The single attribute is as follows:

  role-name—the role that has access to the restricted area.

- **<ip-constraint>**—the IP addresses that can access the restricted areas.
- **<constraint>**—defines a custom constrait. The attributes are:

  class-name—a class that extends com.caucho.http.security.AbstractConstraint.

  init-param—initialization parameters.

<security-role>

This tag is currently not defined.

<env-entry>

This tag is currently not defined.

<ejb-ref>

This tag is currently not defined.

<ejb-local-ref>

This tag is currently not defined.

<message-destination>

This tag is currently not defined.

<locale-encoding-mapping-list>

This tag is currently not defined.

<deployment-extension>

This tag is currently not defined.

Application and Server Tags

<web-app-deploy>

When the WAR files are expanded, they are expanded into the <web-app-deploy> directory. If you don't want the expanded WARs in the same directory as the WARs themselves, use the <war-expand-dir> element to define where they should be expanded. Just like the <web-app-deploy> element, the <war-expand-dir> element is relative to $RESIN_HOME.

<character-encoding>

The default character encoding for Resin is ISO-8859-1. To change the encoding, use the <character-encoding> element:

```
<web-app>
  <character-encoding>UTF-16</character-encoding>
</web-app>
```

<dependency-check-interval>

The Resin server automatically checks to determine whether any configuration file has changed on the server and it should force a reload. The default value is 2 seconds; you should set this value as low as possible for development servers. When a server is moved to a production phase, the interval should be much higher because of the overhead associated with checking for new code. You can change the value using the <dependency-check-interval> element:

```
<web-app>
  <dependency-check-interval>2D</dependency-check-interval>
</web-app>
```

The interval value can use seconds (S), minutes (M), or days (D).

<taglib>

If you have a tab library for a Web application, you can use the <taglib> element to configure the library. The element attributes are:

- **taglib-uri**—the matching URI for the tag library.
- **taglib-location**—the path to the actual tag library, relative to classpath; typically the tag library is found in WEB-INF/classes.

Here's an example:

```
<web-app>
  <taglib
    taglib-uri-'/storefront/store'
    taglib-location='/store.tld'/>
</web-app>
```

<description>

This element describes the Web application and current has no functionality. The following example uses both <display-name> and <description>:

```
<web-app>
  <display-name>My Store Front</display-name>
<description>This is the store front servlet</description>
</web-app>
```

<multipart-form>

In order for Resin to handle multipart forms and file uploads, you must use the <multipart-form> element to enable support. By default, the server does not support multipart forms and file uploads. If the upload limit is exceeded or uploads are disabled, a caucho.multipart.form.error exception is thrown. The element has two attributes:

- **enable**—defines whether support is available. A value of true indicates support.
- **upload-max**—the maximum size of an upload in kilobytes. Default is no limit.

For example, support can be enabled with the following element:

```
<web-app>
  <multipart-form
    enable='true'
    upload-max='1024' />
</web-app>
```

<browser-mapping>

As you know, not all browsers are created equal. If you determine that some of your users are using a browser that needs HTTP/1.0 tags instead of 1.2 or later, you can list these browsers as troublesome using the <browser-mapping> element. The attributes available in this element are:

- **regexp**—a regular expression to match the User-Agent HTTP header.
- **force10**—if found in the element, forces HTTP/1.0.

There is no default <browser-mapping>, but the default resin.conf file includes four commented elements:

```
<browser-mapping regexp="MSIE 4\.0b2" force10/>
<browser-mapping regexp="RealPlayer 4\.0" force10/>
<browser-mapping regexp="Java/1\\.0" force10/>
<browser-mapping regexp="JDK/1\\.0" force10/>
```

<lazy-init>

Resin's default behavior is to load all Web application when the server starts and automatically execute those servlets whose <load-on-init> elements are defined. Here's an example:

```
<web-app>
  <lazy-init>true</lazy-init>
</web-app>
```

<app-dir>

By default, a Web application has a home directory with the same name as the <web-app> element's id attribute. If you need to change the application directory, use the <app-dir> element. The attributes for the element are as follows:

- **id**—the prefix from the URL matching the Web application.
- **url-regexp**—a regular expression to match a URL.
- **app-dir**—default is a subdirectory using the id attribute. The root directory for the Web application.

For example:

```
<host id='company.com'>
  <web-app
    id='/store'
    app-dir='/usr/home/webs/store' />
</host>
```

<secure>

If a Web application can only be accessed from a secure connection, you should set the <secure> element to true. For example:

```
<web-app>
  <secure>true</secure>
</web-app>
```

<regexp>

The Resin server allows the use of regular expressions to match information passed to the application. One such use is the ID of a <host> element. For example:

```
<host
  regexp='([^/]*).company.com'
  doc-dir='e:/pages/$1/docs' />
```

The regular expressions are based on Perl5 with 16-bit strings. You can find more information at www.caucho.com/resin/jsref/regexp.xtp.

<url-character-encoding>

You can use the <url-character-encoding> element to specify the character encoding used by the server to decode an incoming URL. The default is utf-8. To change the encoding as needed, use the element as follows:

```
<host>
  <url-character-encoding>UTF-16</url-character-encoding>
</host>
```

<host>

The <host> element defines specific hosts in an <http-server> element. When a request is made on the server, a match is attempted with all the <host> elements. If a match is found, the configuration for the matched <host> is used. Default is the <server> <root-directory> value. The attributes of the <host> element are:

- **id**—the host name. (Required)
- **regexp**—a regular expression to be used to match an incoming host.
- **root-directory**—defines the root directory for this host.
- **document-directory**—defines the document directory for this host.

If a regular expression is used, you can use replacement variables. Here's an example:

```
<server>
  <host-name="www.mycompany.com, mycompany.com">
  <root-directory>hosts/mycompany</root-directory>
</server>
```

<port>

This element specifies the port the HTTP or srun should listen to. Most HTTP Web servers listen to port 80.

<http>

The Resin server requires the definition of a port for HTTP requests and potentially a port for secure requests. The <http> element handles the definition using a number of attributes:

- **id**—the name of the identifier.
- **host**—the name of the host listening for requests; not needed if localhost. Defaults to all interfaces.
- **port**—the port the server should listen to for requests.
- **openssl** and **jsse-ssl**—defines option for openssl or jsse-ssl.

  ssl—defines whether SSL is enabled.

  ssl2—defines whether SSLv2 is enabled.

  ssl3—defines whether SSLv3 is enabled.

  tls1—defines whether TLSv1 is enabled.

  key-store-type—defines the JSSE key store type. Applies only to jsse-ssl. Default is jks.

key-store-file—defines the JSSE file with certificates. Applies only to jsse-ssl.

password—defines the password needed to access certificates. Also defines an OpenSSL password needed for the key file.

certificate-chain-file—defines an OpenSSL certificate chain.

certificate-file—defines an OpenSSL certificate.

certificate-key-file—defines an OpenSSL key file.

crypto-device—defines the OpenSSL engine.

<srun>

You can designate multiple machines for srun load balancing. To add machines, use multiple <srun> elements. The attributes defined in the element are:

- **id**—the srun identifier.
- **host**—the host when srun is available.
- **port**—the port for the specified host.
- **backup**—backup server definition.

For examples of <srun> see Chapter 19, "Load Balancing and Reliability."

<thread-max>

As requests are sent to the Resin server, threads are spawned to handle the processing. The default number of threads for the server is 200. You can change the thread count with the <thread-max> element:

```
<server>
  <thread-max>500</thread-max>
<server>
```

<thread-min>

Just as there is a maximum number of processing threads, there is also a minimum. The default is five threads, but you can change this value with the <thread-min> element:

```
<server>
  <thread-min>50</thread-min>
</server>
```

<thread-keepalive>

In situations where an external Web server is used to handle page requests and Resin is used to handle JSPs/servlets, you must use a socket connection to pass information between the applications. These sockets are called *keepalive connections*. Resin attempts to reuse the connections as much as possible. The element <thread-keepalive> determines the total number of threads that can be used in the connections. The default is 100; you can change the value as follows:

```
<server>
  <thread-keepalive>500</thread-keepalive>
</server>
```

<request-timeout>

The server waits a default time of 30 seconds for a request. Once the timeout has expired, the request is interrupted. To change the request timeout, use the <request-timeout> element:

```
<server>
  <request-timeout>120s</request-timeout>
</server>
```

<live-time>

When the Resin server is in a load-balancing situation, the <live-time> element determines how long an idle srun connection remains open. When the timeout expires (the default is 10 seconds), the connection is closed. The <live-time> value must be less than <request-timeout>. Here's an example:

```
<server>
     <live-time>60s</live-time>
</server>
```

<dead-time>

As discussed in Chapter 19, "Load Balancing and Reliability," once a server is determined to be dead, the other servers wait a default of five seconds before retrying the potentially dead server. This value can be changed with the <dead-time> element:

```
<serve>
  <dead-time>10s</dead-time>
</server>
```

<connect-timeout>

The Resin server waits a default time period of 30 seconds for a connection between the Web server and the Resin srun. If the timeout is exceeded, the server gives up on the connection. You can change the timeout with the <connect-timeout> element:

```
<http-server>
  <connect-timeout>60s</connect-timeout>
</http-server>
```

<timeout-interval>

The Resin server initiates a disconnection from the client after a default time of 60 seconds. You can use the <timeout-interval> element to change the timeout:

```
<server>
  <timeout-interval>120</timeout-interval>
</server>
```

<accept-buffer-size>

The Resin server listens for client connections on the designated port, such as 80 or 8080. Once a connection is made, an internal socket port is assigned to the remote connection. The server defaults to 256 sockets in the accept buffer the server uses to assign remote connections. To change the number of sockets, use the <accept-buffer-size> element:

```
<server>
  <accept-buffer-size>1024</accept-buffer-size>
<server>
```

<listen>

When the Resin server launches, a listen method call is made. The default value for the total number of listening threads is 5. You can change this default with the <listen> element:

```
<server>
  <listen>25</listen>
</server>
```

The higher the number of listen threads, the greater the required system resources. It is recommended that you change the value in small increments and gauge performance.

<cache>

For performance purposes, you should configure the Resin server to use a cache. The Resin cache acts as a high-performance proxy cache; it will help with both static and dynamic pages. The cache is not activated by default; a specific <cache> element must be located in <http-server>. The cache uses both memory and the filesystem to keep cached pages.

The attributes available in the <cache> element are as follows:

- **path**—the file directory where cached pages not in memory should be stored. Default is <installation dir>/cache.
- **entries**—the total number of entries allowed in the cache also contingent on the size of the cache. Default is 16386.
- **enable**—defines whether the cache is enabled. Default is true.
- **memory-size**—size of memory to use.
- **disk-size**—size of disk to use.

The default resin.conf configuration file defines the <cache> element as follows:

```
<cache dir='cache' size='1024' entries='8192'/>
```

<ping>

One of the hallmarks of a successful site or Web application is uptime. You can use external monitoring packages or the Resin server to monitor site code. The <ping> element defines a set of URLs and conditions for checking on a site. The code behind <ping> is designed to ping the URLs and, after a set number of attempts, bring down the Resin server. In a production setting, the OS uses a server or a script to restart the server automatically. The ping code is executed in a separate thread from Resin, but it remains in the same Java Virtual Machine so problems with the VM will not be detected. The attributes of the <ping> element are:

- **url**—the URL that should be pinged. (Required)
- **sleep-time**—the time to wait between pings. Default is 15 minutes.
- **retry-count**—the number of retries before restarting Resin. Default is 3.
- **retry-time**—the length of time to wait before attempting a new ping after a failed ping. Default is 1 second.
- **class-name**—a custom ping class. Default is com.caucho.http.admin.PingThread.

Here's an example of using <ping>:

```
<server>
  <ping>
    <url>http://localhost:80/store/storefront.jsp</url>
    <retry-count>2</retry-count>
    <retry-time>15s</retry-time>
    <sleep-time>30m</sleep-time>
  </ping>
</server>
```

You can write a custom ping class by extending com.caucho.http.admin. PingThread. One such extension is called PingMailer; it sends an email when a ping test has failed. The following attributes are available in PingMailer, in addition to those already listed:

- **mail-to**—the email address of the recipient. (Required)
- **mail-from**—the sender of the email. Default is resin process user.
- **mail-subject**—the subject text of the email. Default is "Resin ping has failed."

Here's an example of using PingMailer:

```
<server>
  <ping>
    <url>http://localhost:80/store/storefront.jsp</url>
    <retry-count>2</retry-count>
    <retry-time>15s</retry-time>
    <sleep-time>30m</sleep-time>
    <class-name>com.caucho.http.admin.PingMailer</class-name>

    <mail-to>myemail@company.com</mail-to>
  </ping>
</server>
```

<ignore-client-disconnect>

A user of a Web application isn't required to complete transactions or continue viewing your site if a request is taking too long. A user's Internet connection may also be broken using a request. In these cases, you can make the Resin server throw an exception (ClientDisconnectionException) when the client disconnects. The default value is false, which means client disconnect exceptions are not ignored. You can change this value using <ignore-client-disconnect>:

```
< server>
  <ignore-client-disconnect>true</ignore-client-disconnect>
</ server>
```

<forbid-host>

The Resin server can deny access to a list of IP addresses using the <forbid-host> element. The code for forbid is contained in com.caucho.http.security. ForbidHost and has a JNDI value of java:comp/env.caucho/forbid-host. Here's an example that uses the element:

```
< server>
  <forbid-host>145.4.3.2</forbid-host>
  <forbid-host>134.2.33.167</forbid-host>
</ server>
```

<session-url-prefix>

When Resin uses sessions, a URL prefix is used for url-rewriting. The default string is *;jessionid=*. You can change this string using the <session-url-prefix> element:

```
<server>
  <session-url-prefix>;resinsession=</session-url-prefix>
</ server>
```

<alternate-session-url-prefix>

When sessions are used with JSPs, you can define an alternate prefix with <alternate-session-url-prefix>:

```
<server>
  <alternate-session-url-prefix>;J=</alternate-session-url-prefix>
</server>
```

<sticky-sessions>

If your load-balancing solution needs sticky sessions, you can enable them with the <sticky-sessions> element. You can find more information about load balancing in Chapter 19, "Load Balancing and Reliablility." An example of using the element is as follows:

```
<server>
  <sticky-sessions>true</sticky-sessions>
</server>
```

<global-system-properties>

When you use the <system-property> element to provide property values to the Resin-hosted Web applications, the server automatically keeps the properties separate as long as the <system-property> elements appear in individual <host> elements. To turn off this default behavior, use the <global-system-properties> element:

```
<server>
  <global-system-properties>true</global-system-properties>
</server>
```

<session-cookie>

The Resin server uses cookies for authentication and session information. The default cookie name is JSESSIONID. To change the cookie, use the <session-cookie> element:

```
<server>
  <session-cookie>RESINCOOKIE</session-cookie>
</server>
```

<url-length-max>

When the Resin server receives an HTTP URL, it is checked against a default maximum length value of 8192. If the URL length is greater than 8192, the browser is passed an error. If you need URLs that are longer than 8192 characters, you can use the <url-length-max> element:

```
<server>
  <url-length-max>16384</url-length-max>
</server>
```

<jsp> Configuration Elements

The Resin server handles all types of files, including the Resin-specific XTP and servlets. In addition, Resin handles the serving, compiling, and execution of JSPs. You can set a number of configuration options specifically for these pages. All the options are defined under the <jsp> element in the <caucho.com> root.

A total of 11 attributes can be set in the <jsp> element:

- **auto-compile**—defines whether changes made to files with a .jsp extension should be automatically recompiled when the server is executing. Default is true.
- **disable-init-log**—when a <log> element is defined for JSP logging, this option (when false) disables the logging of init() and destroy() methods on JSP objects. This keeps the log from growing too quickly and eliminates garbage in the log. Default is false.
- **jsp-update-interval**—the amount of time the server waits before checking whether a JSP file has been modified. Default is 2 seconds.
- **jsp-max**—the total number of active JSP pages. Default is 1024.
- **precompile**—defines where the server should precompile JSPs during startup. Default is true.
- **require-source**—before a JSP is executed, defines whether the server should check to see if the original source file is available. If not, the compiled JSP is not executed. Default is false.
- **recompile-on-error**—defines whether the server recompiles a JSP if it has previously thrown a java.lang.Error exception. Default is false.
- **recycle-tags**—determines whether the server recycles tags as defined by the JSP 2.0 specification. Default is true.
- **session**—defines whether sessions are activated. Default is true.
- **static-encoding**—defines whether the server precompiles character encoding. If true, auto-compile is forced true. Default is true.

- **velocity**—defines whether Velocity-style syntax can be used in a JSP file. Default is true.

The default <jsp> element in resin.conf is as follows:

```
<jsp
  precompile='true'
  static-encoding='true'
  recompile-on-error='true'/>
```

You can change the attributes in the default <jsp> as needed, and add new attributes.

What's Next

This chapter has taken a comprehensive look at all the Resin configuration options. In Chapter 16, we will take a closer look at the configuration of the internal and external Web servers and how they are used with Resin.

CHAPTER 16

Configuring Your Web Server

The Resin server is really many applications in one. The primary application is a JSP/servlet engine designed to compile and execute server-side code. Coupled with the engine is a full-featured Web server, which handles serving up HTML static pages as well as passing JSP/servlet requests to the Resin engine. The Resin Web server can serve pages faster than some other Web servers, but this isn't always enough to convince an IT department to switch away from another server application.

In this chapter, we look at the interface between Resin and several external servers, including Apache, Microsoft Internet Information Server (IIS), and Netscape's iPlanet. We also take a look at using other server-side languages—like PHP and Perl. In addition, we discuss a Web-based authoring and versioning system called WebDav.

Let's start off with a look at how a plug-in interfaces Resin with an external server.

URL-Dispatching

Before we discuss using another application as a front end to Resin, let's see how a request gets from the client browser through the front-end Web server to the Resin servlet engine. The mechanism that allows an HTTP request to navigate through the applications is called URL-Dispatching.

The three Web servers we discuss in this chapter are Apache, IIS, and Netscape's iPlanet. For each of the servers, a plug-in to the server application is available that handles dispatching of URLs:

- mod_caucho for Apache
- isapi_srun for IIS
- nsapi for Netscape

These plug-ins handle the dispatching of a URL to the Resin engine as well as the transfer of the Request and Response objects. For each of these modules, information is gathered about the current environment from the Resin configuration file. The modules read information from the <host>, <web-app>, and <servlet-mapping> elements.

From <host>, the modules gain information about the current virtual hosts. From <web-app>, the modules learn about the various applications configured on the machine, and they read <servlet-mapping> to learn the selected URLs. The most important tag to the plug-in is <servlet-mapping> because it is able to determine which URLs need to be passed to the Resin servlet engine.

The plug-in finds the <url-pattern> element within <servlet-mapping>. As you've seen, <url-pattern> has the job of matching the URL being requested. A <reg-exp> element is also available, but the Resin plug-ins don't recognize it. Within <servlet-mapping> are two special names that can be used in the servlet-name attribute: plugin-match and plugin-ignore.

Consider the following configuration example:

```
<servlet-mapping url-pattern='/forresin/*'
                 servlet-name='plugin_match'/>

<servlet-mapping url-pattern='/otherpages/*'
                 servlet-name='plugin_ignore'/>
```

These <servlet-mapping> elements tell the Resin plug-in how to handle pages it might be given by a client Web browser. In the first example, the element checks all incoming URLs with the pattern /forresin/*. If it finds this pattern, the plug-in automatically sends the URL to the Resin servlet engine. In the second example, the element checks all incoming URLs with the pattern /otherpages/*. All of these pages are kept with the external server. These directives are useful for directing an entire directory of pages to Resin.

As you'll see shortly, it's also possible to allow Apache's httpd.conf configuration file to handle dispatching duties as well. You accomplish this using the <Location> and SetHandler directives. For example:

```
<Location /forresin/*>
  SetHandler caucho-request
</Location>
```

These directives match all /forresin/* URLs and signal that Resin should handle them.

Apache

Many hosting companies and corporations use Apache as their primary engine for serving HTML and a variety of other page types to their users. However, a third-party application server is needed to handle requests from servlets and JSP files. In this section, we describe the easiest way to connect Resin and Apache to form a system that can serve a large variety of file types. For the most part, we assume that you are already running Apache or are looking to rebuild a server and use Resin as an application server.

Figure 16.1 shows how the two different servers communicate with each other to facilitate the execution of HTML, JSP, and servlets.

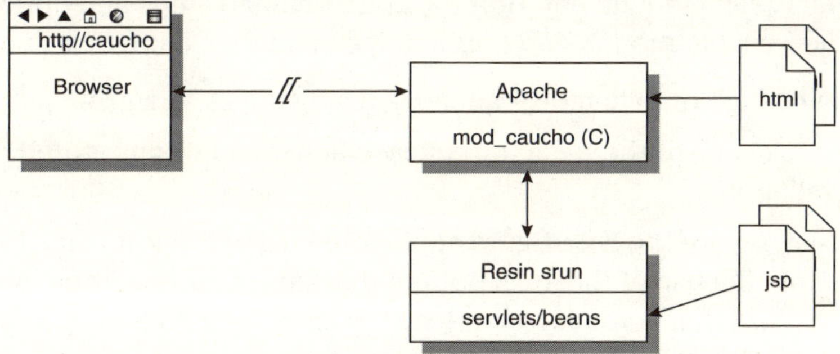

Figure 16.1 The communication structure between Resin and Apache.

The interface between Apache and Resin is accomplished using Dynamic Shared Objects (DSO). DSOs are objects compiled into a general format thus allowing them to be loaded dynamically by those applications that need the object functionality. As we discussed earlier, the mod_caucho shared object works with Apache to direct a client's URL request to the right application.

Installing and Configuring Apache on Unix

By far the most popular Unix Web server is Apache, due to its extensive support and ongoing enhancements. In this section, we show you how to install Apache in a way that allows the mod_caucho SO to be loaded and that tells Apache to direct servlet requests to Resin. The following steps guide you through the installation of Apache. Once you complete these steps, skip ahead to the section "Configuring Apache's httpd.conf."

The following steps assume that you don't already have Apache installed, or that it isn't in /usr/local/apache, or that you didn't compile with DSO support. If this isn't the case, skip to the "Configuring Apache's httpd.conf" section. (We also assume that you have previously installed Resin and Java.)

Step 1—Download Apache from www.apache.org/dyn/closer.cgi/httpd/. For this example, we chose the 2.0 version.

Step 2—Uncompress the downloaded file with gunzip.

Step 3—Untar the downloaded file.

Step 4—Configure Apache using ./configure but with a few options. Here's the configure statement you should use:

```
./configure --prefix=/usr/local/apache --enable-module=so
```

Step 5—Make the server with the make command and install with the command make install.

The previous steps are simple—and vague. We highly recommend that you consult the Apache documentation for more detailed steps and options. Just be sure the --enable-module=so option appears in the ./configure line.

Now you need to compile mod_caucho.so using the following steps:

Step 1—Change to the Resin directory where you initially stored it during installation.

Step 2—Execute the ./configure application using the following command. Note the use of the apxs option; this aids the application during compile. We assume you have Apache installed in /usr/local/apache:

```
./configure —with-apxs=/usr/local/apache/bin/apxs
```

If this configure fails, try

```
./configure —with-apache=/usr/local/apache
```

Step 3—Make the shared object with the command make.

Step 4—Install the object with the command make install. The mod_caucho.so file will be copied to the Apache installation.

Installing and Configuring Apache on Windows

In most cases, Apache will be executed on a Unix-based system. However, some Windows users, rather than using IIS, select Apache as their sole Web server. We have just gone through the process of using Resin with Apache on Unix, so let's do the same thing with Windows. The architecture shown in Figure 16.1 is still valid for a Windows-based system.

Use the following steps to marry Resin and Apache on Windows:

Step 1—Download Apache from www.apache.org/dyn/closer.cgi/httpd/. You can choose either the EXE or the MSI (Microsoft Installer) download. For this example, we downloaded the MSI file. Either save the file to the local hard drive and double-click it, or select the Open option in the download dialog box. You can use either the 1.3 or 2.0 version of Apache.

Step 2—Click through the first Installer Wizard screen.

Step 3—Accept the Apache license and click Next.

Step 4—Click Next at the readme screen.

Step 5—At the Server Information screen, enter the network domain, server name, and administrator e-mail address. At the bottom of the screen, specify whether the server should be installed as a service for all users or started manually by the currently logged-in user. Click Next.

Step 6—For most uses, select Complete Installation and then Next.

Step 7—Select the directory where you want to install the software and click Next.

Step 8—Click Install.

Step 9—When the installation completes, click the Finish button.

Step 10—Using the Services application found in Administrative tools, stop the Apache server.

Configuring Apache's httpd.conf

Next, we need to make a few changes to Apache's httpd.conf file to create the connection to Resin through the shared object file:

Step 1—Browse to the httpd.conf file typically located in c:/program files/apache group/conf.

Step 2—Open httpd.conf.

Step 3—Add the following information to the configuration file near the other LoadModule commands:

```
LoadModule caucho_module <install dir for resin>/libexec/<apache
version>/mod_caucho.dll

# Note, AddModule not needed for Apache 2.0
AddModule mod_caucho.c

<IfModule mod_caucho.c>
  CauchoConfigFile <install dir for resin>/conf/resin.conf
  <Location /caucho-status>
    SetHandler caucho-status
  </Location>
</IfModule>
```

Note that you must place the LoadModule, AddModule, and <IfModule> elements in individual parts of the Apache httpd.conf file. You need to substitute the actual installation directory for Resin in two places and specify the correct Apache version in one place. If you look in the /libexec directory of the Resin installation, you'll see two directories—for example, apache-1.3 and apache-2.0—that are to be used with the correct Apache version. If you are running in a production environment, delete the <Location> elements and values.

Step 4—Close the file.

The Resin mod_caucho shared object reads the specified resin.conf configuration file to determine which URL paths should be transferred to Resin for handling and which should remain with Apache. If you don't want mod_caucho reading the configuration file, you can configure the locations of servlets directly in the httpd.conf file. The location must match the information found in the Resin configuration file. You must make changes to any of this information in both places. The following is an example of what you need to include in the httpd.conf file if you aren't using the resin.conf file:

```
LoadModule caucho_module <install dir for resin>/libexec/<apache
version>/mod_caucho.dll
AddModule mod_caucho.c

CauchoHost localhost 6802
AddHandler caucho-request jsp
<Location /servlet/*>
   SetHandler caucho-request
</Location>
```

Here we find that the caucho_module is loaded and various information about Resin is provided. First we have the CauchoHost option, which is followed by the IP or domain of the Resin server and the port where requests must be sent. Next is an AddHandler option that lets Apache know that all JSP files should be directed to the caucho-request handler. Finally, a <Location> element selects the additional paths that, when matched, also need to be sent to the Resin server.

Four Resin-specific commands are available within Apache's httpd.conf file for handling the connection between Apache and Resin:

CauchoConfigFile <path>—Forces reading of the specified configuration file.

CauchoServerRoot <directory>—Defines the server root.

CauchoHost host port—Defines the host and port where a Resin server can be found.

CauchoBackup host port—Defines the host and port where a secondary Resin server can be found.

By using CauchoBackup and multiple <srun> elements within Resin, you can achieve full redundancy.

Configuring resin.conf

After Apache has been configured, the Resin server needs attention. Two additions might be necessary. If you want to keep your servlets in the same directory as the Apache documents, use the <app-dir> element. In Windows, for example, you'd use the following code:

```
<resin>
  <server>
    <host id=''>
       <document-directory>c:/program files/apache
          group/apache/htdocs</document-directory>
      <web-app id=''>
        <servlet-mapping url-pattern='*.xtp' servlet-name='xtp'/>
        <servlet-mapping url-pattern='*.jsp' servlet-name='jsp'/>
      </web-app>
    </host>
  </server>
</resin>
```

In Unix, this configuration changesyou change only the <app-dir> path:

```
<resin>
  <server>
    <host id=''>
       <document-directory>/usr/local/apache/htdocs</document-
directory>
       <web-app id=''>
          <servlet-mapping url-pattern='*.xtp' servlet-name='xtp'/>
          <servlet-mapping url-pattern='*.jsp' servlet-name='jsp'/>
       </web-app>
    </host>
  </server>
</resin>
```

Testing Apache and Resin

Your last step is to test the configuration. Begin by starting the Apache Web server. You do this either by double-clicking the Apache.exe icon in the Apache installation directory or through the Services application found in the Administrative Tools directory. At this point, you should be able to browse to http://localhost and see the output shown in Figure 16.2.

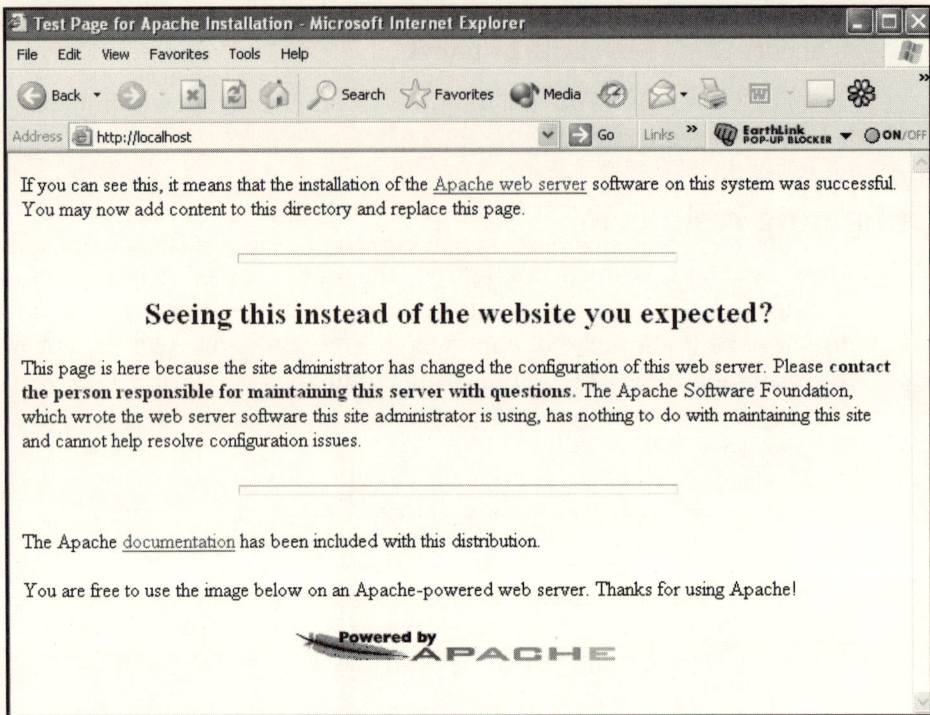

Figure 16.2 Apache test output.

Now start Resin by double-clicking on the httpd.exe icon in the Resin installation directory or starting the Resin server service. Create a new file called test.jsp in the Apache document directory specified in the resin.conf configuration file and add the following JSP code to the file:

```
<HTML>
<BODY>
<%  java.util.Date date = new java.util.Date(); %>

It worked! Today is <%= date %>

</BODY>
</HTML>
```

Browse to the file with http://localhost/test.jsp and you should see the output shown in Figure 16.3. If you don't see the expected output or you receive an error, go over the steps.

Troubleshooting

As you might expect, several things could go wrong when you attempt to integrate Resin with an external Web server. In this section, we consider some of those potential problems.

- One of the more common errors occurs when Resin tells you the document cannot be found. In this case, check to make sure you only have one <app-dir> element in the Resin <http-server> configuration.
- Verify that Resin is configured correctly to use its internal Web server through port 8080.
- Check that caucho-status is enabled in the Resin configuration file and browse to localhost/caucho-status to see if the plug-in is working.
- Make sure Resin outputs a statement saying it is listening on port 6802.
- Be sure the right host is configured in the Resin configuration file.
- Start Resin with --verbose and check the logs in the /log directory.

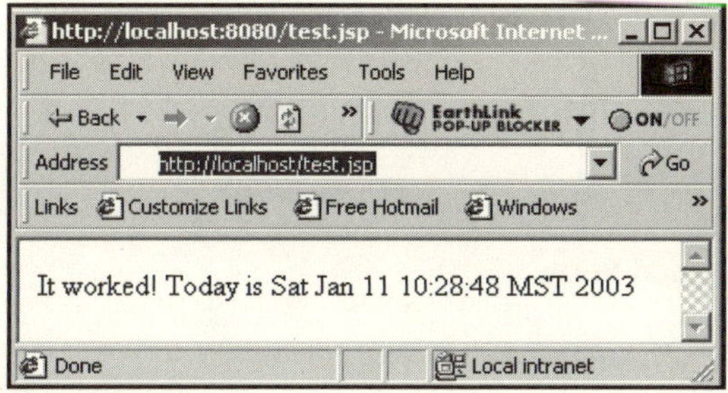

Figure 16.3 Resin/Apache test output.

Virtual Hosts

As you will see in Chapter 17, the Resin server supports virtual hosting with its internal Web server and servlet engine. In one of the virtual hosting scenarios, a separate Java Virtual Machine (JVM) is used for each host to provide the most secure and stable environment possible. When using Apache as a Web server, you need to do a little more work in setting up the virtual hosting with separate JVMs. You might want to skip ahead to Chapter 17 now and come back to this section.

To support separate JVMs with Resin, you typically create multiple configuration files and included those files in a larger one. Each of the configuration files set up the environment for the separate JVMs. You need to let Apache know about the hosts as well. In Chapter 17, we use the configuration files companycom.conf and ourcompanycom.conf. Within the httpd.conf file of Apache, let's set up two <VirtualHost> elements:

```
<VirtualHost company.com>
ServerName company.com
ServerAlias www.company.com
CauchoConfigFile /www/hosts/companycom.conf
</VirtualHost>
```

```
<VirtualHost ourcompany.com>
ServerName ourcompany.com
ServerAlias www.ourcompany.com
CauchoConfigFile /www/hosts/ourcompanycom.conf
</VirtualHost>
```

This configuration tells the Apache Web server to transfer servlet requests for company.com to the Resin server executing under the companycom.conf configuration. All servlet requests to ourcompany.com are directed to a separate Resin server started with the ourcompanycom.conf configuration. Figure 16.4 shows an example of how the requests move.

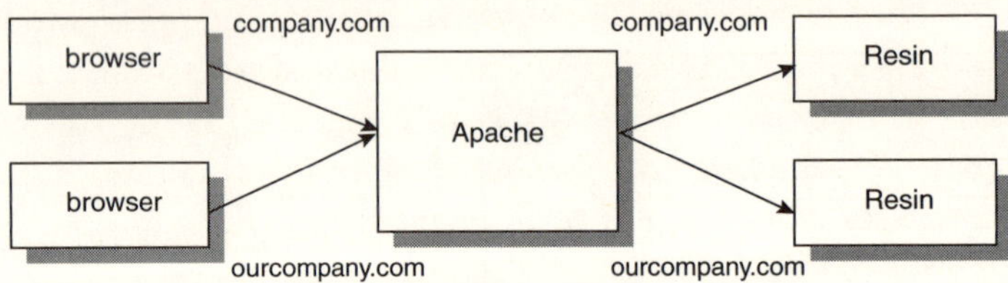

Figure 16.4 Virtual hosting with Apache and Resin.

Error Pages

mod_caucho uses a specific error page if it is unable to contact the primary or any redundant servlet engines. It produces an exception of the type connection; in a production environment, you'll find an <error-page> element in the appropriate Resin configuration file. For example:

```
<web-app>
  <error-page exception-type='connection'
              location='/connection_error.html'/>
</web-app>
```

Using IIS with Resin

On the Windows platform, IIS and Personal Web Server (PWS) are two ways of dealing with requests for client browsers. Each of the servers handle traditional HTML pages as well as one written with Active Server Pages (ASP). Figure 16.5 shows an example of how you can use IIS as the primary Web server front end to Resin acting as a servlet engine (just as we did for Apache). Instead of using a shared object, you use a dynamic link library (DLL) to transfer requests from IIS to Resin.

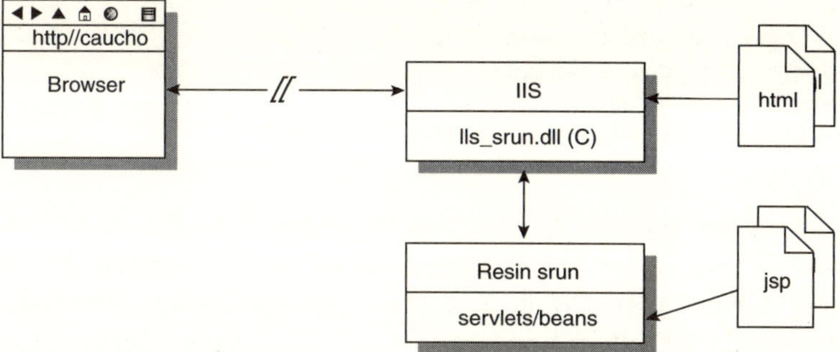

Figure 16.5 Using IIS and Resin.

For this discussion, we assume that you've already installed either IIS or PWS. (In most all cases, the operating system installation process also installs the server.) There are two ways to configure Resin for IIS support: automatically and manually. Let's start with the automatic approach:

Step 1—Browse to the /bin directory of your Resin installation. Double-click on the icon called setup.exe to open the dialog box shown in Figure 16.6.

Resin 1.2 Setup

General

Resin Home C:\data\books\resin\resin-ee-2.1.4

Web Servers

Apache c:\program files\apache group\apache

IIS/PWS c:\inetpub\wwwroot

Netscape

WebSite

OK Cancel Apply Remove

Figure 16.6 The Resin setup dialog box.

Step 2—In the edit line for IIS or PWS, select the correct location of wwwroot and click OK. Setup asks if you want to restart IIS to accept the new plug-in. Click OK.

Step 3—At this point, place in the Resin configuration file all of the configuration information for directories under IIS. This includes all virtual directories. Here's an example:

```
<resin>
  <server>
    <servlet-mapping url-pattern='/servlet/*'
      servlet-name='invoker'/>
```

```
    <servlet-mapping url-pattern='*.xtp'
      servlet-name='com.caucho.jsp.XtpServlet'/>
    <servlet-mapping url-pattern='*.jsp'
      servlet-name='com.caucho.jsp.JspServlet'/>
  </server>
</resin>
```

This configuration lets the Resin server know that the appropriate JSP servlets can be found in the c:\inetpub\wwwroot directory as well as in \servlet. For virtual directories, use the <path-mapping> element to map requests to the right file location.

Testing IIS and Resin

Now start Resin by double-clicking the httpd.exe icon in the Resin installation directory or by starting the Resin server service. Create a new file called test.jsp in the Apache document directory specified in the resin.conf configuration file and add the following JSP code to the file:

```
<HTML>
<BODY>
<%  java.util.Date date = new java.util.Date(); %>

It worked! Today is <%= date %>

</BODY>
</HTML>
```

Browse to the file with http://localhost/test.jsp and you should see the output shown in Figure 16.3. If you don't see the expected output or you receive an error, check over the steps.

Using Netscape iPlanet with Resin

Netscape's iPlanet is a popular Web server on the Unix platform and works as a viable front-end Web server for Resin's servlet engine. In this section, we look at configuring Resin to interface with Netscape. We assume that you have already installed the Netscape server.

Step 1—You need to compile the plug-in for Netscape, which is called caucho_nsapi.so. The first step is to run the ./configure application:

```
./configure --with-netscape=/usr/local/netscape/<https-hostname>
```

We assume that you installed Netscape in /usr/local/netscape. The value for –with-netscape must point to the scripts directory of the installation.

Step 2—When the configure application is finished, build the plug-in with the make command.

Step 3—The make automatically performs the necessary setup for Netscape.

Step 4—Modify resin.conf to use the application directory /usr/local/netscape/htdocs.

To test the installation, start Netscape and Resin. Refer to the previous section, "Testing IIS with Resin," but use /usr/local/netscape/htdocs as the application directory.

Running Netscape iPlanet and Windows

If you are using Netscape iPlanet on Windows, use the setup.exe application as discussed in the section "Using IIS with Resin." All of the work is performed by the setup file, and the plug-in is already compiled.

Hosting a CGI without Apache

So you've been able to convince your management that the internal Resin Web server can be used just as efficiently an external Web server. Now the problem becomes, How do you handle the various PHP, Perl, and Python applications currently floating around your production Web server? While one answer might be to rewrite them as servlets, that may not be the most efficient approach. The next best thing is to find a way to handle all those various page types as well. The CGIServlet and FastCGIServlet external interpreters let you handle page requests and pass them to an appropriate interpreter. In this section, we show you how to incorporate these interpreters with the internal Resin Web server.

CGIServlet

The Resin internal Web server lets you use external interpreters to handle various languages—Perl, for example. A servlet called com.caucho.http. servlet. CGIServlet is used to pass the Common Gateway Interface (CGI) to the environment for processing. The idea is to "execute" the file in the URL request. The first line of the file specifies the application responsible for executing the contents of the file. For example, consider the following Perl script:

```
#!/usr/local/perl
use CGI qw(:standard);
print header();
print "<html>\n<head>\n",
    "<title>Hello!</title>\n",
    "</head>\n",
    "<body>\n\n";
 print "\n</body>\n", "</html>\n";
```

This script tells us that Perl should be used to process the file. We can do the same thing within Resin's internal Web server by placing the following <web-app> element within the configuration file:

```
<web-app>
  <servlet-mapping url-pattern='*.cgi'
       servlet-name='com.caucho.servlets.CGIServlet'/>
</web-app>
```

This new configuration code tells the Resin that when it finds a URL with a page extension of .cgi it should pass the request to the CGIServlet for processing. This servlet in turn "executes" the page against the system's environment. You can easily change the CGI pattern to PL (for Perl) or some other execution.

FastCGIServlet

Look in the /bin directory of your Unix Resin installation and you will find a Perl script called fastcgirunner.pl. This script is designed to be used in conjunction with the Resin internal Web server and a servlet called com.caucho.http.servlet/ FastCGIServlet to allow the execution of server-side CGI code. You can use these components to enable your Resin internal Web server to execute foreign CGI code like PHP.

As an example, let's assume that you want to use Resin as well as PHP. Follow these steps:

Step 1—Obtain the source code version of PHP from www.php.net.

Step 2—Using the directions in the distributable or the PHP Web site, www.php.net/manual/en/install.commandline.php, compile a CGI or command-line version of PHP. Be sure to use the —fastcgi option when compiling PHP.

Step 3—Set your system path so that the PHP executable can be executed by the user your Resin server executes. This might still be root in a development environment or something like "resin".

Step 4—Add the following <servlet-mapping> element to the Resin configuration file:

```
<web-app>
  <servlet-mapping
    url-pattern='*.php'
    servlet-name='com.caucho.servlets.FastCGIServlet'>
    <init-param server-address='localhost:7000'/>
  </servlet-mapping>
</web-app>
```

This <servlet-mapping> tells Resin that if it finds any requests from a client with a page extension of .php, the request should be handled by a servlet called FastCGIServlet. The element tells Resin to redirect the request to port 7000. Of course, you need something on port 7000—and that's the next step.

Step 5—Once Resin is running, open a terminal window and change to the /bin directory of the Resin installation. Execute the fastcgirunner.pl Perl script in the following fashion:

```
./fastcgirunner.pl –port 7000 php
```

This command tells the script to execute and listen on port 7000. When a request comes from port 7000, the script should start and pass the request to the .php executable.

Step 6—Write a PHP script to test the system. Here's an example:

```
#!/usr/local/php
<?php
phpinfo();
?>
```

When writing PHP scripts for the PHP command-line interpreter, be sure to start the script with the path to the PHP installation.

Resin and WebDav

WebDav, commonly called just Dav, is a Web-based authoring and versioning system that allows developers and administrators to change a supported site's primary pages using the Web itself. Most site maintainers are probably familiar with using FTP to upload changed site pages. WebDav was designed to allow multiple users to collaboratively edit and manage the pages on a remote site. You can find much more information on WebDav at www.webdav.org. Many support applications can save directly to WebDav, and some operating systems allow a filesystem link to be created directly to a WebDav-supported site.

Since we've included a section on WebDav in this book, you've probably guessed that Resin supports it. In this section, we look at setting up Resin to use WebDav and how you can interface to the supported site.

Configuring for WebDav

Resin supplies a servlet designed to support WebDav. To activate support, you must explicitly set up the servlet in the configuration file. By default, the servlet requires a user logged into the system that with the role "webdav". The connection defaults to Secure Socket Layer (SSL) for the best security when changing a site's pages. The following example shows how you might configure a WebDav servlet:

```
<servlet-mapping url-pattern='/webdav/*'
   servlet-name='com.caucho.servlets.webdav.WebDavServlet'>
  <init-param enable='write'/>
</servlet-mapping>

<authenticator type="com.caucho.server.security.XmlAuthenticator">
  <init>
    <user>username:password:webdav</user>
    <password-digest>none</password-digest>
  </init>
</authenticator>
<login-config auth-method='basic'/>
```

There are three major components to this configuration. First, note the declaration of the <servlet-mapping> element. In this element, we let Resin know that if a page is requested in the directory webdav, the WebDavServlet should be used to handle the request. Second, we set up an authenticator with a specific username, password, and role for the logged-in user. Third, we set up a <security-constraint> for all the pages within the webdav directory.

Parameters currently available for the WebDav servlet include:

enable—Indicates whether the servlet can read or write to the specified directory; the default is false.

role—Defines the required role for a user using WebDav; the default is webdav.

user—Specifies the user who may use WebDav; the default is none.

secure—Indicates whether writes must be done over SSL; the default is true.

root—Defines the root directory for webdav.

path-source—Defines a custom path.

Configuring Windows' My Network Places

It is possible to map a location with Windows' My Network Places dialog box to a WebDav-supported site. Follow these steps:

Step 1—Open the My Network Places dialog box.

Step 2—Select Tools, then Map Network Drive.

Step 3—Click on the link Create A Shortcut To Web Folder Or FTP Site. A dialog box appears that requests the URL to the site. Enter the site; for example, http://localhost:8080/webdav.

Step 4—Enter the required username and password for our configuration.

Step 5—Once the link has been established in your Network Neighborhood, you can save directly to the link.

What's Next

In this chapter, we took a quick look at how you can use external Web servers with Resin. We also discussed Resin's support of PHP and other Web languages, and explained how to use WebDav with Resin. In the next chapter, we discuss virtual hosting.

CHAPTER 17

Exploring Virtual Hosting

Resin is used in a variety of situations, from development to ISP-based hosting. In many situations, a single server can be used to host Web applications, which execute based on different IP addresses or domains. For example, you might have a company with a domain called company.com and a URL www.company.com that provides basic information. Using the same domain, you could also have the URL stats.company.com as a secure site for handling project statistics.

There is no need to have separate servers for these two different URLs existing on a single domain. In fact, you can take this example one step further and add an entirely new domain called ourcompany.com. This domain can exist on your server along with company.com. This type of hosting, called *virtual hosting*, allows a single server to host many different domains—a common practice with commercial hosting companies. In this chapter, we show you how to configure Resin specifically to handle basic virtual hosting as well as virtual hosting using external Web servers. We also explain how to provide individual virtual machines for each host.

Basic Virtual Hosting

We touched on the concept of supporting virtual hosting in Chapter 15, where we laid out all the elements available in the Resin configuration file. Of particular importance is the <host> element. This element allows you to specify an identifier as an attribute that the Resin server uses to determine if the current <host> element matches the domain within the URL being browsed. For example:

```
<server>
  <host id='www.company.com' />
</server>
```

If a client attempts to browse www.company.com/servlet/store, the Resin server breaks off the domain part of the URL, www.company.com, and attempts to find a match within the <host> elements of its configuration file. If the domain isn't found in the configuration file, the server assumes it doesn't support that particular domain.

You can configure the Resin server to support numerous domains through its internal Web server by specifying more than one <host> element within the <server>. For example, this configuration file is designed to support both the www.company.com and www.ourcompany.com domains:

```
<host id='www.company.com'>
    <root-directory>f:/hosts/company_com</root-directory>
</host>
<host id='www.ourcompany.com'>
    <root-directory>g:/hosts/ourcompany_com</root-directory>
</host>
```

Here we have two different <host> elements. The first one tells the server to match all requests with a domain of www.company.com and use the application directory called f:/hosts/company_com. With this host, browsing to the URL http://www.company.com/store.jsp causes the file store.jsp to be executed from the f:/hosts/company_com directory.

In the same manner, we defined a second host for the domain www.ourcompany.com using a completely different application directory, g:/hosts/ourcompany_com. A URL using the www.ourcompany.com domain finds a file in its specified application directory.

Just as you can use the <root-directory> attribute in each of the <host> elements, you can use all of the elements and attributes defined in Chapter 15 for the <hosts> element in each host definition. This allows each of the hosted domains to have individual configurations that don't interfere with the others.

You can imagine the headache of trying to maintain all the configuration information in a single file. However, as you may recall, you can use the <resin:include> element to include additional files into a single resin.conf file. For example:

```
<resin>
  <server>
    <resin:include href='companycomhost.conf'/>
    <resin:include href='ourcompanycomhost.conf'/>
  </server>
</resin>
```

Instead of using a single resin.conf file with large <host> elements, you keep each of the <host> elements in separate files and include them in the primary configuration file.

Virtual Hosting Using External Web Servers

Our examples thus far have assumed that the internal Web server is being used to pass requests from the client's Web browser to the servlet engine within Resin. As you recall from Chapter 16, you can use several external Web servers as front ends to Resin. This configuration turns Resin into an application server and ignores the internal Web server.

In these situations, you still want to be able to support virtual hosting. Fortunately, whether you're using Microsoft IIS or Apache as a front end, you don't have to modify the resin.conf configuration file—with one exception. Depending on how the domain for a site is set up using static IP addresses as such, you might need to use both the www.company.com and company.com domain strings for a successful match by the Resin server, as shown here:

```
<server>
  <host id='www.company.com'>
    <host-alias>company.com</host-alias>
  </host>
</server>
```

As for IIS, no other changes are required. If you have one host serving pages through IIS, then just add more hosts to provide virtual hosting. Apache, on the other hand, needs a little help when you're specifying more than one host. First, don't change anything in the Resin configuration file—this file does not have to be modified.

However, you do have to add appropriate <VirtualHost> elements within Apache's httpd.conf file. Consider the following snippet using our two sample domains:

```
LoadModule caucho_module /usr/local/apache/libexec/mod_caucho.so
AddModule mod_caucho.c

CauchoConfigFile /home/www/conf/resin.conf

<VirtualHost 134.154.45.65>
  ServerName www.company.com
</VirtualHost>

<VirtualHost 134.154.45.67>
  ServerName www.ourcompany.com
</VirtualHost>
```

In this Apache httpd.conf file, we start by loading the caucho_module and then the Resin configuration file. It is very important that these two steps occur in the order shown in the example. Next, <VirtualHost> elements are defined for each of the domains being hosted. The most important part of these two definitions is the use of ServerName. The value associated with ServerName is the domain name passed to Resin for matching against the various <host> elements in the Resin configuration file. If the values for ServerName aren't accurate, the Resin server will not find the associated <host> configuration.

IP Virtual Hosting

If you don't have a domain name associated with a site but you do have an IP address, you can use it for virtual hosting as well. For example:

```
<http host='184.38.9.22' port='80'
      virtual-host='www.company.com'/>
```

In this example, a sort of mapping occurs between the specified address and a virtual-host domain value. The virtual-host value will be used as a match against the <host> elements in the configuration file.

Providing JVMs per Host

At this point, we must address the issue of security and crash protection. In our previous examples, each of the requests to the Resin server for the domains result in a thread being started and executed with the same Java Virtual Machine (JVM). It is possible to configure Resin to keep all hosts within their own VM and thus provide the ultimate in protection.

Basically, you start two or more Resin servers that execute in their own JVMs. You need to create configuration files for both of our example domains. First, the configuration for www.company.com:

```
<resin>
  <server>
    <cluster>
      <srun host="localhost" port="8800"/>
    </cluster>

    <host id="www.company.com">
       <root-directory>...
       <resin:include href="common.conf"/>
```

Note three things in particular in this configuration file. First, the port being used for srun is 8800. Second, we've defined a <host> element with a specific application directory. Third, we use <path> to pull in common information for the file.

Now the configuration file for www.ourcompany.com:

```
<resin>
  <server>
  <cluster>
      <srun host="localhost" port="8801"/>
    </cluster>

  <host id='www.ourcompany.com'>
    <root-directory>g:\hosts\ourcompany_com</root-directory>
    <path href='common.conf'/>
  </host>
  </server>
</resin>
```

The srun ports and the application directory are the only differences between these two configuration files. Now you need to start Resin using the configuration files. On Windows, you accomplish this by executing the following two commands:

```
httpd.exe —conf ourcompany.conf
httpd.exe —conf company.conf
```

Two Resin servers are started, and each listens on a different srun port. This example assumes you're using an external Web server. If you're using Apache, you have to pull the separate configuration files into the correct <VirtualHost> element, as shown here:

```
<VirtualHost 134.154.45.65>
  ServerName www.company.com
  CauchoConfigFile c:/resin/company.conf
</VirtualHost>

<VirtualHost 134.154.45.67>
  ServerName www.ourcompany.com
  CauchoConfigFile c:/resin/ourcompany.conf
</VirtualHost>
```

What's Next

In this chapter, we explained how to host multiple domains with the Resin server. Virtual hosting allows a hosting company, a development shop, or a company to have multiple independent sites on a single machine using a single Resin server application. In the next chapter, we look at using Resin HardCore, an embedded version of Resin within the Linux kernel.

CHAPTER 18

Using Resin HardCore

For those of you with a daring side to your personality, this chapter introduces Resin HardCore. Written as a Linux kernel module, Resin HardCore brings Web server functionality directly into the Linux kernel for handling HTTP requests with very little overhead.

We cannot stress enough that the techniques we discuss in this chapter are experimental. The kernel module supports only GET HTTP requests, logging, load balancing, and caching. Other major features aren't supported, and if there is a failure in the module, you risk crashing your entire Linux system.

The module works by forwarding all HTTP GET requests to an appropriate Resin servlet engine. The servlet engine is responsible for executing the request and returning the results to the module. Since the module is running in kernel space, the initial processing of the request and transfer to the servlet engine is very fast. Unlike a traditional Web server, though, the module does not do any page processing. The module is an ideal candidate for an easy-to-build load balancer.

Building the Module

The first step in using Resin HardCore is to configure and compile the module. You begin by executing ./configure within the Resin source directory using one or both of these options:

```
--with-linux-src=<source directory>
--enable-linux-smp
```

The first option, which is required, specifies the path to the current kernel source files. If your kernel is designed for multiprocessor operation, include the second option.

At this point, compile the resulting makefile with the make command. After the make completes, locate the file called resin.o in the /libexec directory of the Resin installation. This is the kernel file you need to associate with Linux.

Installing the Module

Change to the root login and execute the insmod application to attach the new module to the kernel. The module defaults to listening on port 80 (which you can change by using the port=<port value> option). An example command is:

```
/sbin/insmod libexec/resin.o
```

Running the Module

Once installed, the module creates a directory called /proc/net/resin. Within this directory are three files: server_port, srun-count, and srun-n. The server_port file contains the port number the module will bind to in order to listen for HTTP requests. You can change the value for your installation. The srun-count file specifies the total number of servlet engines available to send requests. The value in srun-count determines the total number of files defined as srun-n.

So, if the value in srun-count is 2, there should be two srun-n files, called srun-0 and srun-1. Within each of these files you'll find a domain name and IP address for the servlet engine and the port where it should send a request. For example:

```
192.168.1.102 6802
```

Once all of the files are configured correctly, start the servlet engines and browse to a file based on the server where the Linux kernel module has been defined.

What's Next

In this chapter, we looked at Resin HardCore, designed to quickly parse and transfer HTTP GET requests. This Linux kernel module, though experimental, provides low overhead and a simple load balancer. In the next chapter, we look at other mechanisms for achieving reliability and load balancing with Resin.

Load Balancing and Reliability

When you're using a servlet engine and Web server in a production environment, one of the most important factors is response time. Of course, your site won't respond if the server fails or it's been swamped with requests. One solution to this problem is to provide a higher level of reliability and load balancing through additional server machines and duplicate copies of the server software. Resin supports the ability to load-balance requests in just this fashion. In this chapter, we explore several options for providing load balancing within Resin. In addition, we explain how sessions are handled across a server farm.

Sessions

As you know, sessions are designed to hold information about a current user on the site. Probably the best example is a shopping cart on a commerce site. The session keeps track of the cart as well as the user doing the shopping. As each request comes from the user, the right cart needs to be modified.

When all your user requests come to a single Web server and servlet engine, you can keep the Session objects in memory; that way, they can be easily accessed when the user makes a new request. But what happens when a request from the user is sent to different servers? The servers in the farm cannot assume they know anything about the current users because they might be seeing every fourth or even more random requests from the same user. Resin provides three possible solutions: srun indexing, distributed sessions, and TCP-ring distributed sessions.

srun Indexing

Since you know that each request from a user will go to any of the servers in a server farm, one way to handle sessions is to ensure that requests from a user are sent to a specific server based on that user's initial request. With this scheme, a user whose request is handled by server a will always have their requests sent to server a. Server a will have the Session object for the user in memory and be able to handle all of the specific information for the user.

In Resin 3.x, the configuration has changed. The <cluster> element has been introduced to produce a configuration like:

```
<server>
    <cluster>
      <srun server-id='servera' host='192.168.1.101'
port='6802' index='1'/>
      <srun server-id='serverb' host='192.168.1.102'
port='6802' index='2'/>
      <srun server-id='serverc' host='192.168.1.103'
port='6802' index='3'/>
    <cluster>
```

Figure 19.1 shows an example using this configuration.

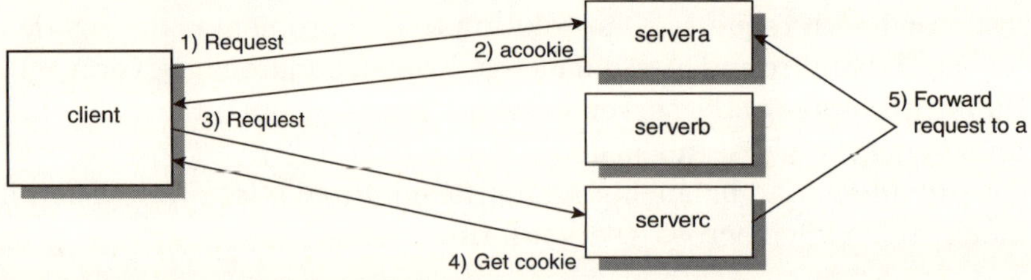

Figure 19.1 srun indexing configuration.

In this configuration, we assume there are three Resin engines running on three different servers. Requests can be made of any of the servers. When a client makes a request, a cookie is saved on the client's machine with the cookie containing a certain prefix. That prefix is used in subsequent requests to indicate which of the three servers should get the new request. If the user is supposed to be handled by serverb but that server fails, the request goes to serverc and the user's session is lost.

Distributed Sessions

One problem with the solution we just described is a lack of reliability provided by the server saving the session in memory. If the box were to fail or even if a Java Virtual Machine (JVM) were to fail, the sessions associated with it would be lost. You need to a way to save the session so that all of the servers can access it regardless of which one receives a request from the user. There are two solutions to this problem: symmetrical sessions and sticky sessions.

Symmetrical Sessions

With symmetrical sessions, most of the session management is assigned to the JVMs. When a client browser makes a request, the receiving JVM pulls the session information from a storage location to update and save it as needed. No management is needed on the load-balancer side of things because the servlet engines don't care whether they have seen a previous request from the current client—they just pull a previously saved session. Figure 19.2 shows an example of how this type of system works.

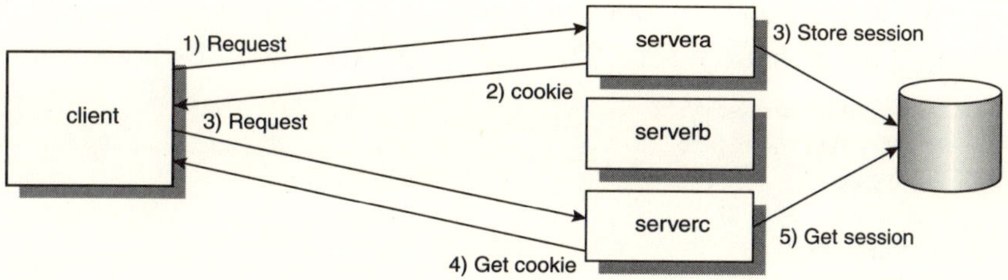

Figure 19.2 Symmetrical session handling.

When a client makes a request, the server stores a cookie on the client and also stores the session in a storage mechanism, such as a database. When another request is made from the same client, the server pulls the cookie and uses the information within it to pull the session from storage. In this scenario, you don't care about any of the previous requests and which server handled it. When building a configuration file for symmetrical session handling, make sure that the <always-load-session> attribute appears in the <session-config> element. This attribute tells the server to load the session of the requesting client for all requests.

The Resin server saves the session data to storage only when an attribute of the session is changed. If have an object as a session variable and you change an internal attribute of the object, the server won't recognize that the session has changed. In this case, you can force a save with the <always-save-session> element. You can also use the <save-on-shutdown/> element to save sessions only when the Resin server shuts down.

Sticky Sessions

Sticky sessions are a combination of the srun indexing and distributed sessions. All requests from a client are sent to a specific server based on a client's initial contact with the server group. At the same time, the session is stored so any server in the farm can obtain it in case that server fails.

Database-Distributed Sessions

Once a server has a session and needs to save it, a storage mechanism must be in place. One of the most popular options is to use a database. While storing the session in a database is relatively easy, there can be a performance issue on a poorly maintained database. To handle any performance issues, you can use a separate server and database solely to handle session stores and retrievals. This is known as *database-distributed sessions*.

To use this approach, you must create a <resource-ref> element in the Resin configuration file for the database server handling session requests. Once you do, the Resin server automatically creates a table in the server and database specified by <resource-ref>. The table will have the following schema:

```
CREATE TABLE session (
  id VARCHAR(64) NOT NULL,
  data BLOB,
  mod_time TIMESTAMP,
  PRIMARY KEY(id)
)
```

The Resin configuration file should look something like the following:

```
<web-app>
  <session-config>
    <jdbc-store>jdbcStore</jdbc-store>
    <always-save-session/>
  </session-config>
</web-app>
```

TCP-Ring Distributed Sessions

As you might guess, the session database server becomes a single point of failure as well as a performance bottleneck. You can still take advantage of load balancing and maintaining secure and reliable sessions through TCP-ring distributed sessions. In this protocol, the servers are logically arranged in a ring. Sessions are distributed throughout the ring, thus providing all servers with copies of all sessions in memory. There is no single point of failure in the system. The configuration is:

```
<resin xmlns="http://caucho.com/ns/resin">
<javac compiler='jikes'/>

<server>
  <cluster>
    <port server-id="a" port='6810' index='1'/>
    <port server-id="b" port='6811' index='2'/>
```

```
      <cluster-store jndi-name="caucho/store"
path="file:/tmp/caucho/qa/session"/>
    </cluster>

    <host id=''>
      <web-app id='/'>
        <session-config persistent-store="caucho/store"/>
      </web-app>
    </host>
  </server>
</resin>
```

File-Distributed Sessions

During application development where servers are reset and applications loaded and restarted, sessions can be lost very easily. To keep the session information available but avoid using a database for storage or multiple servers, you can use a file store. For example:

```
<web-app>
  <session-config>
    <file-store>WEB-INF/sessions</file-store>
  </session-config>
</web-app>
```

This configuration tells Resin to use a directory called sessions to hold all sessions created during the execution of the server. As a session is updated, the new session data is written to the file store. When an application is reloaded or the server is restarted, Resin reads all session information found in the store. You should not use a file store-based solution in a multiserver environment because Resin was not designed for this type of configuration.

Load-Balancing Options

Clearly a production environment needs to have load balancing in order to ensure that an application will be able to support an appropriate load. In this section, we examine a couple of options for load-balancing client requests across a number of servers: hardware load balancing and the use of Resin as a balancer.

Hardware Load Balancing

In a typical production environment where a hardware load balancer is used, there is generally a single Resin server on each of the server machines. The hardware load balancer is configured to send requests in an intelligent manner to the back-end servers. Figure 19.3 shows an example of this configuration.

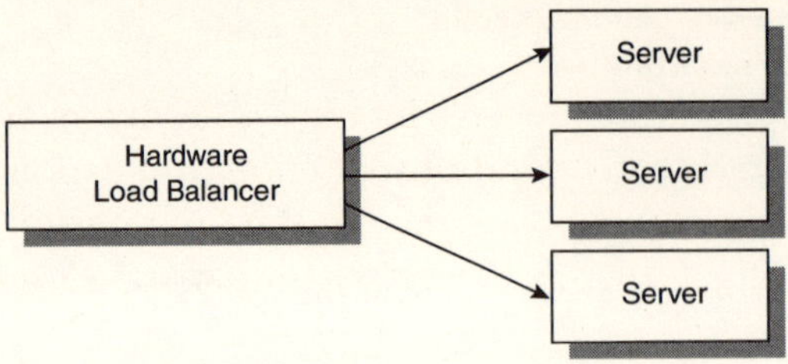

Figure 19.3 Hardware load-balancing configuration.

Since the hardware load balancer doesn't know anything about the requests coming from the client browsers, you must define distributed sessions for all of the Resin servers. With the configuration shown in Figure 19.3, the Resin configuration file would look like this:

```
<resin xmlns="http://caucho.com/ns/resin">
  <javac compiler='jikes'/>

  <server>
    <cluster-definition id='a'>
      <srun id='srun-a' index='2' host='localhost' port='6810'/>
    </cluster-definition>

    <host id=''>
      <web-app id='/'>
        <servlet servlet-name='remote'
                 servlet-class='com.caucho.servlets.LoadBalance-
Servlet'>
          <init-param cluster='a'/>
        </servlet>
        <servlet-mapping url-pattern='/remote/*' servlet-
name='remote'/>
      </web-app>
    </host>
  </server>
</resin>
```

All of the servers use the same configuration file but start in slightly different ways. In a Unix farm, you start the three servers with these commands:

```
Server 1> bin./resin -server resina -pid resina.pid start
Server 2> bin/resin -server resinb -pid resinb.pid start
Server 3> bin/resin -server resinc -pid resinc.pid start
```

On a Windows farm, you use the following startup command lines:

```
Server 1> bin.httpd -server resina -install-as resina
Server 1> net start resina
Server 1> bin.httpd -server resinb -install-as resinb
Server 1> net start resinb
Server 1> bin.httpd -server resinc -install-as resinc
Server 1> net start resinc
```

Using Resin as a Balancer

If you have a production system that doesn't include a hardware load balancer but you still want to provide this kind of reliability, you can use Resin itself and a servlet called LoadBalanceServlet. This configuration uses a machine running Resin that acts as the load balancer, as shown in Figure 19.4.

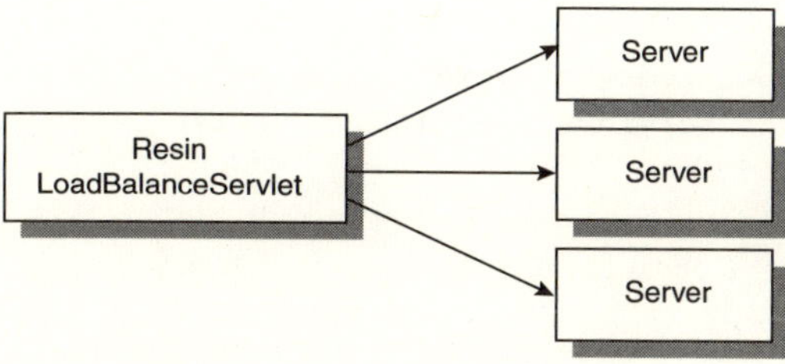

Figure 19.4 Configuring a Resin load balancer.

The LoadBalanceServlet is very flexible, and it allows server groups to be created based on specific requests. For example, Figure 19.5 shows a Resin load balancer that sends requests for /company.com to a server farm and requests for /ourcompany.com to a single server.

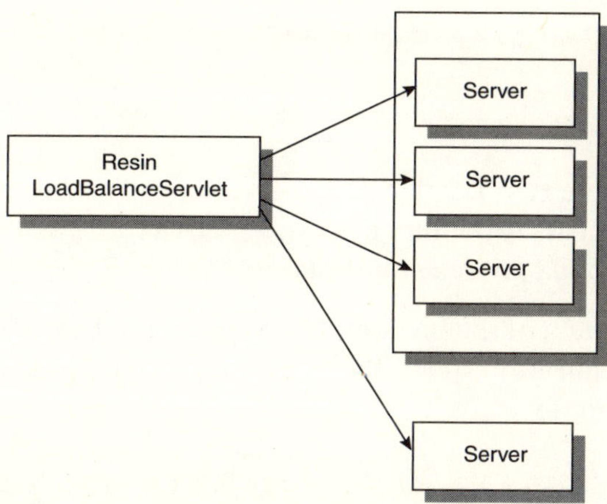

Figure 19.5 A Resin load balancer-specific request.

Not only is the Resin server able to provide load balancing, but Resin's internal cache provides better overall performance for all hosted sites. When configuring a Resin load-balance system, you need two configuration files: one for the load -balancing server and one for all of the back-end servers. Let's consider the configuration in Figure 19.5. The load-balancing configuration is:

```
<server>
  <http port='80'/>
```

```
    <cluster-definition id="a">
      <srun id='resina' index='1' host='192.168.0.1'/>
      <srun id='resinb' index='2' host='192.168.0.2'/>
    </cluster-definition>
    <cluster-definition id="b">
      <srun id='resinb' index='3' host='192.168.0.3'/>
    </cluster-definition>

  <servlet>
    <servlet-name>resingroup-a</servlet-name>
    <servlet-class>com.caucho.servlets.LoadBalanceServlet </servlet-
class>
    <init-param cluster='a'/>
  </servlet>

  <servlet-mapping url-pattern='/company.com/*' servletname=resingroup-
a/>
  <servlet>
    <servlet-name>resingroup-b</servlet-name>
    <servlet-class>com.caucho.servlets.LoadBalanceServlet </servlet-
class>
    <init-param cluster='b'/>
  </servlet>

  <servlet-mapping url-pattern='/ourcompany.com/*'
  servletname='resingroup-b'/>

  <server>
```

In this configuration we have two LoadBalanceServlet servlets executing to handle client requests. Requests for company.com/* go to a three-server farm; requests for ourcompany.com/* go to a single server.

The configuration files for each of the back-end servers defined earlier resemble the load-balancer configuration file without the servlet mapping and session management. For example:

```
<server>
  <http port='80'/>
  <cluster>
    <cluster-group>
      <srun id='resina' index='1' host='192.168.0.1' port='6802'/>
      <srun id='resinb' index='2' host='192.168.0.2' port='6802'/>
      <srun id='resinc' index='3' host='192.168.0.3' port='6802'/>
    </cluster-group>

    <cluster-group>
      <srun id='resind' index='1' host='192.168.0.4' port='6802'/>
    </cluster-group>

  </cluster>
```

```
    <session-config>
      <tcp-store/>
    </session-config>
  </server>
```

Using srun-backup

In those situations where a load balancer or router is used to distribute load to multiple servers and each is running both a Web server and a servlet engine, you can use the <srun-backup> element to provide greater reliability.

When a Web server receives a request, it attempts to send the servlet request to a primary machine. If the request isn't successful, another servlet machine is attempted. For this situation to work, the configuration files must include distributed-session management and use a host attribute in the initial <srun> element to indicate the primary servlet engine. For example:

```
<server>
  <cluster>
    <srun id="resina" port='6802' index="1"/>
    <srun id="resinb" port='6802' backup='true' index="2"/>
    <srun id="resinc" port='6802' backup='true' index="3"/>
    <srun id="resind" port='6802' backup='true' index="4"/>
  </cluster>
</server>
```

Here, we tell the configuration to use the localhost servlet engine as the primary and other servers as backups.

Reliability Options

Most of our discussion so far has been based on the assumption that multiple servers were available. The multiple servers provide not only load balancing but also reliability. We can further increase reliability through multiple servlet engines on the same machine. In this section, we assume you have only a single server but still want to provide reliability through multiple servlet threads.

Figure 19.6 shows an example of how we want to configure a server.

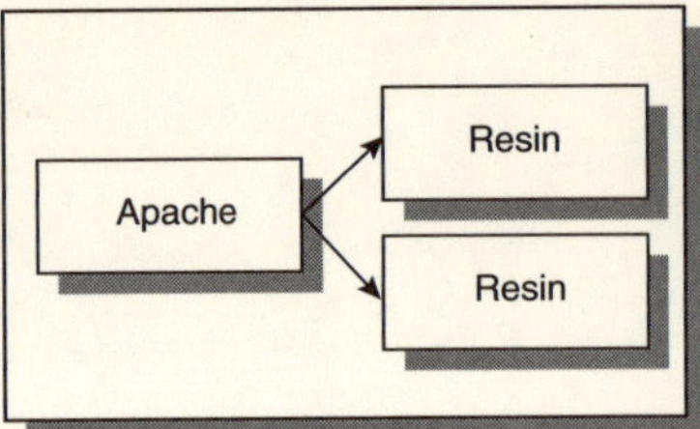

Figure 19.6 A single machine with multiple servlet threads.

The basic idea is if a JVM fails during its execution of one Resin servlet engine, another one will be available to take its place. To achieve this, you need a configuration that uses the <srun-backup> element. For example:

```
<server>
  <cluster>
    <srun id="resina" host="localhost" port="6802" index="1"/>
    <srun id="resinb" host="localhost" port="6803" index="2"
backup="true"/>
  </cluster>
</server>
```

The configuration file is used to start two servers on the same box using the following commands. In Unix:

```
unix> httpd.sh -pid srun1.pid -server resina start
unix> httpd.sh -pid srun2.pid -server resinb start
```

In Windows:

```
c:\resin3.0.2> bin/httpd -install-as resina -server resina
c:\resin3.0.2> bin/httpd -install-as resinb -server resinb
```

This setup assumes that an Apache server passes the servlet requests to the appropriate server instance. See Chapter 16 for more details on setting up Apache with Resin.

Conclusion

That's it! We hope you enjoyed reading the book as much as we enjoyed writing it. You should have learned during your reading that Resin isn't just an application server but a comprehensive package that provides support for JSP, Servlets and EJBs as well as a host of protocols like Hessian and Burlap. You should now have a comprehensive understanding of how to deploy the server and write application for it.

APPENDIX

A

Resin Sources

Caucho provides two ways you can download the Resin server. One option is to download the full-source package. The other option, the "snapshot," is the latest version, but keep in mind that it has not gone through Caucho's full quality assurance cycle. All of the downloads are available at www.caucho.com/download/, as shown in Figure A.1.

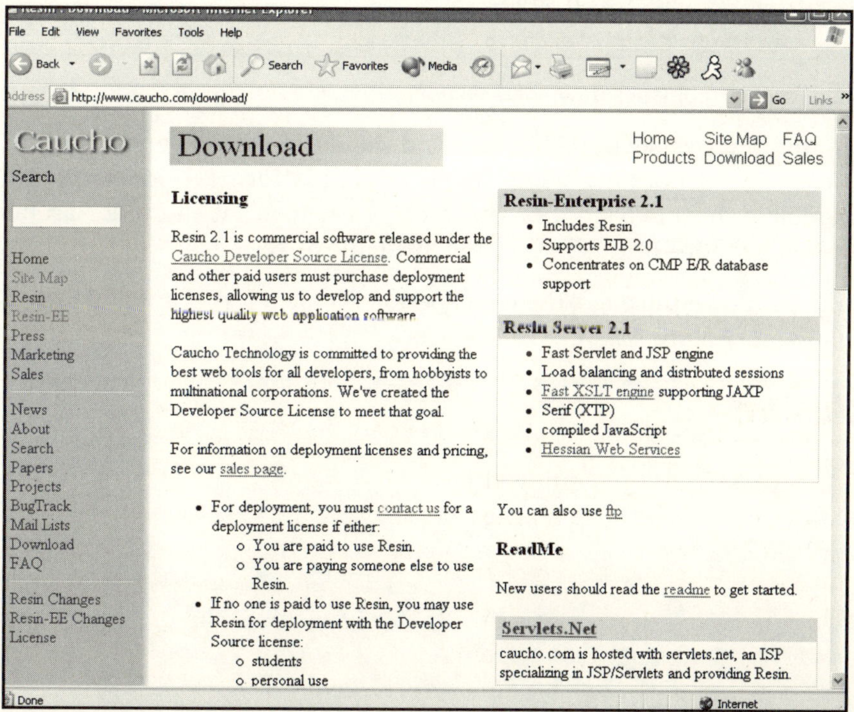

Figure A.1 The Caucho download page.

This page groups the downloads by their function. The first section, shown in Figure A.2, contains links for downloading the Resin binaries.

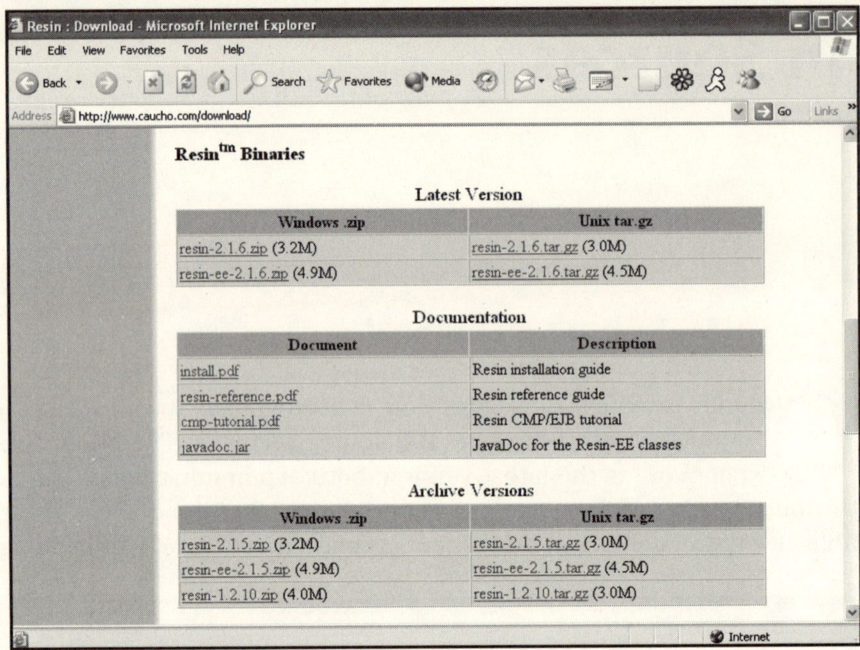

Figure A.2 The Resin binaries download section.

In the Binaries section, you can find the latest tested versions of Resin and Resin-EE for both the Windows and Unix platforms. Documentation is also available on this page. For those of you who want the older archived and tested versions of Resin, they are available as well.

Moving down the page, the next section is called Experimental Snapshots, as shown in Figure A.3.

File Edit View Favorites Tools Help

Address http://www.caucho.com/download/

The experimental snapshot is always the most current version of the code, but it will not have gone through the entire QA cycle.

Experimental Snapshots

Windows .zip	Unix tar.gz	Date
resin-snap.zip (3.2M)	resin-snap.tar.gz (3.0M)	2003/02/04
resin-ee-snap.zip (4.9M)	resin-ee-snap.tar.gz (4.5M)	2003/02/04
resin-3 0-snap.zip (2.3M)	resin-3 0-snap.tar.gz (1.6M)	2003/02/04
resin-ee-3 0-snap.zip (2.3M)	resin-ee-3 0-snap.tar.gz (1.6M)	2003/02/04
resin-1.2snap.zip (2.5M)	resin-1.2snap.tar.gz (1.7M)	2002/08/29

Internet

Figure A.3 Resin's experimental snapshots.

The experimental snapshots are complete systems, but they have not been fully tested. You will find version 3.x's latest snapshots as well as snapshots for the older 2.1 version.

The last section on the page features source downloads, shown in Figure A.4.

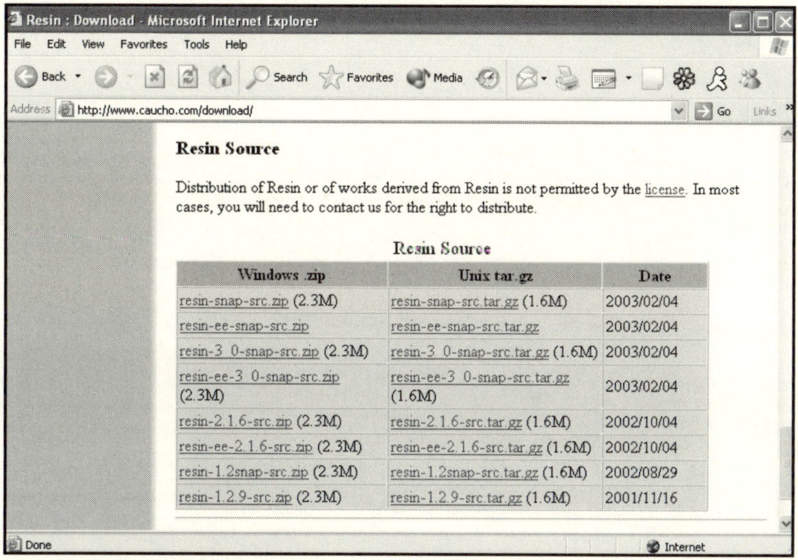

Figure A.4 Resin source downloads.

APPENDIX B

Resin Status

One of the most important aspects of running a Web site that provides information to consumers is reliability. We discussed reliability in Chapter 19 in the form of replicating the servers; in this appendix we discuss another reliability topic: obtaining the status of the Resin server.

Status can be obtained in several ways. An obvious and simple method is to browse various page on the Web site. If the page loads in the browser, then you can be relatively sure the server is operating successfully. If the page doesn't come up, you probably have a bigger problem to handle. A more reliable method for checking your site is Resin's status servlet called ResinStatusServlet.

This servlet isn't available "right out of the box" due to potential security concerns with providing status information. To activate the servlet, the <web-app> configuration information shown in Listing B.1 needs to be added to your resin.conf file.

```
<web-app id='/admin'>
  <allow-admin>true</allow-admin>
  <servlet-mapping url-pattern='/resin-status'
                  servlet-name='com.caucho.servlets.ResinStatusServlet'>
    <init-param enable='read'/>
  </servlet-mapping>
```

Listing B.1 Configuration spec for ResinStatusServlet. (continues)

```
  <!-- only allow the localhost to use the admin -->
  <security-constraint>
    <ip-constraint>127.0.0.1/32</ip-constraint>

    <web-resource-collection>
      <url-pattern>/*</url-pattern>
    </web-resource-collection>
  </security-constraint>
</web-app>
```

Listing B.1 Configuration spec for ResinStatusServlet. (continued)

Taking a moment to look at the configuration, we find that the servlet will be located at the URL of /admin/resin-status. When a user browses to any servlet in the /admin directory, this <web-app> element will come into play.

The first element in the <web-app> hierarchy is <allow-admin> which has a value of true. This sub-element is very important because it allows the servlet to be invoked to have access to the class com.caucho.http.admin.ApplicationAdmin. The ApplicationAdmin class gives the invoked servlet administrative privileges to the executing application. As you can see, this has direct implications for the site's security. A few of the most useful methods available in the ApplicationAdmin class are:

- **void clearCache()**—clears the application cache.
- **int getActiveSessionCount()**—current # of active sessions.
- **Path getAppDir()**—gets the application directory of the current application.
- **ClassLoader getClassLoader()**—returns the applications class loader.
- **HostAdmin getHostAdmin()**—return a HostAdmin object.
- **ServerAdmin getServerAdmin()**—returns a ServerAdmin object.

The last two methods provide even more information about the currently executing application and the server itself. The HostAdmin allows the servlet to obtain information about a virtual host. The second method returns a ServerAdmin object which allows complete administration of the server itself. Methods in this object include:

- **void clearCache()**—clears the system cache.
- **void close()**—closes the server.
- **void restart()**—restarts the server.

There are many additional methods available for obtaining a wide range of statistics about the currently executing server. Looking back at the configuration information from the status servlet, we find that all of the functionality for the ResinStatusServlet can be found in the class com.caucho.servlets. ResinStatusServlet. Because Caucho has made the source code for Resin available, a developer has the option of adding any type of administration control they find necessary for their particular situation.

Due to the security concerns that the administration servlet raises, additional security elements are provided in the <web-app> entry. The <ip-constraint> element is used to limit who can access the servlet. In this case, only browsers that are located on the local machine are able to access the servlet.

Once the configuration file has been updated, use a browser to access the servlet using a URL like:

http://localhost:8080/admin/resin-status

The servlet will display a Web page with a variety of information. Figure B.1 shows the first part of the information returned.

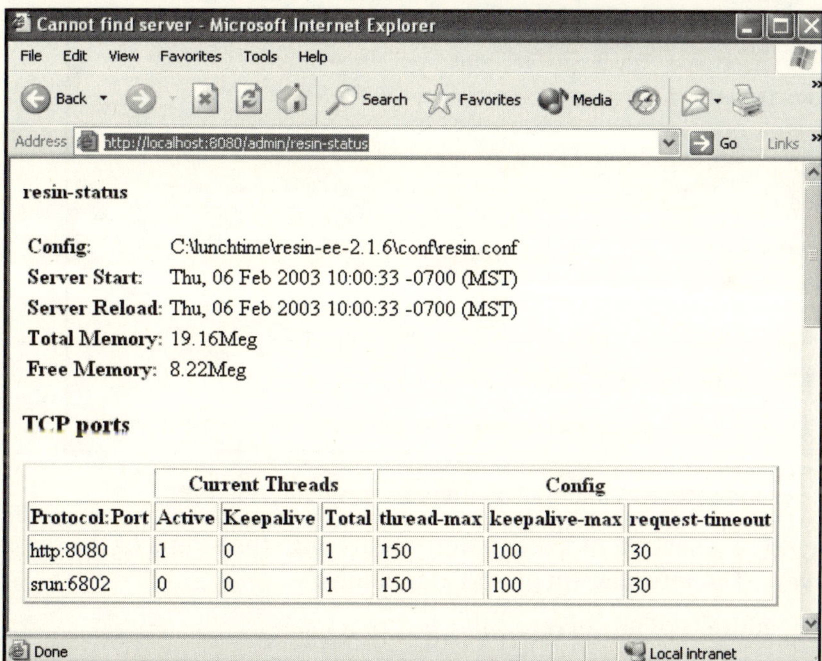

	Current Threads			Config		
Protocol:Port	Active	Keepalive	Total	thread-max	keepalive-max	request-timeout
http:8080	1	0	1	150	100	30
srun:6802	0	0	1	150	100	30

Figure B.1 First section of information from the ResinStatusServlet.

The first section of information returned from the servlet is data about the server itself, including:

- Configuration file used for the server.
- Start time (when the server was executed).

- Reload time (the time the server last reloaded itself).
- Total hard drive space.
- Free hard drive space.

The next section of information details the WEB and srun ports the server is using, as well as information about the threads servicing the ports. For each of the ports, the thread information includes:

- Active threads (total number of threads current servicing requests).
- Keep-alive threads (total number of threads in keep-alive state).
- Configuration values for the threads.

Figure B.2 shows the middle section of information returned by the servlet.

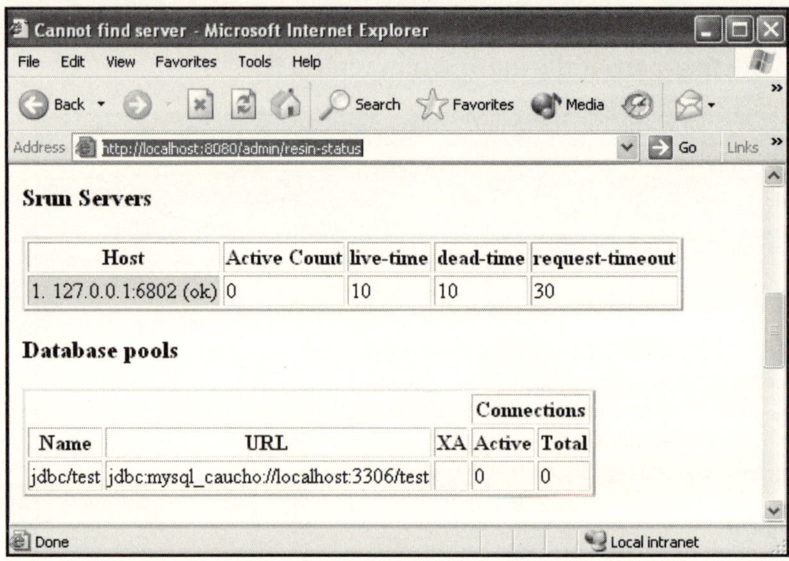

Figure B.2 Second section of information from the ResinStatusServlet.

The second section of information begins with the status of the current srun servers. The information provided includes:

- IP address of all servers.
- Active thread counts for the servers.
- Configuration information for the threads.

The srun server information is followed by database statistics. This section is one of the most critical to verifying your site's overall functionality. The database pools section includes:

- Name of the JNDI resource.

- URL to the database.
- Whether the connection is XA based.
- Active and total connections.

The database stats are important because one of the most resource-intensive activities on your site is database access. These stats will show you which of the JNDI resources are using the most database connections, as well as the most active database host. With this information at hand, you can make the architecture decisions needed to maximize your system's performance.

Finally, Figure B.3 shows the last information returned by the server.

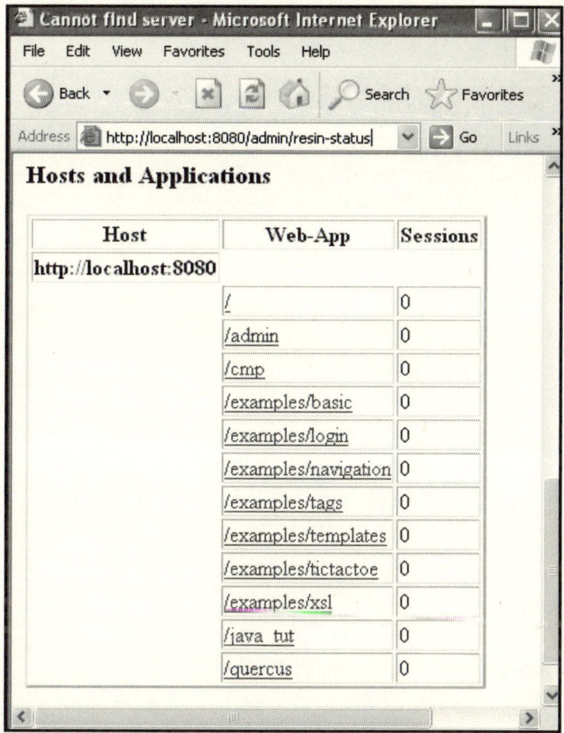

Figure B.3 Final section of information from the ResinStatusServlet.

The final section of information returned from the ResinStatusServlet is a list of all applications broken down by host. If you had virtual hosts on the server, all of the applications for those hosts would be listed as well. The information provided shows the total number of sessions currently active for all applications. As you might guess, this number can be used to determine which virtual hosts and specific applications are most active. Again, this information is very useful for scaling and architecture purposes.

APPENDIX C

Resin and Eclipse

One of the most exciting new IDEs (Integrated Development Environments) is the Eclipse platform, an open source set of highly integrated tools, available at www.eclipse.org. The IDE is designed to be a universal tool which allows open extensible APIs. Using the extension API, plug-ins can be created to provide specific functionality to the Eclipse IDE. A company called Improve has developed an excellent, open source Resin plugin for the Eclipse IDE. This plugin, called the Improve Resin Plugin for Eclipse, offers several key features, including:

- **ResinLauncher**—allows the Resin server to the launched with Eclipse for debugging purposes.
- **ResinProjectWizard**—creates appropriate <web-app> directory structures and classpath.

Installing the Eclipse Plugin

After you have installed Eclipse, download the latest Improve Resin Plugin for Eclipse from www.improve-technologies.com/alpha/resin/. Place the downloaded JAR file into a directory called /fr.improve.eclipse.resin_0.5.2. This directory should be placed within the /plugins directory of the Eclipse installation. In many cases, the full directory structure will be:

```
c:/eclipse/plugins/fr.improve.eclipse.resin_0.5.2
```

After the jar is saved in the new directory, use the following command to extract its contents:

```
jar -xf fr.improve.eclipse.resin_0.5.2.jar
```

There is one more step in the installation process: launch the Eclipse IDE and select Window and Preferences. A dialog will open with various options listed on the left part of the screen as shown in Figure C.1.

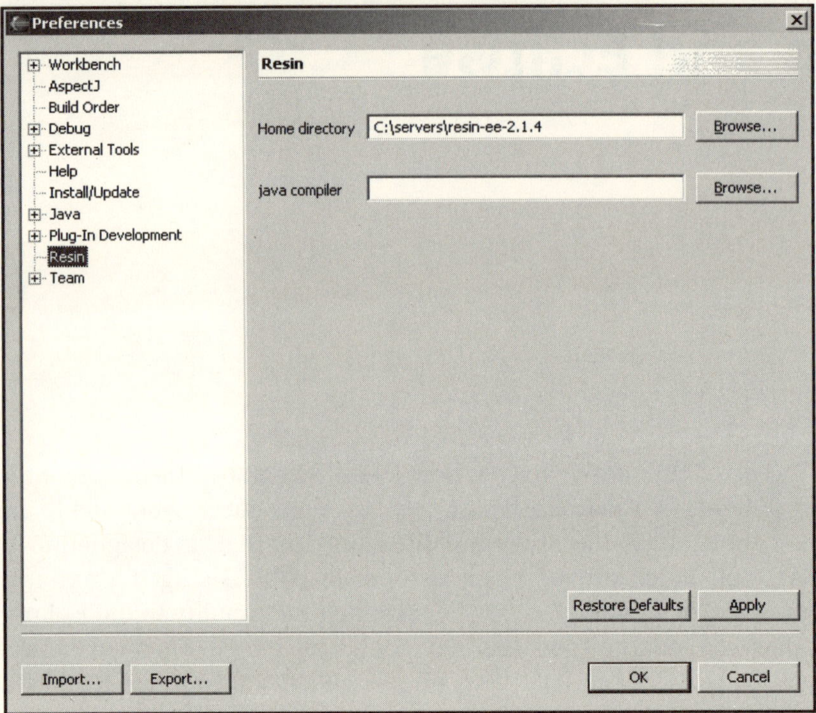

Figure C.1 Preferences dialog.

Select the Resin option form the list; a dialog box with two edit lines will be displayed. On the first line, labeled Home directory, enter the root directory of the Resin installation that Eclipse and the Improve Resin Plugin for Eclipse should use. On the second line, labeled Java compiler, enter the location of the Java compiler you want Eclipse to use. If you don't supply a compiler, the IDE will use the installed JDK. Click on OK to save the preferences.

Using ResinProjectWizard

Now let's walk through how to use the ResinProjectWizard to create a new Resin project. Click on File, New, then Project to bring up the New Project dialog. Click on the Java entry listed on left side of the dialog. The click should reveal one or more wizards on the right of the dialog, one of which is Java Resin project as shown in Figure C.2

Now, either double-click on the Java Resin project entry or single click on the entry and press Next. Either operation will bring up the dialog in Figure C.3

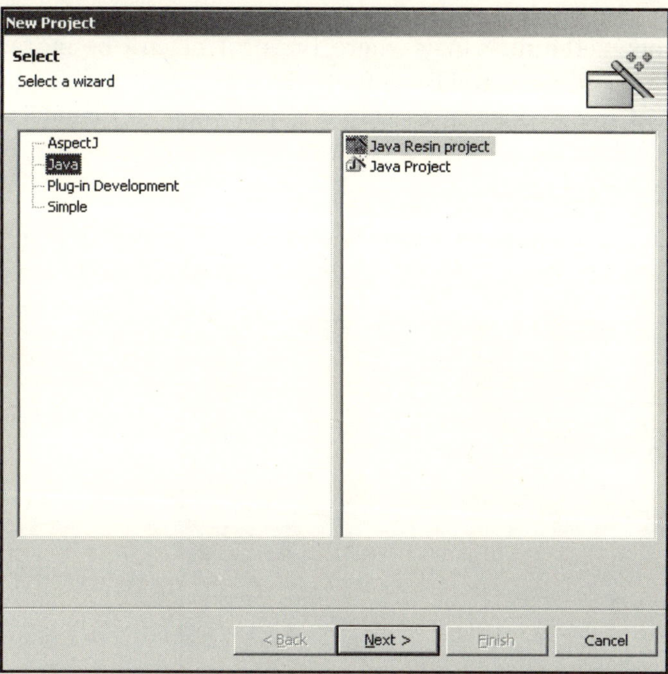

Figure C.2 New project wizard with Resin project.

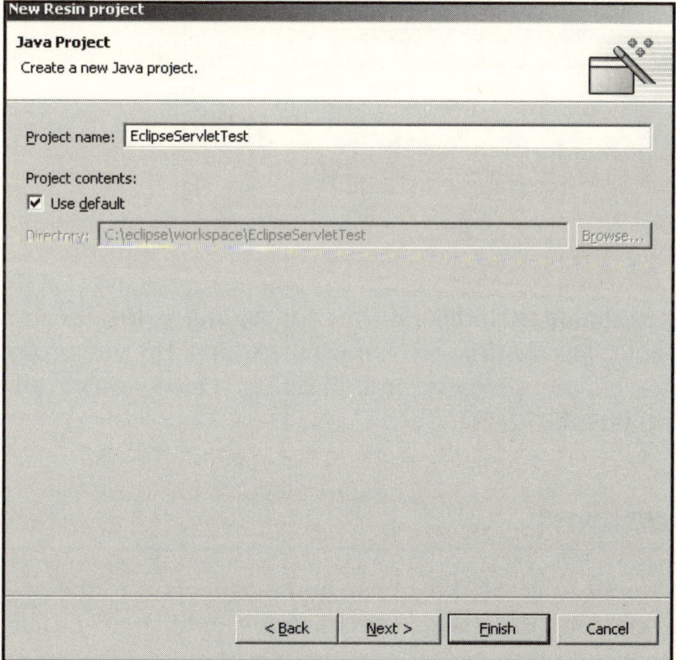

Figure C.3 New Resin project dialog.

Enter a name for your project in the Project name edit line. As you type in the name of the project, the directory where the project will be stored is displayed in the second edit control. By default, the dialog will choose the /workspace directory of the Eclipse installation. If you want to manually enter a specific directory, remove the check in the Use default checkbox, and then enter your own directory path.

Click on the Next button to move to the next dialog. The next dialog is shown in Figure C.4 and allows specific Java settings to be added to the project.

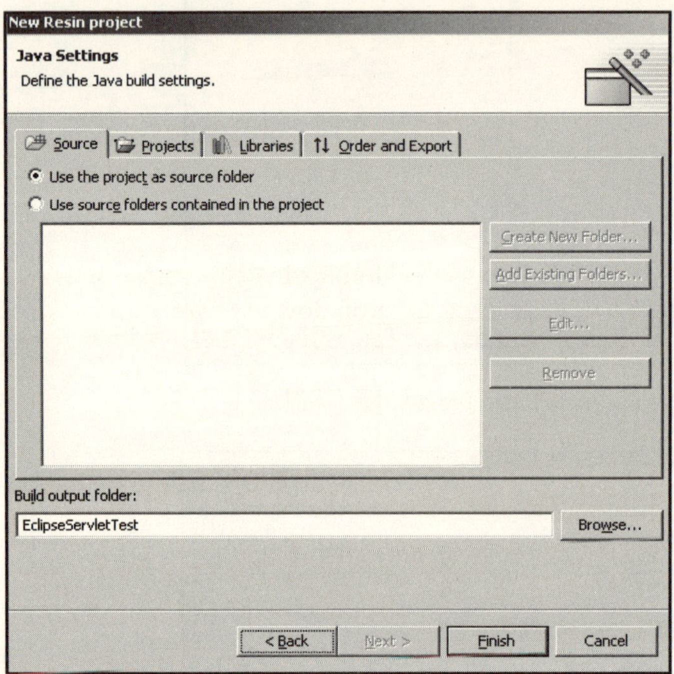

Figure C.4 Java Settings Dialog

The Java Settings dialog includes options for adding paths for the source, additional projects, any additional libraries needed by the projects, and finally the order of the projects and libraries. Once you've added any changes, click on Finish.

Using ResinLauncher

Once a project has been created, you can add a new class to the project and place servlet code into the class. For example, add a new Class called EclipseServletTest and place the code in Listing C.1.

```
import java.io.*;
import javax.servlet.*;
import javax.servlet.http.*;

public class EclipseServletTest extends HttpServlet {
  public void doGet(HttpServletRequest request,
                    HttpServletResponse response)
    throws ServletException, IOException {

    response.setContentType("text/html");
    PrintWriter out = response.getWriter();

    out.println("<title>Hello, World!</title>");
    out.println("<h1>Hello, World!</h1>");
  }
}
```

Listing C.1 Example Hello World Servlet.

To execute the Hello World Servlet within Resin, click on the small arrow just to the right of the Run button. In the drop down menu that appears, click on the Run…entry to bring up the dialog shown in Figure C.5.

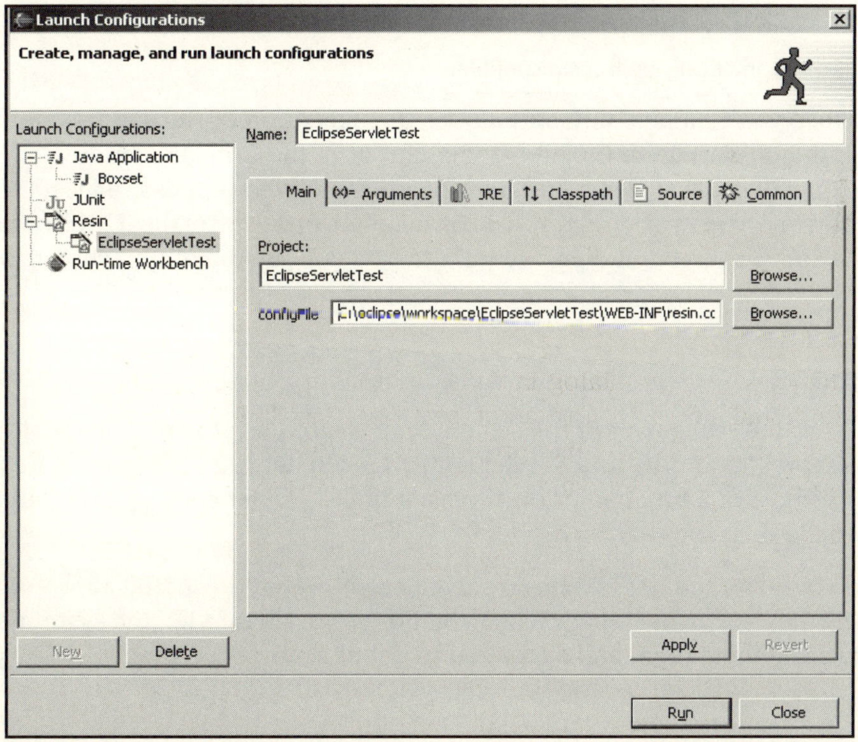

Figure C.5 The Launch Configurations dialog.

The Launch Configurations dialog is important because it shows the various runtime options that can be set, as well as the Resin config file to use when executing the servlet project. The Improve Resin Plugin for Eclipse will automatically create a resin.conf file for the current project and default to that file. If you are just developing your servlets, you can use this file. An example of the file created for our example is shown in Listing C.2.

```
<caucho.com>
  <java compiler='' args="-g"/>
  <http-server app-dir='doc' class-update-interval='2'>
  <http port='8080'/>

  <servlet-mapping url-pattern='/servlet/*'
    servlet-name='invoker'/>
  <servlet-mapping url-pattern='*.jsp'
    servlet-name='com.caucho.jsp.JspServlet'/>

  <web-app id='EclipseServletTest'
    app-dir='C:\eclipse\workspace\EclipseServletTest' />
  </http-server>
</caucho.com>
```

Listing C.2 Automatically built resin.conf file.

Once you've added any options for the execution of the servlet, click on the Run button. Figure C.6 shows the output in the Console window of Eclipse. You will see that Resin has started and is ready to process requests. To see if your servlet works, open a browser and browse to the URL: http://localhost:8080/servlet/ EclipseServetTest. You will see the output shown in Figure C.7

Debugging

Now, the real power of the system comes into play; the plugin enables you to set breakpoints in your servlet code to aid in debugging. Figure C.8 shows an example of a breakpoint that was set in the servlet code and triggered when the URL above was used.

In order to activate the Resin server, select Debug…, set the appropriate config file, and press Debug. When you browse to the servlet, the system will trigger the breakpoint and allow you to debug your code.

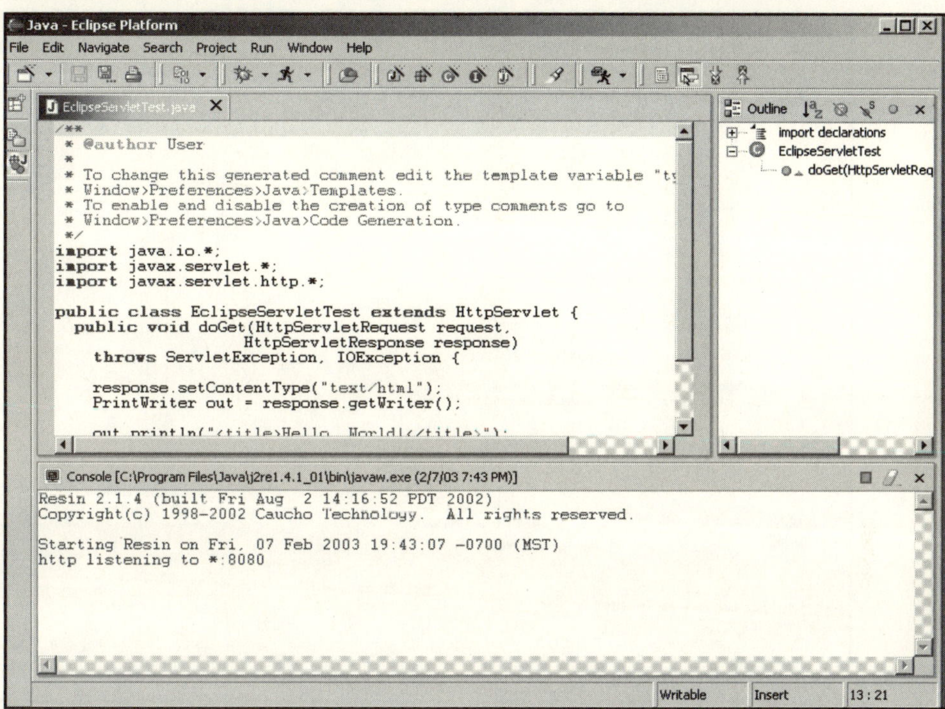

Figure C.6 Resin started within Eclipse.

Figure C.7 The sample servlet executing.

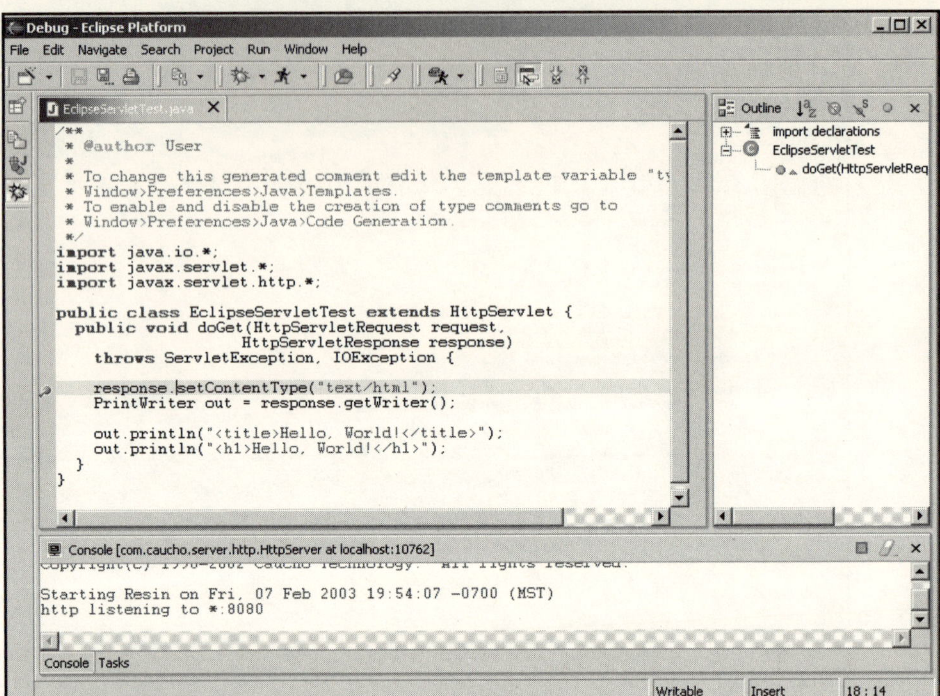

Figure C.8 Breakpoint in the servlet.

APPENDIX D

Burlap and Hessian APIs

This appendix is a developer's quick reference to the Burlap and Hessian APIs.

Package com.caucho.burlap

public class com.caucho.burlap.SerializedExceptionWrapper

extends java.rmi.RemoteException

Constructors

public SerializedExceptionWrapper()

public SerializedExceptionWrapper(Throwable cause, String trace)

Methods

public java.lang.Throwable getRootCause()

public java.lang.String getMessage()

public java.lang.String toString()

public void printStackTrace()

public void printStackTrace(PrintWriter pw)

public void printStackTrace(PrintStream os)

public class com.caucho.burlap.RpcException

extends java.rmi.RemoteException

implements java.io.Serializable

Constructors

public RpcException()

public RpcException(String s)

public abstract class com.caucho.burlap.ObjectStub

extends com.caucho.burlap.BurlapStub

Constructors

public ObjectStub()

Methods

public abstract java.lang.String getBurlapType()

public Handle getHandle()

public EJBHome getEJBHome()

public boolean isIdentical(EJBObject obj)

public void remove()

public java.lang.Object getPrimaryKey()

protected EJBHome _ejb_getEJBHome()

protected boolean _ejb_isIdentical(EJBObject obj)

protected void _ejb_remove()

protected java.lang.Object _ejb_getPrimaryKey()

Fields

protected transient _handle

public class com.caucho.burlap.NoRpcObjectException

extends com.caucho.burlap.RpcException

Constructors

public NoRpcObjectException()

public NoRpcObjectException(String s)

public class com.caucho.burlap.NoRpcMethodException

extends com.caucho.burlap.RpcException

Constructors

public NoRpcMethodException()

public NoRpcMethodException(String s)

public class com.caucho.burlap.NameContextSkeleton

extends Skeleton

Methods

protected void _service(ReadStream is, WriteStream os)

protected void executeUnknown(String method, BurlapInput in, BurlapOutput out)

Fields

protected static dbg

public class com.caucho.burlap.MetaStub

Constructors

public MetaStub()

Methods

public static java.lang.Object call(Path urlPath, String method, Object arg)

public static java.lang.Object call(Path urlPath, String method, Object[] args)

public class com.caucho.burlap.MessageSkeleton

extends Skeleton

Methods

protected void _setObject(Object obj)

protected void _service(ReadStream rawIs, WriteStream rawOs)

protected void _execute(CharBuffer method, BurlapInput in, BurlapOutput out)

Fields

protected static dbg

protected server

protected connection

protected destination

protected session

protected queueSession

protected queueSender

protected topicSession

protected topicPublisher

public class com.caucho.burlap.MarshalExceptionWrapper

extends java.rmi.MarshalException

Constructors

public MarshalExceptionWrapper(String s, Exception root)

Methods

public java.lang.Throwable getRootCause()

public abstract class com.caucho.burlap.HomeStub

extends com.caucho.burlap.BurlapStub

Constructors

public HomeStub()

Methods

public java.lang.String getBurlapURL()

public abstract java.lang.String getBurlapType()

public HomeHandle getHomeHandle()

public EJBMetaData getEJBMetaData()

public void remove(Handle handle)

protected EJBMetaData _ejb_getEJBMetaData()

protected void _ejb_remove(Handle handle)

public class com.caucho.burlap.EJBServlet

extends com.caucho.ejb.EJBServlet

Constructors

public EJBServlet()

Methods

protected java.lang.String getDefaultProtocolContainer()

public class com.caucho.burlap.BurlapWriter

extends BurlapOutput

Constructors

public BurlapWriter(ReadStream is, OutputStream os)

public BurlapWriter(OutputStream os)

public BurlapWriter()

Methods

public void init(OutputStream os)

public void setRemoteResolver(BurlapRemoteResolver resolver)

public BurlapInput doCall()

public void close()

public class com.caucho.burlap.BurlapStubFactory

Constructors

public BurlapStubFactory()

Methods

public BurlapRemoteResolver getRemoteResolver()

public void setWorkPath(Path path)

public Path getWorkPath()

public java.lang.Object create(Class api, String url)

public AbstractBurlapInput getBurlapInput(InputStream is)

public BurlapOutput getBurlapOutput(OutputStream os)

public java.lang.Object lookup(String type, String url)

public abstract class com.caucho.burlap.BurlapStub

Constructors

public BurlapStub()

Methods

public java.lang.String getBurlapURL()

protected com.caucho.burlap.BurlapWriter _burlap_openWriter()

protected void _burlap_freeWriter(BurlapWriter out)

Fields

protected _url

protected transient _urlPath

protected transient _client

protected transient _resolver

public abstract class com.caucho.burlap.BurlapSkeleton

extends Skeleton

Constructors

public BurlapSkeleton()

Methods

protected abstract void _setObject(Object object)

protected void _service(ReadStream is, WriteStream os)

protected abstract void _execute(CharBuffer method, BurlapInput in, BurlapOutput out)

protected void _executeUnknown(CharBuffer method, BurlapInput in, BurlapOutput out)

Fields

protected static dbg

public class com.caucho.burlap.BurlapServerException

extends com.caucho.burlap.BurlapProtocolException

Constructors

public BurlapServerException()

public BurlapServerException(String s)

public class com.caucho.burlap.BurlapReader

extends BurlapInput

Constructors

public BurlapReader(ReadStream is)

public BurlapReader()

Methods

public void init(InputStream is)

public class com.caucho.burlap.BurlapProtocolException

extends java.rmi.RemoteException

Constructors

public BurlapProtocolException()

public BurlapProtocolException(String msg)

public BurlapProtocolException(Throwable rootCause)

Methods

public static com.caucho.burlap.BurlapProtocolException create (Throwable rootCause)

public static java.rmi.RemoteException createRemote (Throwable rootCause)

public java.lang.Throwable getRootCause()

public java.lang.String getMessage()

public void printStackTrace()

public void printStackTrace(PrintStream os)

public void printStackTrace(PrintWriter os)

public java.lang.String toString()

public class com.caucho.burlap.BurlapProtocol

extends ProtocolContainer

Constructors

public BurlapProtocol()

Methods

public java.lang.String getName()

protected HandleEncoder createHandleEncoder(AbstractServer server, Class primaryKeyClass)

protected Skeleton getSkeleton(String uri, String queryString)

protected java.lang.Class getHomeSkelClass(AbstractServer server)

protected java.lang.Class getObjectSkelClass(AbstractServer server)

public class com.caucho.burlap.BurlapParseException

extends com.caucho.burlap.RpcException

Constructors

public BurlapParseException()

public BurlapParseException(String s)

public class com.caucho.burlap.BurlapModel

extends AbstractModel

Constructors

public BurlapModel(String prefix)

public BurlapModel(String namePrefix, BurlapModel root)

Methods

public AbstractModel copy()

public java.lang.Object lookup(String name)

public java.util.List list()

public java.lang.String toString()

public class com.caucho.burlap.BurlapHomeHandle

extends AbstractHomeHandle

Constructors

public BurlapHomeHandle()

public BurlapHomeHandle(String url)

public BurlapHomeHandle(EJBHome home, String url)

Methods

public java.lang.String getServerId()

public EJBHome getEJBHome()

public java.lang.String getURL(String protocol)

public java.lang.String getURL()

public boolean equals(Object b)

public int hashCode()

public java.lang.String toString()

public class com.caucho.burlap.BurlapHandleEncoder

extends HandleEncoder

Constructors

public BurlapHandleEncoder(String serverId, Class primaryKeyClass)

public BurlapHandleEncoder(AbstractServer server, String serverId, Class primaryKeyClass)

Methods

public AbstractHomeHandle createHomeHandle()

public AbstractHandle createHandle(Object primaryKey)

protected java.lang.String getURL(Object primaryKey)

protected java.lang.String createRandomStringKey()

protected java.lang.String encodePrimaryKey(Object primaryKey)

public java.lang.Object objectIdToKey(Object objectKey)

public class com.caucho.burlap.BurlapHandle

extends AbstractHandle

Constructors

public BurlapHandle()

public BurlapHandle(String url)

public BurlapHandle(String url, Object key)

Methods

public java.lang.String getServerId()

public java.lang.String getObjectId()

public EJBObject getEJBObject()

public java.lang.Object getObjectKey()

public java.lang.String getURL()

public java.lang.String getURL(String protocol)

public int hashCode()

public boolean equals(Object obj)

public java.lang.String toString()

public class com.caucho.burlap.BurlapContextFactory

implements javax.naming.spi.InitialContextFactory

Constructors

public BurlapContextFactory()

Methods

public javax.naming.Context getInitialContext(Hashtable environment)

public class com.caucho.burlap.BurlapContext

extends ContextImpl

Methods

protected ContextImpl create(String name, AbstractModel model, Hashtable env)

Package com.caucho.burlap.io

public class com.caucho.burlap.io.QSerializerFactory

extends SerializerFactory

Constructors

public QSerializerFactory()

Methods

public Serializer getSerializer(Class cl)

public class com.caucho.burlap.io.HomeSerializer

extends Serializer

Constructors

public HomeSerializer()

Methods

public void writeObject(Object obj, AbstractBurlapOutput out)

public class com.caucho.burlap.io.EJBObjectSerializer

extends Serializer

Constructors

public EJBObjectSerializer()

Methods

public void writeObject(Object obj, AbstractBurlapOutput out)

Package com.caucho.hessian

public abstract class com.caucho.hessian.ObjectStub

extends com.caucho.hessian.HessianStub

Constructors

public ObjectStub()

Methods

public abstract java.lang.String getHessianType()

public Handle getHandle()

public EJBHome getEJBHome()

public boolean isIdentical(EJBObject obj)

public void remove()

public java.lang.Object getPrimaryKey()

protected EJBHome _ejb_getEJBHome()

protected boolean _ejb_isIdentical(EJBObject obj)

protected void _ejb_remove()

protected java.lang.Object _ejb_getPrimaryKey()

Fields

protected transient _handle

public class com.caucho.hessian.NameContextSkeleton

extends Skeleton

Methods

protected void _service(ReadStream is, WriteStream os)

protected void executeUnknown(String method, HessianInput in, HessianOutput out)

Fields

protected static dbg

public class com.caucho.hessian.MetaStub

Constructors

public MetaStub()

Methods

public static java.lang.Object call(Path urlPath, String method, Object arg)

public static java.lang.Object call(Path urlPath, String method, Object[] args)

public class com.caucho.hessian.MessageSkeleton

extends Skeleton

Methods

protected void _setObject(Object obj)

protected void _service(ReadStream rawIs, WriteStream rawOs)

protected void _execute(CharBuffer method, HessianInput in, HessianOutput out)

Fields

protected static dbg

protected server

protected connection

protected destination

protected session

protected queueSession

protected queueSender

protected topicSession

protected topicPublisher

public abstract class com.caucho.hessian.HomeStub

extends com.caucho.hessian.HessianStub

Constructors

public HomeStub()

Methods

public abstract java.lang.String getHessianType()

public HomeHandle getHomeHandle()

public EJBMetaData getEJBMetaData()

public void remove(Handle handle)

protected EJBMetaData _ejb_getEJBMetaData()

protected void _ejb_remove(Handle handle)

public class com.caucho.hessian.HessianWriter

extends HessianSerializerOutput

Constructors

public HessianWriter(ReadStream is, OutputStream os)

public HessianWriter(OutputStream os)

public HessianWriter()

Methods

public void init(OutputStream os)

public void setRemoteResolver(HessianRemoteResolver resolver)

public HessianInput doCall()

public void close()

public void writeObjectImpl(Object obj)

public class com.caucho.hessian.HessianStubFactory

Constructors

public HessianStubFactory()

Methods

public HessianRemoteResolver getRemoteResolver()

public void setWorkPath(Path path)

public Path getWorkPath()

public java.lang.Object create(Class api, String url)

public AbstractHessianInput getHessianInput(InputStream is)

public HessianOutput getHessianOutput(OutputStream os)

public java.lang.Object lookup(String type, String url)

public abstract class com.caucho.hessian.HessianStub

Constructors

public HessianStub()

Methods

public java.lang.String getHessianURL()

protected com.caucho.hessian.HessianWriter _hessian_openWriter()

protected void _hessian_freeWriter(HessianWriter out)

Fields

protected _url

protected transient _urlPath

protected transient _client

protected transient _resolver

public abstract class com.caucho.hessian.HessianSkeleton

extends Skeleton

Constructors

public HessianSkeleton()

Methods

protected abstract void _setObject(Object object)

protected void _service(ReadStream is, WriteStream os)

protected abstract void _execute(CharBuffer method, HessianInput in, HessianOutput out)

protected void _executeUnknown(CharBuffer method, HessianInput in, HessianOutput out)

Fields

protected static dbg

public class com.caucho.hessian.HessianReader

extends HessianSerializerInput

Constructors

public HessianReader(ReadStream is)

public HessianReader()

Methods

public void init(InputStream is)

public class com.caucho.hessian.HessianProtocol

extends ProtocolContainer

Constructors

public HessianProtocol()

Methods

public java.lang.String getName()

protected HandleEncoder createHandleEncoder(AbstractServer server, Class primaryKeyClass)

protected Skeleton getSkeleton(String uri, String queryString)

protected java.lang.Class getHomeSkelClass(AbstractServer server)

protected java.lang.Class getObjectSkelClass(AbstractServer server)

public class com.caucho.hessian.HessianModel

extends AbstractModel

Constructors

public HessianModel(String prefix)

public HessianModel(String namePrefix, HessianModel root)

Methods

public AbstractModel copy()

public java.lang.Object lookup(String name)

public java.util.List list()

public java.lang.String toString()

public class com.caucho.hessian.HessianHomeHandle

extends AbstractHomeHandle

Constructors

public HessianHomeHandle()

public HessianHomeHandle(String url)

public HessianHomeHandle(EJBHome home, String url)

Methods

public EJBHome getEJBHome()

public java.lang.String getServerId()

public java.lang.String getURL(String protocol)

public java.lang.String toString()

public class com.caucho.hessian.HessianHandleEncoder

extends HandleEncoder

Constructors

public HessianHandleEncoder(AbstractServer server, String serverId, Class primaryKeyClass)

Methods

public AbstractHomeHandle createHomeHandle()

public AbstractHandle createHandle(Object primaryKey)

protected java.lang.String getURL(Object primaryKey)

protected java.lang.String createRandomStringKey()

protected java.lang.String encodePrimaryKey(Object primaryKey)

public java.lang.Object objectIdToKey(Object objectKey)

public class com.caucho.hessian.HessianHandle

extends AbstractHandle

Constructors

public HessianHandle()

public HessianHandle(String url)

public HessianHandle(String url, Object key)

Methods

public java.lang.String getServerId()

public java.lang.String getObjectId()

public EJBObject getEJBObject()

public java.lang.Object getObjectKey()

public java.lang.String getURL()

public java.lang.String getURL(String protocol)

public int hashCode()

public boolean equals(Object obj)

public java.lang.String toString()

public class com.caucho.hessian.HessianContextFactory

implements javax.naming.spi.InitialContextFactory

Constructors

public HessianContextFactory()

Methods

public javax.naming.Context getInitialContext(Hashtable environment)

public class com.caucho.hessian.HessianContext

extends ContextImpl

Methods

protected ContextImpl create(String name, AbstractModel model, Hashtable env)

public class com.caucho.hessian.EJBServlet

extends com.caucho.ejb.EJBServlet

Constructors

public EJBServlet()

Methods

protected java.lang.String getDefaultProtocolContainer()

Package com.caucho.hessian.io

public class com.caucho.hessian.io.ThrowableDeserializer

extends JavaDeserializer

Constructors

public ThrowableDeserializer(Class cl)

Methods

protected java.lang.Object instantiate()

public class com.caucho.hessian.io.QSerializerFactory

extends SerializerFactory

Constructors

public QSerializerFactory()

Methods

public Serializer getSerializer(Class cl)

public class com.caucho.hessian.io.HomeSerializer

extends Serializer

Constructors

public HomeSerializer()

Methods

public void writeObject(Object obj, AbstractHessianOutput out)

public class com.caucho.hessian.io.EJBObjectSerializer

extends Serializer

Constructors

public EJBObjectSerializer()

Methods

public void writeObject(Object obj, AbstractHessianOutput out)

Index

Symbols

+ (addition) operator, 80
$ (expression) (StyleScript), 95
>= (greater or equal) operator, 80
> (greater than) operator, 80
<= (less or equal) operator, 80
< (less than) operator, 80
= (like) operator, 80
* (multiplication) operator, 80
!= (not like) operator, 80
- (subtraction) operator, 80
<%...%> tags, 36

A

abstract-schema-name tag (EJBs), 114
<accept-buffer-size> element, 283
accessing databases
  JSP, 49–50
  servlets, 64–66
<access-log> element, 264–265
account history example, JSP version, 68–71
Active Server Pages (ASP), 2–3
addition operator (+), 80
<allow-admin> element, 330
<alternate-session-url-prefix> element, 286
Ant build files, 155–157
Apache servers, 291
  configuring resin.conf for, 295
  error pages, 298
  testing, 295–296
  troubleshooting, 296–297
  Unix installation/ configuration, 291–292
  virtual hosting, 297–298
  Windows installation/ configuration, 292–295
<app-dir> element, 279
application variable (JSP), 38, 42–43
$ apply-imports (StyleScript), 95
$ apply-templates(select) (StyleScript), 96–97
$ apply-templates (StyleScript), 95–96
ASP (Active Server Pages), 2–3
$ attribute(name) (StyleScript), 97
$ attribute-set(name) (Style-Script), 97–98
<auth-constraint> element, 240
authentication, 6, 231
  building authenticators, 239
  password storage, 236–239
  session timeouts, 236
  specifying password files, 235–236
  XmlAuthenticator, 231–233
    digest authentication, 233–234
    form authentication, 234–235
<authenticator> element, 265
authorization, 239–240
autoFlush directive (JSP), 44
automatic startup, 16–19

B

<base64> tag (Burlap), 166
BasicAPI, 170–171, 180–181. *See also* Burlap; Hessian
beans, 3. *See also* Burlap; Entitlements application example
  counter bean example, 47–49
  deployment descriptors, 113–115
  ejbSelect() method, 124–126
  entity beans, 109–110, 109–110
    changing values of, 126–131
    creating with XDoclet, 152–155
    implementation bean, 112–113
    local home interface, 110–111
    local interface, 111–112
    multiple entity beans, 134–135
  finder methods, adding, 119–124, 157–159
  remove() method, 134
  stateless session beans, 146–149
  table relationships, building, 139–145
  tags, 46–47
  transactions, 145–146
  web.xml file configuration, 116

begin() method (UserTransaction class), 146
binary structure (Hessian), 197
boolean() function (XPath), 81
<boolean> tag (Burlap), 165
boolean structure (Hessian), 197
<browser-mapping> element, 278
buffer directive (JSP), 44
Burlap, 7
  BasicAPI, 170–171
  clients, creating, 171–173, 176–177
  com.caucho.burlap.io package
    EJBObjectSerializer class, 353
    HomeSerializer class, 353
    QSerializerFactory class, 353
  com.caucho.burlap package
    BurlapContext class, 352
    BurlapContextFactory class, 352
    BurlapHandle class, 352
    BurlapHandleEncoder class, 351
    BurlapHomeHandle class, 351
    BurlapModel class, 350
    BurlapParseException class, 350
    BurlapProtocol class, 350
    BurlapProtocolException class, 349
    BurlapReader class, 349
    BurlapServerException class, 348–349
    BurlapSkeleton class, 348
    BurlapStub class, 348
    BurlapStubFactory class, 347
    BurlapWriter class, 347
    EJBServlet class, 347
    HomeStub class, 346
    MarshalExceptionWrapper class, 346
    MessageSkeleton class, 345–346
    MetaStub class, 345
    NameContextSkeleton class, 345
    NoRpcMethodException class, 345
    NoRpcObjectException class, 344
    ObjectStub class, 344
    RpcException class, 344
    SerializedExceptionWrapper class, 343
  downloading, 164
  goals, 163
  serialization, 164
  services, creating
    interface, creating, 173–174
    interface JAR file, 174
    weather service example, 174–176
  tags, 164–169
    <base64> tag, 166
    <boolean> tag, 165
    <burlap:call> tag, 169
    <burlap:reply> tag, 169
    <date> tag, 165
    <double> tag, 165
    <int> tag, 165
    <list> tag, 167
    <long> tag, 165
    <map> tag, 167–168
    <null> tag, 168
    <ref> tag, 168
    <remote> tag, 166
    <string> tag, 165
    <xml> tag, 166
<burlap:call> tag (Burlap), 169
<burlap:reply> tag, 169
BurlapContext class, 352
BurlapContextFactory class, 352
BurlapHandle class, 352
BurlapHandleEncoder class, 351
BurlapHomeHandle class, 351
BurlapModel class, 350
BurlapParseException class, 350
BurlapProtocol class, 350
BurlapProtocolException class, 349
BurlapReader class, 349
BurlapServerException class, 348–349
BurlapSkeleton class, 348
BurlapStub class, 348
BurlapStubFactory class, 347
BurlapWriter class, 347

C

<cache> element, 283–284
Cache-Control HTTP header, 247, 251
cache-mapping, 250–251
<cache-mapping> element, 268–269
caching, 245–246
  cache-mapping, 250–251
  HTTP headers, 247–248
    Cache-Control HTTP header, 247–248, 251
    Expires header, 249
    If-Modified, 250
  metatags, 246–247
  proxy caches, 246, 248
  Web caches, 246
calls, Hessian, 198
$ call-template(name) (StyleScript), 98
<case-insensitive> element, 267
ceiling() function (XPath), 81
CGI (Common Gateway Interface), 1–2
  hosting on Resin Web server
    CGIServlet, 301–302
    FastCGIServlet, 302–303
CGIServlet, 301–302
<character-encoding> element, 277
$ choose(test) (StyleScript), 98–99
<class-loader> element, 257
-classpath option, 22

clearCache() method, 330
close() method, 330
<cluster> element, 258
<cluster-definition> element, 258
CMP (container-managed persistence), 8, 108
  Entitlements application example
    Ant build files, 155–157
    changing entity values, 126–131
    deploying code, 118
    deployment descriptor, 113–115
    ejbSelect() method, 124–126
    finder methods, adding, 119–124, 157–159
    groups bean, adding, 136–137
    login entity bean, 109–110
    login query, 109
    multiple entity beans, 134–135
    removing beans, 134
    running, 118–119
    servlet, creating, 116–118
    setup, 109
    stateless session beans, 146–149
    table relationships, 137–145
    transactions, 145–146
    updating tables, 131–134
    web.xml file, 116
    XDoclet entity bean, 152–155
cmp-field tag (EJBs), 115
<cmr-field> tag, 143
<cmr-field-name> tag, 143
com.caucho.burlap.io package
  EJBObjectSerializer class, 353
  HomeSerializer class, 353
  QSerializerFactory class, 353
com.caucho.burlap package
  BurlapContext class, 352
  BurlapContextFactory class, 352
  BurlapHandle class, 352
  BurlapHandleEncoder class, 351
  BurlapHomeHandle class, 351
  BurlapModel class, 350
  BurlapParseException class, 350
  BurlapProtocol class, 350
  BurlapProtocolException class, 349
  BurlapReader class, 349
  BurlapServerException class, 348–349
  BurlapSkeleton class, 348
  BurlapStub class, 348
  BurlapStubFactory class, 347
  BurlapWriter class, 347
  EJBServlet class, 347
  HomeStub class, 346
  MarshalExceptionWrapper class, 346
  MessageSkeleton class, 345–346
  MetaStub class, 345
  NameContextSkeleton class, 345
  NoRpcMethodException class, 345
  NoRpcObjectException class, 344
  ObjectStub class, 344
  RpcException class, 344
  SerializedExceptionWrapper class, 343
com.caucho.hessian.io package
  EJBObjectSerializer class, 362
  HomeSerializer class, 361
  QSerializerFactory class, 361
  ThrowableDeserializer class, 361
com.caucho.hessian package
  HEJBServlet class, 360–361
  HessianContext class, 360
  HessianContextFactory class, 360
  HessianHandle class, 359–360
  HessianHandleEncoder class, 359
  HessianHomeHandle class, 359
  HessianModel class, 358
  HessianProtocol class, 358
  HessianReader class, 357–358
  HessianSkeleton class, 357
  HessianStub class, 357
  HessianStubFactory class, 356
  HessianWriter class, 356
  HomeStub class, 355–356
  MessageSkeleton class, 355
  MetaStub class, 354–355
  NameContextSkeleton class, 354
  ObjectStub class, 353–354
command-line options, 22–23
$ comment() <<....>> (StyleScript), 99
commit() method (UserTransaction class), 146
Common Gateway Interface (CGI), 1–2
Common Object Request Broker Architecture (CORBA), 4
compiler parse errors, 221–222
<compiling-loader> element, 257
concat() function (XPath), 81
configuration
  <log> element, 26–27
  base configuration file example, 24–26
  configuration files, 30
  error page, 28–29
  HTTP port, 26
  Java compiler, 27–28
  Resin-EE, 108
  Resin server (resin.conf file), 253
    <accept-buffer-size> element, 283

<access-log> element, 264–265
adding comments to, 254
<alternate-session-url-prefix> element, 286
<app-dir> element, 279
<authenticator> element, 265
<browser-mapping> element, 278
<cache> element, 283–284
<cache-mapping> element, 268–269
<case-insensitive> element, 267
<character-encoding> element, 277
<class-loader> element, 257
<cluster> element, 258
<cluster-definition> element, 258
<compiling-loader> element, 257
<connect-timeout> element, 282–283
<context-param> element, 270
<database> element, 258–259
<dead-time> element, 282
default path values, 255–256
<dependency-check-interval> element, 267, 277
<deployment-extension> element, 276
<description> element, 269, 277
<display-name> element, 269
<distributable> element, 269
<ejb-local-ref> element, 276
<ejb-ref> element, 276
<ejb-server> element, 259
<env-entry> element, 260–261, 276
environments, 254
<error-page> element, 274–275
<filter> element, 270
<filter-mapping> element, 270–271
<forbid-host> element, 285
<global-system-properties> element, 286
high-level configuration format, 254–255
<host> element, 280
<http> element, 280–281
<ignore-client-disconnect> element, 285
<javac> element, 266
<jndi-link> element, 261
<jsp> element, 287–288
<jsp-config> element, 275
<lazy-init> element, 278
<library-loader>, 257
<library-loader> element, 258
<listen> element, 283
<listener> element, 271
<live-time> element, 282
<locale-encoding-mapping-list> element, 276
<log> element, 262
<make-loader> element, 258
<message-destination> element, 276
<message-destination-ref> element, 275
<mime-mapping> element, 273–274
<multipart-form> element, 278
<path-mapping> element, 269
<ping> element, 284–285
<port> element, 280
<reference> element, 261–262
<regexp> element, 279
<request-timeout> element, 282
<resin:include> tag, 255
<resource> element, 262
<resource-env-ref> element, 275
<resource-ref> element, 275
<secure> element, 279
<security-constraint> element, 275–276
<security-role> element, 276
<servlet> element, 271
<servlet-mapping> element, 272
<session-config> element, 272–273
<session-cookie> element, 286
<session-url-prefix> element, 286
<simple-loader> element, 258
<srun> element, 281
<stderr-log> element, 262–263
<stdout-log> element, 263
<sticky-sessions> element, 286
<strict-mapping> element, 269
<system-property> element, 266
<taglib> element, 277
<temp-dir> element, 267
<thread-keepalive> element, 281–282
<thread-max> element, 281
<thread-min> element, 281
<timeout-interval> element, 283
<url-character-encoding> element, 279

<url-length-max> element, 287
<web-app> element, 268
<web-app-default> element, 268
<web-app-deploy> element, 268, 276
<welcome-file-list> element, 274
<work-dir> element, 267
XML elements, 254
Resin Web server
CGIServlet, 301–302
FastCGIServlet, 302–303
server restart ping, 29–30
servlets
<servlet> element, 57–59
<servlet-mapping> element, 56–57, 59
WebDav, 303–305
Web servers
Apache, 291–298
IIS, 298–300
iPlanet, 300–301
URL-Dispatching, 289–291
-conf option, 22
connection-wait-time parameter, 214
<connect-timeout> element, 282–283
container-managed persistence. *See* CMP
contains() function (XPath), 81
contentType (JSP), 44
<context-param> element, 270
$ copy() <<....>> (StyleScript), 99
$ copy-of(select) (StyleScript), 99
CORBA (Common Object Request Broker Architecture), 4
count() function (XPath), 81

D

<database> element, 258–259
database access
JDBC, 207–209
JNDI, 209
configuration parameters, 210
library placement, 210
MySQL connections, 211–213
Oracle connections, 213
Postgres connections, 213
Resin configuration file, 210
JSP, 49–50
JSP, connecting through, 217–218
servlets, 64–66
database-distributed sessions, 318
database pooling, 214–216
database reliability, 216–217
<date> tag (Burlap), 165
date structure (Hessian), 197
<dead-time> element, 282
debugging
Apache servers, 296–297
error types
compiler parse errors, 221–222
logic errors, 223–224
run-time errors, 222–223
JIT (Just-In-Time) compilers, 224
logging, 225–227
ResinLauncher, 340–342
rootCause exceptions, 227
standalone debuggers, 228
thread dumps, 227–228
tracing code, 224–225
$ declaration (StyleScript), 100
defaults, 55–56
<dependency-check-interval> element, 267, 277
<deployment-extension> element, 276
<description> element, 269, 277
destroy() method, 54
digest authentication, 233–234
$ directive.page(attributes) (StyleScript), 100
<display-name> element, 269
<distributable> element, 269
distributed sessions, 6, 316–317
database-distributed sessions, 318
sticky sessions, 317–318
symmetrical sessions, 317
TCP-ring distributed sessions, 318–319
div operator, 80
documentation, 24
document parsing
HTML, 205–206
XML, 199–200
changing parsers, 204–205
DOM parsing, 200–203
SAX parsing, 203–204
doGet() method, 54
DOM XML parsing, 200–203
doPost() method, 54
-D option, 23
<double> tag (Burlap), 165
double structure (Hessian), 197
downloading Resin, 325–327

E

echo() method (BasicAPI), 170, 180
Eclipse plugin
installing, 335–336
ResinLauncher, 338–342
ResinProjectWizard, 336–338
@ ejb:bean tag (XDoclet), 153–154, 159
@ ejb:finder tag (XDoclet), 160
@ ejb:home-method tag (XDoclet), 160
@ ejb:home tag (XDoclet), 154, 160
@ ejb:interface-method tag (XDoclet), 154, 155, 160
@ ejb:interface tag (XDoclet), 154, 160
@ ejb:persistence tag (XDoclet), 160
@ ejb:persistent-field tag (XDoclet), 154
@ ejb:persistent field tag (XDoclet), 155

@ ejb:pk-field tag (XDoclet), 154, 160
@ ejb:pk tag (XDoclet), 154, 159–160
@ ejb:relation tag (XDoclet), 160
@ ejb:select tag (XDoclet), 160
ejb-class tag (EJBs), 114
ejb-jar tag (EJBs), 114
<ejb-local-ref> element, 276
<ejb-name> tag, 143
ejb-name tag (EJBs), 114
EJBObjectSerializer class
  Burlap, 353
  Hessian, 362
EJB-QL (Enterprise JavaBeans Query Language), 8
<ejb-ref> element, 276
<ejb-relation> tag, 143
<ejb-relation-name> tag, 143
<ejb-relationship-role> tag, 143
<ejb-relationship-role-name> tag, 143
EJBs (Enterprise Java Beans), 107. *See also* Burlap; Entitlements application example
  configuration tags, 114–115
  deployment descriptors, 113–115
  ejbSelect() method, 124–126
  entity beans, 107, 109–110
    changing values of, 126–131
    creating with XDoclet, 152–155
    implementation bean, 112–113
    local home interface, 110–111
    local interface, 111–112
    multiple entity beans, 134–135
  finder methods, adding, 119–124, 157–159
  remove() method, 134
  scalability, 108
  stateless session beans, 146–149
  table relationships, 137–138
    building, 139–145
    supported types, 139
    unidirectional, 138–139
  transactions, 145–146
  web.xml file configuration, 116
ejbSelect() method, 124–126
<ejb-server> element, 259
EJBServlet class (Burlap), 347
$ element(name) (StyleScript), 100
encoding (response variable), 42
encryption, 6
enterprise-beans tag (EJBs), 114
Enterprise JavaBeans. *See* EJBs
Enterprise JavaBeans Query Language. *See* EJB-QL
Entitlements application example
  Ant build files, 155–157
  changing entity values, 126–131
  deploying code, 118
  deployment descriptor, 113–115
  ejbSelect() method, 124–126
  finder methods, adding, 119–124
    findAll() method, 120–122
    findByOpenCloseDate() method, 123–124
    findByOpenDate() method, 122–123
    with XDoclet, 157–159
  login entity bean, 109–110
    implementation bean, 112–113
    local home interface, 110–111
    local interface, 111–112
  login query, 109
  multiple entity beans, 134–135
    groups bean, adding, 136–137
  removing beans, 134
  running, 118–119
  servlet, creating, 116–118
  setup, 109
  stateless session beans, 146–149
  table relationships, 137–138
    login and groups tables, 139–145
    supported types, 139
    unidirectional, 138–139
  transactions, 145–146
  updating tables, 131–134
  web.xml file, 116
  XDoclet entity bean, 152–155
entity beans, 107, 109–110
  changing values of, 126–131
  creating with XDoclet, 152–155
  implementation bean, 112–113
  local home interface, 110–111
  local interface, 111–112
entity tag (EJBs), 114
<env-entry> element, 260–261, 276
environments, resin.conf file, 254
equal (=) operator, 80
error page, 29
<error-page> element, 29, 274–275
errorPage directive (JSP), 44, 46
error pages, Apache servers, 298
errors
  compiler parse errors, 221–222
  logic errors, 223–224
  run-time errors, 222–223
exception variable (JSP), 38
Expires HTTP header, 249
$ expr(expression), 100
extends directive (JSP), 44
Extensible Markup Language. *See* XML
Extensible Stylesheet Language. *See* XSL

F

false() function (XPath), 81
FastCGI, 2
FastCGIServlet, 302–303
fault() method (BasicAPI), 170, 180
field-name tag (EJBs), 115
file-distributed sessions, 319
<filter> element, 270
<filter-mapping> element, 270–271
finder methods, adding to beans, 119–124, 157–159
<forbid-host> element, 285
$ for-each(select) <<....>> (StyleScript), 100–101
form authentication, 234–235
forms, 40–41
  servlets, 62–64

G

getActiveSessionCount() method, 330
getAppDir() method, 330
getClassLoader() method, 330
getHostAdmin() method, 330
getServerAdmin() method, 330
global invokers (servlets), 66–67
<global-system-properties> element, 286
greater or equal (>=) operator, 80
greater than (>) operator, 80

H

HardCore, 313–314
hardware load balanacing, 319–320
HEJBServlet class (Hessian), 360–361
hello() method (BasicAPI), 171, 181
Hello World example
  HTML version, 34
  JSP version, 34–37
  servlet version, 59–62
  XTP version, 73–76
Hessian, 8
  calls, 198
  clients, creating, 181–182, 188–190
    interface, 182–183
  com.caucho.hessian.io package
    EJBObjectSerializer class, 362
    HomeSerializer class, 361
    QSerializerFactory class, 361
    ThrowableDeserializer class, 361
  com.caucho.hessian package
    HEJBServlet class, 360–361
    HessianContext class, 360
    HessianContextFactory class, 360
    HessianHandle class, 359–360
    HessianHandleEncoder class, 359
    HessianHomeHandle class, 359
    HessianModel class, 358
    HessianProtocol class, 358
    HessianReader class, 357–358
    HessianSkeleton class, 357
    HessianStub class, 357
    HessianStubFactory class, 356
    HessianWriter class, 356
    HomeStub class, 355–356
    MessageSkeleton class, 355
    MetaStub class, 354–355
    NameContextSkeleton class, 354
    ObjectStub class, 353–354
  configuring resin.conf file, 187
  configuring web.xml, 187–188
  downloading, 180
  mobile devices, 190–194
  Python implementation, 196
  replies, 198
  running, 188
  serialization, 194–196, 197–198
  server structure, 186–187
  services, creating, 183
    authentication service example, 184–186
    interface, compiling, 184
    interface, creating, 183–184
HessianContext class, 360
HessianContextFactory class, 360
HessianHandle class, 359–360
HessianHandleEncoder class, 359
HessianHomeHandle class, 359
HessianModel class, 358
Hessian Mux, 196
HessianProtocol class, 358
HessianReader class, 357–358
HessianSkeleton class, 357
HessianStub class, 357
HessianStubFactory class, 356
HessianWriter class, 356
HomeSerializer class
  Burlap, 353
  Hessian, 361
HomeStub class
  Burlap, 346
  Hessian, 355–356
<host> element, 280. *See also* virtual hosting
HTML
  combining Java with, 37
  forms, 40–41
  metatags, 246–247
  parsing, 205–206
  tags, style changes, 92
<http> element, 280–281
httpd.conf file, configuring for Apache, 293–295
HTTP headers, 247–248

I

id() function (XPath), 81
if() function (XPath), 81
$ if(test) <<....>> (StyleScript), 101
If-Modified HTTP header, 250
<ignore-client-disconnect> element, 285
IIS servers, 298–300
implementation bean (entity beans), 112–113
$ import(href) (StyleScript), 102
import directive (JSP), 44, 45
include directive (JSP), 44, 46
info directive (JSP), 44
init() method, 54
<init-param> element, 58
  Hello World example, 61–62
-install-as option, 23
installing
  Apache
    on Unix, 291–292
    on Windows, 292–295
  Eclipse plugin, 335–336
  Resin
    JDK requirements, 11–12
    on Linux, 19–21
    recommended server configuration, 12
    tested configurations, 12
    testing installation, 21–22
    on Unix, 19–21
    on Windows, 14–19
  Resin HardCore, 314
  XDoclet, 151–152
-install option, 23
<int> tag (Burlap), 165
integrating Resin, 12–13
int structure (Hessian), 197
iPlanet servers, 300–301
isErrorPage directive (JSP), 44
isThreadSafe directive (JSP), 44

J

Java, combining with HTML, 37
-java_home option, 23
Java API for XML Processing (JAXP), 199
JavaBeans, 3
<javac> element, 266
Java compiler, 27–28
Java Database Connectivity. *See* JDBC
Java Development Kit. *See* JDK
Java Naming and Directory Interface. *See* JNDI
Java Secure Socket Extension (JSSE), 242–243
JavaServer Pages. *See* JSP
JAXP (Java API for XML Processing), 199
JDBC (Java Database Connectivity), 207–209
JdbcAuthenticator, 236–239
JDK (Java Development Kit)
  obtaining, 13–14
  version requirements, 11–12
JIT (Just-In-Time) compilers, debugging, 224
JNDI (Java Naming and Directory Interface), 209
  configuration parameters, 210
  library placement, 210
  MySQL connections, 211–213
  Oracle connections, 213
  Postgres connections, 213
  Resin configuration file, 210
<jndi-link> element, 261
joining tables, 137–138
-J option, 23
JSP (JavaServer Pages), 3
  application variable, 38, 42–43
  beans
    counter bean example, 47–49
    tags, 46–47
  database access, 49–50
  database connectivity, 217–218
  directives, 44–45
  exception variable, 38
  forms, 40–41
  Hello World example, 34–37
  out variable, 38
  overview, 32–33
  pageContext variable, 38
  request variable, 38
  Resin support, 5, 34
  response variable, 38–40, 41
    encoding, 42
    redirection, 41–42
  scripting languages, 31–32
  session variable, 38, 43–44
  tags, 36
  templates, 67–71
<jsp> element, 287–288
<jsp-config> element, 275
JSP-EL support, 50–51
JSSE (Java Secure Socket Extension), 242–243
JSTL support, 50–51
Just-In-Time (JIT) compilers, debugging, 224
JVMs (Java Virtual Machines), 310–311

L

lang() function (XPath), 81
language directive (JSP), 45
last() function (XPath), 81
<lazy-init> element, 278
less or equal (<=) operator, 80
less than (<) operator, 80
<library-loader> element, 258
like (=) operator, 80
Linux, installing Resin on, 19–21
<list> tag (Burlap), 167
<listen> element, 283
<listener> element, 271
list structure (Hessian), 197
<live-time> element, 282
LoadBalanceServlet, 321–323

load balancing, 6
hardware load balanacing, 319–320
Resin as a balancer, 321–323
sessions, 315
distributed sessions, 316–319
file-distributed sessions, 319
srun indexing, 316
srun-backup, 323
<load-on-startup> element, 58–59
<locale-encoding-mapping-list> element, 276
local home interface (entity beans), 110–111
local-home tag (EJBs), 114
local interface (entity beans), 111–112
local-part function (XPath), 81
local tag (EJBs), 114
<log> element, 26–27, 225–226, 262
logging, 225–227
<log> element configuration, 26–27
logic errors, 223–224
logouts, 240
<long> tag (Burlap), 165
long structure (Hessian), 197
loor() function (XPath), 81

M

<make-loader> element, 258
many-to-many table relationships, 139
many-to-one table relationships, 139
<map> tag (Burlap), 167–168
map structure (Hessian), 197
MarshalExceptionWrapper class (Burlap), 346
matching URLs, 57
max-active-time parameter, 214
max-connections parameter, 214
max-idle-time parameter, 214
max-overflow-connections parameter, 214
max-pool-time parameter, 214
<message-destination> element, 276
<message-destination-ref> element, 275
MessageSkeleton class
Burlap, 345–346
Hessian, 355
MetaStub class
Burlap, 345
Hessian, 354–355
metatags, 246–247
<mime-mapping> element, 273–274
mobile Hessian, 190–194
mod operator, 80
<multipart-form> element, 278
<multiplicity> tag, 143
MySQL databases, connecting to, 211–213

N

name() function (XPath), 81
NameContextSkeleton class
Burlap, 345
Hessian, 354
namespace() function (XPath), 81
Netscape iPlanet servers, 300–301
-nojit option, 23
normalize-space() function (XPath), 81
NoRpcMethodException class (Burlap), 345
NoRpcObjectException class (Burlap), 344
not equal (!=) operator, 80
not like (!=) operator, 80
<null> tag (Burlap), 168
nullCall() method (BasicAPI), 171, 181
NULL structure (Hessian), 197
number() function (XPath), 81

O

objects, attaching to JSP templates, 68–71
ObjectStub class
Burlap, 344
Hessian, 353–354
one-to-many table relationships, 139
one-to-one table relationships, 139
OpenSSL, 240–241
and operator, 80
Oracle databases, connecting to, 213
or operator, 80
$ output(attributes) (StyleScript), 102
out variable (JSP), 38

P

page caching, 245–246
cache-mapping, 250–251
HTTP headers, 247–248
Cache-Control HTTP header, 247–248, 251
Expires header, 249
If-Modified, 250
metatags, 246–247
proxy caches, 246, 248
Web caches, 246
pageContext variable (JSP), 38
$ param(name) (StyleScript), 102–103
parsing
HTML, 205–206
XML, 199–200
changing parsers, 204–205
DOM parsing, 200–203
SAX parsing, 203–204
passwords
specifying password files, 235–236
storing, 236–239
<path-mapping> element, 269
persistence-type tag (EJBs), 114

persistent processes, 2
-pid option, 23
<ping> element, 284–285
pinging servers, 29–30
ping-on-free option (JNDI), 217
ping-on-idle option (JNDI), 217
ping-on-reuse option (JNDI), 217
ping queries, 216–217
ping-table option (JNDI), 217
pooling databases, 214–216
<port> element, 280
ports, 13
  HTTP port, 26
Postgres databases, connecting to, 213
prefix directive (JSP), 45
prim-key-class tag (EJBs), 114
primkey-field tag (EJBs), 115
$ processing-instructions(name) (StyleScript), 103
protection authorization, 6
proxy caches, 246, 248
Python, Hessian implementation, 196

Q

QSerializerFactory class
  Burlap, 353
  Hessian, 361

R

redirection (response variable), 41–42
reentrant tag (EJBs), 114
<ref> tag (Burlap), 168
<reference> element, 261–262
ref structure (Hessian), 198
<regexp> element, 279
<relationship-role-source> tag, 143
relationships (tables), 137–138
  building (Entitlements application), 139–145
  supported types, 139
  unidirectional, 138–139
<relationships> element, 142–143
reliability options, 323–324
<remote> tag (Burlap), 166
Remote Management Interface (RMI), 4
remote structure (Hessian), 198
remove() method (EJBs), 134
-remove-as option, 23
-remove option, 23
replies, Hessian, 198
<request-timeout> element, 282
request variable (JSP), 38–40
Resin
  downloading, 325–327
  features, 5–8
  installing
    JDK requirements, 11–12
    on Linux, 19–21
    recommended server configuration, 12
    tested configurations, 12
    testing installation, 21–22
    on Unix, 19–21
    on Windows, 14–19
  integrating, 12–13
  overview, 4–5
  ports, 13
resin.conf file, 24–25, 253
  <accept-buffer-size> element, 283
  <access-log> element, 264–265
  adding comments to, 254
  <alternate-session-url-prefix> element, 286
  <app-dir> element, 279
  <authenticator> element, 265
  <browser-mapping> element, 278
  <cache> element, 283–284
  <cache-mapping> element, 268–269
  <case-insensitive> element, 267
  <character-encoding> element, 277
  <class-loader> element, 257
  <cluster> element, 258
  <cluster-definition> element, 258
  <compiling-loader> element, 257
  configuring for Apache, 295
  <connect-timeout> element, 282–283
  <context-param> element, 270
  <database> element, 258–259
  <dead-time> element, 282
  default path values, 255–256
  <dependency-check-interval> element, 267, 277
  <deployment-extension> element, 276
  <description> element, 269, 277
  <display-name> element, 269
  <distributable> element, 269
  <ejb-local-ref> element, 276
  <ejb-ref> element, 276
  <ejb-server> element, 259
  <env-entry> element, 260–261, 276
  environments, 254
  <error-page> element, 274–275
  <filter> element, 270
  <filter-mapping> element, 270–271
  <forbid-host> element, 285
  <global-system-properties> element, 286
  high-level configuration format, 254–255
  <host> element, 280
  <http> element, 280–281
  <ignore-client-disconnect> element, 285
  <javac> element, 266
  <jndi-link> element, 261
  <jsp> element, 287–288

<jsp-config> element, 275
<lazy-init> element, 278
<library-loader> element, 258
<listen> element, 283
<listener> element, 271
<live-time> element, 282
<locale-encoding-mapping-list> element, 276
<log> element, 262
<make-loader> element, 258
<message-destination> element, 276
<message-destination-ref> element, 275
<mime-mapping> element, 273–274
modifying for Hessian, 187
<multipart-form> element, 278
opening, 253
<path-mapping> element, 269
<ping> element, 284–285
<port> element, 280
<reference> element, 261–262
<regexp> element, 279
<request-timeout> element, 282
<resin:include> tag, 255
<resource> element, 262
<resource-env-ref> element, 275
<resource-ref> element, 275
<secure> element, 279
<security-constraint> element, 275–276
<security-role> element, 276
<servlet> element, 271
<servlet-mapping> element, 272
<session-config> element, 272–273
<session-cookie> element, 286
<session-url-prefix> element, 286
<simple-loader> element, 258
<srun> element, 281
<stderr-log> element, 262–263
<stdout-log> element, 263
<sticky-sessions> element, 286
<strict-mapping> element, 269
<system-property> element, 266
<taglib> element, 277
<temp-dir> element, 267
<thread-keepalive> element, 281–282
<thread-max> element, 281
<thread-min> element, 281
<timeout-interval> element, 283
<url-character-encoding> element, 279
<url-length-max> element, 287
<web-app> element, 268
<web-app-default> element, 268
<web-app-deploy> element, 268, 276
<welcome-file-list> element, 274
<work-dir> element, 267
XML elements, 254
<resin:include> tag, 255
-resin_home option, 23
Resin-EE, 108
configuring, 108
Entitlements application example
Ant build files, 155–157
changing entity values, 126–131
deploying code, 118
deployment descriptor, 113–115
ejbSelect() method, 124–126
finder methods, adding, 119–124, 157–159
groups bean, adding, 136–137
login entity bean, 109–110
login query, 109
multiple entity beans, 134–135
removing beans, 134
running, 118–119
servlet, creating, 116–118
setup, 109
stateless session beans, 146–149
table relationships, 137–145
transactions, 145–146
updating tables, 131–134
web.xml file, 116
XDoclet entity bean, 152–155
server structure, 186–187
@ resin-ejb:cmp-field tag (XDoclet), 154, 155, 161
@ resin-ejb:entity-bean tag (XDoclet), 154, 160
@ resin-ejb:relation tag (XDoclet), 161
Resin Enterprise, 8
Resin HardCore, 313–314
ResinLauncher, 338–342
ResinProjectWizard, 336–338
Resin server
configuration (resin.conf file), 24–25, 253
<accept-buffer-size> element, 283
<access-log> element, 264–265
adding comments to, 254
<alternate-session-url-prefix> element, 286
<app-dir> element, 279
<authenticator> element, 265
<browser-mapping> element, 278
<cache> element, 283–284
<cache-mapping> element, 268–269

<case-insensitive> element, 267
<character-encoding> element, 277
<class-loader> element, 257
<cluster> element, 258
<cluster-definition> element, 258
<compiling-loader> element, 257
configuring for Apache, 295
<connect-timeout> element, 282–283
<context-param> element, 270
<database> element, 258–259
<dead-time> element, 282
default path values, 255–256
<dependency-check-interval> element, 267, 277
<deployment-extension> element, 276
<description> element, 269, 277
<display-name> element, 269
<distributable> element, 269
<ejb-local-ref> element, 276
<ejb-ref> element, 276
<ejb-server> element, 259
<env-entry> element, 260–261, 276
environments, 254
<error-page> element, 274–275
<filter> element, 270
<filter-mapping> element, 270–271
<forbid-host> element, 285
<global-system-properties> element, 286
high-level configuration format, 254–255
<host> element, 280
<http> element, 280–281
<ignore-client-disconnect> element, 285
<javac> element, 266
<jndi-link> element, 261
<jsp> element, 287–288
<jsp-config> element, 275
<lazy-init> element, 278
<library-loader> element, 258
<listen> element, 283
<listener> element, 271
<live-time> element, 282
<locale-encoding-mapping-list> element, 276
<log> element, 262
<make-loader> element, 258
<message-destination> element, 276
<message-destination-ref> element, 275
<mime-mapping> element, 273–274
modifying for Hessian, 187
<multipart-form> element, 278
opening, 253
<path-mapping> element, 269
<ping> element, 284–285
<port> element, 280
<reference> element, 261–262
<regexp> element, 279
<request-timeout> element, 282
<resin:include> tag, 255
<resource> element, 262
<resource-env-ref> element, 275
<resource-ref> element, 275
<secure> element, 279
<security-constraint> element, 275–276
<security-role> element, 276
<servlet> element, 271
<servlet-mapping> element, 272
<session-config> element, 272–273
<session-cookie> element, 286
<session-url-prefix> element, 286
<simple-loader> element, 258
<srun> element, 281
<stderr-log> element, 262–263
<stdout-log> element, 263
<sticky-sessions> element, 286
<strict-mapping> element, 269
<system-property> element, 266
<taglib> element, 277
<temp-dir> element, 267
<thread-keepalive> element, 281–282
<thread-max> element, 281
<thread-min> element, 281
<timeout-interval> element, 283
<url-character-encoding> element, 279
<url-length-max> element, 287
<web-app> element, 268
<web-app-default> element, 268
<web-app-deploy> element, 268, 276
<welcome-file-list> element, 274

<work-dir> element, 267
XML elements, 254
status, obtaining, 329–333
resin-web.xml file, 30
Resin Web server
hosting CGI on
CGIServlet, 301–302
FastCGIServlet, 302–303
<resource> element, 262
<resource-env-ref> element, 275
<resource-ref> element, 275
resources, documentation, 24
response encoding, 42
response redirection, 41–42
response variable (JSP), 38, 41
encoding, 42
redirection, 41–42
restart() method, 330
RMI (Remote Management Interface), 4
rollback() method (UserTransaction class), 146
rootCause exceptions, 227
round() function (XPath), 81
RpcException class (Burlap), 344
run-time errors, 222–223

S

SAX XML parsing, 203–204
scripting languages, 31–32
$ scriptlet() <<statements>> (StyleScript), 103
<secure> element, 279
security. *See also* Security Manager
authentication, 6, 231
building authenticators, 239
password storage, 236–239
session timeouts, 236
specifying password files, 235–236
XmlAuthenticator, 231–235
authorization, 239–240
encryption, 6
JSSE, 242–243
logouts, 240
OpenSSL, 240–241
protection authorization, 6
virtual hosting, 310–311
<security-constraint> element, 239, 275–276
Security Manager, 7
<security-role> element, 276
serialization
Burlap, 164
Hessian, 194–196, 197–198
SerializedExceptionWrapper class (Burlap), 343
server restart ping, 30
Server-Side JavaScript (SSJS), 2–3
service startup, 16–19
<servlet> element, 55, 57–59, 271
<init-param> element, 58
<load-on-startup> element, 58–59
<servlet-class> element, 58
<servlet-name> element, 58
<servlet-class> element, 58
<servlet-mapping> element, 56–57, 59, 272
<servlet-name> element, 58
servlets, 3–4
configuring Resin for
<servlet> element, 57–59
<servlet-mapping> element, 56–57, 59
database access, 64–66
forms, 62–64
global invokers, 66–67
Hello World example, 59–62
JSP templates, 67–71
life cycle, 53–54
returning XTP pages, 92–93
<session-config> element, 272–273
<session-cookie> element, 286
session directive (JSP), 45, 45–46
sessions, 315
distributed sessions, 316–317
database-distributed sessions, 318
sticky sessions, 317–318
symmetrical sessions, 317
TCP-ring distributed sessions, 318–319
file-distributed sessions, 319
srun indexing, 316
session timeouts, 236
<session-url-prefix> element, 286
session variable (JSP), 38, 43–44
<simple-loader> element, 258
Simple Markup Language. *See* SML
single-tier architecture, 107
SML (Simple Markup Language), 163
$ sort(attributes) <<....>> (StyleScript), 103
SQL
joins, 137–138
maintaining code, 107
sql-column tag (EJBs), 115
sql-table tag (EJBs), 114
<srun> element, 281
srun-backup, 323
srun indexing, 316
SSJS (Server-Side JavaScript), 2–3
starts-with() function (XPath), 81
stateless session beans, 146–149
status (of Resin server), 329–333
<stderr-log> element, 262–263
<stdout-log> element, 263
sticky sessions, 317–318
<sticky-sessions> element, 286
<strict-mapping> element, 269
string() function (XPath), 81
<string> tag (Burlap), 165
string-length() function (XPath), 82
string structure (Hessian), 197
StyleScript, 94–95
$ (expression), 95

$if(test) <<....>>, 101
$ apply-imports, 95
$ apply-templates, 95–96
$ apply-templates(select), 96–97
$ attribute(name), 97
$ attribute-set(name), 97–98
$ call-template(name), 98
$ choose(test), 98–99
$ comment() <<....>>, 99
converting XSL to, 94–95
$ copy() <<....>>, 99
$ copy-of(select), 99
$ declaration, 100
$ directive.page(attributes), 100
$ element(name), 100
$ expr(expression), 100
$ for-each(select) <<....>>, 100–101
$ import(href), 102
$ output(attributes), 102
$ param(name), 102–103
$ processing-instructions(name), 103
$ scriptlet() <<statements>>, 103
$ sort(attributes) <<....>>, 103
$ template(match), 104
$ text() <<....>>, 104
$ value-off(select), 104
$ variable(name), 105
substring-after() function (XPath), 82
substring-before() function (XPath), 82
subtract() method (BasicAPI), 171, 181
subtraction (-) operator, 80
sum() function (XPath), 82
symmetrical sessions, 317
<system-property> element, 266

T

tables
relationships, 137–138
building (Entitlements application), 139–145
supported types, 139
unidirectional, 138–139
transactions, 145–146
updating (Entitlements application), 137–138
<taglib> element, 277
tag libraries, 50–51
tags
<base64> (Burlap), 166
<boolean> (Burlap), 165
Burlap, 164–169
<burlap:call> (Burlap), 169
<burlap:reply> (Burlap), 169
<date> (Burlap), 165
<double> (Burlap), 165
EJBs, 114–115
<int> (Burlap), 165
JSP, 36
beans, 46–47
<list> (Burlap), 167
<long> (Burlap), 165
<map> (Burlap), 167–168
<null> (Burlap), 168
<ref> (Burlap), 168
<remote> (Burlap), 166
<string> Burlap), 165
style changes, 92
table relationships, 142–143
XDoclet, 153–155, 159–161
<xml> (Burlap), 166
XSL (Extensible Stylesheet Language)
matching with attributes, 89–91
<xsl:apply-imports> tag, 82–83
<xsl:apply-templates select="mode="> tag, 83
<xsl:attribute name="name-space="> tag, 83
<xsl:attribute-set> tag, 83–84
<xsl:call-template> tag, 84
<xsl:choose> tag, 84–85
<xsl:comment> tag, 85
<xsl:copy of> tag, 85
<xsl:copy use-attribute-sets=""> tag, 85
<xsl:element> tag, 85–86
<xsl:for-each select="">, 86
<xsl:if test=""> tag, 86
<xsl:import href=""> tag, 86
<xsl:param name=""select=""> tag, 87
<xsl:processing-instruction name=""> tag, 87
<xsl:sort> tag, 87
<xsl:stylesheet> tag, 87–88
<xsl:template> tag, 88
<xsl:text> tag, 88
<xsl:value-of select="" disable-output-escaping=""> tag, 88
<xsl:variable> tag, 88–89
TCP-ring distributed sessions, 318–319
<temp-dir> element, 267
$ template(match) (StyleScript), 104
templates (JSP), 67–71
testing installations, 21–22
$ text() <<....>> (StyleScript), 104
thread dumps, 227–228
<thread-keepalive> element, 281–282
<thread-max> element, 281
<thread-min> element, 281
three-tier architecture, 107
ThrowableDeserializer class (Hessian), 361
<timeout-interval> element, 283
tracing code, 224–225
transactions, 145–146
translate() function (XPath), 82
troubleshooting
Apache servers, 296–297
documentation, 24
error types
compiler parse errors, 221–222

logic errors, 223–224
run-time errors, 222–223
JIT (Just-In-Time) compilers, 224
logging, 225–227
ResinLauncher, 340–342
rootCause exceptions, 227
standalone debuggers, 228
thread dumps, 227–228
tracing code, 224–225
true() function (XPath), 82

U

unidirectional table relationships, 138–139
Unix, installing Resin on, 19–21
<url-character-encoding> element, 279
URL-Dispatching, 289–291
<url-length-max> element, 287
<url-pattern> element, 57
UserTransaction class, 146

V

$ value-off(select) (StyleScript), 104
$ variable(name) (StyleScript), 105
-verbose option, 23
virtual hosting, 7, 307–309
Apache servers, 297–298
with external Web servers, 309–310
with IP addresses, 310
providing JVMs, 310–311

W

weather service example, 174–177
web.xml file, 30
EJBs, configuring for, 116
modifying for Hessian, 187–188
<servlet> element, 57–59
<init-param> element, 58
<load-on-startup> element, 58–59
<servlet-class> element, 58
<servlet-name> element, 58
<servlet-mapping> element, 56–57, 59
<web-app> element, 55, 268
<web-app-default> element, 55–56, 268
<web-app-deploy> element, 268, 276
Web application defaults, 55–56
Web caches, 246
WebDav, 303–305
<web-resource-collection> element, 239
Web servers, 6
Apache, 291
configuring resin.conf for, 295
error pages, 298
testing, 295–296
troubleshooting, 296–297
Unix installation/configuration, 291–292
virtual hosting, 297–298
Windows installation/configuration, 292–295
IIS, 298–300
iPlanet, 300–301
URL-Dispatching, 289–291
Web services
Burlap, 7
Hessian, 8
<welcome-file-list> element, 274
Windows
installing Resin on, 14–19
Windows service startup, 16–19
<work-dir> element, 267

X

XDoclet, 8
Ant build files, 155–157
creating entity beans, 152–155
expanding beans with, 157–159
installing, 151–152
tags, 153–155, 159–161
XML (Extensible Markup Language), 5–6, 76–77
parsing, 199–200
changing parsers, 204–205
DOM parsing, 200–203
SAX parsing, 203–204
<xml> tag (Burlap), 166
XmlAuthenticator, 6, 231–233
digest authentication, 233–234
form authentication, 234–235
xml structure (Hessian), 197
XML Templates. *See* XTP
-X option, 23
XPath, 77–80
expressions, 80
functions, 81–82
<xsl:apply-imports> tag, 82–83
<xsl:apply-templates select="mode="> tag, 83
<xsl:attribute name="namespace="> tag, 83
<xsl:attribute-set> tag, 83–84
<xsl:call-template> tag, 84
<xsl:choose> tag, 84–85
<xsl:comment> tag, 85
<xsl:copy of> tag, 85
<xsl:copy use attribute-sets=""> tag, 85
<xsl:element> tag, 85–86
XSL (Extensible Stylesheet Language), 5–6. *See also* StyleScript
tags
matching with attributes, 89–91
<xsl:apply-imports> tag, 82–83
<xsl:apply-templates select="mode="> tag, 83
<xsl:attribute name="name-

space="> tag, 83
<xsl:attribute-set> tag, 83–84
<xsl:call-template> tag, 84
<xsl:choose> tag, 84–85
<xsl:comment> tag, 85
<xsl:copy of> tag, 85
<xsl:copy use-attribute-sets=""> tag, 85
<xsl:element> tag, 85–86
<xsl:for-each select="">, 86
<xsl:if test=""> tag, 86
<xsl:import href=""> tag, 86
<xsl:param name=""select=""> tag, 87
<xsl:processing-instruction name=""> tag, 87
<xsl:sort> tag, 87
<xsl:stylesheet> tag, 87–88
<xsl:template> tag, 88
<xsl:text> tag, 88
<xsl:value-of select="" disable-output-escaping=""> tag, 88
<xsl:variable> tag, 88–89
<xsl:for-each select="">, 86
<xsl:if test=""> tag, 86
<xsl:import href=""> tag, 86
<xsl:param name=""select=""> tag, 87
<xsl:processing-instruction name=""> tag, 87
<xsl:sort> tag, 87
<xsl:stylesheet> tag, 87–88
<xsl:template> tag, 88
<xsl:text> tag, 88
<xsl:value-of select="" disable-output-escaping=""> tag, 88
<xsl:variable> tag, 88–89
XTP (XML Templates), 73
Hello World example, 73–76
returning from servlets, 92–93
style changes, 92